The publisher gratefully acknowledges the generous contribution to this book provided by the Music in America Endowment Fund of the University of California Press Foundation, which is supported by a major gift from Sukey and Gil Garcetti, Michael Roth, and the Roth Family Foundation.

Making the Scene

Making the Scene

Contemporary New York City Big Band Jazz

Alex Stewart

UNIVERSITY OF CALIFORNIA PRESS
Berkeley Los Angeles London

University of California Press, one of the most distinguished university presses in the United States, enriches lives around the world by advancing scholarship in the humanities, social sciences, and natural sciences. Its activities are supported by the UC Press Foundation and by philanthropic contributions from individuals and institutions. For more information, visit www.ucpress.edu.

University of California Press
Berkeley and Los Angeles, California

University of California Press, Ltd.
London, England

Portions of this book have been previously published in "Contemporary New York City Big Bands: Composition, Arranging, and Individuality in Orchestral Jazz," *Ethnomusicology* 48.2 (Spring/Summer 2004): 169–202.

Library of Congress Cataloging-in-Publication Data

Stewart, Alex, 1952–
Making the scene : contemporary New York City big band jazz / Alex Stewart.
p. cm.
Includes bibliographical references (p.), discography (p.), and index.
ISBN: 978-0-520-24953-0 (cloth : alk. paper)
ISBN: 978-0-520-24954-7 (pbk. : alk. paper)
1. Big band music—History and criticism. 2. Big bands—New York (State)—New York. I. Title.
ML3518.S74 2007
784.4'8165097471—dc22

2006025497
MN

Manufactured in the United States of America

16 15 14 13 12 11 10 09 08 07
10 9 8 7 6 5 4 3 2 1

This book is printed on New Leaf EcoBook 50, a 100% recycled fiber of which 50% is de-inked post-consumer waste, processed chlorine-free. EcoBook 50 is acid-free and meets the minimum requirements of ANSI/ASTM D5634–01 (*Permanence of Paper*).

Dedicated to Marci Jane Stewart (1950–1972)

CONTENTS

ILLUSTRATIONS

TABLES

PREFACE

As a young saxophone player coming up during the 1970s in Boston, I took little interest in big bands. My record collection contained no Buddy Rich, Maynard Ferguson, or Woody Herman. Although I owned a few compilations of Basie (mostly for the Lester Young on them) and Ellington (mostly for the great tunes on them), my passion was John Coltrane, and through him I discovered Dexter Gordon, Charlie Parker, Sonny Rollins, Bud Powell, Lester Young, and many others. It was a difficult time to be a jazz musician. Almost none of the friends I had known in high school listened to jazz. A gig at a club in Cambridge might pay $7, if anything. The best-paying steady "jazz" gigs were in the burlesque clubs in Boston's notorious Combat Zone. Nevertheless, nothing could divert me from my goal. All I cared about was mastering the art of improvisation. I dedicated myself to transcribing and learning the solos of my idols and hanging out and sitting in with the older, more experienced players at Wally's, a black club on the edge of Roxbury.

Still, I remember trying to play in every big band I could. I'm not sure what attracted me to them. Certainly it was not familiarity with the repertoire or ambitions to land a job in one of the few remaining touring bands. Instinctively I must have known that certain musical skills were more easily acquired in a big band: reading music at sight, improving intonation, learning to phrase and breathe with other players, and developing a stronger sense of swing. Perhaps I wanted to be a part of something larger, to become absorbed into something more powerful, to play more of an accompanying role—something that, unlike members of the rhythm section, horn players rarely do in small groups.

Only later, after moving to New York City, when big bands had become an important part of my musical life, did I begin to explore classic big band recordings in their own right: for their ensemble styles, for their distinctive players, and, above all, for the creativity and ingenuity of their arrangers. I performed in numerous big bands and toured Europe and North America with the Lionel Hampton Orchestra. Eventually, first as a graduate student at the Manhattan School of Music and later as a teacher in a university, I studied classic scores and began writing my own arrangements.

Most young musicians today have far more experience playing in big bands than I did at their age. For some, the experience begins as early as grade school. Still, I frequently encounter young college students who, like me years earlier, show little enthusiasm for big bands. Sometimes this lack of interest stems from having played inferior arrangements or working with a mediocre director. Some students have a stereotypical view of big bands as loud, unwieldy ensembles with blaring trumpets and bashing drums. They may find big bands stifling, detest the "regimentation," and crave more opportunities for soloing. Most have little idea of what goes into making a great band: the indispensable role of each player in contributing to the overall ensemble and the great arrangements, preferably by someone who knows intimately the personalities and idiosyncrasies of the individual players. Even those students with no intention of pursuing big bands professionally come away from the experience with improved tone, greater discipline, and new ideas.

At different times jazz may have been dominated by either one or the other, but throughout most of its history both small and large groups have been vital. Even during the height of the big band craze, leaders preserved small groups within their big bands. Benny Goodman had his trio and quartet; Artie Shaw, the Gramercy Five; Count Basie, the Kansas City Six and Seven; and Tommy Dorsey, the Clambake Seven. At the dawn of the bebop, or modern jazz, era, rather than reject big bands in favor of small combos, Gil Evans, Dizzy Gillespie, and Neal Hefti were quick to adapt the innovations of bebop to orchestral jazz by contributing arrangements to the Claude Thornhill, Gillespie, and Herman bands. The history of jazz shows a constant exchange of concepts and practices between small and large groups. Experience in one informs the other.

Despite the fact that more than fifty years of vital, progressive, and innovative big band jazz separate us from the swing era, most people consider big bands synonymous with this bygone time. Over the past seven years, when I have told people that I am working on a book on New York City big bands, almost no one has guessed that the book might be about contemporary bands. The usual response is, "Oh, I love swing music!" or "My father is really into the big bands." Among scholars and jazz writers the reaction is virtually the same; they assume that my project is a historical study. Even the musicians I approached for interviews might have made this mistake had I not made it clear that I was interested in *their* involvement in big bands.

Musicians react differently because they instantly understand the reasons for my interest. Big bands are an important part of their lives; for most, hardly a week passes without several phone calls inviting them to a rehearsal or gig. Apart from the big band, the only kind of jazz performance where large numbers of musicians traditionally congregate is the jam session. A more open form of "small group" jazz, the jam session focuses mainly on competitive improvisation. Like some big bands (such as those devoted primarily to rehearsal), the jam session tends to be structured around the interests of the musicians rather than the audiences. Both these events bring players together for improving skills, exchanging ideas, and building professional relationships. But important differences remain. From a social perspective, big bands require considerable advance planning, and participants must be invited. In contrast, jam sessions are more spontaneous. Nearly anyone can sit in, although repeat performance might be discouraged if one does not play at the requisite level or follow proper protocol. Ralph Ellison called the jam session "the jazzman's true academy," but for many jazz musicians, the words of Dizzy Gillespie still hold true. Reflecting on his early years, Gillespie said, "In those days we had several means of access to experience. Big bands were one, jam sessions were another, I tried to get plenty of both."[1]

The growth of jazz education helped to compensate for dwindling opportunities for on-the-job training in commercial big bands. Early programs at Berklee in Boston, Indiana, Miami, and North Texas State began to produce skilled players and composers. In recent years two of the country's leading jazz programs emerged in New York: the Manhattan School of Music and the New School. Just outside the city, William Paterson College in New Jersey and the State University of New York at Purchase have attracted aspiring jazz musicians. Recently Juilliard, in conjunction with Jazz at Lincoln Center, instituted its first jazz program. Along with the constant flow of players that traditionally have come to New York to test their mettle, these programs have fed the city's ever-expanding networks of big bands.

Since 1997 I have interviewed more than eighty people. Unlike many studies on jazz, I have tried to draw musicians from widely varying backgrounds (age, gender, ethnicity), social networks, and styles. Other than striving for diversity, my approach has not been particularly systematic; often one interviewee would suggest another, or gaps in my knowledge and research would lead me to another source. Without these musicians and other contributors who gave generously of their knowledge and time, this book, the prime purpose of which is to represent their discourse and knowledge, would not exist.

I express deep gratitude to my colleagues at the University of Vermont: Wayne Schneider, who scoured the manuscript with a singular devotion to detail and style, and Patricia Julien, who examined the text and music examples with similar dedication. John Gennari's and Henry Martin's comments on earlier drafts of several chapters helped to steer the book in new directions. John Murphy, Christopher Washburne, and Rob Walser supplied valuable input at later stages. I tapped Bill Kirchner's encyclopedic knowledge of big bands both at the outset of this project and, for help with some final details, especially the discography, as the manuscript neared completion. David García and Benjamin Lapidus offered suggestions for the chapter on Latin bands. The University of Vermont funded two excellent research assistants, Joseph Gresser and Peter J. McConville, at a crucial time. During a Fulbright fellowship to Mexico in 2006–7, Philip Tamberino covered for me by making some final checks on citations as the manuscript was going into production. In earlier phases of this project, a grant from the Graduate Center of the City University of New York helped to support my writing, and guidance from my teachers Steven Blum and Peter Manuel and the rest of the dissertation committee (David Olan, Richard Kramer, Michael Mossman, and Scott Reeves) helped immeasurably as my ideas were beginning to coalesce. All shortcomings, of course, remain my sole responsibility.

In addition, I would like to thank Lynne Withey of the University of California Press for her initial enthusiasm for the project and especially the music editor, Mary Francis, and her assistant, Kalicia Pivirotto, for seeing it through the long process of peer review and editorial committee approval. Senior editor Rachel Berchten, who oversaw the editing and production, and Sheila Berg, copyeditor, improved the manuscript immeasurably. Chalon Emmons helped with some final corrections before the book went to press.

Any list of people to whom I am indebted must include my mother and father, for without their kindling of interest and support for my musical inclinations, my life surely would have taken a different path. My brother David's big ears and unique musical style served as inspiration. Most important, I express my deepest appreciation to my partner, Yin, and children, John and Zora, both for their tolerance of my absenteeism during long periods and for the joy they have brought during welcome respites from my work. To them, and especially my sister, Marci, who first told me about Coltrane, I dedicate this book.

AUTHOR'S NOTE

SOURCES

Quotations from individuals identified in the text, unless otherwise noted, appear without formal citation. A list of interviews along with their dates can be found in Sources at the end of this book. Occasionally I have withheld a person's identity, either by request or because of the sensitive nature of the material.

PITCH NOMENCLATURE

For the pitch nomenclature used in this book, italic letters are used exclusively when discussing specific pitches within a defined range or octave. Non-italic capital letters denote pitch classes, not specific pitches. All pitches from middle C and above are indicated in lowercase italics. For pitches beginning at the C an octave above middle C, a superscript number indicates the number of octaves above middle C (i.e., c^2 indicates the C two octaves above middle C). All pitches below middle C are in uppercase italics with a subscript number indicating the number of octaves below middle C (i.e., C_2 is the C two octaves below middle C).

Intro

"THE BIG BANDS ARE BACK" proclaims a bumper sticker or the liner notes to a CD. Many of us have heard and have good reason to be skeptical of this refrain, voiced sporadically in the years since the swing era (roughly 1935–46).[1] Yet, despite the persistence of powerful discourse dismissing big bands as anachronistic, irrelevant, or even anti-jazz, big bands have remained vital to jazz musicians, especially in New York City. Throughout the decades following the swing era, big bands appeared regularly in ballrooms, concert halls, and jazz clubs. Recording and broadcast studios mediated the sounds (but not always the images) of orchestral jazz to the public. In television shows, film sound tracks, and commercials, the big band sound has continued to signify urbane sophistication. Even when there was little hope of performing publicly, composers carefully assembled ensembles if only to hear their own music. Perhaps most important, a rich rehearsal band scene has thrived in which musicians make contacts and exchange knowledge.

During the 1990s, big band activity in New York mushroomed as the Lincoln Center Jazz Orchestra, the Carnegie Hall Jazz Band, the Mingus Big Band, and bands led by composers such as Maria Schneider gained international recognition. Interest in big bands spills over stylistic categories: repertory orchestras performing the classic works of Ellington and other "great masters," established mainstream ensembles such as the Vanguard Jazz Orchestra, Latin bands such as Chico O'Farrill's, and free-spirited avant-garde groups led by Oliver Lake, William Parker, and others.[2] Performances occur in rarefied concert halls on the Upper West Side, mainstream midtown clubs such as Birdland in Times Square, and cutting edge venues such as the Knitting Factory and other downtown establishments. In 1997–98 alone, as illustrated in the appendix, I identified over eighty-five active big bands in New York (not including many dance and nostalgia bands).[3] Big bands dominated the 1998, 2001, and 2004 International Association of Jazz Educators conventions held in New York, and many of New York's most recognized big bands appeared.

Improvisation may have attracted the most attention from jazz listeners and writers, but the esteem accorded jazz composers, both past and current, seems to be rising. Works by Jelly Roll Morton, Duke Ellington, and Gil Evans have been fastidiously transcribed and published. Classic arrangements by Thad Jones, Oliver Nelson, and others, long unavailable, have been reprinted. Composers such as Maria Schneider, Jim McNeely, Michael Abene, Slide Hampton, Bob Brookmeyer, Paquito D'Rivera, and Kenny Werner receive commissions to write for and conduct jazz orchestras all over the world. Some perceptive critics have noticed a changing emphasis in jazz. According to Ben Ratliff, "the music, across the board, is deep in its compositional phase, . . . [which] doesn't just mean old repertory; it means new music that can survive, as written, into the future."[4]

With more players and a wider palette of instrumental color than small groups, big bands provide composers with the fullest range of resources available in jazz. Not so obviously, despite their decline as full-time employers, big bands also offer players the opportunity to develop, maintain, or sharpen skills. For sixteen musicians to swing and groove together, they must phrase, accentuate rhythms, and breathe as a unit. Playing in large ensembles can also promote better intonation and a richer tone. The ability of a large group of musicians to interact cohesively, which requires years of paying dues, tends to be undervalued by critics and dismissed as mere "craft," as opposed to the "art" involved in improvisation. To the critic Francis Davis, "chops and sight-reading skills" are "superficial" and overvalued by musicians.[5] Yet these competencies are vital for achieving both professional status within the mainstream jazz field and high-paying gigs in the theater and recording industries.

The existence of a large number of bands in New York allows musicians to approximate the experience that could still be found in road bands until the late 1960s. Sam Burtis, trombonist with the Smithsonian Jazz Masterworks Orchestra and Chico O'Farrill's Afro-Cuban Jazz Orchestra and former leader of the Mingus Big Band, says, "If I want to, I can rehearse with a big band every day of the week here."[6] Women could say the same thing, though some complain that they cannot get beyond being substitutes in many bands. Because of a paradoxical combination of limited options (continued sexism in the music industry) and economic incentives ("girl bands" are marketable), many women have developed their talents within their own professional scene apart from male-dominated networks, and few women have made the move into elite circles. The relationship of avant-garde bands to professionalism is more nebulous; the values engendered in these playing environments (stylistic innovation and creative group interaction) have less obvious relevance in the marketplace.

Experience in big bands changes the way players think about improvisation. They learn to make concise statements within limited space. They begin to shape their solos; the arrangement provides a point of departure and a clear destination and, often, background figures to feed off. Most of all, soloing in a big band builds strength. Waiting for a turn to solo, surrounded by fifteen or so peers, is like sitting in a pressure cooker. As the tenor saxophonist Joe Lovano relates about his long experience playing in big bands, from Woody Herman's to Carla Bley's, "When you got up and stood on your own two feet, you had to say something after someone else just played. That's a very important thing in the development of your personality as an improviser and for the music, period. That's why big bands are so important to play in."

There are also substantial social reasons for the existence of big bands. Big bands occupy central positions in the networks within which New York City jazz musicians compete for recognition and economic survival. In these networks musicians trade job referrals, exchange favors, and share knowledge. Often, on smaller band gigs, each musician plays a different instrument; in big bands, however, saxophone players can network with other saxophone players, trombone players can network with other trombone players, and so on. Work is not limited to the jazz field; rather, musicians' abilities in different styles often qualify them for other kinds of work, including Broadway shows, popular music recordings, salsa bands, and club dates. Networks differ greatly not only in style preferences but also in ethnic makeup, race and gender integration, aesthetics, education, and political activism.

Underlying musicians' widespread interest in big bands may also be a fundamental, yet often unacknowledged, desire for legitimation. Parity with symphonic musicians (in terms of steady income, benefits, and better working conditions) is but one outward sign of acceptance in the greater project of gaining recognition for jazz as a "serious" art form alongside large-scale European-derived genres such as symphony, opera, and ballet.[7] Just as sizable orchestras enhanced the prestige of European cities, big bands can dynamically announce the arrival of jazz as a cultural force and symbol of civic pride. Perhaps the prominent display of large groups always carries something of this social meaning. As more and more cities have built performance centers, big bands can fill their spaces with sound and their stages with musicians better than can small groups.[8] In the case of all-women bands such as Diva, the sight of sixteen women playing brass, bass, and drums undermines stereotypes concerning "masculine" instruments. For avant-garde musicians, big bands provide a clamorous retort to more conventional musicians or listeners who might question their competence (especially during an era of "neoclassical" revival in jazz).

So why, then, are big bands seen as an anachronism, a throwback to the swing era? The relegation of big bands to the past is so complete that big band music has its own category, separate from jazz, in the statistics collected by the record industry (RIAA) and reflected in the layout of the bins in many record stores. A customer looking for a Count Basie or Duke Ellington CD may not find it in the jazz section.

THE "DEATH" OF THE BIG BAND

Ironically, their very success may be reasons that big bands' continued importance in the jazz universe is often overlooked. In their heyday big bands marched victoriously out of the Great Depression across the world stage like the platoons of Americans fighting in World War II. In a market increasingly unified by national broadcasting networks and record distributors, the first superstars were born. While contributing to the dissemination of African American musical culture, the swing industry profited white bandleaders, promoters, and corporations more than its African American originators.

Benny Goodman, playing a "hotter" style of jazz, attracted legions of young fans. In 1937 the swing industry took in nearly $80 million. Record sales surged from 10 million in 1932, past predepression levels, to 130 million in 1941.[9] Star sidemen commanded high salaries as leaders competed for their talents. Caught up in the frenzy, ambitious players rushed to form their own big bands. As one example of this trajectory, Cootie Williams moved from Duke Ellington to Benny Goodman in 1940 and a year later formed his own successful band. It might have seemed to many promoters, ballroom managers, and musicians that this boom would last forever.

And then, almost without warning, at least as this narrative conventionally unfolds, the big bands came to an abrupt and catastrophic end. In the space of a mere four weeks, beginning in December 1946, seven prominent bands broke up: those led by Woody Herman, Jack Teagarden, Les Brown, Benny Carter, Harry James, Tommy Dorsey, and the King of Swing himself, Benny Goodman. Many lesser-known bands were also casualties. Although some of these leaders regrouped over the next several years, most were never again to stand in front of regularly touring orchestras. As a period of employment for vast numbers of musicians, especially saxophone, trumpet, and trombone players, the swing era would never be duplicated.

Not surprisingly, books on big band jazz focus on the "golden age," chronicling a steady curve upward into the war years until the sudden collapse in the years immediately after World War II. An early chapter in George T.

Simon's important guide to big bands (first published in 1967) is titled "The Rise, the Glory and the Decline." Albert McCarthy, in *Big Band Jazz* (1974), begins with "Early Syncopated Bands" (James Reese Europe) and the "First Flowering" (Fletcher Henderson), devotes several chapters to "The Swing Era," and concludes with "The End of an Era—The Decline of the Big Bands."[10]

Even as the popularity of the swing big bands was rising, a countermovement was taking root in the form of renewed interest in more traditional styles of jazz. In the late 1930s Eddie Condon and even big band leaders such as Tommy Dorsey formed "Dixieland" groups. The New Orleans cornet player Bunk Johnson was "rediscovered." Writers such as Winthrop Sargeant and Rudi Blesh attacked big bands as a commercial corruption of true jazz, a formulization by slick arrangers of the improvisation and riffs of the New Orleans and "traditional jazz" they loved. "Large scale jazz can never be hot jazz," wrote Sargeant. "The larger the scale, in fact, the colder the product." Like many white jazz enthusiasts, Sargeant's preferences were predicated on assumptions of racial difference, such as associating composition and literacy with the forces of civilization and spontaneous improvisation with instinctual abandon. "With the formation of large ensembles and of complex orchestrations there enter the factors of deliberation, rehearsal, discipline and so on," Sargeant continued. "Our old enemy the notational system begins to assert its sway. Technique begins to be more precise, and performance more self-conscious." The swing fad, though it marked a return "toward the primitive art of Negroid improvisation" celebrated by Sargeant, "like most fads . . . [had become] sophisticated and conventionalized."[11] In the rancorous debates that flared in the jazz press, defenders of the swing bands labeled proponents of Dixieland jazz "moldy figs."[12]

Equally contemptuous of the swing bands but opposing this reactionary point of view were the writers who championed the new angular and dissonant style of jazz, bebop, that seemed to burst on the scene in 1945. One writer explained, "It's a difficult music to play and understand. That's why our young musicians, better schooled than yesterday's swing men, are turning to it once they find that swing is a pushover." For their part, swing enthusiasts complained about bebop: "You can't sing it, and you can't dance to it."[13] Picking up many of the same criticisms earlier leveled at swing, their fundamental disagreement over the direction of jazz notwithstanding, both the "moldy figs" and champions of the bebop revolution found themselves in a strange alliance against their common enemy, the "rampant commercialism" of the swing industry.[14]

A 1947 broadcast of a concert on Rudi Blesh's "This Is Jazz" show pitted the "house" band (New Orleans–style musicians such as Wild Bill Davison and Warren "Baby" Dodds) against a group of modernists (including Charlie Parker, Dizzy Gillespie, and Lennie Tristano). Promoted by the critic

Barry Ulanov as "the first battle of jazz styles," of "moldy figs vs. moderns," the contest excluded the swing bands, dismissing them as "the commercial middle ground."[15]

Bernard Gendron has argued that the similar discursive formations used by both factions played a significant role in the transformation of jazz from entertainment to "art."[16] As some jazz composers and orchestra leaders attempted to transform the big band format from functional dance music to "serious" art, Norman Granz and other impresarios promoted the jam session, not the jazz orchestra, as concert music. When big bands did appear in concert halls, fans still expected to hear their favorite songs. If the bands obliged, the audiences sometimes did "violence to the conventions of concert etiquette by dancing in the aisles." Moreover, not only was the dance band tainted by connections to the body, but, as Scott DeVeaux points out, the jam session was romanticized "as a 'pure' form of jazz because the musicians played not for money but for their own artistic fulfillment."[17]

The dual assault of revivalists and modernists and the inability to shed the dance band image had the effect of permanently relegating the big band to a lesser status in jazz. From these points of view, the big band era came to be seen as an aberration, a decade of excess sandwiched between two periods of "authentic" jazz. The modernist position was articulated most forcefully by Ross Russell in a series of articles in *The Record Changer* (1948–49). Characterizing the innovators of bebop as "disillusioned large band sidemen whose creative impulses led them back to small band jazz," Russell wrote:

> Bebop is the music of revolt: revolt against big bands, arrangers, vertical harmonies, soggy rhythms, non-playing orchestra leaders, Tin Pan Alley—against commercialized music in general. It reasserts the individuality of the jazz musician as a creative artist, playing spontaneous and melodic music within the framework of jazz, but with new tools, sounds, and concepts.[18]

Allowing that the "new ideas" and "harmonic levels" of the beboppers may have "filtered into the jazz language through the offices of the swing arranger," Russell maintained that "the beginnings of bebop" were best viewed "as a simplification of big band instrumentation," adding that "the whole idea of experimentation demanded an absolute minimum number of voices."[19] Russell and other modernists viewed the decline of big band jazz in terms of aesthetic depletion. The musical resources of this style had been used up, a process accelerated by the commercial success of big band jazz during the swing era that spawned imitators rather than innovators. According to the part-time jazz writer Hsio Wen Shih, "artistically, swing had died" even earlier than "the decline of the 'band business' after the end of World War II. By the early 1940's the gradual elimination of stylistic variations had killed big-band jazz. It was a death by entropy."[20]

In his highly influential 1963 book, *Blues People,* LeRoi Jones (Amiri Baraka) continued this discursive thread:

> The tasteless commercialism of most of the swing bands had rendered them virtually incapable of serving as vehicles for any serious musical expression. . . . The autonomy, even anarchy, of the small band was not only an instinctive return to the older forms of jazz, but it must certainly have been a conscious attempt by these young musicians to secure some measure of isolation from what they had come to realize by now was merely cultural vapidity.[21]

According to this thinking, if spontaneous improvisation, that is, "freedom," is the essence of jazz, then small groups, because they typically allow more space for improvisation, must be more "jazz." Moreover, by associating this "cultural vapidity" with assimilative inclinations of middle-class blacks, Baraka linked the big band to racial and class distinctions.[22] "Swing music, which was the result of arranged big band jazz, had almost nothing to do with blues, had very little to do with black America, though that is certainly where it had come from" (164–65). The primary culprit was the arranger. "Spontaneous impulse had been replaced by the arranger, and the human element of music was confined to whatever difficulties individual performers might have reading a score" (181). In his important investigation of orality in jazz, Ben Sidran argued that whereas written texts stifle individuality, in "the oral mode of perception, . . . individuality . . . actually flourishes in a group context."[23] In fact, bebop, in his view, resulted from "the demand within oral culture for individuality above all else—heightened by the conformity of urban society" (87). Both Jones and Sidran, quoting Ross Russell, credit Lester Young with "replenish[ing] the stream polluted by the arrangers and thus making possible the even more complex rhythmic development of the bebop style."[24] Bebop, while revolutionary, marked a return to the "oral," "spontaneous," and "individualistic" roots of jazz.[25] DeVeaux notes that, other than the music of a few canonized artists (Ellington, Basie, and Lunceford), "much that went under the banner of swing" came to be regarded as "trivial, threadbare, or hopelessly commercial."[26] When Martin Williams assembled the *Smithsonian Collection of Classic Jazz,* besides a quick nod to early big band recordings by Fletcher Henderson and Benny Moten, recordings by this holy trinity were the only orchestral jazz he included.

The big band has not fared much better in contemporary discourse. Gunther Schuller claims that "jazz orchestral styles atrophied" and that "very little of truly innovative achievement in arranging concepts can be claimed after 1960." DeVeaux dismisses big bands' significance to "aspiring jazz musicians," stating that a "jazz orchestra of fifteen or more musicians suggests either nostalgia . . . or the sterility of the university 'lab band.' "[27] Jazz education makes an easy target. Bruno Nettl begins with the assumption that big band jazz has "a very modest role in the outside world of jazz" and concludes that the university's emphasis on big bands "does not really correspond to the important types of jazz heard in the real musical world."[28] In the *Jazz Grove* Gary Kennedy laments that "'jazz education' has yet to reach any of the artistic goals that the term would imply" and lays much of the blame for "stylistic narrowness" and the resulting "generic professional musicians" squarely on big bands. Mike Vax writes, "The essence of jazz music is creativity and improvisation. These attributes are best learned in a smaller environment than a big band rehearsal."[29] The criticism of big bands is situated along racial fault lines, as jazz education festivals are condemned for featuring "big bands, white repertory and white performers," instead of small groups and "the central black-American traditions of jazz."[30] Some of these criticisms have merit; deficiencies in the training and experience of many jazz band directors and their selection of repertoire warrant vast improvements. But rather than suggest ways to improve and expand the orchestral jazz curriculum, most seem to identify big bands as the problem.

To jazz musicians, big bands—"the symphony orchestras of jazz"—are simply larger groups and, as such, are style-neutral. In the impresario George Wein's words, "Each era has different approaches to big band playing that all come out of the jazz psyche. They're a total reflection of whatever the jazz mode is at any given time." The founder of the Newport Jazz Festival and the world's preeminent producer of jazz festivals from Nice to Tokyo, Wein has promoted big bands in various enterprises over the years. Even if "big band music is not in vogue," he explains, "there are so many big bands around because musicians love to play great arrangements. They will come to rehearse for nothing to play great arrangements." If romantic fantasies of lack of mercenary motivations are a test of commitment to an art form, then big bands have proven they pass muster as well as the jam session.

With the end of the swing era, big bands garnered less attention in the music industry, but they were still important features of the musical topography of the United States. They remained prominent fixtures where ample budgets could support them, on television variety shows, in Las Vegas, and in the military. Despite hardships, big bands endured, backing up popular singers, recording in the studio, traveling on the road, and, on the grassroots level, as rehearsal bands or playing for dances. New York City, in particular, persisted as a center for big band activity.

Writings on post-1940s big bands have been sparse, except for histories of specific bands that survived beyond the swing era—such as the Ellington, Basie, Herman, and Kenton orchestras. Bill Kirchner's collection of contemporary big band music for the Smithsonian partially fills this huge void. His accompanying booklet provides insightful program notes and historical perspective on dozens of creative and vital bands that were active at various times from the 1940s through the 1980s. Unfortunately, this important work is currently out of print.[31]

Like most jazz scholarship and critical discourse, the growing ethnomusicological literature on jazz has concentrated on improvisation in small groups. By contrast, big bands open a window onto musical practices and social interactions discussed much less often in jazz studies: jazz musicians' interest in composition, the collaborative or dialogic relationship between improvisers and composers, and players' approaches to interpretation of precomposed music. Paul Berliner touches on some of these topics in his magnum opus, *Thinking in Jazz: The Infinite Art of Improvisation,* but purposely confines most of his discussion to "small group practices."[32] Although not unique to big bands, these issues surface more conspicuously in large ensembles.

Jazz has been celebrated for its emphasis on "personal freedom put . . . at the service of group conception."[33] In her study of "mainstream" small jazz groups, Ingrid Monson has noted "two levels on which this individual-versus-group tension operates: the relationship of the soloist (who may be a rhythm section member) to the rhythm section, and the relationship of each individual to the remainder of the rhythm section."[34] Big bands considerably complicate these dynamics not only because of their additional sections of players (trumpets, trombones, and saxophones) but also because of the important role of the composer and the arranger. This book explores how jazz musicians have dealt creatively with the tension between individual and large-scale collective expression: How are the goals of the composer and the arranger reconciled with those of the performer in an idiom in which the performer's role not only as interpreter but also as improviser remains central? How do composition and performance practices converge to yield differing concepts of ensemble blend? Perhaps most important, how do concepts of individual autonomy relate to processes of self-discovery and identity formation in jazz?

INDIVIDUALITY AND BLEND

At the beginning of the penultimate chorus of his 1931 recording of "I Got Rhythm," Louis Armstrong calls out "Every Tub!" to cue the entire band to begin improvising. Both Ellington (1933) and Basie (1938) recorded big band pieces they named "Every Tub."[35] These words, taken from the saying "Every tub sits on its own bottom," resonated deeply with many African American jazz musicians. The saying signified not only "self-reliance" or "self-realization" but also spoke to the value many jazz musicians placed on retaining a distinctive sound and sense of individuality in all musical situations. This individualism in jazz, as in African American music and culture in general, is rooted in the figures of the itinerant rural bluesman and the country preacher.[36]

When playing in small groups, musicians face fewer obstacles to upholding the ideal of individualism. Solo space is plentiful, and ensemble passages are less densely orchestrated. In big bands the constraints of ensemble playing to various extents temper jazz musicians' desires for individuality and personal expression. Still, the principle of one person to a part is inviolable. Jazz musicians never share music stands, as in a symphony orchestra, and everyone must read from his or her own book. Although a few composers have experimented with larger ensembles (and unorthodox instruments, for jazz), each section of the winds has an upper limit of four or five—enough instruments for each section to stand on its own harmonically, without doubling any part except the top melody (usually an octave lower).

Throughout the history of jazz, players, bandleaders, composers, and arrangers have reconciled the twin demands of individual and ensemble in very different ways. Some leaders, such as Benny Goodman or Artie Shaw and, to a somewhat lesser extent, Count Basie (post-1950), have striven for a meticulously coordinated and polished blend in which each section of the band, and at times the entire band, attempts to sound "as one." Lead players were prominent, and selected improvisers stood out during their allotted solo space before merging back into the ranks. In the Ellington orchestra the requirements of group cohesion were balanced with Ellington's aesthetic of maintaining his players' sonic identities. Writing for *Down Beat* in 1939, Ellington explained, "Those things we have to say, we try to express musically with the greatest possible degree of freedom of inspiration and individuality. We thus attempt to achieve a form of individual expressiveness presented by the entire band, both as individuals and as a whole."[37] The most heterogeneous ensembles—for example, the Sun Ra Arkestra and other avant-garde bands, as well as the Mingus Big Band—elevate individual freedom above group coordination, often to the point of eliminating any semblance of ensemble cohesion.[38]

The most polished bands follow an aesthetic similar to that of the classical symphonic tradition. Players cultivate darker sounds that are more easily blended, work obsessively to correct tiny idiosyncrasies in the intonation of their instruments, and develop a fluid and consistent technique in all registers. In performance they coordinate attacks and releases, interpret rhythms exactly the same, and follow a rigorous and constantly shifting hierarchy of the lead trumpet and their section leaders. At the other extreme, ensemble sections may at times resemble a boisterous party or noisy argument in which individuals strive to make their voices heard above the crowd. Instead of working to "tame" their instruments, players delight in their instruments' idiosyncrasies, ignoring slight intonational discrepancies or possibly lingering on a note just for its funny sound.

Many listeners have difficulty appreciating the full spectrum of blending styles. To some, the more individuated approach sounds sloppy or unprofessional, while to others, the more homogeneous blend seems sterile and mechanical. What may be difficult for lay listeners can be impossible for musicians. Because they spend much of their musical lives immersed in one style or the other and their livelihood depends on its mastery, players tend to disparage blending practices different from their own. Instrumentalists who have not learned how to subjugate their own personalities "for the greater good," as the trumpeter and arranger Michael Mossman puts it (somewhat facetiously) and follow the nuances and subtleties of phrasing, articulation, breathing, and intonation of their section leaders will not be successful in circles that value such skills. Similarly, these musicians might seem too reserved or lacking in personality to find acceptance in bands that prize more individuated styles of blend.

Despite widespread acknowledgment that notation barely captures jazz performance practice, few studies have focused on jazz musicians' approach to interpretation of written parts. Jazz musicians mentally convert notated rhythms from "straight" to swing and, sometimes, to complex polyrhythms, simultaneously adding timbral, inflectional, and accentual effects at appropriate moments. In the typical jazz score articulations and dynamics are barely indicated. Oral and written traditions merge as musicians, through experience playing together, are enculturated in different blending styles and aesthetics of ensemble cohesion. In different jazz worlds compositional techniques and blending performance practices closely mirror each other.

The wide range of blending styles found in jazz presents special problems to directors of school jazz bands and repertory ensembles that perform diverse repertoires. Now that the availability of arrangements has expanded, educators, in particular, need to understand and be able to convey to their students the very different demands of music played by, for example, the Mingus and the Bob Mintzer big bands. Some may have found, as have I, that students enjoy playing music that permits a degree of abandon and may have difficulty making the transition back to arrangements that require more careful blending. On the other hand, others (such as Wynton Marsalis) worry that too much emphasis on homogeneous blending produces bland, "cookie cutter" musicians.

This study relates blending styles not only to enculturated performance practices of musicians but also to compositional decisions. Different procedures require differing degrees of intonational, timbral, accentual, and rhythmic conformity. Complex chord structures, polyphony in which clarity of individual lines is desired, for example, demand appropriately experienced players. More individuated playing styles work successfully with unisons, open and less complicated voicings, and simpler, often repetitive, figures or riffs.

An important principle underlying much African music is the combining of relatively simple parts into a cohesive, sophisticated whole. Individual parts often remain aurally distinguishable through distinctive timbres, pitch allocations, or rhythmic patterns.[39] Many writers have described such individuated ensemble styles as characteristic of African diasporic musical cultures.[40] Rather than view these practices as static "retentions" or "survivals" of African culture, recent ethnomusicological theory has emphasized music's active role in giving "voice to racial difference."[41] Indeed, throughout the history of jazz, ensemble blend has been an important marker of racial identity. William Russell wrote of Bunk Johnson's style (and by extension, Buddy Bolden and New Orleans jazz):

> All the parts are played in a sort of pseudo unison, or at least the parts are in similar rhythmic values. Of course they never are in true unison nor are they hit off rhythmically together, and naturally almost every sin known to European musical culture is committed—lack of precision, out of tunefulness, smears, muffs—in other words we have with us once again the well-known "sloppy New Orleans ensemble."[42]

During the swing era, although much of this "sloppiness" was toned down, blending style continued to resonate with racial difference. In Sidran's words, "The large Negro bands . . . attempted to maintain a 'group feeling' that was a function of individual personalities."[43] According to Benny Goodman's former personal secretary (as well as saxophonist and jazz historian), Loren Schoenberg, Goodman and Artie Shaw complained about the Ellington band's intonation. Schoenberg notes, "They [Ellington's band] played with a looseness and with less of the 'professional' sheen than Goodman and Shaw would have ever permitted." Emphasis on individual autonomy in jazz and African American musics not only accentuated non-European or "African" elements in the racial imaginary; it also allowed creative intervention in dominant discourse that constructed all blacks and racial others as the same. Many jazz musicians, whatever their racial and ethnic backgrounds, continue to find jazz attractive for its emphasis on self-discovery and individuation.[44]

JAZZ AND GENDER

While styles of ensemble blend have been important musical signifiers of racial identity, within the almost exclusively male or homosocial universe of jazz, concepts of individual autonomy also are bound up intimately with masculine roles. For African Americans, jazz became an important site for construction of black masculinity that offered the possibility of undermining and subverting prevailing stereotypes rooted in minstrelsy and mass-mediated entertainment. At the same time, jazz became an important field in which white men could define themselves in relation to the perceived or imagined differences of African Americans.

Recent gender studies in music, finding much relevance in the work of the feminist theorist Judith Butler, emphasize the performative aspects of gender and sexuality—that "the gendered self is the cumulative result of *performances*" (original emphasis). Butler posits that to be culturally intelligible, genders must "in some sense institute and maintain relations of coherence and continuity among sex, gender, sexual practice, and desire." Feminist musicologists working in classical music have begun unraveling the complex interplay of these elements in classical music composition and performance.[45] Such work has barely begun in jazz, despite the obvious importance of male identity formation in the idiom.[46] In classical music femininist approaches often have met fierce resistance as they infringe on the supposed purity of "absolute" music. Similarly, encroachments by feminist theory into jazz studies have threatened established hierarchies of expertise among jazz collectors, discographers, critics, historians, and the like. In my conversations with male *musicians,* however, I often have found an openness, almost a fascination with the topic of gender.

Some writers have warned of the danger of discussing gender only when women musicians are involved. As Lucy Green notes, "The gender of a female performer in many contexts, and of a female composer in most contexts, unlike the gender of the male musician, becomes an object of interest, an overt, and often problematic, part of the musical meanings themselves."[47] As a male musician and scholar, I have observed this tendency in myself, and to some extent this book has fallen into this trap despite my best intentions. My conversations with female musicians have made me more aware of gender as it operates in all-male spheres. For example, just as the sight of an all-white big band in New York can raise the hackles of many observers (white as well as black), the fact that a jazz orchestra is all-male no longer escapes my notice. The tendency to focus on difference, in this case on gender as it applies to women, has the effect of helping us to better understand how gender operates in male jazz composition and performance. The female jazz musicians I interviewed, however, although invariably patient with my questioning, showed an evident, understandable fatigue with discussing the topic of gender.

When not talking about "women in jazz," many writers interested in gender have focused on misogynist or hypermasculinist discourse, such as is found in the autobiographies of Miles Davis and Charles Mingus.[48] While extreme cases such as these may expose gender's role in the articulation of power, I am also interested in a broader range of gendered discourse and musical styles available to jazz musicians. For example, while some jazz musicians have foregrounded their abilities to compete in aggressive, fast, and loud styles, many others have emphasized lyrical and laid-back qualities generally considered less macho. That these musical qualities are often gendered is clear in musicians' choices of metaphors (for example, "playing with balls"). Despite the overall tendency to favor "masculine" styles, individualism and contrarianism are thoroughly ingrained in the jazz ethos, and many musicians have carved out distinctive musical identities by foregrounding the "less masculine" side of these oppositions.

Unlike classical music, jazz has seemed more open to the possibility of female composers. Perhaps, because it is a more private activity and, as Green points out, because of its somewhat lesser status vis-à-vis improvisation, jazz composition fit more easily into accepted patterns of female domesticity.[49] Female composer-arrangers (for example, Lil Hardin Armstrong, Mary Lou Williams, and Toshiko Akiyoshi) have participated in jazz over nearly its entire historical span.[50] Beginning in chapter 6 with discussion of the composers Maria Schneider, Carla Bley, and Jim McNeely and continuing in chapters 7, 10, and 11 with the Mingus band, all-women bands, and the Lincoln Center orchestra, gender increasingly occupies my attention.

As some musicians, scholars, listeners, and critics are beginning to recognize, women's participation is the most critical issue facing jazz in the twenty-first century. Although most observers would agree that the number of female instrumentalists has grown significantly since the 1980s, female jazz musicians face continued resistance to their full participation. Given the existence of the large and often separate social networks in New York's jazz scene, like racial integration, sexual integration in jazz may prove elusive.

JAZZ SCENES: COLLABORATION AND COMPETITION

In jazz links between composers and players have been more direct than those typically found in classical music. Many jazz composers prefer to write for their own carefully chosen ensembles and are intimately involved in the realization of their works.[51] Ellington was hardly the exception when he identified individual players by name, not by instrument, on his scores and parts. Musicians frequently evaluate big band arrangements according to whether the music sounds "generic"—that is, written for a universal pool of competent players, as is most classical music, or customized or designed exclusively for a certain group of players. In the composer and pianist Jim McNeely's memorable words, "It's great to write for a band and see the faces on the score page."[52]

The process is circular: composers' approaches to coordinating the actions of individual players are also determined by the distinctive performance styles of the players for whom they write. Performers and leaders often become actively involved in editing, adapting, and reinterpreting works. Many of the best ensembles strike a balance between the players' desire for freedom of expression and the composers' need for control. This collaboration takes many forms: when the composer and performer work together directly, the performer extemporizes on a composition ("improvises"), or the performer interprets a musical text.[53] Clear distinctions between composer and performer, composition and improvisation, begin to break down as composerly authority becomes more diffuse.

In practice the realization and dissemination of a work of art requires the cooperation of a large network of people. In big bands this network includes not only composers and players but also managers, record executives, copyists, club owners, critics, and philanthropists. The "works," of course, are performances as well as compact discs. To maintain these collaborative art worlds, leaders depend on large networks of players. Because of the meager financial incentives they are able to offer, leaders build long lists of substitutes, usually through recommendations from their regular players. The resultant flow of personnel maintains a degree of "interchangeability." Musicians develop similar competencies, common understandings, and conventional practices. Older, more established players, with their larger networks, stick together.[54] The social networks that make up New York City big bands have varying degrees of stability within them and separation between them. To the extent that aesthetics, traditions, and performance practices differ substantially, there is little interchange of musicians between these scenes.[55] The language in which differences between networks is articulated includes such familiar dichotomies as innovative/traditional, avant-garde/mainstream, non-conformist/conservative, artistic/commercial, and untrained or amateur/skilled or professional.

Because resources flow through social contacts, the most successful musicians tend to have the largest personal networks. According to a recent National Endowment for the Arts (NEA) study, jazz networks in New York are prone to be very large (average size 223.8, compared to only 65.8 in San Francisco). Big bands offer jazz musicians, especially recent arrivals to New York, a chance to acquire social capital quickly by coming into contact with a large number of musicians. Although jazz musicians are more racially inclusive than other groups in the Unites States studied by similar methods, the study confirms that "racial and ethnic boundaries have been maintained in New York; with each group having positive affiliation toward itself (homophily) and negative affiliation toward the other."[56] Moreover, "jazz musicians have a high contact pattern because they hang out together, but . . . it is often by musical style that they do so" (I:4). Although male and female jazz musicians interact increasingly, the study notes, "in New York there are independent male and female music scenes" (III:56). The large jazz universe in New York, estimated at 33,003 persons (I:6), means that jazz musicians can easily put together big bands within the groups with which they feel the strongest affiliation and explains the presence of many bands that are all or predominantly white or black, male or female.[57]

Some scenes, for example, all-women bands and Lincoln Center, have rather clear social boundaries because of hiring policies. Jazz worlds also tend to be kept apart by clustering around different venues, such as the "downtown" scene at the Knitting Factory and what might be called the "mainstream" scene in Greenwich Village or at Birdland off Times Square. African American and Latino groups often congregate uptown in Harlem or El Barrio. Mainstream rehearsal bands gather at the Local 802 union hall. Each jazz scene, or school of activity, tends to have characteristic composing and arranging techniques and performance practices.[58]

In addition to interchange of personnel, interaction among jazz scenes involves communication: exchange of ideas, competition for audiences and resources, how musicians in different networks distinguish themselves from each other, and how they interpret their actions. Competition among jazz scenes has become more intense since jazz acquired legitimacy, however reluctantly bestowed, in the academy and other institutions of "official" culture. The ascendancy of Jazz at Lincoln Center raises the aspirations of many jazz musicians. At the same time, its success has become the focal point of bitter disputes concerning allocation of financial resources and representation of white musicians, women, and the avant-garde.[59]

Individuals' viewpoints and actions also should be understood in relation to their positions in various fields—jazz, criticism, academia, business, politics, and so forth.[60] For example, because of their positions outside the jazz field, critics and scholars tend to undervalue the importance of big bands and the skills prized by the musicians within them. Inversely, musicians dismiss perfunctorily the opinions of writers whom they believe have a vested interest in promoting certain artists or styles. The views of nonmusicians are marginalized. Musicians, along with the jazz press, also have little respect for academic writing they see as jargon-laden and overly theoretical. Such thoroughly ingrained modes of acting and thinking inhibit easy movement among greatly differing scenes and understanding of other points of view within the separate fields.

My discussions with composers, arrangers, mentors, leaders, and players explore their contention as well as their cooperation with each other. These interviews ground this book in the social contacts and associations of musicians rather than in the exploration of aesthetic issues solely through musical analysis. Nearly all the musicians who have participated in this study have shared their insights and experiences eagerly.

Much of my information also has been derived through traditional techniques of participant observation. My more than fifteen years of activity as a saxophonist in the New York area inform much of my narrative. I have also attended numerous performances and rehearsals strictly as an observer. In addition, I have gleaned important information from press releases, musicians' magazines, reviews, scholarly studies, scores, transcriptions, liner notes, recordings, and videotapes, which are documented in notes and in the bibliography. The recent NEA-sponsored study, *Changing the Beat,* has provided quantitative data that supports much of my more qualitative research.

Most of the bands studied in this book were active during the late 1990s. Some, such as the Carnegie Hall Jazz Band, have ceased to exist. In the meantime other important bands have sprung up. Leaders such as Jimmy Heath, Charlie Haden, and Mike Longo have started or reconstituted bands. The Dave Holland Big Band has emerged as a leading jazz ensemble. Though I have tried to maintain contact with many of my original informants, inevitably scenes change as musicians come and go, as bands break up and new ones are formed.

COMPOSITION, ARRANGING, AND IMPROVISATION

In dominant Western musical cultures, as codified in intellectual property laws, composition, arranging, and improvisation are conceptualized as distinct, hierarchically related activities. In actual practice the three processes are often difficult to unravel. The jazz idiom, as the cooperative worlds involved in jazz make clear, intertwines composition and improvisation in complex and creative ways. Though in some arrangements composer and improviser remain fairly distinct, in the work of many musicians the distinctions between these roles are blurred. As discussed in chapter 8, many "experimental" or avant-garde composers intentionally undermine the hierarchical relationships of these activities.

In a classic essay Nettl proposed that composition and improvisation be understood as opposite ends of a continuum rather than as distinct processes.[61] "Composition," derived from the Latin verb *componere* (put together), implies the assembling and structuring of musical ideas. Along with "invention" or original creation, composers draw upon and rework materials from their own experience. The process of fixing compositions in their final form, particularly in notation or in recorded medium, allows for reflection, revision, and refinement. Improvisers, while responding creatively to unforeseen circumstances, are rarely totally spontaneous and typically rely on formulaic material, habitual patterns, and premeditated strategies. Seen in this way, improvisation could be considered a type of composing, or "composition in real time." Within any given music culture, improvisation and composition typically share common stylistic conventions, procedures, and theory. To distinguish between composition and improvisation, as Stephen Blum points out, "we need at least a rudimentary understanding of what the performers are expected to accomplish and of how they prepare themselves to meet those expectations."[62] In fact, a more flexible conception of composition is the norm in most of the world's music cultures as evidenced in sung oral poetry, religious and ritual ceremonies, dance suites, laments, competitions, and so forth. In many musics of southern and western Asia, for example, melodic motifs are subjected to repetition, simple variation, extension, contraction, and sequential treatment.[63]

The composition, as a metaphysical entity, remains fixed from performance to performance, retaining a degree of permanence, whereas improvisation is experienced as immediate and ephemeral. The composition is valued as an object; improvisation is valued, if at all, as a process. Copyright law legitimizes the "superior" status of composition. Improvisation is considered part of the performance and, hence, protectable only under the significantly lower status of the recording copyright or as a derivative work akin to an "arrangement" of the composition.[64] Of course, the reality is not that simple: improvisations can be fixed in recordings and transcriptions and can be copied, learned, studied, and analyzed. Composers, especially in popular idioms, seldom use notation. Works are constructed in the recording studio, where "improvisations" can easily become part of the "composition." Compositions, especially in oral traditions, are subject to variation even when passed down through the most rigorous pedagogy.

Like improvisation, arranging should not be conceptualized as fully separate from the process of composing, or "putting together." Some arrangements so radically transform the original piece that it is recomposed beyond recognition. Some supposedly original compositions borrow so heavily from other compositions that they could be seen as arrangements (perhaps even subjecting their authors to infringement lawsuits). To be considered arrangements, works must retain some connection with the works on which they are based, even if at times the relationship seems tenuous. Intellectual property laws and their interpretation have accorded arranging a status somewhere between that of composition and improvisation. Arrangers obtain clearance from the holder of the copyright on the original composition. The property rights of the owner of the original composition remain supreme. As I discuss later, the hierarchical status accorded these activities has profoundly affected jazz musicians' attitudes toward their work.

A central task of the jazz arranger is combining precomposed material with improvisation. Soloists usually play alone with the rhythm section, in effect creating a small group within the big band. Leaving the rest of the band out of the arrangement during extended solos can allow a sense of compositional narrative to be lost. Arrangers use such techniques as background melodies or riffs (short repetitive patterns), "send-offs" or interludes between solos, and sustained chords or "pads" to maintain a more orchestral texture. In some bands members of the orchestra contribute to the arrangement by making up riffs on the spot. In fact, some jazz compositions that have evolved during performance have been based entirely on riffs. The Count Basie Orchestra of the 1930s was known for such collective composition.

A fundamental concern is the structure of the solo section itself. Traditionally, jazz musicians have favored strophic harmonic frameworks in which to improvise. Most often these were based on blues or thirty-two-bar popular song forms. Composers may wish to be free of such restrictions during the composed sections of the work, so that they may more freely explore motivic development and contrapuntal textures. However, suddenly inserting a chordal pattern for the solos that has not been used in prior sections makes the improvisation seem less a part of the arrangement. Possible solutions are to introduce free or modal solo sections or create vamps (short, repeated sequences of chords) based perhaps on similar harmonic gestures in the composition.

In addition to combining composition and improvisation, jazz arranging typically involves three interrelated activities: orchestration, rhythmic reinterpretation, and reharmonization. Arrangers distribute parts to different instruments, thicken lines with harmony, or compose new countermelodies and, sometimes (especially with music from other idioms), adapt rhythms to the grooves of swing or Latin jazz. The Carnegie Hall and Mingus bands have specialized in new arrangements of older repertoires (some in the former group virtually *recomposed* the original work). Even with radical changes, if the piece remains recognizable and carries associations with previous versions, it will invite comparison in a way that a newly composed piece will not. Some scholars see the reworking of earlier material in the postmodernist context of parody or the African American practice of versioning or signifyin(g).[65] Rearranging is a time-honored tradition in jazz, as illustrated in Jelly Roll Morton's "King Porter Stomp," which was adapted by Fletcher Henderson and Benny Goodman. Ellington's works were subject to continual revision, as can be seen in his musicians' abundant markings on their parts or heard in the numerous versions of recorded tunes.[66]

Rigid conceptualization of the roles of composition, arranging, and improvisation and failure to understand the dialogic processes involved in much jazz composition have led some writers to conclude incorrectly that a composer such as Ellington was not a composer at all. For example, in a much-maligned book, James Lincoln Collier devotes three hundred pages to Ellington's music only to conclude that, through his manipulation of sidemen and other "ingredients," Ellington was more like a "card shark" or "master chef" than a composer.[67] Similar questions challenging Marsalis's authorial role in composing his own works (such as *Blood on the Fields,* discussed further in chapter 11) continue to circulate in contemporary jazz scenes and prove the durability of traditional conceptions of composerly authority.

Much of the difficulty of understanding jazz composition comes from unawareness of the fundamental hybridity of jazz as a cultural form. Paul Gilroy argues for the central role of black musical expression in reproducing a "distinctive counterculture of modernity," or Afro-modernism. By standing both *inside* dominant culture and *apart from* it, people of African descent (the "black Atlantic") contributed to and absorbed elements of modernist discourse while offering strategic alternatives.[68] The position of jazz composers is complicated by this legacy of "double consciousness" in African American culture. While procedures and ideals highly valorized in Western art music, such as motivic development, organic unity, and attention to formal structural, are commonly found in jazz, through their incorporation of improvisation jazz composers relinquish some control over their works.[69] The fundamental hybridity of Afro-modernism is nowhere more apparent than in the dialogic relationship between composers and performers and the complex admixture of compositional, arranging, and improvisational practices common in jazz. In the pages ahead, this book examines how this legacy continues to inform the work of many jazz musicians.

CATEGORIES OF BIG BANDS

Musicians often distinguish among big bands according to their functions. Of the seven types, five remain fairly common in New York: rehearsal bands, working bands (mostly part-time since very few full-time bands remain), dance bands, school bands, and, the newest rubric, repertory orchestras.[70] Studio bands, or bands assembled expressly for the purpose of recording, have become less common as recording budgets for jazz have continued to shrink. The few road bands remaining have less relevance to this study because their members are most often away from New York. These classifications are not mutually exclusive and may overlap. Most players play in more than one kind of band, and many (myself included) have played in all seven.[71]

Rehearsal bands seldom perform publicly and exist mainly for composers and arrangers to hear their work or for players to keep up their chops. To some extent all the other types of bands, except for school bands, could be considered subcategories of working bands, because their players receive some remuneration (however minimal) for performance. As musicians use the term, and as it is used in this book, *working bands* refers to standing ensembles that work in clubs and may occasionally go on short tours or record a CD. Dance bands appear in different venues—dance clubs and ballrooms—and perform a specialized repertoire. Repertory bands perform a broad repertoire in much the same way that classical orchestras present the works of the "great composers." Indeed, the founders of repertory emulated the model of the symphony orchestra not just in the way they selected material but also in terms of gaining public and institutional support. Repertory orchestras differ from another type of working band, often referred to as a "ghost band" by musicians, that tours under the name of a deceased leader (such as Count Basie, Duke Ellington, or Glenn Miller) and performs a more limited repertoire. School bands combine some of the characteristics of rehearsal and working bands because their regular rehearsals (often several a week) culminate in public performances.

These distinctions reflect the way bands approach their material and the kinds of venues in which they seek to perform. Although these categories may seem self-evident, in practice they can be misleading. For example, most "rehearsal" bands seldom rehearse, at least in a systematic manner. Instead, because they do not perform publicly, their rehearsals assume more of the characteristics of a performance. Some rehearsal bands aspire to become working bands. As they begin to gig more often, rehearsals may become less frequent. Many orchestras that musicians refer to as "working" bands in reality have little work, but they rehearse even less. Bands with regular gigs almost never rehearse privately, unless they have an important engagement or a new, difficult piece of music. This study devotes considerable attention to important working bands in New York, such as the Vanguard Jazz Orchestra, the Maria Schneider Jazz Orchestra, and the Mingus Big Band. Repertory orchestras have evolved very different approaches to the performance of historical material, and most have seen the developing of new works as central to their mission. Because they may tour frequently, repertory bands could also be considered road bands, except that most maintain a significant presence at home through their attachment to institutions such as Lincoln Center or Carnegie Hall.

Of these categories, repertory orchestras have generated the most controversy. Their prominence and their receipt of public money have led to demands that they represent all of jazz's diversity. A related issue is whether classic scores should be "preserved" and performances re-created or whether they should be reinterpreted by the group currently performing them. Some musicians worry that by making jazz a "consecrated" art form in the manner of classical music with a share of governmental subsidy and private philanthropic support, it will become fossilized with an "official" canon of great works and a pantheon of great (mostly dead) artists.[72] For jazz to remain vital, they believe, traditions must be replenished through the commissioning of new music instead of venerating a finite set of fixed artifacts. Furthermore, many musicians have resisted musical direction that insists on slavishly recreating note-for-note the solos on the original records. As the repertory movement has matured, many of these concerns have evaporated as musicians have discovered creative possibilities within the constraints of different historical styles.

OVERVIEW

Big bands form an arena in which views on many issues in jazz today are expressed and acted out—issues such as how to define the boundaries of jazz, recognition of its African American roots and contributions from other ethnicities, gender roles, access to funding, and the relative values of tradition and innovation. Interpretation and reenactment of historical jazz (through the repertory movement) have become increasingly important. In the process a new kind of jazz musician is taking shape: one who is fluent in diverse historical styles, though at the expense, some may feel, of finding an innovative voice. It is not the purpose of this book to take sides in these and other debates but to present the issues by studying the social networks of the players, leaders, and composer-arrangers and their concomitant musical styles, ideologies, and rhetorical strategies.

Chapter 1 explores some of New York's many jazz venues and considers such basic issues as the size and instrumentation of big bands and why big bands have remained important in New York. Using the typology discussed above, chapter 2 looks behind the scenes—at venues and rehearsal spaces—while providing historical perspective on the types currently active. Musicians discuss their training and influences and their competition for work and recognition. Their discourse reveals how perceptions of musical and social boundaries are inflected by racial difference. The rise of repertory jazz orchestras is examined in chapter 3 in the context of the changing cultural significance of jazz, growth in performing arts centers, shifting patterns of funding by philanthropic and governmental agencies, and expanding corporate sponsorship. Chapter 4 goes inside a big band, the Vanguard Jazz Orchestra (VJO), to experience musicianship from the vantage point of each chair. The traditions of the VJO, the longest-lived contemporary New York big band, began in the Thad Jones/Mel Lewis Orchestra and have continued to evolve over four decades of performances. Members and their substitutes constitute a formidable network of musicians, active in a large number of New York bands, as well as the Broadway theater and recording industries. Chapter 5 follows many of these same players into a very different situation, the now-defunct Carnegie Hall Jazz Band, directed by Jon Faddis. Comparing the leadership in this band with the more cooperatively run VJO (as well as taking a glimpse back at the leadership styles established by Thad Jones and Mel Lewis) yields insights into different approaches to musical direction. Chapter 6 examines recent developments in arranging and composition, with an emphasis on innovative techniques and formal structures. Chapter 7 looks at the Mingus Big Band. In keeping with the spirit of her late husband, Sue Mingus has assembled musicians from diverse social networks and backgrounds. In her role as artistic director, she presides over the "gunslingers" of the Mingus band as they recreate the hypermasculinist, competitive atmosphere that was integral to the Mingus ethos. In the avant-garde or experimental bands studied in chapter 8, Andrew Hill and William Parker deconstruct boundaries between composition and improvisation, further elevating the musical freedom of their musicians. Chapter 9, by looking at the careers, lives, and music of Chico O'Farrill and Ray Santos, enters a jazz world that thrives on hybridity. Latin jazz bands test musicians' mastery of the harmonic and melodic complexities of jazz as well as the rhythmic matrices of Latin music. While musical and social heterogeneity may rule, divisions arise more from neocolonial political economies and nationalistic impulses than from racial or ethnic background. Chapters 10 and 11 explore two relatively isolated jazz scenes (at least in personnel): all-women bands and the Lincoln Center Jazz Orchestra. Gathering in all-women groups contradicts the goal of many female musicians to move into mainstream jazz circles while providing opportunities to gain valuable experience. A concluding section of chapter 10 discusses the common perception of a rise in women's participation in jazz in the context of persistent narratives characterizing women as "emergent," even after many decades of contributions. Chapter 11 includes analysis of Marsalis's Pulitzer Prize–winning oratorio, *Blood on the Fields,* and the relationship of this work to his efforts to build an orchestra in the Ellington mold. I address the questions, why did he let go his original all-star band to work with young, mostly inexperienced players from outside New York, and how does *Blood* reflect changes in his musical thinking and his ideology? The conclusion to this book, or Outro, engages in conversation some of the recurrent ideas of the previous chapters, suggests a few practical applications of this study, and sounds some unresolved themes.

One of the highest forms of praise that a jazz ensemble can receive from other musicians is that it sounds like a *band,* with the length of the vowel stretched in proportion to the quality of the group. Bands that have acquired neither a personality through performance of a distinctive repertoire (often written expressly for them) nor a highly developed sense of ensemble playing (usually achieved through playing together for a long time) are dismissed as "generic." In the following pages, I explore how a band becomes a *ba-a-a-nd.*

Chapter 1

New York City Big Band Scenes

Monday night is musicians' night. With Broadway theaters dark, the weekend club dates finished, and many residencies at nightclubs running Tuesday through Sunday, on Monday nights jazz musicians gather to perform and listen to the music that interests *them.* Though a thriving tourist industry may supply clubs with a stream of foreign and domestic visitors, on Mondays the venues are much freer of "amateur" clubgoers than later in the week. In an atmosphere of camaraderie and release from the week's accumulated frustrations, jazz musicians cram themselves onto tiny bandstands to play in big bands.

A cool Monday evening, October 1997. A friend and I decide to take a walk around Greenwich Village to check out a few of these big bands.[1] Within a radius of a few blocks, half a dozen bands are performing in a wide range of styles. Beyond the Village, more than we can possibly visit in a single night, an even more astounding variety of bands are performing in the downtown and midtown scenes.

We begin our big band tour at the Village Vanguard, where the journeyman Vanguard Jazz Orchestra (formerly the Thad Jones/Mel Lewis Orchestra) has appeared weekly for more than forty years. Even on Monday night the club is packed with tourists (mostly European and Japanese), and musicians and friends of the band congregate in the back near the bar. The leader, John Mosca, counts off a Thad Jones classic, "Big Dipper." After an eight-bar intro played by the saxes and trombones, an extended piano solo by Jim McNeely launches the evening's opening number. For several minutes, while the rest of the band sits idly by and the rhythm section warms up, the audience waits in suspense. When the brass and reeds finally enter, the crowd explodes in approval. We stay for the first set, an interesting mix of classic material from the band's library and brand-new arrangements written for the band by McNeely.

Just down the street at Sweet Basil, a predominantly black thirteen-piece group, the Spirit of Life Ensemble, though maybe not, strictly speaking, a big band, plays "creative jazz with a world beat." The group includes several percussionists and a singer. Though only a few doors away, the music seems to come from a completely different world. Instead of complex, hard-swinging, expertly rendered arrangements, we hear mostly Latin-flavored pieces, rather minimally arranged but played with enthusiasm.

A few blocks away, at Visiones, Maria Schneider guides her band through her intensely personal compositions. Her unique style of conducting has captivated the small crowd gathered there. As we enter she is talking about growing up in Minnesota. She describes her fears associated with a bomb shelter that was in her parents' house (the door to which was beside her bed) and shares intimate details about her life. The band then launches into "Bombshelter Beast," the first part of an extended suite based on Schneider's childhood memories.

We stay for only one piece so that we can race downtown to the Knitting Factory in time to hear the Oliver Lake Big Band. When Lake is not playing alto saxophone sideways to the audience, he makes strange gestures and hand signs to the band. Apparently the band has learned a secret code, for they respond with glissandos, staccato blips and blaps, long drones, and other unusual effects. A singer joins the band, her intonation somewhat unsettling to our ears. In one of the most memorable performances of the evening, Ku-umba Frank Lacy takes a wild solo, at one point removing parts of his trombone.

After several pieces we take a cab uptown to Times Square to catch another composer, Toshiko Akiyoshi, and her orchestra at Birdland. This spacious and comfortable new jazz club has instituted a big band policy featuring Chico O'Farrill's Afro-Cuban Jazz Orchestra on Sunday nights and Duke Ellington's Famous Orchestra—under the direction of Duke's grandson Paul Mercer Ellington—on Tuesday nights. Along with her husband, the tenor saxophonist and flutist Lew Tabackin, Akiyoshi has been leading her own band since 1974. Though not sharing intimate details of her life, Akiyoshi draws on her background by incorporating elements from traditional Japanese music. Her music reminds us of the VJO in the bop-styled lines and virtuosic demands made on the players. But, unlike the VJO, most of whose members solo in the course of an evening, Akiyoshi features Tabackin on most of the solos. Her band, made up of some of the best young Broadway pit players and jazzmen in town, glides through her difficult arrangements with apparent ease.

We do not have time (and would not have been able to get tickets anyway), but a little farther uptown at Lincoln Center, far removed from the crowded stages and dingy clubs of the Village, the tuxedo-clad Lincoln Center Jazz Orchestra (LCJO), under the direction of Wynton Marsalis and hosted by Ed Bradley, is performing for Vice President Al Gore and his wife and a host of other luminaries—raising a million dollars for Jazz at Lincoln Center in the process. Later we hear that after the concert the LCJO played another set for the assembled socialites and dignitaries on the terrace of the State Theater, proving that a jazz big band can still fulfill one of its original functions, providing social dance music.

We end our tour back in the Village, around the corner from where we started, at another subterranean club, aptly named Small's. Remembering that Small's serves only tea and fruit juice, we pick up a bottle of wine. In this late-night, bohemian atmosphere, the Jason Lindner Big Band, a group made up of young European Americans, African Americans, Israelis, and a female trombonist, performs for an equally youthful, enthusiastic audience. The contrast with the Akiyoshi, Schneider, and Vanguard bands is pronounced. Here the emphasis is on the soloists; the arrangements, though interesting, occupy relatively little performance time.

We have to save for a future Monday tour Howard Williams at the Garage and the Chuck Clark Little Big Band at the Internet Café. And while Monday evenings remain the prime time for big band activity, numerous other big bands, some with international reputations (such as the Carnegie Hall Jazz Band, the Mingus Big Band, Chico O'Farrill's Afro-Cuban Jazz Orchestra, and bands led by John Fedchock, Bobby Watson, and Frank Foster), appear around town, some regularly, others sporadically. Although they do not perform frequently in their home city, two all-women big bands are also based in New York: Diva (No Man's Band) and the Kit McClure Band. All week long a procession of big bands can be found rehearsing in the Local 802 Union Hall or uptown at Boys Harbor.[2] In October 1997, the month of our tour, nineteen bands rehearsed at the hall.

NEW YORKESTRAS

New Yorkers' imaginations operate on a large scale. At gatherings of the city's social elite, the size of the band remains a measure of status and wealth. New York club date agencies continue to sell bands by the number of pieces; the ballrooms of posh hotels have rather large minimums negotiated with the musicians union, Local 802.[3] The abundance of musicians, capacious venues such as grand ballrooms and concert halls, and demands of the entertainment industry for arranged and elaborate music have stimulated the appetite for large ensembles.

"There's far more of everything in New York City," says David Berger, who has been active as a player, composer, and leader since the early 1970s. "It's much easier to fill them [big bands] in New York because there are so many players." Bill Kirchner hardly exaggerates when he states, "Only in New York is it possible to have big bands from certain apartment buildings." Jazz musicians have taken over buildings in Brooklyn, and in Manhattan 350 West 55th Street has long been occupied by musicians, and Manhattan Plaza has provided subsidized housing for hundreds of people in the arts since the mid-1970s. The number of big bands in Boston, Chicago, San Francisco, New Orleans, and Los Angeles, the only other cities with enough jazz musicians to support a fair number of bands, is dwarfed by the number in New York. The appendix gives a far from exhaustive list (omitting many dance and nostalgia bands) of big bands active in New York in 1997–98.

New York is also distinguished by its players' high level of musicianship. The intensely competitive environment pushes players to improve. A "New York caliber" band, according to Kirchner, has "killers in every chair," not just in a few featured positions. Every horn player is likely to be an accomplished soloist and improviser as well as a proficient section or lead player. Bandleaders can draw from a large pool of solid and imaginative rhythm section players. To unify the members of a band in a common conception of swing, the drummer and bass player must provide a strong foundation and intense groove. A good big band drummer not only reads proficiently but also is strong enough to pull everyone together, a much more difficult task than in a small group. Too much activity from the rhythm section can throw the band off balance or obscure the arrangement's figures.

As might be expected, New Yorkers have a highly developed sense of place. The frequency with which jazz musicians invoke "New York" in their band names and album titles indicates the extent to which they associate the city's name with excellence. A few examples are John Fedchock's New York Big Band, the Manhattan Symphony Jazz Orchestra, the BMI New York Jazz Orchestra, Clem DeRosa's New York City Big Band, Bill Watrous's Manhattan Wildlife Refuge, CDs titled *Latin from Manhattan* by Bob Mintzer and *New York City Jazz* by Bill Warfield. Some big band aficionados outside of New York may question the city's big band hegemony, but these challenges do little to temper New Yorkers' sense of superiority.[4]

Many jazz musicians in New York feel joined to an orchestral tradition that encompasses a wide range of styles, nationalities, ethnicities, and performance contexts. Sam Burtis, veteran trombonist with many repertory orchestras and other big bands, thinks big bands are "a repository of the New York tradition," and his remarks reflect the awe felt by many musicians for the rich and diverse legacy of the city:

> I've been in New York since 1970 or '71 and I feel like I'm the beneficiary of a playing tradition that goes back to the early 1900s, maybe even earlier, an ensemble playing tradition with the Sousa/Goldman kind of band, theater players, all of the Italians that came over and the German bands, and the black bands, the Spanish bands all of which were large ensembles playing entirely

> different music. But the cream of those bands became the studio players of the teens, the twenties and thirties, which then became the jazz players of the thirties, forties, and fifties. Artie Shaw and Tommy Dorsey were in the studio before they started their bands, Glenn Miller and most of those cats in New York. . . . And all these musicians have come to New York, hundreds and hundreds and hundreds and they've all left a little spore. A little vibrato from [lead trumpeter] Conrad Gozzo, high range from [trombonist] Urbie Green, triplets from [trumpeter] Joe Wilder; there's this amazing performance tradition. It's so joyous to play that people form bands and do it for free, although they would rather be paid!

From the concert bands mentioned by Burtis to the prejazz "syncopated orchestras" of James Reese Europe in the early years of the twentieth century through the bands of Paul Whiteman, Fletcher Henderson, and Duke Ellington in the 1920s, large ensembles thrived in New York. As jazz moved from small New Orleans–style groups into larger dance bands, arrangers coordinated the larger number of players. By the time Whiteman came to New York in 1920, he had already engaged Ferde Grofé to provide "symphonic jazz" arrangements. Whiteman's phenomenal success prompted others to follow suit: Ellington, Fletcher Henderson, Jean Goldkette, and others formed dance bands playing arranged jazz. The dance bands gradually grew in size and, with some exceptions, became standardized in instrumentation. By the 1930s and the legendary competitions at Harlem's Savoy Ballroom between Chick Webb, Cab Calloway, and Benny Goodman, the big band had arrived at what remains its standard format: fifteen to eighteen pieces divided into trumpet, trombone, reed, and rhythm sections.

Louis Armstrong's arrival in New York in 1924 to join the Fletcher Henderson band helped to transplant the rhythmic principles of jazz into the early big band as the soloists and rhythm section absorbed Armstrong's intense but relaxed New Orleans swing feel. Don Redman, working in Henderson's band, and others successfully incorporated these "hotter" rhythms in their arrangements for large ensembles. Duke Ellington performed at the Hollywood and Kentucky clubs on Broadway (1923–27) and entertained the segregated audience at Harlem's Cotton Club (1927–31), where he developed his "jungle-style" music in addition to playing revues by white songwriters such as Jimmy McHugh and Harold Arlen. As the popularity of dance bands rose, even Armstrong appeared exclusively with big bands from about 1929 on, until he formed the first of his "all-star" sextets in 1947.

To audiences, orchestral jazz remained bifurcated between "sweeter," sentimental bands, which some swing era writers derisively referred to as "Mickey Mouse" bands, and the hotter swing-oriented dance bands. In reality, most bands played at least a little of both styles. Ellington composed gentle mood pieces as well as torrid dance charts. In live performances, Jean Goldkette's orchestra, despite the lack of evidence in their recordings, played in a hotter style. According to some witnesses, Goldkette's ensemble outplayed the Fletcher Henderson Orchestra in a battle of the bands in New York's Roseland Ballroom in 1926.[5] Goldkette also helped to organize both black and white orchestras. He hired Redman away from Henderson to form McKinney's Cotton Pickers, an important black dance band, and he founded the Orange Blossoms, which evolved into the influential white band, the Casa Loma Orchestra.

In the late 1920s the once-thriving music scene in Chicago was dying. A crackdown on speakeasies and the closing of cabarets and theaters in that city, along with the installation of Vitaphones and other new sound technologies in theaters across the country, put many musicians out of work. The growth of radio and the emergence of national booking agencies based in New York led many to migrate to New York in search of employment. Eddie Condon, Gene Krupa, and Joe Sullivan were among an influx of white midwesterners who had cultivated the hot style. Other musicians came to town with touring bands. Ben Pollack and his "Californians" arrived in New York in early 1928. Pollack, who had picked up much of his band in Chicago, brought Benny Goodman (clarinet) and his brother, Harry (bass), Jimmy McPartland (cornet), Glenn Miller (trombone), Bud Freeman (tenor), and other top players. The trombonist Jack Teagarden soon joined Pollack for an engagement at the Park Central Hotel, where the band was billed as Ben Pollack's Park Central Orchestra. In a move that anticipated his work for Goodman several years later, Redman provided some hot arrangements for Pollack's band.[6] Audiences in Harlem in the early 1930s danced frenetically to the Cab Calloway and Jimmie Lunceford bands. Lunceford's band, billed as the "Perfect Swing Band," relied on the first-trumpet playing and superior arranging talents of Sy Oliver.

As Linda Dahl made clear in her groundbreaking book *Stormy Weather: The Music and Lives of a Century of Jazz Women,* not only did women have a greater presence as sidepersons in all-male groups than is generally recognized, but all-women bands have existed from the earliest years of jazz, perhaps an outgrowth of "all-girl" minstrel and vaudeville groups.[7] In the 1920s groups such as the Parisian Redheads (also known as the Bricktops) headlined theaters like New York's Palace, and the trombonist, pianist, arranger, and conductor Marie Lucas led various female groups at the Lafayette Theater. In the swing era leading dance bands such as Ina Ray Hutton (the Blonde Bombshell) and the Melodears, Phil Spitalny's "Hour of Charm" Orchestra, and the International Sweethearts of Rhythm performed and occasionally auditioned members in New York. In 1943 the Darlings of Rhythm, a black "all-girl" big band was formed in Harlem, by a former member of the Sweethearts, the saxophonist Lorraine Brown.[8]

Latin big bands began to emerge as a major force in New York during the 1930s after "The Peanut Vendor" (1931) became a national hit and incited the "rhumba" craze.[9] Don Azpiazú appeared with his Havana Casino Orchestra on Broadway and Xavier Cugat opened at the Waldorf Astoria. The growth of Latin bands brought Latino musicians to New York and led to a productive exchange of jobs and ideas between them and North American musicians. For example, working together in Cab Calloway's Orchestra, Dizzy Gillespie and Mario Bauzá established a relationship that helped to lay the groundwork for the first important jazz fusion, Latin jazz, in the 1940s.[10]

Because New York was the center for music publishers, booking agencies, and broadcasting industries, many big bands were based there. Leaders recruited and auditioned players, recorded in studios, and broadcast on radio shows in the city. New York attracted regional bands that wanted to become national bands. The city had large venues: the Savoy, Roseland, the Paramount, movie theaters (which featured big bands between movies), and major hotels. During extended engagements, which came as a welcome relief after weeks of road travel, bands could record there, broadcast live on radio (and later television), and be reviewed in newspapers and magazines.

For example, following its debut at Roseland after coming from Kansas City via Chicago in 1936, the Count Basie Orchestra kept New York as its home base throughout the ensuing decades of constant touring. Ambitious to raise his orchestra's status above that of a regional or "territory band," perhaps at the impresario John Hammond's urging, Basie expanded the band. He and the band also performed "stock arrangements" of popular songs, played shows, and acquired more intricate arrangements from New Yorkers such as Jimmy Mundy. But the more economical style of southwestern, blues-infused jazz and an emphasis on exciting solos gave the band its distinctive style. Reviews and live broadcasts over the CBS radio network during the band's residency at the Famous Door on Fifty-second Street in 1938, propelled Basie to international prominence.[11]

Although bands playing in a sweet style retained more mass appeal, the hot bands gathered increasing support, as was made resoundingly clear in Benny Goodman's reception at the Palomar in 1935. The greater commercial rewards reaped by white bands raised issues over white appropriation of black styles, despite the inclusion of a few African American players in the Goodman, Charlie Barnet, and other bands. Still, as Kirchner points out, big band jazz was an outgrowth of "much cross-pollination between the black and white orchestras."[12]

With the collapse of the market for touring bands in the late 1940s, big bands continued to be assembled for studio recording sessions. In New York Gil Evans, Manny Albam, Benny Carter, J. J. Johnson, John Lewis, and others recorded their arrangements with all-star big bands. Record companies featured their leading musicians with large ensembles. For example, Sonny Rollins and John Coltrane recorded with brass sections and Thelonious

Monk recorded with a ten-piece band.[13] Between 1957 and 1962, the collaboration of Gil Evans and Miles Davis produced some of the most venerated orchestral jazz in the jazz canon: *Miles Ahead, Porgy and Bess,* and *Sketches of Spain.* Another great Latin dance "invasion" in the 1950s, the mambo, brought bands led by Pérez Prado, Tito Rodriguez, Machito, Tito Puente, and others.

Over the decades many New York musicians found work and gained valuable experience in the orchestras of Lionel Hampton and Illinois Jacquet until the leaders' deaths in the early 2000s. Gerry Mulligan's Concert Jazz Band (1960–64) featured the arrangements of Bob Brookmeyer and included among its principal soloists Clark Terry. Terry founded his own ensemble, which became known as the Big B-A-D Band, in the late 1960s, which continued until 1987. The broadcasting networks maintained several full-time bands in New York until 1972, when the last of them, the NBC Orchestra, moved with the *Tonight Show* to Los Angeles. The trumpeter Thad Jones and the drummer Mel Lewis founded the Thad Jones/Mel Lewis Orchestra in 1965. Determined to establish a viable working and touring band, they called on some of the leading studio and broadcasting musicians of the day. The ensemble went on to become the most influential big band of the 1970s and continues (as the VJO) to play a central role among New York big bands.

In the mid-1960s the Jazz Composers Guild Orchestra, led by the composers Mike Mantler and Carla Bley, performed and recorded avant-garde orchestral jazz, and in 1968 Bley wrote and arranged much of the politically oriented music for Charlie Haden's Liberation Music Orchestra. In the 1970s jazz lofts such as Sam Rivers's Studio Rivbea and James Dubois's Studio We provided outlets for creative jazz composition. From 1972 to 1984 "experimental" musicians found sanctuary at Karl Berger's Creative Music Studio in Woodstock, New York, about two hours from the city. Visiting teachers such as Leo Smith, Anthony Braxton, and George Lewis held workshops to discuss their compositions. Instrumentation of ensembles tended to be haphazard, and students wrote for whatever players were enrolled. The pianist Muhal Richard Abrams, founder of the Chicago-based collective of avant-garde musicians, the Association for the Advancement of Creative Musicians (AACM), moved to New York in 1977 and led and composed for both small and large groups. Beginning in the early 1980s Cecil Taylor led an influential big band.

The 1960s and 1970s also saw the first stirrings of the repertory movement with Orchestra U.S.A., Ron Roullier's New York Jazz Repertory Orchestra, George Wein's New York Jazz Repertory Company, and Chuck Israels's National Jazz Ensemble. Through all this activity and beneath the public's radar, musicians formed rehearsal bands simply for a chance to play great arrangements, meet other players, or keep up their chops. Burtis, who participated in the repertory movement early on by way of the National Jazz Ensemble, says that big bands have remained vital in New York precisely because they provide a connection to its rich performance traditions:

> It has do with the fact that those rehearsal bands, those big bands, those Monday night gigs and by extension the repertory bands are the only place where you can learn that tradition in a concentrated manner. I mean you can go out and play club dates and you'll get a drib here and a drab there and there are working big bands—Machito's band, the Latin bands, some of the swing bands, some of the Monday night bands that have gone on to be more than that—but if I want to I can rehearse with a big band every day of the week here.

Like many other established jazz musicians in New York City, Burtis has actively participated in big bands, even when receiving little or no pay for his services. He explains that musicians of all levels benefit from big bands:

> It's the place where young musicians learn their craft and more experienced musicians keep it sharp. All the time that I've spent playing $40 gigs and $100 gigs and no-dollar gigs are the things that enabled me to go into a recording session.

The presence of many gifted players, the relative ease with which they could be organized into big bands, and the opportunities for media exposure also attracted composers and arrangers—the central figures in orchestral jazz. Aspiring arrangers could apprentice or study with established masters. Work in film, television, or radio provided valuable experience. Writers heard their music played by musicians who were able to make it sound as good as it could. As composers were inspired to write more challenging music, they pushed musicians to greater creative and technical heights.

SIZE AND INSTRUMENTATION

In contrast to the tremendous variation typical of classical orchestras, big bands seem remarkably consistent in size and instrumentation. By adhering to convention, composers and arrangers render their music more widely playable. Perhaps most important, the instruments traditionally taken up by jazz musicians have remained relatively limited: trumpets, trombones, and saxophones (often doubling on other woodwinds); and in the rhythm section, piano, bass, drums, and guitar.

Within the norm of fifteen to eighteen players, the brass is split into two groups of four (rarely five) trumpets and three or four trombones (two or three tenor and usually one bass).[14] The reed section has five players (two alto, two tenor, and one baritone saxophonist, sometimes doubling on clarinets or flutes). Piano, bass, drums, and, sometimes, guitar make up the rhythm section. The players in each section of winds follow a principal player, known as the "lead," who generally plays the top voice in the harmony and determines dynamics, phrasing, articulation, and other stylistic matters. Along with drummers, many of whom became bandleaders (Chick Webb, Ray McKinley, Buddy Rich, Louie Bellson, Mel Lewis, and others), these highly skilled section leaders are the most important and "in demand" players of the big band.

Though the minimum number of instruments for a big band is subject to some debate, Andy Farber, saxophonist and arranger, states assuredly, "A big band is anything above a dectet." While this limit may result from the fact that few people know the Latin prefixes for the numbers eleven and above (a hendectet?), historically, nonets and dectets have been identified as distinct from big bands. Musically speaking, a band of eleven with three in the rhythm section (piano, bass, drums) leaves eight slots for horns, which can be divided equally into four brass (three trumpets and one trombone, or two of each) and four saxophones—voices sufficient for four-part writing in each section. The Ellington Orchestra of the early 1930s included eight horns (five brass and three reeds), and Ellington frequently added a trombone (usually Juan Tizol on valve trombone) to his saxophones to get four voices (for example, "It Don't Mean a Thing," 1932).

A unit of only eleven pieces will not be as powerful as a more conventional big band that consists of at least six brass and five saxophones. Moreover, the three added pieces enable the arranger to score for three autonomous sections (three trumpets, three trombones, and five saxophones), spread harmonies over a wider compass (from bass trombone or baritone sax on the bottom to high trumpets on top), and write sax solis in either five-part harmony or the traditional four-part, double-the-lead voicings (as in the group Supersax, which specialized in such harmonizations of transcribed Charlie Parker solos).[15]

Very often financial resources dictate band size. Elimination of only a few pieces can make a group economically viable. After leaving Stan Kenton in 1953, the trumpeter Maynard Ferguson experimented with various instrumental configurations, eventually settling on two fewer trombones than the standard four and eliminating one alto sax but keeping the trumpet section intact. This favoritism to his own instrument had musical reasons: his stratospheric playing required support from a full battery of trumpets voiced in their upper registers. Today, even with further cuts in his band (now only two saxes and one trombone remain), he still carries three trumpets.

For the arranger Don Sebesky, who played trombone in the original Ferguson band, the challenge was "trying to make the band, given the limitations of the instrumentation, sound bigger." He explains, "Maynard only had two trombones and that was a severe limitation. Kenton had demonstrated that the trombone was the heart of the big band, that's what gives it the substance, the inner heart. Since we only had two, we lost a lot of body that way. Everything was very trebly and upper register. We had a hard time grounding it. . . . We had to do all these tricks with orchestration that you normally wouldn't have to do with more horns at your disposal."[16] Slide Hampton, who also played trombone and arranged for the band, found that the instrumentation provided a sufficient number of voices for him to express his ideas harmonically: "When you have three trumpets [not including Ferguson], two trombones, and four saxes, you have as many notes as you would use if you were using a full ensemble." Fewer horns eliminated some of the parts-doubling that often occurs between sections in the band's midrange. "Sometimes a big band can sound kind of heavy," Hampton says, "but Maynard's ensemble was the right size to be able to achieve everything I wanted musically.... [A]lthough it was small, the result sounded big. And exciting!"[17]

When Bill Warfield accepted a regular job at the Metropolitan Café in 1995 he cut several pieces from his band because of budget and space limitations. As a model for his new instrumentation, he chose the Ferguson orchestra, a favorite band of his youth. The change in band size forced him to rearrange his charts. When he wanted a "trombone" section, he voiced the baritone sax and one of the tenor saxes with the two remaining trombones. Sax solis that had been voiced in five-part harmony lost one part, and those that had been in four parts with the lead doubled at the octave simply had the doubled part eliminated.

Mike Mantler's Jazz Composer's Orchestra in the 1960s was one of the few jazz orchestras to depart radically from conventional instrumentation. According to Carla Bley, Mantler staffed the band using a "Noah's Ark" principle: "Two of each.... That was Mike Mantler's orchestrating thing. It was two trumpets and two tenors and two altos and two flutes and two French horns and two trombones and, I don't know, just two of everything." In putting together his eleven-piece band (twelve, if you include his occasional trombone playing), Joey Sellers also thought in pairs of instruments. He delights in the band's symmetry, explaining that it builds outward from a core of two tenor trombones to two lower instruments (bass trombone and baritone sax) to two midrange instruments (alto and tenor sax), up to two higher instruments (trumpets). His writing does not always keep these pairs intact; he actually prefers cross-sectional pairings (trumpet and sax, baritone sax and flute, trombone and sax, etc.). His original concept grew out of instrumental limitations he faced as a young writer when he was in high school.

Although most leaders would prefer full-sized bands, they do not necessarily want their ensembles always to sound, feel, or behave like a large ensemble. Contemporary big band composers and leaders often extol a small-group aesthetic of lighter textures and subtle rhythms. After all, for extended periods during solos, a big band actually *is* a small group. The saxophonist-composer Oliver Lake says, "I take the same attitude about arranging for big bands as I do in the smaller groups. I'm just tryin' to approach it as openly as I can, and not feel like I have to follow any kind of big band formula or format because that's been done so much, and done well." Laughing, he adds, "Using my original music, that means automatically it's gonna turn out sounding different than a traditional big band." For a big band album with the Bill Warfield band, the guitarist Dave Stryker replaced the regular drummer with Jeff Hirshfield immediately before the studio date because he wanted a "lighter" touch. On the CD *Treasure Island,* Bob Belden also used Hirshfield to try to make his "big band swing like a small group."[18]

In his Little Huey Creative Music Orchestra, William Parker seeks to preserve some of the freedom of the small group. For *Mayor of Punkville,* a CD recorded in 1999, he organized his ensemble into seven sections, or "stations": (1) trombones, (2) trumpets, (3) baritone sax and tuba, (4) soprano sax and tenor sax, (5) alto saxes, (6) drums, and (7) bass. The number of players varies; on his 1997 CD, *Sunrise in the Tone World* (recorded in 1995 at the Knitting Factory), some pieces have as many as twenty-five musicians. The saxophone players may double on flutes or clarinets, and occasionally he adds piano and a vocalist. Parker explains that "these sections can be compared to the branches of a tree, branches that lead back to a main body that is rooted in the soil called sound." Players in each station have "the freedom to create their own part if they feel the part they would create is better than the written part at that moment."[19]

Instruments not traditional to jazz occasionally have figured prominently in an arranger's sonic identity. Drawing on his early experience writing for the Claude Thornhill Orchestra, Evans expanded his sonic palette through unusual voicings and combinations of instruments. "It was essentially a French horn band," said Evans of the Thornhill group. "Trumpets and trombones would play in derby-hats to avoid vibrato" and were combined with the French horns and reeds, often clarinets, to produce a variety of distinctive sonorities.[20] In his later work for Miles Davis, he added tuba and expanded the woodwind section, using double reeds and alto and bass flutes. His protégée, Maria Schneider, has managed to tease new timbral dimensions out of the big band format by "trying to make it sound orchestral instead of sectional." In 1997 she had an opportunity to write for the Metropole Orchestra in Europe. "It felt great, not having to try so hard to create varied colors. The many instruments, including strings, were like a 'super' set of Crayola crayons."[21] The reed players in her own band double on oboe, English horn, flutes (including alto and bass), clarinets (including bass and contrabass), and other woodwinds.

Strings remain a largely unexplored resource in jazz (with a few notable exceptions: recordings of Charlie Parker and Clifford Brown with strings, Stan Kenton's forty-three-piece Innovations in Modern Music Orchestra, and, more recently, Wynton Marsalis's *The Midnight Blues,* etc.). In the past, strings in jazz arrangements worked ineffectively because the string players couldn't swing. Arrangers restricted their string parts to long-value notes ("footballs" or "pads"). With jazz and classical programs coexisting in many conservatories and music departments, perhaps more string players will become experienced in swing rhythms.

The pianist Hank Jones, who has had a long-standing interest in performing with strings, appeared with a thirty-two-piece orchestra at Lincoln Center in September 1998. Wynton Marsalis has pursued collaborations with his fellow Lincoln Center constituent, the New York Philharmonic. Though the big band will remain the favored outlet of expression for orchestral jazz, other possibilities of instrumentation likely will be explored, especially with the funding available to Lincoln Center. Nevertheless, the inherent problem for strings and other orchestral instruments is that they are not loud enough. The large sections needed to compete with jazz instruments, such as saxophones, brass, and drum sets, run counter to the jazz aesthetic of one musician to a part. Necessary volume can be achieved with the use of microphones, but amplification causes blending problems with other, nonamplified instruments.

Some of these problems were apparent when Sue Mingus unveiled her new ensemble at Birdland dedicated to exploring the "compositional" side of Mingus's music on 2 March 1999. Billed as an alternative to the "boisterous, bluesy bebop" played by her "downtown" band, the Mingus Orchestra features "acoustic instruments you don't ordinarily hear in jazz."[22] This "orchestra-in-the-making" (Sue's words), like many of Charles's projects, and like the Mingus Big Band, is an ongoing public experiment. The instrumentation of this group (including bassoon, bass clarinet, and, in the beginning, cello) raised issues of balance and blend that rarely confront the big band. For example, the bass clarinetist, Roger Rosenberg, voiced his frustrations to me about not being heard during the group's initial performances. The challenge, in one musician's words, has been to retain the energy of Mingus's music without "cutting the balls off it."[23] Microphones have been added and subtracted, drummers have been put on brushes instead of sticks, and instrumentation has been changed.

When writers depart too far from convention they risk difficulty hearing their works performed or obtaining a publisher. Such considerations constrain even those musicians most open to experimentation. Inspired by Eric Dolphy's arrangements for John Coltrane's *Africa Brass* album, Oliver Lake included two French horns in his earliest compositions for big band. He was forced to reconsider the instrumentation when he "couldn't find the French horn players all the time." He also realized that if he wanted other bands to play his music he would have to "write for what was there." The AACM, as Lewis Porter notes, "developed an aesthetic that involved openness to a whole range of sounds and instruments [and] rebelled against the restrictions of bebop instrumentation."[24] Very few other groups have followed suit. In my interviews, some musicians with avant-garde leanings seem perplexed by the issue. "It's a good question," says the saxophonist Jorge Silvester. "There should be more ways of getting a big band, I mean with a different instrumentation. . . . I guess it's just traditional."

Many forces conspire to keep the size of bands small. There are few incentives for enlarging them. Although bands occasionally deploy five trumpets (the LCJO has often used five since Marsalis resumed his place in the trumpet section), virtually no bands follow the Stan Kenton model of five trombones. More than five players in each of the wind sections would require continual doubling of parts.

Adding percussion to an existing band is another story. Most often conga, timbale, and other percussion parts are unnotated, and the players simply add another layer of density to the groove and learn the breaks and hits of the arrangements aurally. Dizzy Gillespie receives credit for being the first to incorporate a conga player (Chano Pozo) in a traditional big band. Latin big bands—in the tradition begun by Don Azpiazú and Xavier Cugat and continued by Beny Moré, Tito Puente, and others—always include additional percussionists. Bob Mintzer and Sue Mingus supplemented their bands with percussionists for their albums *Latin from Manhattan* and *¡Que Viva Mingus!* respectively. Oliver Lake is considering doing some concerts with added African and Latin percussion players.

In big bands every musician retains a degree of autonomy not always found in large ensembles in other idioms. Although each player is part of the larger unit, each chair also has a clearly defined space within the band. This independence has contributed to what Charles Mingus described as "the kind of [distinctive] musicianship that has developed from each instrument [in jazz]."[25]

Players must nonetheless surrender a portion of their individuality to the section leaders, especially the lead trumpeter. Along with the drummer, this player is the central musician in the band, perhaps even more important than the concertmaster in a symphony orchestra. Many musicians would agree with the bandleader and trumpeter Dean Pratt "that in order to put together a great big band you must start with a lead trumpeter with both stamina and leadership, a drummer who can not only swing but has the instinctive ability to propel the band, and then everything else will take care of itself."[26] Some big band authorities, such as Kirchner, consider the bass equally important. Because they typically remain very much in the background, the bassists' contribution often goes unrecognized. Of course, the foundation in pulse and intonation they provide is not unique to big bands, but it is fundamental to virtually all jazz groups. Next in importance to these players are the other section leaders, the lead alto sax and the lead trombone, and the low instruments, the baritone sax and bass trombone (if present). Ultimately, to field a "New York caliber" big band, *all* chairs must be occupied by musicians who are not only expert on their instruments but also cognizant of their differing roles.

During the big band era, the art of ensemble playing was highly respected by musicians and audiences. Fans knew the personnel of their favorite bands as well as they knew the rosters of their major league baseball teams, and they followed the movement of stars from band to band much as they would trades between ball clubs. Tommy Dorsey carried this analogy further, comparing "a dance band to a football team. In the backfield he put the soloists, the obvious stars. And in the line he put his lead men—first trumpet, first sax, and first trombone—along with the four men in his rhythm section—the pianist, guitarist, bassist, and drummer." As this description makes clear, the rest of the band, the nonimprovising, lower section players, went unrecognized. "These were strictly supportive players," says the jazz writer George T. Simon, "their lives filled with little glamour and seldom any overt appreciation."[27] Because few of these musicians were adept at improvisation, they had little hope of becoming hot players. Their only chance for stardom was to become section leaders. This ambition drove the players to develop their sound, sight-reading ability, and other skills as they jockeyed for these positions. Sitting next to an accomplished lead player was a valuable apprenticeship for an aspiring player. Nevertheless, these lesser-known musicians had to understand and play their supportive roles well, or the section leaders could have them replaced.

In most contemporary New York City big bands, nearly *all* players are accomplished improvisers. During a typical performance, almost everyone is featured on at least one arrangement. Because players have this outlet, they are less driven to become section leaders. The sharp division between soloists and lead players and the rest of the band is much less pronounced today because many players are able to adapt to different roles. Chapter 4 examines some of these roles in detail in the Vanguard Jazz Orchestra. But first we look at the traditions behind New York's rehearsal and working bands and the development of repertory orchestras.

Chapter 2

Behind the Scenes

Training, Rehearsals, and Gigs

Paquito D'Rivera says with characteristic irony, "Every time I want to have some fun (and lose some money!), I organize a big band." D'Rivera typifies jazz musicians' attitudes toward big bands by revealing, in the same breath, his joy and his frustration.[1] For many jazz musicians, especially leaders, big bands are a money-losing venture. If this weren't enough, for some of the listening public, association with big bands carries a certain stigma. Gary Giddins has noted the tendency since World War II and the emergence of bebop for critics to look to small groups for innovators. Big bands, by contrast, were considered "home to solid professionals . . . who lack[ed] originality." By way of illustration, Giddins describes the career of Joe Lovano, who, despite recognition from his peers during a "long apprenticeship" in numerous big bands, began to receive widespread acclaim only after leading his own small groups.[2] But, as Lovano discusses below, his apprenticeship played a critical role in the formation of his musical conception. He mentions Parker, Gillespie, and Coltrane as examples of innovators who played in big bands, then adds, "There've only been a few cats who didn't have that much big band roots behind them." Since the end of the swing era, three main avenues have remained for musicians to get that experience: school bands, rehearsal bands, and part-time working bands including dance orchestras.

SCHOOL BANDS

Known variously as "stage" or "dance" bands, the big band was the first form of jazz to get its foot in the academic door. Large groups allowed for greater participation. Written scores and emphasis on ensemble playing fit easily with existing pedagogy. Little thought had been given to formalized methods of teaching improvisation. The jazz program at North Texas State (now the University of North Texas), usually given credit as the nation's first (1947), was initially conceived to train dance band players. During the 1950s, many musicians who settled down after years of touring with swing bands became music teachers, bringing stage bands to the public schools. Big bands took their place among other large ensembles: choruses, symphonic bands, and orchestras. State and county music teacher organizations, the International Association of Jazz Educators, and, more recently, Jazz at Lincoln Center sponsored festivals and annual competitions. By including more students, large ensembles were better suited for these events: selecting even the "best" seventeen players is difficult in a state with as many jazz students as New York.

In suburban communities such as Long Island, young, mostly white music students now begin playing in their first big bands in the fifth or sixth grade. As an adjudicator for various jazz festivals, I heard many elementary and middle school bands. Much of the music written for this age group is sadly deficient, though some arrangers and educators are working to remedy the situation. Students who are just beginning to learn how to read music struggle with an entirely different approach to the interpretation of notation—swing rhythms. Most of the youngsters' lack of experience listening to swing compounds the problem. The teachers themselves may have similar limitations, and, having very little idea of what to play in these ensembles, they select arrangements of rock songs. Even with these problems, by the time they graduate from high school, many students have played in fairly advanced bands. Directors with a devotion to jazz and a competent "farm system" in the lower schools may turn out excellent bands year after year.

In stark contrast, in the more ethnically diverse New York City public schools, since the budget crisis of the 1970s, music and other arts programs have been decimated.[3] Teachers who had directed orchestras, bands, and other ensembles were reassigned to state-mandated general music classes. Professional-quality instruments owned by the schools were locked in closets from which many were pilfered. Unless they studied outside of school, few students received instrumental training. The most accomplished of these students could audition for LaGuardia High School for the Performing Arts, glorified in the 1980s TV series and musical *Fame*. The highly selective big band at LaGuardia, in the heart of the theater district on Forty-sixth Street, incubated the talents of a fortunate few. Many graduates of this school have gone on to become prominent New York jazz players. In 1984, in a relocation that further concentrated arts education in the city, the high school moved into its own nine-story building at Lincoln Center.

New York City came late to jazz education on the college level. Until the late 1980s the most prominent jazz programs in the country were found in Boston, Miami, Indiana, or Texas. Prevailing wisdom dictated that one should study first in the hinterlands and defer a New York debut until ready to "make a splash." New arrivals continued their education through private lessons with a master player or making the rehearsal band scene. The few jazz workshops available were ensemble classes at Lynn Oliver's studio on Eighty-ninth and Broadway and improvisation classes taught by Barry Harris.

Today jazz programs flourish in the New York area. Programs advertise their proximity to the "jazz capital of the world." In 1984 Dick Lowenthal established the Jazz and Commercial Music program at the Manhattan School of Music (MSM), which became a template for other schools.[4] By assembling a stellar faculty of New York players, Lowenthal attracted seasoned New York professionals interested in a college degree, as well as ambitious young students from far and wide. Like other more established jazz programs, the big band was the flagship ensemble that featured prominent guest artists and represented the school at conferences and competitions. By 1988 MSM supported three big bands, and students competed for spots in the "A band," or top ensemble. Practically overnight this group became one of the most highly regarded "student" ensembles in jazz, rivaling the One O'Clock Band at North Texas. At various times the band's roster included John Riley, Todd Coolman, Ryan Kisor, Chris Potter, Jon Gordon, Doug Purviance, Bob Keller, Steve Slagle, and Tony Kadleck.

Other New York area schools that assemble accomplished big bands include William Paterson, New York University, Columbia University, City College, Long Island University (Brooklyn Campus), Hofstra, Five Towns College, and SUNY Purchase. Although students at most other schools are also required to play in a small group every semester, the New School has emphasized combos. Many groups are dedicated to the performance of specific repertories: Art Blakey and the Jazz Messengers, Herbie Hancock, the Ellington small groups, Horace Silver, and so forth. Since combining with the Mannes School, the New School has become one of the largest jazz programs in New York City—yet it has only one traditional big band. Many of its students receive little or no big band experience.[5] Among prominent New York City music schools, only Juilliard remained without a jazz program. But in 2000 it too joined the fray, when Wynton Marsalis announced a two-year jazz diploma program. Enrollment at Juilliard was limited to the requisite instrumentalists for one big band, plus two additional rhythm sections. Members of the Lincoln Center Jazz Orchestra comprise most of the faculty.

School bands have helped to structure the social networks of New York City big bands as bonds among players often lead to lasting professional relationships. For example, when Arturo O'Farrill Jr. was asked by Marsalis to form the Afro-Latin orchestra for Jazz at Lincoln Center, O'Farrill recruited several of his former schoolmates from LaGuardia. In the 1990s Bill Warfield and other MSM alumni formed bands largely comprised of former fellow students. Schools outside New York continue to have an enormous impact on the jazz scenes of the city. The two colleges with the oldest jazz programs,

North Texas and Berklee (founded in 1954), emphasized big band performance and became recruiting grounds for bandleaders such as Woody Herman and Maynard Ferguson. Coming to New York after graduation or time on the road, musicians often seek out former classmates. For example, the saxophonist, composer, and record producer Bob Belden, who attended North Texas and later traveled with Woody Herman, recruited North Texas and Herman alumni when he formed his own band in New York. In the 1980s many graduates of the University of Miami's jazz program began to arrive in New York. Maria Schneider and the Nuyorkestra have drawn heavily from this pool of musicians.

Some of the best students gain entry into elite professional networks through the recommendations of their teachers. Most college big bands also feature guest artists in special concerts, which give students a chance to play with prominent musicians in rehearsals, workshops, and performances. Well-known players also draw larger audiences to school performances and publicize their programs. Occasionally students are discovered by visiting artists. For example, the trombonist Wayne Goodman first came to Marsalis's attention during a presentation of Ellington's *Sacred Concert* at MSM. Marsalis later recruited Goodman for his jazz oratorio, *Blood on the Fields,* and eventually the Lincoln Center Jazz Orchestra. Because guest artists typically bring their own music, the notion of jazz as a living tradition is reinforced: instead of relying solely on written texts, students connect directly with a living master.

In addition to familiarizing students with basic repertoire, college bands perform students' arrangements and new works commissioned from established arrangers. Most jazz students study composition and arranging, as well as improvisation and other performance-related courses. Typically, composition and arranging courses culminate in a major project, such as a big band arrangement, performed by the college big band so that the students can hear their work. In this way, many college students with little previous interest have discovered a love for composing. For example, when Magali Souriau first arrived at Berklee from France in 1990, she considered herself a pianist. After studying with Herb Pomeroy, she "discovered about writing and fell in love with it." After graduating she came to New York and put together her own band. Now, like many players who have become leaders, Souriau seldom plays so that she is free to conduct. Composers and arrangers are key to the livelihood of rehearsal and working bands in New York. Without new and inspiring compositions, many of the best players would lose interest.

REHEARSAL BANDS

Before New York City emerged as a center for jazz education, players gained valuable experience and made contacts by participating in rehearsal bands.

A glance at the careers of several prominent musicians illustrates the importance of the rehearsal band scene to aspiring players since at least the 1960s.

The trumpeter Bob Millikan arrived in New York from Indianapolis in 1963 at the age of seventeen, "without any great expectations," after spending a summer on the road with the Warren Covington band. He immediately fell into a thriving rehearsal band scene:

> There were tons of rehearsal bands. I can't remember the names of them, but I remember playing in like eight different rehearsal bands. It was really wild and I loved it. I was just a kid. It was better than working. I would have been perfectly content spending my life doing that. Playing with really great players, playing a lot of arrangements that I wouldn't have had a chance to play anywhere else except maybe in a college band.

In those days musicians could acquire a comprehensive musical education without attending a college or music school—by simply hanging out, taking a few lessons, playing in as many bands as possible, and picking up gigs in New York's bustling music industry. The rehearsal bands, Millikan says, were "a great way to learn how to play and a great measuring stick to see how you're progressing." He "loved the camaraderie, the sheer entertainment of being around the cats and playing the music."

In the thriving society, jazz, and commercial music scene of the late 1960s and early 1970s Millikan was fortunate to play with many of his idols. In addition to their house bands, the Waldorf Astoria, the Copacabana, the Plaza, and the Americana engaged orchestras to play shows. Millikan says, "I met Snooky [Young] when working at the Waldorf. Occasionally acts would come in, like Peggy Lee or something, they'd bring in their own trumpet player. It didn't seem like such a big deal at the time, but I really enjoyed it because I was young and it was chance to play a lot of good acts. Unfortunately the scene started to disappear by 1973 or 1974." Millikan also subbed in the newly formed Thad Jones/Mel Lewis band and played in Bill Berry's New York Band, as well as working bands led by Fred Waring Jr., Ron Roullier, Bill Watrous's Manhattan Wildlife Refuge, and Al Porcino's Band of the Century. Some of the other important rehearsal bands in the 1960s and 1970s were led by Chuck Israels, Rick Wald, Billy Byers, David Goodkind, Dave Mathews, Jerry Kale and Julie Schwartz, and Dave Berger. A band called the New Americans, started around 1973 by the Russian immigrant Alex Rogov, featured other immigrants (such as the trumpeter Valerie Ponomarev). Now widely recognized as one of the top two or three lead trumpeters in the city, Millikan has performed on literally hundreds of jazz recordings—for Bob Mintzer, Bill Warfield, David Berger, and a host of others. All this activity has yet to earn Millikan a puff piece in *Down Beat* or an entry in the *Jazz Grove*. Like so many important contemporary big band players, his contribution to jazz has been largely overlooked.

By the 1970s growing numbers of musicians formally schooled in jazz programs came to New York. When the drummer John Riley arrived in September 1976 after attending North Texas, he was "able to do weddings and stuff like that right off the bat." But only through the rehearsal bands did he meet "a lot of great musicians who started to open some doors up for more artistically satisfying work." Because he had learned to be "a fairly good reader" in college and was "hungry to play," he soon found he "was getting called to do several bands every week." Often they would rehearse at Charlie's Tavern, on Fiftieth Street between Broadway and Eighth Avenue, where a lot of the older studio musicians gathered between recording sessions:

> I remember meeting Clark Terry, Grady Tate, Frank Wess, Bobby Rosengarden, George Duvivier. Those guys would hang out in this place, so the owner was sort of friendly to musicians and he made the back room available for rehearsals. None of these places had drums and it was always a lot of dues to take drums to do one of these rehearsals, that didn't pay any money, that weren't leading directly to any gigs. So it seemed like there weren't that many drummers that were good readers who were inclined to partake in these things.

Despite the hardship of transporting his drums on the subway from his apartment on Broadway and Eighty-sixth Street, Riley became a regular on the scene, eventually assuming the drummer's chair in the Bob Mintzer Big Band and the Vanguard Jazz Orchestra and working frequently in the Carnegie Hall Jazz Band.

As players acquire more gigs, they tend to drop out of rehearsal bands and seem unaware that a thriving rehearsal band scene continues as new bands spring up and fresh players take their places. In my interviews I frequently heard older, established musicians express nostalgia for the era of the "great" rehearsal bands—almost invariably coinciding with the time they arrived in New York. But young musicians aspiring to move up the ladder still congregate in the many rehearsal bands of the city.

The experience of the multireed player Jay Brandford illustrates how players can combine enrollment in a school program and participation in rehearsal and working bands in order to gain a foothold in the New York jazz scene. Brandford had been active in his hometown of Boston but, like many musicians, yearned to try his hand in "the big time." In 1991 he enrolled in the master's program at MSM. Almost immediately he became active in the big band scene:

> That same fall I got a chance to substitute with Clifford Jordan's big band for a few weeks. That was in a club near Union Square, Condon's. This was their Monday night big band for many months. In the saxophone sections Jerome Richardson played lead, Sue Terry played second, Charles Davis played tenor, and of course Jordan played tenor. There may have just been four saxophones. When Jerome Richardson was going to be out, I think for surgery or something

> like that—he was going to take some time off from playing—Sue Terry played lead and invited me to sub on second.

Brandford had met Terry while subbing in another band, possibly Charli Persip's. Although he does not remember the exact sequence, he subbed a few times with Toshiko's band in rehearsals in the first few months he was in the city. He also played with the trumpeters Bill Mobley and Kenny Rampton, who "rehearsed a little bit and taped some arrangements they had written." As a newcomer to New York, it was an exciting time for him: "That was the ebb and flow, that was the blood circulating in the jazz world—musicians playing together in these rehearsals! I was meeting and hearing so many people and finding out about the high level of musicianship. It was great!" Brandford became one of the most active saxophone players in New York big bands, playing regularly or subbing in the David Liebman band, the VJO, the Ellington Orchestra, Dave Berger's Sultans of Swing, and many others.

The rehearsal band scene in which Millikan, Riley, and Brandford participated has remained remarkably constant, despite changes in the music industry and in jazz. Bands are divided into two fairly distinct types: those playing original compositions and arrangements and those playing—in Millikan's words—"the charts that everybody likes." In the 1960s and 1970s established arrangers such as Billy Byers and Don Sebesky, as well as aspiring writers such as David Berger, put together bands in order to hear their arrangements, a practice that continues today. In bands that do not play original music, leaders assemble "books," or collections, of their favorite charts through barter, theft, or transcriptions of recordings. Few bands play music that is commercially available. Many prized arrangements have been circulating among bandleaders for years. Lynn Oliver, whose rehearsal studio was frequented by Gerry Mulligan, Horace Silver, the Basie Band, and many others, built a formidable library by photocopying the charts of every band that passed through. When the legendary European-based big band led by Kenny Clarke and Francie Boland folded, the tenor saxophonist Billy Mitchell inherited some of the book, which he brought back to the United States and eventually contributed to a rehearsal band on Long Island. As one indication of how closely leaders guard their music collections, the leader of this rehearsal band kept a voodoo talisman with the music as protection from would-be thieves. Because many arrangements were never published or are out of print, collectors often traffic in barely legible photocopies and poorly copied manuscripts.

Ironically, most rehearsal bands do not rehearse in the usual sense of the word: they typically play through charts one after another without stopping to rehearse. What they practice is reading at sight. Musicians develop the ability to adapt to lead players' and drummers' accents, pitch inflections, swing feel, and changing dynamics. Section leaders must make instantaneous decisions regarding interpretation. Players follow customary, yet usually unspoken, rules, such as "All quarter notes are played short, unless otherwise marked." The most acclaimed section leaders develop distinctive styles. Players accustomed to working under them know what to expect.

Historically, little rehearsal time is allotted for much of the work jazz musicians do, such as shows, concerts, and club dates. Musicians take great pride in getting it right the first time. Asking to go over something again requires courage; the player making the request may be suspected of having made a mistake. Practicing a passage (such as a sax soli) typically involves getting the notes down and rarely involves discussion of the subtler aspects of interpretation. Lead players who are consistent in their phrasing and interpretation of note length, accents, and dynamics are more easily followed but yield a product listeners may find too predictable. In some bands the leader cultivates a more mindful and open climate by frequently asking the players if they would like to go over something again.

One type of rehearsal band, sometimes referred to as a "workshop band," does not seek work but exists solely for the purpose of playing new music, usually composed by its members. The BMI New York Jazz Orchestra, sponsored by the performance rights organization BMI, provides opportunities for professional and semiprofessional musicians to learn composition and arranging techniques. In the twelve years since its founding in 1988, more than three hundred musician-composers participated. At Local 802 on the last Tuesday of every month from September through June, workshop members, led by the composer-teachers Bob Brookmeyer (until he left for Rotterdam in 1990), Manny Albam (until his death in 2001), and Jim McNeely, gain valuable feedback by hearing each other's arrangements. Like many school bands, the BMI orchestra occasionally brings in guest artists. For example, in July 1998, to commemorate the workshop's tenth anniversary, the orchestra performed participants' compositions at Merkin Hall with featured soloists Jon Faddis and Phil Woods.

Some younger musicians, perhaps as a result of their college training, have rejected the paradoxical situation that rehearsal bands do not actually rehearse. In school they became accustomed to breaking down sections, discussing finer points of articulation, dynamics, and balance, and frequently stopping if necessary. When the Nuyorkestra was founded at the end of 1995, according to Steve Kenyon, lead altoist, "we tried not to think of it as a rehearsal band." The band does not rehearse every week "just for the sake of rehearsing" and always tries to have some kind of job on the horizon as a specific goal. The band, Kenyon points out with some pride, actually practices arrangements: "A lot of the older bands don't really know how to rehearse anyway, so the problems never get fixed."

Until recently leaders needing rehearsal space rented privately owned studios, met during the day in the nightclubs where they perform, or obtained space in a church, school, or other facility. Local 802 finally acquired a building in midtown in 1992 (Phil Ramone's former A&R Studios on Forty-eighth Street), after leasing offices for most of its existence. The ground floor of the facility offers a spacious rehearsal room, complete with a small stage equipped with a piano and a mostly nonfunctioning bar. The availability and affordability of Local 802's rehearsal space has contributed to the growth of big bands. Requirements are few: the person renting the room must be a member "in good standing," and no recordings can be made (except of "the walkman type").[6]

Because the rehearsal space is located near the main entrance, everyone entering and leaving the building hears the bands. Many linger for a moment to listen. Leaders wishing privacy will not choose this space. During rehearsals, well-known musicians pass through on their way to pick up checks at the cashier window of the recording department upstairs. As might be expected, the bands that rehearse at the union are representative of union membership. Union members tend to be musicians active in work that gives them the wherewithal to support unionization (Broadway shows, society gigs, studio work, classical orchestras, etc.). Most jazz and Latin gigs do not generate enough income to warrant union involvement, which includes benefits and dues, and musicians active exclusively in those scenes have little reason to join the union.

Despite the relative paucity of union work in the jazz idiom, the NEA survey *Changing the Beat* found that a remarkably high 70 percent of Local 802 members identified themselves as jazz musicians. This fairly large number of musicians (estimated at 7,360) still only constitutes about 22 percent of the total number of jazz musicians in New York.[7] Most Local 802 jazz musicians are white. Despite making up nearly 33 percent of the total jazz population in New York, only 17.3 percent of union jazz musicians are African American.[8] Besides playing jazz, both union and nonunion jazz musicians eke out livings performing in bar bands, Latin groups, a wide variety of ethnic musics, and club dates.

Because players must accumulate minimum contributions every six months in order to qualify for union health plans, union members are motivated to seek union work, primarily Broadway shows, studio work, and society club dates. These union requirements may have the unintended consequence of pulling musicians away from the jazz scene, compelling them to turn down more musically satisfying but lower-paying jazz gigs in order to meet union minimums. For some of these players, the rehearsal band scene offers a creative outlet.

Stylistically, the rehearsal band scene is predominantly mainstream. Musicians congregate in rehearsal bands primarily to gain the very skills not highly valued in avant-garde circles. Avant-garde composers tend to assemble their bands only when they have gigs. The avant-garde stands, almost by definition, in opposition to normative procedures, and many of its composing and performance practices are antithetical to those found in more conventional big bands. In some of these bands rehearsing is seen as counterproductive, as inhibiting spontaneity or enforcing conformity.

Also characteristic of the rehearsal band scene, at least at the union hall, is the striking dominance of all-white or nearly all-white bands. Jay Brandford observes:

> I think that the rehearsal band scene closely matches the commercial, money-making scene, like the bands that make money, the cats that get to work on Broadway, or that get to be part of bands that actually do little tours, like Toshiko's band and so on. And that is by far a very white scene, that commercial side of it. And I think that, for whatever reasons, traditionally—you know how it is—you call the people you're used to calling, you're used to being comfortable with, and so that's been white, mainly white, and it's gonna stay mainly white. And I think that the rehearsal band scene reflects that segment of the community.

The racial homogeneity of these bands is not by conscious design; in fact, many leaders of all-white bands express the desire to involve more black players. Brandford notes, "I can remember occasional conversations with guys running rehearsal bands saying, 'Man I feel like I don't know that many black players. Who should I call, Jay. Give me some names of some black trumpet players.' And then they call them and they say, 'Those guys are too busy!' " Although it is difficult to verify how much effort they actually have made, white leaders often complain that "high-level" black players turn them down. Asking a stranger to invest time and transportation costs in a project that offers no remuneration feels awkward and may generate tensions, especially given the historical context of racial exploitation. Leaders seem more comfortable staying within their established networks or letting band members send their own subs.

Some black players—busy or not—decide the rehearsal band scene is a waste of time. Brandford suggests:

> Some may think, "What's the point of getting involved? It doesn't translate into money-making gigs because the white people will still tend to call the people they're familiar with." It seems like being active in the rehearsal bands, you may get to play a lot with some of the people who have real lucrative work, but that doesn't mean that the trumpet player sitting next to you is gonna call you to sub in his Broadway show. They're very careful about sharing that work. A lot of black players feel that it's a racial thing, but it's not so clear; it's more nebulous than that.

In the first place white jazz musicians outnumber black musicians. As Brandford observes about his own instrument, "There aren't nearly as many black saxophone players as there are white players around." Furthermore, when musicians call subs for paying gigs, they tend to call people they hope will reciprocate. The most established players rarely take someone less experienced under their wings. On the other side, many white players feel they stand little chance of being hired in the black jazz scene. The end result is that, with some notable exceptions, big bands in New York still divide along racial lines.

The saxophonist and clarinetist Bill Easley, a fourth-generation musician who toured with Mercer Ellington before coming to New York, has never been interested in rehearsal bands: "This is not a hobby. I've been doing it since I was thirteen years old. I take the business end of it pretty seriously. Not that I don't like to play, but it's not about fun and games. This is what I do for a living." He attributes his serious attitude to black experience:

> How the music developed in the first place was out of survival. You didn't become a jazz musician because it was cool, and because it was something fun and exciting to do. People did it because that was the only opportunity that was open to them. The music that evolved out of that type of situation, it didn't come out of textbooks or studies, it came out of life experience. It was a positive reaction to an adverse situation that evolved over a period of a hundred years.

Easley recognizes that younger black players, many of whom have come through jazz education programs, have grown up in a different climate. Eddie Allen, a trumpeter, saw benefits to starting a rehearsal band and basing it in the union hall. When he re-formed his band in 2002, according to Brandford, "he made a point of calling for the most part black players," explaining that he wanted "black players to start circulating and getting to know each other a little bit more." Allen wanted to lower people's expectations, so he explicitly identified it as a rehearsal band. He explains:

> Some of the bands I've been in, it's obvious that they're rehearsal bands, but they don't want to admit it. Then you start weighing, "I'm spending this much money to rehearse. It's taking up so much of my time. Am I paying for parking?" All those kind of things become a factor, and this person keeps sayin', "We're not a rehearsal band." So if we're not a rehearsal band, then incomewise, I shouldn't be goin' in the hole. So as long as I say it's a rehearsal band, I never have to worry about anybody being annoyed saying we're not working. If a job does come in, it's actually like a surprise.

To keep the players' interest, Allen decided to feature a different conductor-composer for each rehearsal. Brandford welcomed the chance "to play some music by some people [he] didn't expect to ever get to play music by, like Muhal Richard Abrams." Band members Cecil Bridgewater and Howard Johnson and guests from outside the band, such as Rufus Reid, Jimmy Heath, and James "Jabbo" Ware, brought in their music. People passing by noticed something different. Allen says, "The white musicians would come in and they'd say, 'Whose big band is this?' " He started to get calls to sub in other bands at the union hall, and often he would be pleasantly surprised to see that other members of his band were also there. He explains:

> There are a lot of rehearsal big bands out there, and I don't know if they assume the black musicians don't want to play in them, or we can't read well enough, but we wouldn't get the calls. And now they see this big band there and say, "Oh, OK. I didn't know he could read."

According to Allen, even some of the black members of the band seemed surprised to see musicians such as the bassist Dwayne Burno and the drummer Carl Allen, who "play with all these small groups, like Jackie McLean, Benny Golson, come in and sight-read a book."

Allen comments on the paucity of black players on the white rehearsal band scene: "I think part of it is an old-school stigma that people just don't want to let go. They think black guys can play in a small group but can't read well enough to play in a big band, or something like that." Although this stereotypical view persists in some circles, some white leaders have confided to me their difficulty finding black musicians whose playing will "fit in." "Fitting in" is often less a question of reading ability than interpretation, especially in jazz, where musical notation fails to convey swing feel as well as articulation, dynamics, and phrasing. Just what "fitting in" means is, of course, central to understanding the processes at work in the formation of the social networks of jazz performers, and it is a subject that receives attention throughout this book.

Besides Local 802, the other affordable rehearsal studio in Manhattan, Boys Harbor, perhaps because of its more uptown location at Fifth Avenue and East 104th Street, tends to attract more ethnically and stylistically diverse bands. The facility, which runs programs for local young people, began renting space to musicians in 1980. There are no requirements (such as union membership) for its use, and rates are reasonable.[9] There is little traffic of musicians through this building, and rehearsals are not on display as they are at the union hall. Most of the bands are jazz or Latin groups, though a few R&B groups also rehearse here.

The singer, bandleader, and arranger Nancie Banks began rehearsing her band at Boys Harbor in 1989. Banks, joined by her husband, the trombonist Clarence Banks, when he was not on the road with the Basie band, assembled a core group of mostly African American players. In recent years she also brought more women into the band. When she first thought of starting a band, Banks was not sure she was ready, so she approached one of her mentors, Gil Fuller, for advice. He told her not to wait. "It takes a long time to develop a band sound," Banks recalls Fuller's counsel. "If you wait until you're ready, it will be too late." In fall 1999 she released her third CD. Like most leaders, she prefers to think of her band as a working band rather than a rehearsal band. When asked the number of jobs she plays in a year, she refuses to make an estimate, saying simply, "Just put down, 'Not enough.' "[10]

WORKING BANDS

As has probably become evident, the classification of a band as either "rehearsal" or "working" is not always clear—even to the musicians involved. Rehearsal bands become working bands as they begin to work. Some bands billed as working bands by their leaders are considered more as rehearsal bands by their band members, because they rehearse far more than they work. If they begin to work steadily, many bands stop rehearsing altogether, thus becoming more clearly working bands.

As a band develops a nucleus of musicians who know the book, there is less need to rehearse. Steve Fitzko, co-leader of the Fitzko/Kinslow Band, explains, "There's no reason to keep playing over and over charts that you already know. Unless you're learning new music, you might as well have cats just show up at the gig." There is also a danger in overrehearsing: the music gets stale, or the better players may lose interest.

When they do rehearse, working bands such as the Vanguard Jazz Orchestra and the Maria Schneider, Chico O'Farrill, and Dave Holland bands may practice in the club on the afternoon of the gig, meet at Local 802 or Boys Harbor, or, if they can afford it, at Carroll's rehearsal studios on West 41st Street. Carroll's has been operating for more than sixty years and is available to leaders on short notice. In 2006 the rate for a room large enough to accommodate a big band was $62 per hour, which is prohibitive for most rehearsal bands. Road bands, recording bands, and other commercially viable bands rehearse here, especially if they need to block off a large number of rehearsals in a short period for an upcoming tour or studio date. The union and Boys Harbor facilities are generally reserved far in advance.

Musicians also frequently meet in schools, churches, and bars to rehearse—especially in the suburbs. Diane Moser, leader and pianist with the Jazz Composers' Orchestra, barters for space at a church in Montclair, New Jersey, by writing and performing a "big piece" for them every year. Schoolteachers provide access to school facilities for many bands. Neighborhood bars offer players the opportunity to play informally for a small audience. In contrast, the LCJO and CHJB, although they occasionally have used Carroll's Studios because of scheduling problems, typically have rehearsed in more rarefied atmospheres. The CHJB met in the vast open space on the top floor of Carnegie Hall (large enough to easily accommodate a large orchestra and chorus), and, before the completion of its new facility in Columbus Circle, the LCJO rehearsed in Kaplan Penthouse at Lincoln Center and the cavernous rehearsal stages deep inside the Metropolitan Opera House.

On a club gig leaders sometimes take a chance sight-reading new music in public. When the band used to do three sets on Monday nights at the Vanguard, Mel Lewis read through new arrangements on the last set after most of the audience had left.[11] Sight-reading on the gig can also be useful for refocusing the band's concentration, if its members have become bored or attention has wandered. This strategy is not without dangers: disastrous train wrecks may result.

Some charts are designed with a high degree of readability (familiar rhythms, comfortable range, etc.). Every working band needs at least a few of these charts for occasions when a large number of substitutes are filling in. This "comfortable" style of arranging is frequently found in vocal charts. Working with various bands and often carrying their own books, singers typically perform only two or three songs per set, often without rehearsal.

For many leaders, a steady gig is a money-losing proposition. A standard arrangement with clubs provides that the bands receive only the money collected at the door. If a leader guarantees each player $20, he or she is more likely to get good players who otherwise would be reluctant to participate. Many bands are subsidized by their leaders. Loren Schoenberg estimates he spent $11,000 on one recording. "My band, to this day, has always cost me money, I will be perpetually in the red for it," he says. One evening at the Internet Café a friend and I were the only people in the audience after the first set. With a cover of $5 and a band payroll of at least $200, it is easy to understand why the leader commented to me, "I don't know how long I can afford to keep my band working."

Other tribulations come with leadership. The versatile drummer Jimmy Madison, who has made his mark with musicians as varied as Lionel Hampton, Rashaan Roland Kirk, and James Brown, recalls how he became a reluctant co-leader of an eighteen-piece band with the Bulgarian trombonist Angel Rangelov in the early 1980s:

> Angel came in and said, "Vee are going to make band." I said, "Wait a minute, I don't want to *make band.* I'm already *making band.*" But somehow he conned me into it, and we formed the Angel Rangelov/Jimmy Madison Big Band. We played a lot at the Blue Note on Monday nights. We would have special guests like Ray Barretto, or Pepper Adams, or Paquito D'Rivera—various horn players. And a lot of times we had some of those guys *in* the band! I imagine we had just about everyone who was worth a damn in New York play in that band. 'Cause Angel knew everybody, it was scary. And he had this way of getting people to do things.

Although Rangelov fronted the band, wrote the arrangements, and handled bookings, Madison helped with promotion, calling musicians, and setting up:

> It was a lot of work, I mean, holy shit. We used to go down there [the Blue Note] on Mondays, and to make a big band stage you had to move half the tables in

> the room out the back door and then put them back again after the night was over. Angel and I did that ourselves. We only rehearsed when Angel could scratch up some money to rehearse somewhere—somebody's loft or occasionally a rehearsal studio.

For all their troubles, the band never received much recognition outside of New York. Eventually the band folded. Madison, somewhat relieved, went back to being a sideman.

To avoid these aggravations, some bandleaders shun public performance, concentrating instead on building reputations through recordings. John Fedchock, who first gained recognition as a trombonist and writer for Woody Herman, used to book his band until he became convinced that his time might be better spent writing and performing. Bob Mintzer's band was one of the first contemporary New York big bands to achieve notoriety but in nearly twenty years has rarely played steady engagements. All these bands could be considered studio bands, except for the fact, as the trumpeter Dean Pratt points out about his band, they have had stable personnel for a long time and occasionally appear at clubs, festivals, and clinics.

Studio bands were among the most important entities for the propagation of orchestral jazz after the decline of the full-time bands. Most were assembled for specific recording projects and had no life outside the recording studio. A look at the personnel on these sessions reveals the same names cropping up time and time again—players with similar competencies who were accustomed to working together and thus required little or no rehearsal time. Composer-arrangers such as Oliver Nelson, Nelson Riddle, Henry Mancini, Gerald Wilson, Billy May, and Quincy Jones relied on these networks of musicians to produce their albums of big band jazz in the 1950s and 1960s. Their style of writing usually adhered to certain conventions of phrasing, articulation, and swing that facilitated recording. As described by the players, "the charts played themselves." This form of praise signified that the music flowed naturally and presented little in the way of pretentiousness or artifice. Unlike writing that demanded extensive rehearsals and frequent performance, this style was matched to the competencies and conventions of the collaborative art worlds that performed it.

While it lasted the studio system served players, composers, and record companies well. Composer-arrangers received a budget for an album from a record company. Sometimes the music would be planned around a certain theme, concept, or featured soloist(s). Studio time was booked and contractors hired the musicians, usually from their regular rosters. The allotted money covered all the production costs: part copying, recording, album jacket design, and, perhaps, even promotion.

Live engagements sponsored by the Music Performance Trust Fund (MPTF) provide another source of work for big bands. These moneys, which the recording industry supplies as a result of the settlement of the 1942 musicians' recording ban, subsidize public performance and usually require a cosponsor to contribute half.[12] Some New York City big bands seek MPTF dates, but because the pay is low (about $70 for a two-hour job, ironically well below union scale) and the conditions of playing outdoors are often poor (wind-blown music, noisy traffic, and bad acoustics), some players have lost interest in this work. Concerts in public spaces are also sponsored by real estate corporations, Jazzmobile (a Harlem-based organization that sponsors concerts around the city, especially in minority neighborhoods), and, most recently, Lincoln Center through its summer series in Damrosch Park. Pay for the sidemen on these jobs ranges from the MPTF rate to $200. Clearly, the economics of big bands work against leaders and sidemen. Nightclubs do not bring in enough money to pay union scale or benefits.

As in rehearsal bands, the racial homogeneity in New York's working big bands may seem surprising, given the ethnic diversity of New York and the multicultural background of jazz itself. Predominantly or totally white big bands (such as Toshiko Akyoshi's, Maria Schneider's, Bill Warfield's, Dave Liebman's, and Bob Mintzer's, to name only a few) or black big bands (Eddie Allen's, Charli Persip's, the Ellington Orchestra, etc.) seem more the rule than the exception. For leaders, the makeup of their band is extremely personal, especially when they are performing their own compositions. In Bill Easley's view, "As much as things have changed with integration, there's still a difference in black and white, and anybody that doesn't know that or can't see that, is really naive. Cultural difference, feeling difference, emotional difference, a lot of differences." The ideal of integration, as desirable as it is to most musicians, seems to falter when confronted by social, cultural, and musical realities.

Halfhearted attempts at diversity smack of tokenism: a big band with only one black or female member is unlikely to feel very integrated. In defense of its affirmative action policies before the Supreme Court, the University of Michigan Law School argued that a "critical mass" of minority students was crucial to ensure a significant contribution to the classes. Greater numbers not only provide a higher comfort level for minorities but also resist members' being "pigeonholed as racial spokesmen."[13] In big bands "critical mass" would probably mean a minimum of three or four members. Easley recalls, "They look for a token or they hire black musicians so they can make something look authentic. That always makes me think how stupid it is. Many times I'm in bands and that's why I'm there because they need the appearance of some color. That doesn't necessarily thrill me." Brandford reflects on being the only musician of color called for the David Liebman band:

> I know that's why I was there, at least I'm there as a half a black person. I didn't ask her, but I'm guessing that's why Laurie Frink was there [as a woman]. You

> know, that they want to have some kind of appearance of diversity. I mean she should be there because she plays so great. But there are so many guys who are closer to Dave Liebman's circle who it seemed would have been more likely to be called.

Musicians chosen for their ethnicity or sex, whatever the motivation, may feel insecure, especially if they are the only minority persons. Brandford admits to worrying, "OK, they didn't call me because they want me and my sound, they just need to call somebody who's not white who they feel comfortable with. I think in a lot of situations I feel like I look for some other reason, rather than taking stuff for the good, clean reason, like it's great if they go out of their way to show that they appreciate me and are willing to invest a little bit in this idea of diversity."

Racially *balanced* bands might be defined somewhat roughly as no more than two-thirds black or white. Prominent New York bands that have met this criteria include the Carnegie Hall Jazz Band, the Mingus Big Band, and the Dave Holland Big Band. The Lincoln Center Jazz Orchestra, despite being criticized for underrepresenting white musicians, actually has met this standard throughout most of its history. Representation of female musicians is another matter. Of the above bands, only the CHJB has had a woman as a regular member.[14]

Raw percentages and numbers are only part of the picture. Integration is also a matter of perception. Because the professional music scene in New York is based so much on social connections, personal recommendations, and, increasingly, relationships formed in schools, leaders and players stay within established social orbits. As I discuss in the next chapter, leaders seeking public and private support may find themselves under considerable pressure to diversify their personnel. Meanwhile, lack of financial resources impedes efforts to reach out; a certain audacity is required to "cold-call" someone to make a rehearsal that does not pay and may lead to low-paying gigs at best.

The meager remuneration in big bands affects the musical product in other subtle ways. Leaders may be less inclined to discipline their band members or may reward them with solo opportunities. Carla Bley, who features only a small core group of soloists in her band, says, "That's what's wrong with big bands. There's too many boring solos because of that sense of fairness. The reason they're using fairness is because nobody's getting paid. So you say, well you've gotta give the baritone player the solo, even though the baritone player cannot solo. Maybe he doesn't even want to solo, but has to try because it's 'fair.' " Excessive soloing can lead to a lapse in the attention of the other players or cause listeners to lose their sense of the composition. In an earlier era, when leaders commonly provided full-time work or put together bands for a recording, dependency was in the other direction: players relied on leaders as employers. Joey Sellers found the players in Los Angeles much more content to just play their parts. "In New York," he says, "everybody's an *artist,* or thinks he's a star. They always want to know, 'How much solo space will I have?' " Players who do not put the ensemble first, either through laziness or lack of skill, are not welcome in most New York bands, regardless of their virtuosity as soloists. Millikan dismisses them as "cats just waiting around for the next solo."

In big bands a dozen or more players may be idle for extended periods. Ideally, soloists and other band members listen attentively to each other. Many soloists play as much for their peers onstage as they do for the audience. In one well-known New York big band, a tenor player is the featured soloist on most of the tunes, though the band has many other accomplished improvisers. His playing may sound fresh and exciting to the public, but band members criticize him for "playing the same things in the same spots night after night." Soloists in big bands have essentially two audiences, and one might conclude that this player has chosen the public over the band.

For Millikan, listening to soloists is one of the best parts of a gig. As lead trumpeter, he often rests during solo sections. "Being able to play lead in these bands gives me an opportunity to hear great jazz players without paying for it. 'Cause I got to work with the best, Freddie [Hubbard], or Dizzy, or whoever," he says. Although he would love to be a soloist himself, recognizing his own strengths and weaknesses, he admits, "I wouldn't have been there unless I was playin' lead."

While impressive soloing in itself might not be enough to get a permanent spot in a big band, it can help someone to get a foothold. Though he was never a great sight-reader, Joe Lovano's soloing abilities earned him a place in the Woody Herman band in 1976 and helped to launch his jazz career:

> My sight-reading was terrible! I thought Woody was going to send me home immediately. I mean there was no rehearsal or anything. The audition *is* the gig. That first gig in St. Louis was in a parking lot out in a mall somewhere. The music was blowing, but I knew some of the songs from my dad's records and stuff. I was in Sal Nistico's old chair, which I knew had some stop-time solo choruses on "Caledonia." I knew some things about the book that saved me [laughs], because the music's blowing around and, boom, Woody just calls, "Four Brothers," and kicks it off. And you're on it. Luckily Woody was the kind of leader that heard your sound and your personality. He wasn't a real judgmental cat in lot of ways like in a technical way. He listened to your feeling and sound. I saw him do that with a lot of players. Luckily he gave me a chance to really get into the music and learn the music. It's not even a thing of just sight-reading the notes either, it's like playing with the feeling of the band. And trying to blend. After that first concert Woody asked Frank [Tiberi], "So what are we gonna do about this guy?" Frank looked at him and said, "Did you hear him *play?*" So he gave me a chance. Now I think a band like Buddy Rich's would have

> been a lot different. You play your part and it's played more strict. I wouldn't have fit in the same.

Lovano's career has been unusual in the sense that he has participated in a stylistic range of big bands almost as wide as exists. After the Herman band, Lovano played in the Mel Lewis Orchestra, Carla Bley's big band, Charlie Haden's Liberation Music Orchestra, and Mario Bauzá's and Machito's Latin bands; more recently, he toured with the LCJO. Big band experience leads to more than the development of ensemble skills. Lovano discusses how his work in big bands informed his conception of soloing:

> When I started to really emerge in some of these bands I had had already a kind of a history playing in more free music and in the bebop school. When I started to play in a big band, I absorbed the music around me that other people were playin' and started to really feed off the energy and the ideas that other cats were playing. It gave me a lot of inspiration about how to approach my little solo moment, playing with a sense of orchestration. When I would come out of an ensemble part and how I could use that as a springboard into my solo excursions and then knowing what was gonna follow, or what background, that gave me a conception about leading somewhere, developing solos within the framework of the piece. That's always been a strong foundation of my playing. Playing in big bands helped crystallize a lot of that stuff. And gave me a conception of *how* to play and not just deal with *what* to play.

DANCE BANDS

Nearly all the bands discussed thus far perform music for listening, not dancing. Most are so far removed from the original function of big bands—social dance music—that the rare sight of a couple getting up to dance is greeted with shock or amusement. Few leaders would go so far as Stanley Kay, manager of the all-women band Diva, who has been known to run into the audience to intercept would-be dancers and politely ask them to stop, insisting that the women in his band play "concert" music. As this rather extreme example illustrates, efforts to elevate jazz to an art solely for listening, like classical music, have involved disconnecting the music from the body and movement.

The swing dance revival provided important opportunities for jazz musicians to acquire big band experience. The movement began in the early 1970s, around the same time that jazz musicians began to explore historical repertoires by forming repertory bands. Even as the number of veteran big band players and fans from the 1940s dwindled in New York (from death or retirement to Florida), the discovery of swing dancing by a younger generation breathed new life into the dance band scene. One of the earliest swing revival bands, the Widespread Depression Orchestra, began with a group of college students in southern Vermont in 1972. Band members wore fedoras and period clothes. By the 1980s the "jazz resurgence," fed largely by the growth of jazz education, had brought many young players to New York, some of whom worked in bands such as Vince Giordano's Nighthawks, the Stan Rubin Orchestra, the Loren Schoenberg Big Band, and New York City Swing. The movement began to garner mass media attention through Joe Jackson's album of Louis Jordan tunes, *Jumpin' Jive* (1981).

Rubin's band illustrates how the swing revival, in addition to providing opportunities for younger musicians to play and exchange ideas with older performers, confronted some of the same issues facing the emergent repertory movement. The clarinetist Stan Rubin became a fashionable leader on the New York society circuit after fronting a band at Princess Grace's wedding in Monaco in 1956. His formation of a big band in 1973 contributed to the swing revival in New York. He commissioned transcriptions from the recordings of swing era arrangements, including the improvised solos, of Basie, Goodman, Artie Shaw, and others. Before brain surgery abruptly ended his playing career, Rubin performed the transcribed solos exactly and insisted that other band members do the same. By the time I was playing in the band on its steady gig at the swing dance venue, Swing 46, in the late 1980s, the musicians frequently complained to each other about not being able to improvise their own solos. When Rubin was present, often only for the first set or two, arrangements were played lockstep and soloists re-created the solos note for note. As soon as Rubin left, the band was transformed: the charts were opened up for extended soloing.

Although a significant crossover of personnel between repertory orchestras and swing bands exists because of their mutual interest in historical material, the big band dance subculture is somewhat removed from larger big band art worlds. Venues have dance floors, and the requirements of the dancers determine repertoire and tempos. While swing dance enthusiasts are not necessarily jazz fans, the audience is remarkably pan-generational and, at least in New York City, interracial. Defying the generation gap in musical tastes and culture that emerged after World War II, the swing dance movement has brought throngs of young people in their teens and twenties together with dancers their parents' and grandparents' ages. At Swing Society events the dance floor reverberates with an intricate choreography of young and old, black and white, dressed in all styles of attire.

The New York Swing Dance Society (NYSDS), founded in May 1985 as "a not-for-profit arts organization dedicated to the revival and promotion of swing dancing to live Big Band music," sponsors weekly Sunday evening dances at the Irving Plaza (on Irving Place at Fifteenth Street) and other locations. Ironically, in light of the society's dedication to big bands, because of limited funds and high overhead, the amount of money allotted for each gig forces leaders to cut the size of their bands, pay less to each player, or supplement the payroll out of their own pockets.

While "straight" jazz has moved farther from dance and popular music since the 1940s, Latin jazz in the same period has remained close to its dance roots. Tito Puente, for example, until his death in 2000, despite his strong interest in jazz, performed primarily dance engagements. No matter how cramped the space, audience members could be expected to be on their feet. Even a band as oriented to "concert" music as Chico O'Farrill's Afro-Cuban Jazz Orchestra, with its tempo and meter changes and adventurous harmonies, occasionally played dances. Arturo O'Farrill Jr., who has directed his father's band since its re-formation in 1995, estimates that about a third of the band's book is danceable. On the rare occasions the band is hired to play for a dance, he simply stretches out these charts by allowing extended soloing.

Attitudes related to the dialectic between "the functional" and "art" are thoroughly ingrained in Western culture.[15] In 1998 Marsalis and Jazz at Lincoln Center inaugurated a project to reintegrate jazz music and dance. Perhaps their success in establishing jazz in the concert hall made them more confident about acknowledging and reinvigorating the dance tradition in jazz. Recognizing that much of the repertoire they hope to canonize, especially the music of Ellington, was conceived and performed as dance music, they saw swing dance as an opportunity to rebuild popular support for jazz. A video and CD recorded at the Supper Club in 1998 *(Live in Swing City: Swingin' with Duke)* features a carefully staged nightclub scene in which dancers interact with the LCJO through their choreography and shouts of approval. In winter 2000 the orchestra played an entire tour of swing dances on college campuses. Although at one time plans called for one of the venues in Jazz at Lincoln Center's new home at Columbus Circle to have a dance floor, as the swing dance phenomenon waned, the idea was dropped.

Though the swing dance revival and the repertory movement occasionally converged through their common interest in big bands, overlapping repertories, and reliance on many of the same skilled practitioners, these tandem movements were motivated by very different impulses. I now turn to the repertory project, probably the most significant development in jazz over the past three or four decades.

Chapter 3

The Rise of Repertory Orchestras

In a 1970 Sunday *New York Times* article, Martin Williams, director of the Smithsonian Institution's Performing Arts Division and the Smithsonian Press, appealed to such "august cultural centers" as Lincoln and Kennedy Centers to incorporate jazz in their programming. "When are they going to realize," he queried, "that if they are really going to stand for art and culture in this country, they are going to have to recognize jazz."[1] Williams's vision included plans for residencies by major composers and artists (Ellington, Basie, and other leaders were still alive), founding of repertory orchestras, transcription and publication of musical scores, and commissioning of new works. The realization of this dream, albeit with a somewhat narrower scope, took a long and circuitous journey of two decades.

Williams's plea articulates two basic impulses behind the repertory movement. Preserving through performance the great works of jazz was ostensibly the first and main goal of repertory orchestras. For this task, the pioneers of the repertory movement had an obvious model—the symphony orchestra. This model also served a second, loftier ambition: the desire to elevate the stature of jazz and African American culture in general. Efforts to celebrate the history and cultural meaning of jazz also brought worries. Would the music atrophy? Was creation of a "living jazz museum" a form of "musical necrophilia,"[2] more in the order of Western classical music's worship of its past? Would jazz become even farther removed from its popular base, appealing only to a small elitist audience? If jazz is elevated as an *African American* art form, then what is the role of white jazz musicians? Does public financing require inclusiveness in race, gender, and programming? Debate over these issues became more heated during Jazz at Lincoln Center's meteoric ascendancy in the 1990s. But first musicians grappled with more immediate concerns. Should recorded solos be re-created or newly improvised?

What would be the role of new compositions and arrangements? Should leaders build standing orchestras or draw on specialists for concerts on specific themes? Above all, the pioneers were preoccupied with how to finance their dreams.

EARLY ATTEMPTS

Precedents for the jazz repertory movement can be found as far back as the 1930s. Bill Kirchner suggests that the Bob Crosby Orchestra, a cooperative unit led by Bing's brother and largely consisting of former members of Ben Pollack's band, could be considered a repertory ensemble because it played mostly big band arrangements of Dixieland jazz. Benny Goodman and John Hammond's famous 1938 "Spirituals to Swing" Carnegie Hall concert reflected a growing consciousness of "jazz history," though as a recorded idiom jazz was barely a couple of decades old.

A film short of Duke Ellington in 1935, *Symphony in Black* (RKO), presented the maestro and his orchestra in a formal setting akin to a symphony orchestra concert. Hammond, Goodman, Ellington, and Eddie Condon began the move to transplant jazz from the saloon to the concert hall, an early phase in jazz's legitimation.[3] Stan Kenton pursued the stage band concept, promoting big band jazz as listening rather than dance music. Gerry Mulligan, along with Clark Terry and Bob Brookmeyer, formed the Concert Jazz Band.

By the 1960s and 1970s, coinciding with the rise of Black Nationalism and Pan-Africanism, black musicians and writers became more vocal in proclaiming the African American origins of jazz and decrying the conditions under which it was played. LeRoi Jones exposed an entertainment industry that rewarded white practitioners of jazz more generously than its black originators.[4] Max Roach, one of the most influential and skilled percussionists in jazz, vented his accumulated anger in an article, "What Jazz Means to Me," which described jazz as "the cultural expression of Africans who are dispersed on this North American continent." He continued, "The term 'jazz' has come to mean the abuse and exploitation of black musicians; it has come to mean cultural prejudice and condescension. . . . What 'jazz' means to me is . . . small dingy places, the worst kinds of salaries and conditions that one can imagine."[5] Archie Shepp and others preferred the term "Great Black Music." Charles Mingus castigated inattentive audiences in noisy clubs.[6] Rashaan Roland Kirk tore apart a piece of furniture on national television as he attacked the media for ignoring jazz.[7] Not all efforts to elevate the image of jazz were confrontational. The polite, tuxedoed attire of the Modern Jazz Quartet (founded in 1952), led by the pianist and composer John Lewis, complemented the understated swing and clean timbral quality of vibraphone and piano. Lewis was involved with Gunther Schuller in the fusion of classical and jazz styles (Third Stream) and, in 1962, founded the short-lived Orchestra U.S.A. primarily as an outlet for original composition.

The New York Jazz Repertory Orchestra, probably the first modern repertory big band, was born out its founder's frustrations with the thriving commercial music industry that, at that time, employed many jazz musicians. In 1959 the pianist and composer Ron Roullier immigrated to New York from London with hopes of making his mark in the city's jazz scene. He soon found himself preoccupied with more lucrative commercial work, especially jingles. "Here I am in New York with all these great players and all we're doing is 58 seconds of music at the most," he realized. "There were a number of rehearsal bands around, but it was like taking a number at the laundry to get your music played, so Willis Conover and Burt Collins and a couple of people said why don't you get your own band going." Roullier spoke to Phil Ramone about rehearsing at A&R Studios on Forty-eighth Street, and they began meeting when the studio was not booked, usually weeknights after midnight. "A lot of the guys, like Tommy Newsom and Eddie Shaugnessy, who came aboard later, were doing the *Tonight Show,*" Roullier explained. As in many of the repertory bands that followed, the initial impetus behind the project was to play original music, not the "classics" exclusively: "The idea was to present a cross section of the repertory: Basie, Ellington, Dizzy Gillespie, Johnny Carisi's chart on 'Israel,' plus some new works, some of my things, and others." A concert at Town Hall in 1967 and a requiem for Martin Luther King Jr. in 1969 cost Roullier "a whole fortune of money" and a second mortgage on his house. The lesson was not lost on Roullier: "I was very naive about the jazz business. . . . You're doing a very ideal kind of a thing, and the idea is if the music is that wonderful everybody will recognize that and support it." As Roullier and others discovered, finding support for repertory jazz orchestras would not be easy.

The National Jazz Ensemble and the New York Jazz Repertory Company

In 1973 New York newspapers reported the near-simultaneous founding of two orchestras dedicated to the performance of jazz repertory—Chuck Israels's National Jazz Ensemble (NJE) and George Wein's New York Jazz Repertory Company (NYJRC). The headline of an article announcing the NJE by the *New York Times* jazz critic John S. Wilson posed the question, "The Great Jazz Dream—Can It Come True?" The subheading asked, "Will New Yorkers support jazz regularly in the concert hall?" A few months later, perhaps overoptimistically, he provided the answer in the title of a piece on the NYJRC: "If the Symphonies Can Do It, So Can Jazz."[8] Though their approaches differed greatly, both the NJE and the NYJRC gradually fizzled out after a financial struggle through the better part of the decade.

The opening concert of the NYJRC at Carnegie Hall in January 1974 was eagerly anticipated in the press. A writer for the *New York Times* waxed enthusiastically, "it would be hard to overstate the promise inherent in the first concert." The company, made up of "more than one hundred talented musicians," promised to take on "anything from traditional to avant-garde jazz and . . . to incorporate everything from country to rock." Four musical directors with widely divergent tastes—Stanley Cowell, Gil Evans, Sy Oliver, and Billy Taylor—were engaged to harness the creative energies of an equally diverse group of musicians that included Clark Terry, Roy Eldridge, Bobby Hackett, Sam Jones, Ron Carter, Sam Rivers, Stanley Turrentine, Zoot Sims, Roy Haynes, Art Blakey, Elvin Jones, and Jaki Byard. A series of fifteen concerts was planned for the first season, some on specific themes—"Jazz in the Rock Age" or "Swing Street: 52nd Street Revisited"—and others devoted to the works of specific musicians—Duke Ellington, Cecil Taylor, or Jimi Hendrix. Concerts would also feature guest artists: Lennie Tristano, George Russell, Oliver Nelson, and others.[9] Sponsorship came from grants from the New York State Council on the Arts and the NEA, and Carnegie Hall provided a generous subsidy under its rent remission program with the city.[10] An even more ambitious series of twenty-six concerts was planned for the second year.

The first year got off to a rocky start. As George Wein recalls, "The original concept was total catholicity of approach. A concert could have avant-garde music and traditional music in the same program." The problem was that various themes and styles attracted completely different audiences. Wein says, "The ones that came to see Armstrong and the traditional didn't want to see contemporary music." After losing $40,000 in the first season, pressure mounted. The *New York Times* in 1974 quoted Wein as saying that the next season would "be a do-or-die stand" and that it if it failed, it would be "many years before any type of funding [would] be available for this type of thing again." Wein made fundamental changes. Hoping to boost attendance, he reduced ticket prices from a range of $3.50 to $7.50 to a top price of $5.50. The previous year each director had had complete control of his part of the program, leading to a lack of cohesiveness in the series—a freedom that, according to the *Times* article, "sometimes resulted in the use of the concerts as a personal platform for the musical directors." Wein established a planning committee that worked out programs in detail and then assigned them to different directors. Concerts were built around a single theme.[11] Wein explains, "We decided that the concerts needed to have individual appeal. That's when we created our greatest concerts, whether it was our George Russell concert, or the Louis Armstrong things that Dick Hyman did for us. We did a Bix Beiderbecke concert, of course we did Goodman, we did Jimmie Lunceford, we did Ornette Coleman, we did a lot different things." Over the next several years the company performed everything from original music to tightly crafted rearrangements and note-for-note transcriptions of classic works.

Wein claims to have poured considerable amounts of his own money into the project over the objections of many of his associates: "In those years I was doing reasonably well. My company got mad at me because whatever little profits we had (and we didn't have many), I put a lot of money—one year I put as much as $80,000 or $90,000—in the jazz repertory company." Because Wein was in the business of jazz promotion and concert organizing, impressions of conflict of interest arose over the mingling of public money and his own funds: "It was always a very upsetting thing to me, and I remember saying to them, 'Look if I was in the clothing business and I gave money to jazz, I'd be a patron. But because my business is jazz and I give money to jazz, then it's a conflict of interest. I don't quite understand that. What I'm doing is one thing and what the NYJRC is doing is another thing.' I was very, very upset about that because I believed in the NYJRC." The funding from New York State abruptly stopped after Gil Evans failed to produce a work on Wilhelm Reich that the State Council had commissioned. The Council notified Wein that he was "in default." As Wein recalls it:

> I said, "What do you mean, we're in default? Of what?" You're in default 'cause you got the money to do the Wilhelm Reich thing. I said I didn't get the money to do the Reich thing, Gil Evans did. "But it was funneled through you." They held us in default and that's when they stopped the funding. I said to Gil, "Let's do a concert, just give me some music, we'll call it the Wilhelm Reich piece." He wouldn't do it.

While funding dried up and the connection to Carnegie Hall withered, the NYJRC continued to appear sporadically at Wein's jazz festivals until a final tribute to Louis Armstrong at Jimmy Carter's White House in 1980. By this time the band had acquired a stabler personnel roster.[12] As Dick Hyman delved further into re-creating classic repertory, musicians were expected to play transcribed solos from the recordings. A story told by Mike Zwerin, who played trombone in the band, conveys the absurdity of this situation, especially to some of the older members of the band. In a rehearsal trombonist Britt Woodman struggled to read a difficult transcription only to eventually recognize it as one of his own solos from the Ellington band.[13]

Unlike Wein's NYJRC, the NJE did not have either a preexisting promotional network or a cozy relationship with a prestigious concert hall. Chuck Israels had originally planned to inaugurate his repertory project in 1976 to coincide with the Bicentennial, because, as he wryly told Wilson of the *New York Times* at the time, he hoped "people and institutions might be looking for intelligent ways to spend money then." He decided to move his project forward several years when he received an unexpected offer of $15,000 from Joseph Leavitt to do two programs at Wolf Trap Farm outside Washington, D.C. The inaugural concerts proved a harbinger of some of the difficulties ahead. When the band arrived they discovered they were merely the opening act for Sarah Vaughan the first night and part of a high school and college band workshop the second night. Israels confided to Wilson, "We made the mistake of putting together a serious program when what they needed was a light, short thing. Instead of spending $15,000 on those concerts, we'd have done better to spend $5,000 and saved $10,000 for the future." When Israels applied for a grant from the New York State Council on the Arts to present five concerts at Alice Tully Hall, he was told he must have specific dates. He then rushed out to reserve five Wednesdays with a deposit of $1,250 of borrowed money. Israels used the fact that the State Council had given Wein $55,000 to pry loose a share for his orchestra.[14]

The NJE was a more traditional big band than the NYJRC in the sense that it had set personnel and musical direction. Israels felt the NYJRC was not really a repertory orchestra because it called in specialists to do different kinds of music rather than have a fixed membership that learned how to play across styles and eras. Just as "symphony concerts have Mozart and Bartók in the same evening," Israels saw no reason why a jazz orchestra could not play "everything from Armstrong to Miles Davis." His motivation was not so much ideological as practical: "It came from the understanding that there is no longer any popular support for this music. Therefore, if you want it to survive at all, you're stuck with institutionalizing it. The model was an economic model, as well as a cultural model."

David Berger, who was hired by Israels to supply transcriptions and play fourth trumpet, recalls that playing classic repertoire was not an end in itself but a strategy for performing original music. Israels agrees:

> To a large extent that's true. Two things happened. One is that I wanted to measure my own music against Ellington's music, and Gil Evans and all of this wonderful stuff, sometimes succeeding in my own mind, and sometimes not. The other idea was that by having a repertory band I could subsidize an ensemble of people who would be there ready to play a new piece of mine, and that I wouldn't have to pay for that simply with my own resources. I could justify public support for the band by the fact that I was not doing just my music.

Conceived broadly as a jazz composers' orchestra, in addition to repertory, the NJE performed Berger's and Israels's music, as well as original arrangements and compositions by Bob Brookmeyer, Herb Pomeroy, Tom Pierson, Bob James, and others.

Israels had led a band in his own compositions in the late 1960s. That group received favorable reviews when it subbed at the Vanguard for several Mondays in 1968 while the Thad Jones/Mel Lewis Orchestra toured Japan. But Israels simply could not hire his old band for the NJE: "It had guys in it who were interested in playing my stuff but would *not* have been interested in playing Jelly Roll Morton's music." In fact, finding musicians to play such a wide range of music was not easy. Israels had less difficulty finding "guys who were usually playing older stuff, who were happy to be asked to play newer stuff. That was fairly common. But the other way around was less common." He explains, "They were brought up, as I was, to think that one developed a particular style and concentrated on a particular musical idiom and became identified with it." He remembers being "quite surprised by Gerry Mulligan's willingness and ability to play Pee Wee Russell and Monk, and everybody else. That was not a common model at all." "Personally," he continues, "I looked askance at that for a long time."

Although Israels's original motivation may have been somewhat mercenary, over time he and the band became more comfortable with the repertory concept:

> It changed. It was first the idea of being able to justify support, and then, it became interesting. But I didn't know how interesting it was going to be until I did it. I had no idea what it was going to sound like to play "Black Bottom Stomp" next to "Four and One." Until I did it. Then I thought: this is really interesting—that we can do this, that the juxtaposition is so informative to us.

Selections from the band's two albums, carefully ordered by Israels to create some of these "interesting juxtapositions," were rereleased on CD in 2002.[15]

From the start, the idea never was to copy improvised solos from the records or "to reenact archaic ways of playing." Israels still believes, as he did in 1973, that "if it's a masterpiece, there's enough room for interpretation."[16] Looking back, Israels says:

> You know it was a judgment call every time. And I thought that everything was up for either preserving or rethinking. Great musical architecture can stand a number of interpretations. The purist approach to that is not necessarily the one that communicates the idea the best. On the other hand, it's a little hard to conceive of playing Ellington's music better than Ellington's band did, because that was a particular collection of music designed around the people in the band. So do you take the concept of making the music sound the way it is now on record, or do you take the concept of designing it around the people that you have at the moment, which was a big element of Ellington's aesthetic? Which part of it do you steal?

Like other early repertory orchestras, the NJE lacked organization. Israels was hard pressed to devote time to fund-raising in addition to all the other duties that came with leading a band and maintaining an active playing career. Berger described the somewhat haphazard pursuit of government subsidy: "He just lucked into some New York State Council on the Arts and National Endowment for the Arts funding in the beginning, and every year it got less and less. One year we got a tour of colleges in New York State and that was great, and one in South Carolina. We also had four concerts every year at the New School." The U.S. economy was not strong throughout most of the 1970s, and jazz had not yet acquired the kind of status that would attract corporate sponsors.

Israels was working mostly on his own as he tried to build this "cultural institution"— without a staff, a board of directors, or offices. In addition, he says, "I never had the kind of business partnership that I could trust to understand what I was doing and pursue things in the right way." The competition with the NYJRC for recognition and funding was lopsided: Wein had organization, connections, the relationship with Carnegie Hall. During this period, Israels and Wein tended to avoid each other, though their relationship went back to 1954 in Boston when Wein ran the club Storyville and Israels was just starting out.

Both Wein and Israels were also competing with other arts groups for money. During the 1970s, funding institutions, especially in the public sector, attempted to correct long-standing inequities of support for minority cultural activities. Jazz, which was becoming recognized as an African American art form during the 1960s and 1970s, seemed a logical way to funnel money to a community that historically had been neglected. Unfortunately for white jazz musicians, these policies effectively denied support for their work. Israels, in particular, because his band was almost entirely white, felt he could not compete with organizations such as Collective Black Artists and Jazzmobile: "We were after the same money. And those were basically black organizations so they could provide the funding organizations with the recipients that the funding organizations were really interested in having. That was a political problem that I never solved."

The competition for funding was only part of the problem. In this racially charged climate, black bandleaders might be criticized for "hiring white guys when there were brothers out of work." Even black musicians who worked with mostly white bands felt the heat for "selling out." Israels wanted a more integrated band, but it seemed that "many of the African American guys who were able to do this music were busy doing other things and more successful and didn't have time to do it." Berger recalls, "We had a lot of black guys who went through the band, but they just didn't stay." Others were called but could not make the dates. Building a "band sound" required consistent personnel, so a strict attendance policy was instituted. Israels also consciously avoided raiding "Thad and Mel's band," although he did use the alto and tenor saxophonist Gregory Herbert. Israels admired Herbert, whom he considered "an enormous friend": "He stood up to criticism from some of his contemporaries, stood up to criticism of my band and wouldn't stand for listening to it without saying something." Eventually, Herbert left to take a better-paying gig with Blood, Sweat and Tears.

Some young black jazz musicians were pursuing more avant-garde or experimental styles of jazz and had little interest in developing the skills required by more traditional jazz or repertory. For a while Israels worked with the trumpeter Jimmy Owens, until they split over artistic differences. Owens recommended black players Israels felt did not fit in the band. Mentioning John Stubblefield as an example, Israels says, "I needed somebody who could play a Lester Young part and do a variety of things and feel comfortable about it, and he couldn't do it."

In 1977 the ensemble began a residency at the New School. The first concert appropriately featured Gerry Mulligan, who had helped to inspire Israels to form the NJE. The remaining concerts of the four-concert season featured the singer Carrie Smith, the pianist Tommy Flanagan, and the tenor saxophonist Michael Brecker.[17] The ensemble gave its final concert at the New School in 1981. Later that year Israels "threw in the towel" and moved to the West Coast when his wife, Margot, was hired by the San Francisco Opera Company. Looking back, Israels realizes that his ambition "to have the equivalent of the New York Philharmonic" was an impossible task for a single individual. "It wasn't a lack of vision, it was a lack of ability to achieve the vision."

Soon after the NJE and NYJRC were formed, the repertory movement received added impetus with the death on 24 May 1974 of the most prolific composer and orchestra leader in jazz. With Duke Ellington's passing, many jazz enthusiasts, critics, scholars, and performers feared that, in Gary Giddins's words, Ellington's music would "be confined to record collectors and libraries."[18] Schuller, another moving force in the repertory movement, observed that a music that is no longer performed live is doomed to extinction.[19]

After his father's death, Mercer Ellington assumed leadership of the band. "We were in danger of losing our way," Mercer recalled to Francis Davis in 1986. "There were new men in the band, and the men who knew his music by heart were on the way out. . . . What I had to do was restore the library, by hiring arrangers to transcribe older pieces from records."[20] Mercer enlisted the aid of David Berger, who had recently begun transcribing pieces for Israels. Because Ellington was able to retain the members of his orchestra for so long, in many cases for three or four decades, and because much of the music was constantly revised, parts were often illegible, fragmentary, or missing altogether. Even in the Ellington orchestra, arrangements that had always been somewhat fluid were being transformed into fixed texts.

The American Jazz Orchestra

After the NJE and the NYJRC withered in the late 1970s, the jazz repertory movement lay fallow until 1985, when the writer, film producer, and critic Gary Giddins decided to establish an ensemble. After observing that "the idea of a stable big band music that keeps its eye on the future while celebrating its past is long overdue," he called for the creation of jazz orchestras that could "be maintained in the same houses and by the same boards of directors that conserve philharmonic orchestras."[21] In May he received a letter from Roberta Swann, director of the Great Hall at Cooper Union, asking if they could meet. After they attended a concert together Swann mentioned her desire to have a modernist ensemble in residence. Giddins responded, "The hell with that! Everybody's doing that! If you love jazz so much, do something innovative! Put Cooper Union behind an institutionalized jazz orchestra!" Echoing the earlier discourse of Israels, Martin Williams, and others, Giddins proclaimed, "It could function just like a philharmonic, only instead of Beethoven and Schubert, it would play Ellington and Mingus!" Swann and Giddins decided to pitch the idea to the president of Cooper Union, Bill Lacy. A few weeks later, to their pleasant surprise, he approved their proposal without hesitation.[22]

Giddins articulated what had become the central questions of repertory performance: "Should a conductor feel obliged to mimic every orchestral idiosyncrasy of an earlier era? Should an arrangement be opened for expanded improvisation? Should classic solos be retained or orchestrated?" Though he perhaps underestimated the lingering power of these issues, dismissing them as mere "details," Giddins was prescient in his realization that the answers would continue to come, as they had in the NJE and the NYRJC, through trial and error.[23]

On 12 May 1986 the American Jazz Orchestra (AJO) presented its opening concert before a full house of nearly one thousand. On the program was the music of Fletcher Henderson, Ellington (featuring a performance of *Harlem* conducted by Maurice Peress), Lunceford, Basie, and Gillespie (with a recently commissioned fantasy on Gillespie themes by Slide Hampton). At first, as was the case in the NYJRC, the personnel for the AJO was drawn from an eclectic pool of musicians. From his work as Benny Goodman's personal manager and leading his own band (which Goodman used for a while in the mid-1980s), Loren Schoenberg knew Giddins and became involved in the project. Schoenberg describes the first AJO as "a kind of a jazz critic's dream": "We had Ted Curson and Craig Harris [trombonist with Sun Ra, David Murray, and others]. I mean this was the only saxophone section in the world that had Walt Levinsky and Hamiet Bluiett, myself, Jimmy Heath, Frank Wess, and [John] Purcell." With the divergent styles of the players Giddins had chosen, the band found it difficult to coalesce into a unit.

A concert featuring Benny Carter was scheduled for early 1987 for which he was commissioned to write a new piece of music. By this time Mel Lewis had joined the band. According to Schoenberg, "Mel was such a big presence and authority that he became a guru to Gary and even to John Lewis. So we began to shape the personnel of the band: [trumpeters] Marvin Stamm, Bob Millikan, Virgil Jones, John Eckert; [trombonists] Eddie Bert, Bobby Pring, [Jimmy] Knepper, sometimes Jack Jeffers. In the reeds the regulars were me,

Danny Bank, John Purcell, Bill Easley, and Jerry Dodgion. Dick Katz was on piano, Ron Carter on bass, and Howard Collins on guitar. . . . Then [Benny] Carter came out. The concert was a big splash."

Giddins continued to pursue a wide range of interests in his programming but with greater stylistic compatibility among his band members. As Schoenberg recalls, "Gary realized that you could not construct a band just made up of your favorite players, that you had to get good section players and consequently a band picked of jazz names would not necessarily make a good big band." Schoenberg gradually assumed the roles of contractor, orchestra manager, and assistant conductor.

With its clear connections to Cooper Union, the AJO was the first institutionally based jazz orchestra. Nevertheless, organizational problems persisted. According to Schoenberg, "Part of the tragedy of the AJO, which is something that was averted with the Smithsonian and Lincoln Center bands, is that we really had no one who really knew how to do fund-raising. Gary gave birth to the band and is a great writer, of course, and Roberta Swann was in charge of the hall at Cooper Union and John Lewis was John Lewis, a great pianist and composer. And I was me. But none of us knew about fund-raising, and ultimately that was one of the real causes of the downfall of the AJO. We kind of thought it would just happen."

Like other repertory orchestras, the AJO needed to build a band library. A grant from the Irene Diamond Fund funded the effort. Schoenberg remembers, "Around 1987 Dan Morgenstern obtained a grant, and approached me to help with the selection of both the material and the transcriber. We hired Mark Lopeman to do the transcriptions. Mark transcribed one hundred big band arrangements that Dan and I chose. And this became pretty much the mother lode of the library of the AJO." Many of those arrangements eventually found their way into the Smithsonian and Lincoln Center bands.

By 1988–89 the band was performing four or five concerts a year at Cooper Union and personnel remained fairly steady. A wide variety of guests passed through for various concerts. Younger players had an opportunity to play with and learn from older players. In 1989 a series of preconcert lectures and interviews was introduced. "A lot of what happened at Jazz at Lincoln Center came out of reaction to some of what we were doing," Schoenberg says. "Wynton [Marsalis] and Stanley [Crouch] came to some of the concerts. Reaction, both positive and negative, gave them an impetus for getting an orchestra together. But with the AJO there was always a feeling of a good opportunity missed. Because these things were not well attended or publicized, it began to be frustrating." The Cooper Union venue was far from ideal. Patrons complained about the uncomfortable seats and the columns that blocked the view of the stage.

Giddins's fellow critics thought these were not the only problems. Critics are supposed to be disinterested, and Giddins's involvement with the band led Francis Davis to protest, "The potential for conflict of interest (and for the *appearance* of it, which can be just as damaging) is, of course, enormous."[24] The musicians in the AJO were more concerned that the conflict between Giddins's dual role as critic and bandleader might affect the trajectory of the band than lead to biased reporting. According to Schoenberg:

> Gary had the strength of his own convictions, as befits a critic of his magnitude. There were conflicts where Gary's independence as a journalist may not have been in the AJO's best interests. The band just died a slow death, the venue was working against us. There was no strong funding. A labor of love can only go so far. Unfortunately, it fell apart in 1992.

Schoenberg also recalls that "although there was a good feeling at the concerts, a bit of a problem philosophically between [him] and some of the players with John [Lewis] and ultimately with Gunther Schuller, was this whole problem of 'authenticity.' " For the AJO's second album, *Ellington Masterpieces,* the band was "instructed to play the written solos," a policy that continued when they did a week at the Blue Note soon after. In Schoenberg's opinion, Lewis and Schuller "sometimes stultified the creative impulses of all these great players":

> Consequently you end up with a band with the same attitude as if they're playing a show. That's not what it's about. If I'm playing "Cottontail" and I want to play Ben Webster's solo, I'll play it, and if I want to play my own solo, I'll play it. And if I want to play a mixture of the two, I'll play it. I'll do whatever the hell I want to do that way. We have something that is honest and keeps the players creatively involved in the process.

The only "aesthetically viable" way to "authenticity," in Schoenberg's view, is to "hire the right musicians, and when it comes to the solos and to all that kind of stuff, let them make up their mind what they want to do."

After the demise of the AJO, Schoenberg continued to perform with the newly established Smithsonian Jazz Masterworks Orchestra (SJMO) in Washington, DC., under the direction of Schuller and David Baker. At least in the beginning Schuller was even more rigid than John Lewis about re-creating every detail of the recordings. A review of a rare New York appearance of the SJMO in 1994 praised his thoughtful presentation but noted, "Mr. Schuller probably couldn't have made a living leading a dance orchestra—he rarely lets the music become exhilarating."[25] Schoenberg was eventually hired by Jazz at Lincoln Center as an artistic consultant, and he has filled in as conductor or player in rehearsals and a few concerts. He was reunited with John Lewis in two concerts in February 1999 featuring music from the Blanton-Webster era of Ellington. Giddins appears to have given up producing concerts and has returned to writing and other related projects.

LINCOLN CENTER AND CARNEGIE HALL

With the inauguration of Lincoln Center's *Classical Jazz* in summer 1987, Martin Williams's dream of a jazz orchestra linked to an "august cultural institution" started to become a reality. The first season began modestly enough with a three-night program. Alina Bloomgarden, an executive at Lincoln Center, produced the first concert in association with WBGO, New York's public radio station devoted to twenty-four-hour jazz programming). Wynton Marsalis, then only twenty-five years old, was hired as artistic director, and his intellectual mentor, Stanley Crouch, was hired as "artistic consultant." The second season, which expanded the series to five nights, from Friday, 5 August, to Wednesday, 10 August, set the tone for future concerts as a salute to "great jazz artists, including Duke Ellington, composer/arranger Tadd Dameron and drummer Max Roach," and an evening of " 'Standards on Horn,' headlined by Mr. Marsalis." A press release touted the series as "celebrating the introduction of 'Jazz,' the new men's fragrance from Yves St. Laurent," which was inspired, according to the president of the perfume company's U.S. branch, "by the joie de vivre, air of improvisation and inventive style that characterizes jazz as a musical form." George Weissman, chairman of Lincoln Center for the Performing Arts, was quoted, "*Classical Jazz* reflects Lincoln Center's commitment to fresh ideas and new audiences." Bloomgarden and Marsalis hired Berger to conduct an "all-star big band including many Ellington alumni" in a concert of some of the maestro's "less frequently performed works."[26] When he was interviewed for the job, Berger was asked how he would approach the music. "Well, I have a different point of view from Gunther Schuller," he responded. "I don't want to re-create the records, I want the guys to play their own shit and play it like it's their music." According to Berger, Marsalis immediately made up his mind: "You got the gig." Berger conducted the band until he was fired in 1993.

An important milestone for Jazz at Lincoln Center came in 1991 when Lincoln Center announced that it was creating a jazz department as the initial step in the anticipated establishment of a "new jazz constituent." A front-page article in the *New York Times* began, "Duke Ellington, Charlie Parker and Thelonious Monk are to have a place alongside Bach, Beethoven and Mozart." Admitting that he was only a recent convert to jazz, Nathan Leventhal, president of the center, was quoted: "But I've learned a lot. . . . There is as much richness and variety in Duke Ellington as there is in Mozart."[27] Lincoln Center's press release noted, "This new constituent would be the twelfth member of the Lincoln Center family and would become the first constituent created by Lincoln Center since both the Film Society and the Chamber Music Society were founded in 1969." Rob Gibson, previously director of the Atlanta Jazz Series and the Montreux Atlanta International Music Festival, was hired as the director of the new department. After a year of "intensive study and deliberation," the Committee on Jazz at Lincoln Center, "an *ad hoc* group comprised of members of Lincoln Center's Board as well as leaders from the music, educational, business, government and funding communities," recommended that Lincoln Center devote $1 million annually to the jazz department by the mid-1990s. With this important seed money and support, Jazz at Lincoln Center was poised to become a major cultural institution.

Soon Jazz at Lincoln Center employed more staff than musicians, an important step in the life of any aspiring arts organization. In 1998 the LCJO performed "more than 125 concerts in 100 cities on five continents."[28] Perhaps not as elegant as a new men's fragrance (but certainly more widely used), the consumer credit arm of Sears—Discover Card—became the major sponsor for Jazz at Lincoln Center. After the announcement in 2000 of plans to build a new performance center at Columbus Circle, Coca-Cola, the investment bankers Allen & Company, the Office of the Mayor, the New York City Council, and several foundations came forward to pledge over $10 million each.

All this money, especially when some of it flows from government coffers, has intensified demands for its recipients to be more representative of diverse points of view and populations. In 1991, after declaring jazz a "rare and valuable American treasure," the U.S. Congress appropriated $242,000 to establish the Smithsonian Jazz Masterworks Orchestra. In Washington complaints mounted that too many players came from New York and were white. Rather than applaud its substantial accomplishments, many in the jazz community have attacked Jazz at Lincoln Center for its narrow view of jazz (that is, for ignoring newer music such as jazz-rock fusion and the avant-garde), the perceived exclusion of white composers and musicians, and a "new boy network" of patronage that hires musicians and commissions works from Marsalis and his friends. These attacks frequently degenerated into counting exercises on both sides. In a February 1994 article in the *Washington Post,* the jazz writer, Richard Harrington, noted that "of 78 titles in the current touring canon, only five are by white composers."[29] When confronted on the race issue during his debate with James Lincoln Collier in August 1994, Marsalis listed all the white members of his band and the white lecturers and guest artists who had appeared at Lincoln Center.[30]

More recently, outcry has arisen over the lack of female permanent members. Lara Pellegrinelli wrote in the *Village Voice* that despite the furor over "accusations of nepotism, reverse racism, and age discrimination[,] . . . what nobody seems to have noticed is the profound and unchanged absence of women from the bandstand." Pellegrinelli also criticized the procedure by which musicians are hired for the orchestra: "Although Marsalis refers to auditions, the LCJO has never had one. Positions are not advertised. There is no formal hiring procedure. As in the majority of big bands past and present, hiring takes place by word of mouth, through personal recommendations. Sometimes the musicians get a foot in the door by subbing—on referral—or by sitting in at rehearsals." Comparing the LCJO with other Lincoln Center constituents, and with classical orchestras in general, Pellegrinelli called for "blind auditions, where unknown musicians play behind a screen, . . . [such as] required by the International Conference of Symphony and Opera Musicians." Pellegrinelli argued that the public funding received by Jazz at Lincoln Center "provides compelling reasons for their consideration."[31]

In response to these complaints, decisions about what and whom to include are portrayed as "purely artistic." Marsalis states flatly, "I hire orchestra members on the basis of merit."[32] Said former executive director, Rob Gibson, "We have to deal with the level of music that is about aesthetics, and that's what we're going to do. It has nothing to do with skin color." He conceded, however, that the ultimate goal is to expand the audience: "Do they actually believe that including some avant-modernists in what we try to do is the difference in whether this music succeeds? We're talking about a 90-year-old art form that accounts for barely 4 percent of recorded sales. We're still trying to get Duke Ellington and Louis Armstrong across to the general populace!"[33]

As controversy continued to swirl around Marsalis, Crouch, and Jazz at Lincoln Center, the one competitor capable of challenging their hegemony was eliminated. For ten years, however, while the Carnegie Hall Jazz Band was active, New York was blessed with two major repertory jazz bands. Although the Carnegie Hall band attempted to give the Lincoln Center orchestra a run for the money (literally), one cannot help feel that the full potential of this competitive relationship was never realized.

The Carnegie band began several years after the Lincoln Center effort. In 1991 Judith Arron, executive director of Carnegie Hall, asked George Wein to initiate a jazz series, and he decided to once again try his hand at establishing a big band. As had Alina Bloomgarden, Wein engaged a trumpet virtuoso, Jon Faddis, to be his musical director. From here the similarities ended. Although both Marsalis and Faddis had been black wunderkinder, Marsalis was an outsider, the most prominent of a batch of young upstarts propelled to the top of the jazz world by their record companies in the 1980s—before, in the view of many, they had paid proper dues. Faddis, on the other hand, had apprenticed in numerous large ensembles—beginning when he was eighteen years old with the Lionel Hampton Orchestra and continuing with the Thad Jones/Mel Lewis Orchestra, Gil Evans, Charles Mingus, Wein's NYJRC, and Dizzy Gillespie.

The CHJB's debut at the hall on 22 October 1992 made clear that Faddis and Wein had set a different course from that of the LCJO. For one thing, the CHJB, as if to emphasize its brash brass, called itself a "band" rather than an "orchestra." Like the NYJRC, the band not only performed classic repertory but also showcased "classic tunes in refreshingly novel forms." Though he intended to build "on the legacy of the great big bands of the 1930s and 1940s," Wein's stated goal was "to present those classics in new and musically challenging arrangements specifically written for it."[34] With a keen sense of the hall's traditions, Wein exploited material that related to its history. For example, the band performed Ellington's *Black, Brown and Beige,* which premiered at Carnegie Hall in 1943, and commissioned updated rearrangements of classic warhorses such as "Sing, Sing, Sing" from Benny Goodman's legendary 1938 *Spirituals to Swing* concert.

As the band's second season got under way, a reporter for the *New York Times* noted the pressure to "establish an identity at once as distinctive as, and distinct from, its better known counterpart, . . . the Lincoln Center Jazz Orchestra."[35] In its first concert that year the band closed the first set with the original arrangement of "Sing, Sing, Sing." The second set opened with a startling new version of the same piece. The saxophonist, David Liebman, came onstage to perform an arrangement of Goodman's classic, completely rewritten by Jim McNeely for soprano saxophone instead of clarinet. The new, impressionistic, sometimes unrecognizable version seemed more inspired by John Coltrane's extended duets with his drummer, Elvin Jones, than by Goodman's with Gene Krupa. Many audience members walked out. Nevertheless, in the view of the *New York Times* jazz critic, Peter Watrous, the evening was the start of "an essential process: the reworking of original source material, with no sense of restraint. . . . It was exhilarating; the repertory movement all of a sudden had new potential."[36] Rather than keep most of the work "in-house," like the LCJO, Wein and Faddis commissioned arrangements and compositions from some of New York's most esteemed arrangers, including Frank Foster, Maria Schneider, Michael Abene, Slide Hampton, Randy Sandke, and Jim McNeely. Although he occasionally sprinkled a few less experienced players in the band, Faddis favored seasoned, experienced players. A four-concert series was presented at Carnegie Hall each season (usually October to March). Through its connections to George Wein's Festival Productions, the band also appeared on the festival circuit in Europe and the United States. Like the LCJO, a wide variety of jazz guests were featured, ranging from Doc Cheatham, Clark Terry, David Liebman, and Joshua Redman to the vocalists Diana Krall, Kevin Mahogany, and Nnenna Freelon. However, Wein's invitations to artists such as Gloria Estefan, Jonathan Butler, and Dave Grusin were criticized for pandering to commercial tastes. Watrous, for one, denigrated the Grusin concert as "pop entertainment . . . [that] called into question the whole idea of serious institutional jazz programming."[37]

Despite its stellar lineup and musicianship and despite acclaim from musicians, the CHJB often fared poorly in the press and in public perception. Band members were particularly frustrated that Lincoln Center got most of the attention. I have frequently heard members complain that "x" (any one of a number of players in the CHJB) had more experience than all of Marsalis's musicians put together. Frank Wess, Dennis Wilson, and Byron Stripling served in the Basie band; Gary Smulyan and Stripling, in the Herman band; Slide Hampton, in the Maynard Ferguson Orchestra; and on and on.[38] The CHJB also felt that its style, more Basie than Ellington, was a disadvantage. Ellington's stock has risen sharply in recent years, as he has been celebrated as "America's greatest composer." As evidenced in its choice of repertoire, its performance practices, and Marsalis's ventures in composition, the LCJO is modeled on the Ellington Orchestra. A commonly mentioned difference between the Ellington and Basie styles is the relative prominence of the reeds and brass. In a review of a January 1999 concert at Carnegie Hall, Watrous criticized the CHJB as being more of a "brass orchestra without much dynamic subtlety."[39] Lead alto, Dick Oatts, is unapologetic about the CHJB being a "brass-powered band." "This is what our sound is," he says. "Woodwinds are nice colors, but a lot of these reviewers are hearing Duke Ellington. They're listening to Wynton's thing over there and thinking this is the way it should be at Carnegie. Hey, it's a different sound. There's beauty in both." Oatts and his colleagues felt that the CHJB was not treated fairly, "that Jon devoted a lot of time and put together an incredible band, only to be attacked." The deciding factor was "money, how much money the Lincoln Center band has, as opposed to the Carnegie band. If we had the money, the writers would want the CHJB." Although foundations such as the Irene Diamond Fund made significant contributions, the fundraising efforts did not come close to the phenomenal success achieved by their rivals.

Their competition for funds and recognition reflected deeper rivalries. The names Carnegie Hall and Lincoln Center brought not only prestige but also distinct traditions, philosophies, and organizational hierarchies. The long-smoldering feud between these institutions went back decades, to the defection of the New York Philharmonic from Carnegie Hall to the newly constructed Lincoln Center in 1960. To make way for the new complex, which included an opera house, a home for ballet, a theater, a concert hall, a performing arts school, a special branch of the New York Public Library, and four thousand luxury apartments, seventeen blocks of brownstone tenements and storefronts (including Thelonious Monk's family apartment) were torn down and entire streets closed off.

With the departure of the Philharmonic, Carnegie Hall itself barely escaped the wrecking ball of urban renewal mania. Initially, Carnegie Hall struggled to fill the hundred nights a year vacated by the Philharmonic. Two things helped to save it: the notoriously bad acoustics at Lincoln Center and rediscovery of Carnegie Hall's rich history. The hall had a long tradition featuring African American music, going back to James Reese Europe's appearance with his 150-piece Clef Club Orchestra in 1912. The absence of a resident orchestra occupying the hall four nights a week actually became something of a blessing, allowing even more diversity in programming. Over the next thirty years the facility gradually became less of a rental hall and turned more and more to production. The staff grew from a mere seven full-time employees in 1960 to more than two hundred by 2000. Development, education, artistic direction and programming, subscription, marketing, ticketing, and production departments were added. In 1986 a full-time curator was hired to collect and display memorabilia and artifacts for the 1990–91 hundredth anniversary season.[40] Carnegie Hall's executive director, Judith Arron, asked Wein to produce two concerts of jazz and folk music as part of the celebration. Afterward, when she asked Wein to introduce a jazz program to Carnegie's annual season, rather than book a series of jazz artists, Wein pitched the idea of a resident big band. Faddis had organized and led the hundredth anniversary jazz band. Wein remembers, "He did an incredible job. They gave us a budget per concert and that's how it started. Jon was the musical director, and I was, I guess, whatever, the executive director."

Unlike the NYJRC, the Carnegie Hall Jazz Band was a set unit. A single individual was clearly in charge of musical direction. Although the NYJRC also had a relationship with Carnegie Hall (through the city's rent remission program), now, because CHJB bore the name of its institutional sponsor, the relationship was unequivocal. Carnegie, with its burgeoning staff, would support the band with marketing, production, and education programs. Wein explains the difference: "The Carnegie Hall Band was presented by Carnegie Hall. The NYJRC was presented by the NYJRC with a little help from Carnegie Hall." Wein's role and financial relationship were also more clearly defined. Now on the board of Carnegie Hall, instead of contributing and raising money directly for the band, he channeled it to the central fund for Carnegie Hall.

Jazz at Lincoln Center, as a constituent of Lincoln Center, retained a degree of independence from the parent institution. Unlike Carnegie Hall, which acted as a rental agency and produced a wide variety of concerts, each constituent of Lincoln Center was freer to pursue its own narrow interests. Shoppers in the Lincoln Center mall could select from a variety of cultural wares: from opera or ballet to symphony or jazz orchestras, each with its own full-time departments devoted to marketing and promotion, production, fund-raising, and education. Moreover, each had its own board of directors. With a dedicated staff and with its affiliations with other Lincoln Center constituents, Jazz at Lincoln Center acquired stratospheric levels of funding.

The Carnegie Hall Jazz Band may have been vanquished on fund-raising and critical fronts, but on the playing field the Lincoln Center Jazz Orchestra did not always emerge victorious. In the competitive spirit of the battles of the bands at the Savoy Ballroom and the "cutting contests" of Kansas City, the bands met head to head twice, in 1994 and 1995. Wein organized both events at Avery Fisher Hall as part of his JVC Jazz Festival. According to him, the leaders and musicians of both bands enthusiastically welcomed the chance to compete musically.

The two contests highlighted differences between the two bands in personnel, musical direction, and repertoire. Watrous described the action in his reviews for the *New York Times:*

> With the two groups facing each other on stage, Mr. Faddis's charges started the proceedings, moving through a suitelike composition by Garnett Brown called "Wat's So" that quoted liberally from Miles Davis. Mr. Faddis underscored his band's strengths, a lush, cogent sound, and declared the group's identity by performing a modern piece outside of the jazz canon.
>
> Mr. Marsalis declared his in turn with a set of three pieces by Duke Ellington—"Happy Go Lucky Local," "Afro Bossa," and a section of "The Nutcracker" Suite—that unquestionably crushed the opposition. Using Ellington's arrangements in a contest like this is like having divine intervention on one's side.

Faddis apparently made several tactical errors by answering a "housewrecking" vocal by Milt Grayson with a lighter arrangement orchestrated for flutes and attempting to sing a few blues choruses himself. A final trumpet battle between Faddis and Marsalis brought the audience to its feet in approval. Still, the general consensus agreed with Watrous that in the first concert "there was blood left on the stage . . . , and most of it belonged to the Carnegie Hall Band."[41]

For their rematch a year later, the Carnegie band's strategy focused on its strengths. In the first half the band came out swinging with a set of impeccably executed Basie arrangements from the 1950s and 1960s. Once again Lincoln Center responded with its versions of Ellington classics. But in the intervening year, many changes had come to the LCJO. Bill Easley, who played with the Lincoln Center band in both contests, explains, "By the second year, now you've got a big turnover in the personnel. And you don't have some of the elements in the Ellington vein. The prior year, you had another band. Britt Woodman [lead trombone], Norris Turney [alto saxophone], I mean that's enough right there!" Besides these Ellington veterans, Easley adds, the previous year's band featured seasoned Ellington specialists Art Baron and Lew Soloff. As I discuss in some detail in chapter 11, Marsalis had fired most of his all-star band and replaced them with younger, less experienced players. Ellington's music—never easy to pull off—provided little advantage to the LCJO this year. The mood of the audience resembled that of a prizefight more than a jazz concert. David Berger, who was in attendance, reports that after the first set a man several rows in front of him stood up and loudly announced, "Carnegie Hall—one, Lincoln Center—nothing!"

In the second set the contrasts were even more stark. Marsalis opened with Ellington's "Wild Man Moore" featuring himself on several bluesy choruses, and the Carnegie band pulled out its abstract, postmodern version of "Sing, Sing, Sing." Carnegie's guest soloist, David Liebman, unleashed aggressive, almost atonal ideas during an extended solo. McNeely's arrangement called for the entire band to mimic Liebman's lines with freely improvised passages. In his turn, as if to say anyone can do that, Marsalis, whose contempt for free jazz is well known, taunted the Carnegie band with a freely improvised section of his own. The drama concluded with a version of Ellington's "Diminuendo and Crescendo in Blue," as the two bands exchanged rhythm sections and brought up soloists Lew Tabackin and Claude "Fiddler" Williams.

In Easley's opinion, both bands took the contests a little too seriously. "It's not the same thing as a boxing match. There should be a little more love in it." While the Carnegie band was playing, he worried that maybe he should not show how much he enjoyed their playing: "I'm up there dancing in my seat to the other band, and I'd have to catch myself, 'Oh, maybe I shouldn't do this.' " The next day the LCJO left for a European tour. Easley recalls:

> We're there at the airport and there's a group of guys standing there, and I happen to walk by and they say, "Oh we're licking our wounds." And I don't even want to *talk* about that. I go somewhere else. But later on the tour Wynton did happen to ask me, "Bill, who do you think won the battle?" I said that to be perfectly honest, I really don't care. Because I don't play music to battle.

Battle or not, Watrous concluded that "New York is profoundly lucky to have two bands working at such a level of excellence."[42] Unfortunately, with the score even at one contest each (in the opinion of most observers), the two bands were not to meet again. Wein lays much of the blame on Carnegie Hall and Lincoln Center administrators: "A lot of people didn't want it to happen. You know there's a certain rivalry between Lincoln Center and Carnegie Hall anyway, and if the press says one beat the other the other people say well we don't need that, both say why are we doing this. We can't win anything, and, if we lose, we lose." Not only were the managements of the two institutions uncomfortable with the idea of bringing their rivalry into the open, outright musical competition was likely quite foreign to them. In the Western classical tradition, the competition occurs behind the scenes; when the curtain goes up, everything is "settled" and seemingly serene. Imagine the "unseemly" spectacle of two symphony orchestras slugging it out with different versions of Mozart. The performance in jazz music is often competitive by its very nature.

Even without meeting head to head, the intense rivalry between the bands continued for another seven years until Robert Harth, who had taken over direction of Carnegie in 2001, abruptly announced that Carnegie Hall would drop the big band in favor of promoting a series of small-group concerts. A stunned Jon Faddis responded, "I think the main emotion for a lot of musicians, myself included, is one of pain rather than anger."[43] For Wein, Faddis, and the band, the last concert was a poignant event. Wein recalls, "They walked out on the stage and before they even sat down the people gave them a long round of applause. . . . [T]he guys got tears in their eyes." He has been criticized for not fighting harder. But Wein, with a businessman's pragmatism, believes that he and his musicians have more to gain by staying in the game:

> You don't fight when you know you're going to lose. The board was not behind the band, the administration wasn't. And all I could do would be to shoot my mouth off and I wouldn't make any friends, I'd just lose. I'm not a rebel in that respect. My importance to everybody is to keep working the way I'm working because it's better for a lot of people that way. People aren't unhappy to see me come around, you know what I mean. If I come around something might happen. I want to keep it that way.

Harth was deliberately vague about the reasons for the band's dismissal: "It goes all over the map. The Carnegie Hall Jazz Band represents a big band sound, which is a sound we would probably have at Carnegie Hall from time to time."[44]

The September 2003 opening of a new, smaller, 640-seat venue, Zankel Hall, blasted out of the Manhattan bedrock beneath Carnegie Hall, promised the possibility of offering more jazz concerts with greater stylistic variety on a reduced economic scale. Faddis questioned the administration's commitment to jazz: "It seems, especially recently, that Carnegie Hall wants to be considered a classical house in the European tradition. I don't think a lot of board members or employees of Carnegie feel that the Carnegie Hall Jazz Band fits within those parameters."[45]

Despite being downplayed by Harth, financial matters surely seem at the root of the decision. As was well documented in the New York press, Harth's predecessor, Xaver Ohnesorg, in the spirit of late 1990s excess, ran up tremendous debt. The ensuing economic slump and the terrorist attack of 11 September 2001 compounded the financial difficulties of Carnegie Hall as well as other institutions. Looking to stanch the flow of red ink, Harth found the Carnegie Hall Jazz Band an obvious choice for elimination. As the only ensemble bearing the Carnegie name, the CHJB stood apart from other Carnegie Hall productions. Carnegie had to pay for arrangements, as well as absorb production and rehearsal costs. With Jazz at Lincoln Center receiving most of the limelight, about to open a new performance center a couple of blocks away, and eclipsing the CHJB in just about every area—educational programs, marketing, subscriptions—at least in the jazz arena, Carnegie Hall seemed destined to come up short in its rivalry with Lincoln Center.

The LCJO and the CHJB (until its demise) have benefited from bearing the imprimatur of New York's premier concert halls. Reflecting on his time as drummer with the Carnegie band, John Riley found its reception unlike anything he had ever experienced: "The name 'Carnegie Hall' gave a certain 'world-class' endorsement to the band that opened doors for us. When we went to foreign countries the president of the country would come to the concert and invite us back to his complex. We always had invitations to embassies, things like that." Although not always well received at home, "the band definitely had a high level of status on the road." Wein pledges to "continue to book Jon's band. It will be the Jon Faddis Band." It is doubtful that the name "Jon Faddis," though it carries considerable clout in the jazz community, will propel the former Carnegie band as far.

To the bitter end, Jon Faddis persisted in staking out different territory from Jazz at Lincoln Center. The legacy of the Carnegie Hall Jazz Band, he said, was "in accord with the guiding principle of the Carnegie Corporation," quoting from the institution's own mission statement, "to 'promote the advancement and diffusion of understanding.' " He offered a eulogy in *Down Beat* that emphasized the CHJB's diversity and inclusiveness:

> More than 135 musicians have performed as members of the CHJB. These musicians are from many cultures, races and religions, and their ages and experiences vary greatly. . . . I am proud that the CHJB included women (both as featured artists and as regular members of the CHJB) and that it showcased women who compose in a prestigious venue denied them too often and for too long.

No doubt thinking of Jazz at Lincoln Center's patronage of Marsalis and his circle, Faddis added:

> George Wein and I made a priority of ensuring that commissions for new arrangements and compositions were shared among many talented writers, because there are as many ways to perceive and to play jazz as there are voices and ways to pray to God.[46]

Stanley Crouch and Wynton Marsalis, in keeping with Lincoln Center's traditional aloofness, have aggressively pursued a narrower view of jazz. Compare Faddis's statement with the words of Crouch lashing out at those who "love to assert, over and over, that everything is relative and jazz is whatever you choose to call it."[47] Jazz at Lincoln Center has eschewed questionable forays into "pop entertainment"[48] while steadfastly pursuing its canonical equivalents of the Western classical pantheon celebrated by other Lincoln Center constituents.

The above discourse is in step with the cultural warfare in the United States over the past forty years. I will return to the ideology of Marsalis and Jazz at Lincoln Center, but for now it suffices to note that their spectacular success must be attributed in part to the timeliness of their rhetoric during an era of ascendant neoconservative values.[49] Not coincidentally, one of the primary battlefields on which the culture wars have been fought concerns the role and nature of public arts funding in the United States.

FUNDING

From the single-handed ventures of Ron Roullier and Chuck Israels to the Jazz at Lincoln Center colossus, the rise of repertory jazz orchestras must be situated in the context of fundamental changes in the music industry and the general growth of nonprofit performing arts institutions in the United States. Early efforts to establish repertory orchestras occurred during the pivotal period of the early 1970s, when jazz musicians seemed forced to choose between more commercial styles of jazz, pursuing subsidies, or leaving the country or the business altogether. At the same time, funding for nonprofit arts institutions was mushrooming.

As hard times descended on the jazz community, the club scene shrank and record sales dwindled. Critics wondered if jazz would survive. Sales of rock LPs soared from under 30 percent of market share in 1966 to over 50 percent in 1969.[50] "Underground" and previously unknown rock groups were signed and promoted in a feeding frenzy, as large record companies moved in first to satisfy and later stimulate this appetite. Even *Down Beat,* during this period, featured cover stories on such nonjazz performers as the Who, Ginger Baker, Hendrix, Ike and Tina Turner, and Jethro Tull. Albert McCarthy wrote in his monthly column in 1970, "It is simple to write of the poor situation in which jazz finds itself, but less easy to suggest any way out of the impasse." He regretted having been "in the past . . . slightly contemptible of the popularisers" and wished jazz could "regain its multi-faceted appeal and . . . move away from any concept of becoming purely art music."[51]

Amid accusations of selling out, musicians such as Miles Davis and Herbie Hancock turned to jazz-rock and funk. But others did not have to look far to see another route to survival. The second half of the twentieth century was bringing a tremendous expansion in the nonprofit arts scene in the United States. Beginning in the late 1950s large metropolitan areas constructed huge performing arts complexes, such as Lincoln Center and the Los Angeles Music Center. From the 1960s well into the 1990s, hoping to revitalize decaying urban centers, smaller cities and communities established arts organizations and built performance venues at an accelerating pace. Civic pride was not the only reason for this cultural expansion. Corporations sponsored arts centers in order to lure executives to smaller cities. This growth was accompanied by increasing participation in the arts as arts education expanded and baby boomers swelled the ranks of amateur and professional artists. Between 1970 and 1990 the number of self-described professional artists nearly doubled, from slightly more than 700,000 to almost 1.4 million.[52]

After World War II the United States emerged as the world's premier economic and military power. Cold war rivalries dictated that the United States be a "cultural" leader as well. Average Americans, not just wealthy patrons and connoisseurs, should be educated in European-style "high" arts. The Ford Foundation, under W. McNeil Lowry, developed an ambitious plan to promote the arts beyond major metropolitan centers like New York and to raise standards of professionalism through support to conservatories and arts schools. Leveraged funding, or matching grants, ensured that ever greater amounts of money flowed into arts organizations. Unlike Europe, which had long traditions of governmental support for the arts, public funding in the United States met resistance. The New York State Council on the Arts, which modeled its approach on Lowry's, was founded in 1960. On the federal level public arts funding took longer to establish and from the beginning generated controversy. Many questioned the government's role in supporting the arts on ideological grounds. Didn't the "survival of the fittest" ethos of free enterprise dictate that arts organizations should succeed or fail on their own? One congressman, apologizing for his "ignorance," questioned the elitist selection process by asking, "What are the arts?"[53] Although a proposal to create an advisory council on the arts failed to pass, the Kennedy administration, which garnered considerable political capital from the arts community, managed to appoint a special consultant to the president for the arts. In the aftermath of the Kennedy assassination, along with Lyndon Johnson's Great Society program, a national arts council, the NEA, modeled after New York's, was finally established in 1965. Over the next decade the budget of the NEA swelled, especially under the somewhat unlikely aegis of Richard Nixon, who oversaw an eightfold increase in the budget to $64 million by 1974.[54] The vast majority of funds to support music continued to go "to those organizations whose repertoire and personnel reflected European classical music traditions, and similar patterns were followed in the support of opera, museum, and theater organizations."[55] In 1973, responding to demands for greater diversity, the NEA established the Expansion Arts program to support racial and ethnic minority and rural arts programs. By 1987 minority artists, institutions, and projects were receiving 13 percent of the NEA budget. As government largesse began to flow into "populist," as well as "cultivated," arts, tension was often expressed in terms of "excellence" (the codeword for Euro-American mainstream) versus "access" (the codeword for everything else).[56]

Grants were awarded by peer review or panels of artists within the various disciplines (music, art, theater, etc.). Jazz gained more autonomy when, in 1976, Billy Taylor and Gunther Schuller managed to separate jazz, folk, and ethnic music from the main music panel, and the bassist Larry Ridley was named the jazz panel's chair. Ridley faced the daunting task of building an umbrella organization for jazz musicians so that they could receive funding. To this end, the National Jazz Service Organization was established in 1984, both to administer grants and to form an advocacy group for more funding.[57] Among its founding members were David Baker (president) and Donald Byrd (vice president). One of the problems, according to Clint Eastwood, a longtime friend of jazz who served on the NEA during the seventies, was that most of the grants required "matching funds." Unlike European-style arts, jazz did not have traditional patrons. "A tremendous amount of money was spent on opera," Eastwood said, "because the wives of C.E.O.'s had their opera groups and were raising tons of money."[58]

Just as jazz was making inroads into the worlds of government subsidy and philanthropy, the structure of government funding was changing. With Reagan's election in 1982 on a platform of shrinking the federal government, the NEA was high on his budget director David Stockman's "hit list." Although major cuts were avoided temporarily when major Republican arts patrons interceded, the NEA, in a move to decentralize arts funding, transferred an increasing share of its budget to the states. As the "culture wars" heated up and controversy erupted over taxpayer support of "obscene" projects (Andres Serrano's "Piss Christ" and Robert Mapplethorpe's nude photographs), Congress considered ways to change the review process, and opponents of public arts funding demanded further cuts or even total elimination of the NEA. Not only were they opposed to governmental arts patronage on ideological grounds, but neoconservatives saw it as rewarding artists on the left of the political spectrum. While direct federal support began to decline, private contributions climbed dramatically, and nonprofit arts organizations became more dependent on individual and corporate largesse.[59]

During the U.S. economic boom of the 1990s, corporate and individual support soared. The total amount contributed to the arts in the United States from the private sector in 1997 was an estimated $1.2 billion, up from $875 million three years earlier.[60] Though this philanthropy was heralded by some as proof of continuing economic vitality in arts funding despite deep federal government cuts, support generally favored those institutions on the top rungs of the ladder. Corporations look for artistic products with high visibility and name recognition to link with their manufactured products. For example, in 2001 Brooks Brothers, aiming "to project a younger image," provided the onstage suits, ties, and dress shirts for Marsalis and his band.[61] A recent recipient of a Presidential Award for support of the arts, John Bryan, CEO of the Sara Lee Corporation, described the profit motive behind contributions:

> There are a couple of reasons the arts are especially effective for corporations. One is the opportunity to identify with the quality image that the cultural aspects of our lives project. Our business is a simple one of creating value by building brands, and to large extent this happens in the art world. The name

> on a painting tells you, "This is an original thing." It gives you trust in that bit of art, even though it may not be obvious to you why this piece is better than another. The name gives you confidence. The same is true of a brand. So identifying with art is a fantastic opportunity.[62]

The relationship between brand-name consumerism and support for recognized artists is clear and unequivocal.

Less established artists suffered further in 1996, when Newt Gingrich and the Republican-controlled Congress slashed the NEA's budget by 40 percent. Congress prohibited grants to individuals except for "Literature Fellowships, American Jazz Masters Fellowships, and National Heritage Fellowships in the Folk & Traditional Arts." The preceding year, seventy-five Jazz Fellowships totaling $545,000 had been awarded to support "jazz performance, composition, study and special projects." At least twenty-two of these grants directly supported jazz composition projects. The next year, fewer small grants were doled out, and, except for three Jazz Masters Fellowships, individual artists received nothing. Rather than incubate talent, most of the money went to "name" institutions and to honor lifetime achievements in jazz.[63]

Corporations are moving away from unrestricted gifts and instead target specific areas for support.[64] Support is linked to business and marketing strategies. When ChevronTexaco announced it would no longer support the Metropolitan Opera's Saturday afternoon live radio broadcasts, ending the longest-running commercial sponsorship in broadcast history (1931–2004), its spokesperson cited a desire to "focus more of our resources directly with the countries and markets where we do business."[65] In 2001, while Jazz at Lincoln Center received $3 million in public money (from federal, state, and local governments)—not an insignificant amount, especially in jazz—it received over $25 million from the private sector (much of it earmarked for Jazz at Lincoln Center's new home in the gleaming new headquarters of Time Warner/AOL). In exchange for pledging $10 million, the Coca-Cola Corporation underwrote Dizzy's Club Coca-Cola, "a venue for ensemble performances and education, as well as informal gatherings, seminars, and other events."[66] The Coca-Cola logo, paired with Gillespie's iconic trumpet with upturned bell, marks the entrance to the 2,500-square-foot room that has views of the Manhattan skyline and Central Park.

The fund-raising for the Carnegie Hall Jazz Band paled by comparison. According to Wein:

> Mrs. Diamond was the major contributor. There were really no other major contributors. I had a couple of parties and raised about ninety or a hundred thousand dollars in $5,000 gifts, $2,000 gifts, from some of my friends, you know. The concept of jazz getting private aid is new. That is one of the great

> contributions of Lincoln Center Jazz, the first organization that ever got individuals to make donations for jazz. Corporations and individuals. People giving million-dollar gifts. They've raised fortunes of money. That's the most important thing that's ever happened to institutionalize jazz in the American arts scene.

The vast sums of money raised by Jazz at Lincoln Center have enraged many of the jazz "have-nots." On the internet, an anonymous writer calling himself the "jazz pariah" and other jazz musicians vent their anger in weekly "Diatribes." Marsalis bears the brunt not only because he is at the top but also because musicians do not feel they can compete fairly. In one posting (ca. 1998), a concert and record producer of "alternative" jazz claimed that "a few greedy scumbags" were eating up money that used to be more evenly distributed among artists in the jazz community. "The $25,000 gig replaces five $5,000 gigs and the sponsor saves the production costs on four shows."[67] The rage is palpable, but are institutions such as Jazz at Lincoln Center really taking funding that would have gone to other jazz projects? In response, David Berger wonders, "Were they getting money from Discover Card? I don't think so."

As classical and jazz musicians shared stages of the same cultural institutions, they also became intertwined in their business relationships. Bookings of jazz artists began to be handled by the same agents that manage classical artists. Herbert Barrett Management established a jazz department in 1994 with Myles Weinstein as its director. In addition to the one hundred thirty classical musicians on its roster, including the Guanieri and Orion Quartets, the office has represented the Mingus Big Band, the Jazz Messengers (under the direction of Benny Golson), Eliane Elias, Ramsey Lewis, Steve Turre, and Billy Taylor. Barrett Management was able to draw on its long experience in the classical field to book jazz artists in concert halls as well as in traditional jazz venues such as clubs and festivals.

Marsalis embodies the cultural equivalence of jazz and classical music. Raised in a jazz family (his father, Ellis, is an established pianist in New Orleans; his brothers Branford, Delfeayo, and Jason play saxophone, trombone, and drums, respectively), he studied classical music most of his life. At fourteen he performed the Hummel concerto with the New Orleans Philharmonic. Three years later, in 1979, he headed north to the Tanglewood Music Festival in Lenox, Massachusetts (where he dazzled Gunther Schuller and played under Leonard Bernstein), and to New York to attend the Juilliard School. In 1984 he became the first musician to win Grammys in both jazz and classical music for his album *Think of One* (recorded 1983) and a recording of concertos by Haydn, Hummel, and Mozart (recorded 1982). Marsalis moved easily from philharmonic to combo. When he spoke on the value of jazz, he had credibility. There could be no better choice to lead the crusade to elevate jazz as "America's classical music."

The high revenues needed to keep large performing arts centers afloat make them increasingly dependent on "superstars." The explosion in the number of artists helped to create a "superstar market," in which a tiny number of performers earn huge salaries while the vast majority barely survive. Superstar markets "exist in labor markets where small differences in ability lead to large differences in compensation. This occurs when information about talent becomes so accurate—or marketing of a particular artist as 'the best' so common—that demand coalesces around a very few stars, driving their wages far above those of everyone else in the field."[68] A recent study predicts that "static or even declining funding streams" will force medium-sized performing arts organization out of business as a small number of large nonprofits in major metropolitan areas seek to maximize earned revenues and rely on advertising and marketing campaigns promoting celebrity performers.[69] Jazz at Lincoln Center has benefited not only from the Lincoln Center name but also from its association with Wynton Marsalis, arguably one of the few remaining superstars in jazz.

Since Lowry's groundbreaking initiatives on behalf of the Ford Foundation in the 1950s, support for the arts has gradually shifted from the *supply* side to the *demand* side.[70] As artists and performance centers proliferated and their quality improved, arts sponsors realized that they needed to concentrate more on nurturing audiences through arts education. One of the most important sources of funding has been the Wallace/Reader's Digest Fund. According to its mission statement, a central goal is "to make the arts an active part of people's everyday lives." One long-term project, the Power of Participation, "is committed to encouraging audience-building practices among interested arts groups."[71] A major component of the Doris Duke Foundation's JazzNet, a consortium of fourteen jazz presenters across the United States, "seeks to develop new and younger audiences for jazz through grants that support . . . National Public Radio's jazz programming and Web site [and] Public Service announcements and programs that focus on contemporary jazz for younger audiences, and a national public service campaign promoting arts education with the Ad Council."[72] To help build appreciative audiences, the Duke Foundation granted $1 million in 1999 to support Ken Burns's *Jazz*. An initiative that more directly supports jazz musicians is Duke's grants to Chamber Music America (CMA) for "composer/performer led ensembles" in the "creation and presentation of original music." Unfortunately, because CMA's guidelines exclude ensembles of more than ten pieces, big bands are ineligible for these grants.[73] The Irene Diamond Fund offered direct support to musicians in addition to education activities (40 percent of the fund's resources were earmarked for "minority education"). Because the fund was designed to be depleted over a ten-year period, most of the funds have been dispersed. Unfortunately, at least for the many underemployed jazz musicians, from an arts funding administrator's point of view, offering direct support to jazz musicians when the market is already glutted makes little sense. In the long term, rank-and-file jazz musicians will benefit if these audience-building efforts are successful.

Since the 1970s jazz musicians have built ever more sophisticated webs of support among public and private funding organizations. Playing the funding game requires sophisticated strategies—emphasizing minority participation, designing educational components. In the present environment experts predict that both small, neighborhood-based projects requiring small investments and large "name" institutions will flourish while medium-sized organizations will suffer. This phenomenon already affects symphony orchestras in smaller cities, which have been forced to "cut staff, budgets, and entire seasons."[74] The causes are widespread: economic downturns, bad management, bloated staffs, high musicians' salaries, declining public and private funding. Some observers posit more fundamental problems: the growing irrelevance of repertoires rooted in European high arts traditions in an increasingly diverse society, unimaginative programming that endlessly recycles canonical masterpieces, and contemporary composers unconcerned with reaching audiences.[75] Perhaps, in this time of shrinking budgets, support for big bands—"the symphony orchestras of jazz"—may be doomed. Or does orchestral jazz, with its African American roots, its legacy of multicultural participation, its vibrant worlds of active composers, and its history of popularity with American mass audiences (admittedly somewhat distant), hold promise for the future?

Chapter 4

On the Inside

The Vanguard Jazz Orchestra

From the mid-1960s to the present the Thad Jones/Mel Lewis Orchestra and its later incarnations as the Mel Lewis and Vanguard Jazz Orchestras have been at the heart of the New York jazz scene.[1] Whether as full-fledged members or regular substitutes, affiliation with these bands has marked for many musicians an important rite of passage, signaling their entry into the highest professional ranks. Outside regular Monday nights at the Village Vanguard, current and former members reunite in Broadway shows, recording studios, and jazz groups. Steeped in the ensemble traditions of "Thad and Mel's band," their musicianship traces elaborate patterns of leading and following, merging and emerging, and filling and staying out of musical spaces.

HISTORY

The extraordinary partnership of the cornetist, flugelhornist, and trumpeter Thad Jones (1923–86) and the drummer Mel Lewis (1929–90) created one of the most forward-looking and certainly most durable big bands in modern jazz.

Jones, along with his younger and older brothers—drummer Elvin and pianist Hank—emerged from the fertile Detroit jazz scene in the 1950s. Thad's brief stint in 1952 subbing for Clark Terry in the Count Basie Orchestra eventually led to a more permanent position two years later. The Basie band provided a platform for Jones to develop arranging and composition skills and mature as a soloist. During this period, he was probably best known for his memorable solo (beginning with an off-the-wall quote of "Pop Goes the Weasel") on the enduringly popular "April in Paris" (1955). But, as the several albums under his own name during the 1950s attest, Jones's primary interest lay in extending the harmonic and melodic dissonance of bebop.[2] He became a protégé of Charles Mingus, who dubbed him "Bartók with valves" and raved about his ability to take "classical techniques . . . and make them swing."[3] Mingus featured him in his Jazz Composers Workshop (1954–55) and on two eight-inch discs on his Debut label.

Like Jones, Mel Lewis was attracted to progressive postbop jazz. At the age of nineteen he left his hometown of Buffalo, New York, to tour with the Boyd Raeburn orchestra, known for its forward-looking style.[4] Lewis subsequently performed in dance bands led by Alvino Rey, Ray Anthony, and Tex Beneke, before joining what might be considered the most ostentatiously progressive big band, the Stan Kenton Orchestra, in 1954. After settling in Los Angeles in 1957, Lewis played in Terry Gibbs's and Gerald Wilson's modernist big bands while building a thriving studio career performing in numerous small groups.

Lewis came to New York in 1960 to play in Gerry Mulligan's Concert Jazz Band, where he was united with Jones in late 1963. After struggling for several years to keep the thirteen-piece group working, Mulligan disbanded after a tour to Japan in 1964. In fall of that year Jones and Lewis briefly together led a group that included future TJ/ML Orchestra members Pepper Adams, Jerry Dodgion, Quentin Jackson, and Benny Powell.[5] In 1965 Basie commissioned Jones to write an album's worth of material. Apparently, the charts were thought too adventurous or complex for the band, and the project was scrapped. Basie, however, allowed his former band member to keep the scores and parts, and that fall Jones teamed up with Lewis to form a band. Because of the busy schedules of the players, many of whom had steady jobs in the thriving network television and studio recording industries, the band rehearsed late on Monday nights (usually from midnight to three or four in the morning). The seven charts written by Jones for Basie ("The Second Race," "The Little Pixie," "A-That's Freedom," "Low Down," "Back Bone," "All My Yesterdays," and "Big Dipper"), along with other Jones originals and contributions from Brookmeyer, formed the core repertory of the band.[6] On Monday, 7 February 1966, Jones and Lewis unveiled their new band at the Village Vanguard. Calling it simply "the Jazz Band," John Wilson reviewed the band's premier in the *New York Times*. Stating emphatically, "Don't sell the big bands short yet. Not in New York, at least," Wilson described its enthusiastic reception as "reminiscent of the great jazz days on 52nd Street":

> This all-star band—it includes Bob Brookmeyer, Hank Jones, Richard Davis, Snooky Young and Jerome Richardson among others—ripped through Thad Jones's provocative, down-to-earth arrangements with the surging joy that one remembers in the early Basie band or Woody Herman's First Herd. Those were young bands whose skills sometimes could not keep up with their desires. But these are old pros, having a wonderful time and rising to each other's challenges.

Wilson, who compared the group to the latest version of the "Dorsey 'ghost bands' " (led by the trombonist Urbie Green) that also debuted that week, wrongly predicted that the band was "not likely to leave New York." He referred to the group's origins as a "rehearsal band," noting that "because these musicians have regular jobs, they can only get together once a week." Few would have expected the band to become a permanent institution. With what in retrospect seems classic understatement, Wilson concluded that the Monday night engagements would continue "for the next few weeks at least."[7]

As the band's prestige grew and bookings and short tours increased, the rehearsal band label, with which Jones and Lewis were never happy, faded away.[8] Throughout the 1970s, with Thad Jones fronting the band, the TJ/ML Orchestra was unquestionably the leading big band in jazz. Abruptly, in 1979, Jones departed to assume leadership of the Danish Radio Big Band, and the band became the Mel Lewis Orchestra. Lewis brought back the trombonist and composer Brookmeyer as musical director and led the band from behind his drumset.

In 1990 Lewis succumbed to cancer. Knowing that the work would drop off as it had after Jones's departure, band members feared that the orchestra would become, in the words of one, "like another rehearsal band." Members urged the group to continue doing outside gigs, not just the Monday nights at the Vanguard, fearing that if the band stopped growing and developing, it would turn into a ghost band surviving on its past reputation. "After a lot of discussion," states John Mosca,

> it was decided to change the name of the band. That was kind of traumatic because we had this attachment to both of them. We wanted to emphasize the fact that we were going to keep moving on and not simply be repertory and do the things we had always done, which I think is a spirit that both Thad and Mel would approve of. We've taken pains to make sure that people know that this is the band that was started by Thad and Mel. We try to keep that on all of our publicity and we really love playing Thad's music. That's still the core of the band's musical personality. Each set kind of revolves around one central heavy big chart of his.

With three of the longest-tenured members serving as a board of directors, the players formed a not-for-profit corporation and renamed themselves the Vanguard Jazz Orchestra.[9] In the years under Jones's and Lewis's leadership, band members came and went with frequency as the "stars" received better offers and many younger players "graduated" to other jobs. In the years since the band became a "cooperative," few members have left.[10] Still, temporary personnel continue to flow through the band. A Monday night without a generous sprinkling of substitutes is a rare occurrence.

Although many in the Vanguard audience probably come to hear the exciting soloists, the main prerequisite for playing in this band is not solo artistry but the ability to fit in. Good soloists, as the lead alto Dick Oatts explains, are given "a little grace period so they can listen and hopefully they'll hear it: they'll listen to me, they'll listen to [lead trumpeter] Earl Gardner." But if substitutes cannot put the group first, they will not be called back. This requirement still leaves plenty of room for individuality. Tone colors need not be uniform; they must complement each other through combinations of bright and dark timbres. Oatts explains, "The Vanguard band is kind of like a jazz small group, so we all kind of take our different sounds from small groups and put 'em in there." The small-group aesthetic also applies to the VJO rhythm section, which is equally comfortable accompanying a soloist or driving the entire ensemble in a shout chorus.

VERTICAL STRUCTURES AND DENSITY

The Vanguard Jazz Orchestra grows out of the Basie tradition, not least because of cofounder Thad Jones's long tenure with Basie (1954–63). Many of the original members of the band also spent time with Basie, most notably his "concertmaster," the lead trumpeter Snooky Young. The bands shared an emphasis on rhythmic propulsion. As in the Basie band, the rhythm section was always one of the main attractions of the TJ/ML Orchestra, and despite their complexity, Jones's compositions have an unfailing forward momentum. Both leaders also gravitated toward blues and "rhythm changes" (tunes based on the chords of "I Got Rhythm"), and Jones absorbed much of Basie's attitude toward leadership (see chapter 5).

Although Jones's arrangements were rejected by Basie, his pieces shared with those of Basie's arrangers in the 1950s and 1960s (e.g., Billy Byers, Neal Hefti, and Sammy Nestico) an emphasis on brass and certain formal structures (such as opening with a piano solo). "I think the period I spent with Basie prepared me musically for the time I spent with Mel," Jones told Gary Giddins in 1985. "When I had just joined Basie my ideas were fragmented. . . . I just wrote ideas that would be scattered through a piece. Neal Hefti—I always give him credit for this—made me aware . . . that maybe I should do a little more with form. And then I noticed that all the other writers did the same thing! They had that form, and that's why their pieces were meaningful not only to the public, but to themselves as writers."[11] Comparing Nestico's arrangements for Basie with those of Jones and his successor, Bob Brookmeyer, for the Jones/Lewis/Vanguard Orchestra, Wright finds the main differences in the use of harmonic dissonance and the "degree of departure from normal 32-bar song and head-and-variation forms." Wright concludes that "the differences among the three writers seem small in comparison with their similarities." For each, "rhythmic invention is of primary importance, . . . good registers and idiomatic writing for the instruments"

EXAMPLE 1. "Second Race," mm. H7–8 (Thad Jones).

have been used, and each section of the band is voiced to "sound harmonically good when heard by itself."[12]

Example 1, from Jones's original blues "Second Race," illustrates a standard orchestrational texture for full ensemble. The trumpets are voiced in major triads (except for the fourth chord) with the color tones doubled, in this case the sharped ninths[13] (e.g., C/A^{7}).[14] Like a tripod, they stand solidly on their own, but they do not necessarily indicate the underlying harmony. The trombones are harmonically complete, but they *only* indicate the underlying chords, none of the coloration. The saxes, on the other hand, give something of both: they outline the basic harmony and provide the sharp-nine flavor. Variations on this style of chord voicing can be found in Jones's writing for full ensemble, but most of his charts embody this sectional approach.

When two or more sections play different melodic lines, usually only one line is harmonized. Possibilities include voicing the brass in harmony while the saxes play a unison line, or voicing the saxes and trombones in harmony with the trumpets in unison The brass sections lend themselves to unison writing because they comprise identical instruments, although writers must avoid extremes in range if they expect a good sound. In writing unison lines for saxophones, however (if they don't want to break into octaves), arrangers are limited to about an octave and a half: from around $D^{\flat}$ to $a^{\flat}$, the lowest note of the alto to the highest of the baritone.

Bob Brookmeyer, who became composer-in-residence after Jones's departure, veered toward twentieth-century classical techniques and away from standard thirty-two-bar forms. Some band members complained that he strayed too far from the founder's principles.[15] Unlike Jones's writing, Brookmeyer's is far less idiomatic and less imbued with blues feeling. His influence also spread through teaching, and two of the composers discussed in chapter 6, Maria Schneider and Jim McNeely, studied with him. After Lewis's death in 1990 the band began performing Brookmeyer's music less often. One band member explains that much of his music is too "dark" for what is basically a "feel-good band." Jones's music continues to form the core repertoire of the band. McNeely, the current resident composer (and a former protegé of Brookmeyer), descends from both traditions. A composition titled "Thad" on the 1997 CD *Lickety Split* pays tribute to Jones by quoting themes from more than a dozen of his tunes. McNeely preserves more of Jones's idiomatic qualities while still drawing on Brookmeyer-like experiments in heightened dissonance, expansion of forms, and development of atonal melodic cells.

CONFIGURATION

In addition to the arranger's distribution of notes, where players sit determines what they hear.[16] Dick Oatts says, "You know, you can switch one book over, like when I moved from playing first tenor to second alto, and, man, the whole band sounded different." Players hear whomever sits closest: on either side, behind, and, to a much lesser extent, in front of them. The musicians situated on the end away from the rhythm section are the least immersed in the sound of the band. In the saxophones, for example, the baritone player connects to the rest of the section through the second tenor (in the standard setup). A weak link here disrupts the baritonist's connection to the lead alto's phrasing and articulation.

The main consideration in setting up the band is the need for certain members to hear one another, both within and between sections. Traditionally, the most frequent soloists sit closer to the rhythm section. Lead players must be located in the middle of their sections. Figure 1 gives the standard seating arrangement used in most big bands. The rhythm section occupies stage right (the left from the audience's perspective) so that the piano lid opens toward the audience.

During the swing era, variations on this seating arrangement were not uncommon. For example, in a 1938 film short, Jimmie Lunceford positioned the brass stage right (and the trombones behind the trumpets) and the saxophones stage left.[17] The drummer and the pianist perform in the center of the stage, separating the brass and the reeds. Variations in the configuration of the band were especially common in films (the sound was often overdubbed), but during the dance band's heyday, even for their live

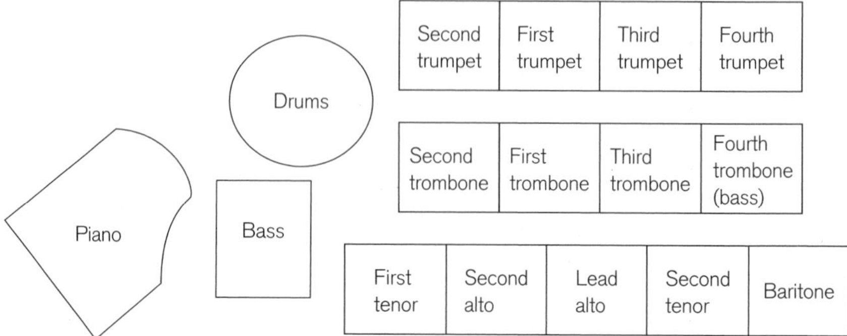

Figure 1. Conventional big band seating configuration.

engagements, bandleaders sometimes experimented with new eye-catching setups.

Though a few contemporary bandleaders have continued to experiment (Wynton Marsalis in the early years of the LCJO tried positioning the sections differently), the configuration of the band's sections shown in Figure 1 has become standard. "Over the early years of jazz nearly every conceivable configuration was tried," says David Berger. "There is a reason why everyone sets up like this now—it's the only way everybody in the band found that they could hear the players they needed to hear."

Although most leaders follow this general configuration, within sections they occasionally vary the seating order (see below). In many bands, and the Vanguard Jazz Orchestra is no exception, members of sections occasionally pass parts among themselves, especially in the brass. Still, as conceived by arrangers and leaders, each chair plays a distinct role in the ensemble.

The Trumpet Section

Standing in the back row, the trumpets are sonically the most prominent section of the band. As the top voices of the harmony, their bright, penetrating sound carries through to the audience even in the largest venues. The trumpets dominate the reed and trombone sections by virtue of their position immediately behind and above them. Because of the emphasis on range and power, brass instruments (especially trumpets) require intense physical routines. Chops (highly developed facial and labial musculature) must be built through diligent practice and guarded from abuse through overblowing. Faced with the ever-present danger of permanent damage to their lips, brass players follow elaborate warm-up and even warm-down rituals.[18]

In big bands the lead trumpeters shoulder a huge responsibility—leading most ensemble sections and bringing the entire band to climax—which almost invariably means playing loud and high. Krin Gabbard, in his study of jazz in American film, describes players who attempt "to overwhelm the competition with pitch, volume, and speed" as "trumpet jocks."[19] Perhaps this reputation for a locker room mentality is justified in other ways. Because of the intense physical demands and their location farthest from the bandleader, some trumpeters release tension through wisecracks, practical jokes, and other antics.

Stereotypical images notwithstanding, the trumpets do not always play with loud, bright, searing sounds. Brass players vary their tone colors by attaching a variety of mutes to the bells of their horns. The most common mutes in jazz are the cup, straight, harmon, bucket, pixie, plunger, and derby or hat. The cup yields a woody sound and blends well with flutes and clarinets. The straight mute produces a metallic sound. With its more cutting edge, the straight mute is useful for "punches" and can substitute for the cup mute when more sound is needed. The harmon, equipped with an adjustable stem that produces a nasal sound, is used without the stem by most jazz players. The softest of all the mutes used in jazz, the harmon, is less frequently called for by arrangers in section work. It requires close placement of a microphone and is especially effective for quiet, intimate readings of ballads. As part of his signature cool, distant sound, Miles Davis became identified with the harmon (sans stem). By opening and closing plunger mutes on the bells of their horns, players create wah-wah effects. Simply a toilet or sink drain plunger with the handle removed, these mutes can be acquired in any hardware store.[20] The pixie, a small straight mute that is inserted completely inside a brass instrument's bell, generates a funkier sound, especially when combined with a plunger, and growling effects à la Ellingtonians James "Bubber" Miley and Joe "Tricky Sam" Nanton. The bucket, a hollow mute filled with gauze, is clipped onto the bell in order to get a soft and distant sound, an effect that can also be simulated by playing into the stands. In one chart often played by the VJO, "ABC Blues," the composer, Bob Brookmeyer, instructs the brass to play "deep [in] stands." During this section, the trumpets point their bells straight down toward the floor. Because mutes tend to alter the pitch, players using them constantly make adjustments. Mutes are physically demanding, so arrangers need to be aware of range and endurance problems. Brass players hear subtle differences in mutes and develop preferences for specific makers and models. Ed Neumeister has gone so far as to bring his trombone to a hardware store to try different plungers.

The most important thing for any trumpet section is "to have a style," according to the trumpeter Glenn Drewes. The Vanguard Orchestra's trumpets, led by Earl Gardner for nearly thirty years (since 1976), evince a relaxed, laid-back feel. Their musical style reflects the collegial atmosphere in the section. "Everyone helps each other," according to Drewes. "There are no egos, no hassles."

Lead Trumpet. In the wrong hands the lead trumpet can be an instrument of pain—straining the player's chops and tormenting the listener's ears. Although they consider a strong high register essential, most musicians regard such things as phrasing, swing feel, sound, and consistency equally vital. The great lead trumpeters have been known for the musical personalities they have imposed on their bands. They are in the unique position of having no one to whom they "listen up"—when playing, the lead trumpet almost always holds the top voice. This demanding role requires occasional relief, and trumpet sections usually designate a secondary lead player. The second trumpet typically provides this service. Sometimes even the third or fourth player may step in.

The Vanguard Jazz Orchestra's illustrious pedigree of lead trumpeters extends back from Earl Gardner through Al Porcino to Danny Stiles and Snooky Young (of Count Basie and *Tonight Show* fame). Gardner's long tenure enabled him to mold the entire band, not just the trumpets, in his image. In contrast with, for example, the Buddy Rich Orchestra, whose leader insisted on a more aggressive "on top of the time" feel, the VJO under Gardner takes a more fluid approach to time, often "sitting back" and delaying phrases. Gardner milks important points of arrival for their drama. Tensions are slightly stretched, resolutions minutely deferred. "The first time you play in the section," says Drewes, "you think you're on Mars, you forget how to count."

The Vanguard's trumpet section (and by extension, the band) is distinguished by other characteristic performance practices: fat quarter notes, long falls, and sparing use of shakes. Not surprisingly, jazz musicians often attack notes more percussively than do classical musicians. In jazz the symbol ^ denotes a sharp attack and short note, usually cut off abruptly (in contrast, many classical teachers instruct wind players *never* to cut off a note with the tongue). In other bands this practice, when carried to an extreme, results in a harsh, choppy style. The Vanguard Jazz Orchestra typically plays such notes "fatter." If Gardner hangs over slightly on the final note of a phrase (which he often does), the rest of the band knows not to follow him. The trumpet players also use longer fall-offs (a descending glissando at the end of a note). In some bands the trumpet sections develop distinctive styles of shakes—for example, the Ferguson band (slow and extremely wide, sometimes an octave) and the Rich band (fast and narrow). Drewes notes that under Gardner shakes are rarely used.

In a comparative study of the Vanguard Jazz Orchestra's lead trumpeters, Petruzzi described Jon Faddis's tone as "extremely compact, . . . well focused, . . . bright and searing." Snooky Young's sound was "concentrated and intense but somewhat broader" and "projecting a vocal quality." Porcino's tone "varied the most ranging from vibrant and forceful [his nickname was "the General"] to warm and relaxed." Gardner's tone quality, according to this writer (himself a lead trumpeter), "was the broadest of the four and less dense." Tone quality varies not only from player to player but also within individual performances. As Petruzzi noted, "In general, the sound produced by each performer was usually warmer, darker, and less intense in unison passages to allow for an optimal blend with others." Young's and Porcino's tone varied the most. Gardner varies his tone color less but also uses vibrato most frequently, which gives "his tone added warmth and energy."[21] John Riley, VJO drummer, says appreciatively, "Earl has a sound that sort of engulfs everything, I'm not talking about volume, but timbre. It's a very encompassing and inviting color in his sound that draws everything together, that draws all the instruments toward it."

Lead trumpeters work closely with the drummer. In the VJO Riley considers that he and Gardner "are a team that really directs and controls the dynamics and the vibe of the band." When Riley joined the band at the end of 1991, Gardner, from his position in the back of the band near the drummer, helped Riley to learn the band's routines. Riley explains:

> A lot of the music had evolved from what was written on the paper in the twenty years or so, and Mel wasn't reading the parts, so he wasn't modifying or correcting or adjusting them according to the evolution of the stuff. So I would be looking at the music, which was more or less in its original state, even though things had been changed. Earl would be very generous in his guidance of what was happening dynamically, when to use sticks, when to use brushes, which phrases were going to be laid-back. He would either be giving me a verbal "heads-up" or a physical signal to watch out that something was going to happen.

This communication began to flow in both directions, as Riley more actively collaborated in their partnership: "As time has gone on, the music has continued to evolve, and I can hear that sometimes I will phrase something a particular way that might be a little different than what had been happening and I can hear him pick up on that, but these things are very subtle."

Second Trumpet. The primary duty of the second trumpet is to provide support for the lead player. When playing parts in close harmony, as the lead soars into the upper register, the second traces a trajectory immediately below. Parts must be played confidently, yet not overpoweringly. Lead trumpeters, who are under constant pressure as the dominant voice of the band, insist on the vital role of the second player. Without a strong second, the lead player may feel isolated and extended far above the band. Lead players take great interest in who occupies this chair, preferring someone familiar with their style, or at least sensitive and quick to follow.

Joe Mosello, an alumnus of Maynard Ferguson's band and an active performer in numerous Broadway pit orchestras, took over this chair in 1980. An accomplished lead trumpeter in his own right, Mosello both supports and provides occasional relief for Gardner. In many bands the second trumpet (especially when not the secondary lead) is also an important soloist (e.g., Sonny Cohn in the Basie orchestra from 1960 to 1990). Other specialties may include plunger and wah-wah effects.

Third Trumpet. In the Vanguard band the third chair, held by Glenn Drewes since 1983, is "kind of a utility chair, . . . you get to do a little of everything—lead, jazz and section playing." The third trumpet generally plays inner parts that are in a comfortable range. Important qualities are a warm sound in the middle register and an ability to blend. Drewes describes his parts as "bastard notes, the strange notes of the chord that don't go where you expect them to go." In this band the third chair is considered, along with the fourth, one of the "jazz chairs." Traditionally, in the Vanguard the third player was the more "inside" player and the fourth the "outside" or more harmonically adventurous soloist.[22] Drewes is also occasionally called on to play lead, after the first and second trumpets. Once in a while he moves to the first chair but only if the first and second players are absent, a situation that can be somewhat nerve-wracking with at least two subs in the section. A versatile player, Drewes thrives in the third chair. Being able to "wear a lot of hats" enables one to take a lot of different kinds of gigs and is important, he feels, for survival in the highly competitive scenes of New York.

Fourth Trumpet. Traditionally, in many bands the fourth trumpet was considered the "jazz chair," although setting aside specialized chairs for improvising soloists is somewhat anachronistic today. In the Vanguard Orchestra a tradition of brilliant soloists evolved around this chair: Marvin Stamm, Tom Harrell, Cecil Bridgewater, Jim Powell and, currently, Scott Wendholt. Although Wendholt has played second and third a few times, he says he "never wants to play lead" and is content sitting in the fourth chair and soloing frequently. He is often featured on harmonically difficult or complex arrangements, such as are often written by McNeely.

The parts written for the fourth chair often extend to the lowest notes in the trumpet's range. As mentioned above, when triadic voicings are used, the fourth usually doubles the lead an octave lower. Some trumpet players do not like playing this chair because they believe that low notes might hurt their "high chops."

The Trombone Section

When Don Sebesky calls the trombone section "the heart of the big band," he speaks from his experience as an arranger, not from prejudice as a former trombonist.[23] Not only do the trombones sit in the center of the band,

EXAMPLE 2. "A-That's Freedom," mm. 33–36 (Hank Jones; Thad Jones, arr.). Transcription by the author.

between the reeds and the trumpets, but they also provide a strong harmonic foundation for the rest of the winds. In concerted ensemble textures the trombone section usually functions to spell out the basic harmonies (as in Example 1, above). In shout choruses and other full band orchestrations, the trombones typically occupy the bottom voices. At other times the section may provide a "comping" background underneath soloists, similar to what might be played by a pianist's left hand. Occasionally, arrangers bring the trombones to the forefront to state a melody in their warm, glowing tone.

No horn swings *harder.* The large cups of trombones' mouthpieces permit very percussive attacks. Four trombones swinging and grooving together can generate enough excitement and energy to drive the entire band (one reason trombones are so prevalent in salsa). Of course, playing with a strong attack requires a certain style of writing. John Mosca, lead trombone with the VJO, says, "It's incumbent on the arranger to have the spacing good, otherwise you can't do that cause you'll make mud. The harder you hit it, it just keeps getting muddy." In Jones's "A-That's Freedom" the trombones comp à la Basie guitarist Freddie Green but with a slightly more martial flavor (according to Kirchner, the "A" in the title refers to the "stuttering," anticipated note in the bass trombone every two measures).[24] (Example 2.)

Trombones also potentially sound smooth, sweet, mellifluous. No instrument is better suited for the warm, luminescent interpretation of a ballad (witness Tommy Dorsey's theme, "I'm Getting Sentimental Over You," or Ellington's lead trombonist Lawrence Brown's performance of "All Too Soon"). Whether playing a harmonized soli (e.g., Ellington's "Slippery Horn" and Kenton's "Here's that Rainy Day") or "pads" (long tones) in the background, a good trombone section melds together, radiating warmth. Sebesky often looks for this kind of sonority from the trombones. Mosca describes it as "almost foggy stuff": "He commonly has us playing euphonium, which is less centered; it's a small tuba. Three guys playing euphoniums, that's a big whoof of a sound. There's not much point on it. And he'll have us play trombones with hats over the bell. It's a more diffuse sound."

In the conventional setup (as in Figure 1), the trombones sit in the same order as the trumpets immediately behind them. The lead trombone sits

Fourth trombone bass	Third trombone (bass or tenor with trigger)	Lead trombone	Second trombone

Figure 2. Vanguard trombone seating.

near the center of the section, and, in addition to the lead players, each trombone hears the correspondingly numbered trumpet behind him or her. The Vanguard Jazz Orchestra trombones are arrayed with a slight difference. Instead of sitting on stage left, the bass trombonist, Douglas Purviance, is located next to the rhythm section, so that he can better hear the bass (see Figure 2). In this configuration, the baritone sax and bass trombone wind up on opposite sides of the band, producing a stereo effect on those rare occasions (at least in Jones's writing) when they are both playing the same line. Ed Neumeister exploits this positioning in his arrangement of Billy Strayhorn's "Daydream" by alternating a low pedal back and forth between the two instruments. A drawback to this seating configuration is that the two players cannot hear each other as well as in the more typical setup where the bass trombone sits immediately behind the baritone (Figure 2). For much of its history, the VJO had two bass trombonists, but, apart from some of Brookmeyer's arrangements, most of the repertoire does not require two bass trombones. Mosca characterizes the doubled bass 'bones as "an experiment that didn't lead anywhere."

Lead Trombone. As is the case with the lead alto saxophone, the first trombone must be both a forceful leader and a sensitive follower. When playing full ensemble passages or with the trumpets, this player must "listen up" to the lead trumpet. "You're basically tethered to the lead trumpet player," says Mosca. "One of the conceptions is to communicate the lead trumpet player's thing into the trombone section, when you're playing together." This dual role—simultaneously following and leading—was Mosca's main function when he briefly left the TJ/ML Orchestra to play lead in Buddy Rich's band in 1977: "In that band, the music was written much more as a whole brass section. The trombone section was cut out very rarely as a different section." When Mosca rejoined the TJ/ML Orchestra Jones asked him how many trombones were in Rich's band: "I said three, and he said, 'Wow, I can't understand how you could not have four.' Because, first, of course, he heard those big chords, and also he wanted the trombones out to do separate things. Kenton also really had a lot of trombone section features." These independent passages offer the lead trombone occasional moments of freedom. Like the lead trumpeter, the lead trombonist needs a fully developed high range (generally up to d^1), consistency in interpretation, and a strong, clear sound.

To facilitate high notes, lead players usually use a smaller bore horn and mouthpiece.

When Mosca joined the TJ/ML Orchestra in 1975 Billy Campbell played lead. Because they were contemporaries and Campbell had a somewhat idiosyncratic approach, Mosca did not model his lead style on Campbell's. Mosca's conception of lead playing derived from listening to recordings and his experiences playing in "the rich rehearsal band scene" in New York during the early 1970s: "I had gotten a lot of experience playing with great lead trumpet players, Jerry Kale and Al Porcino, and great lead trombone players like Bobby Burgess (one of Kenton's top guys)." From the records he "always liked the way Earl Swope played. He had a real jazz conception. He played with Woody [Herman] and in one of Buddy's first bands." Mosca liked his "big sound" and the fact that he was more of "a jazz player playing lead." However, Mosca picked up some of the TJ/ML tradition "as a kid coming to hear the band." "I liked the way Garnett Brown played lead," Mosca remembers. "He was a real strong lead player."

Second and Third Trombones. The second and third chairs generally have similar roles in the section. Both use larger bore horns to play inner parts within a fairly close range. Jones often voiced these two trombones in half-step "grinds" between the seventh and the thirteenth and the sharped ninth and major third in a dominant chord or a whole-step apart as between the major third and flatted fifth. Such close intervals require an exacting sense of pitch from both players.

As with the trumpets, the second player may function as a secondary lead. Ellington's second trombonist, Joe "Tricky Sam" Nanton, a master in the art of using pixie and plunger mutes to produce growling, wah-wah effects, was known for his "talking" style. Following this precedent, many leaders have tried to find at least one similarly skilled trombone player for their bands. Quentin "Butter" Jackson replaced Nanton in the Ellington band and for a time brought this style of playing to the TJ/ML Orchestra.

Ed Neumeister, the Vanguard's second trombonist (until he departed for Europe in 1999), is an accomplished plunger player and provided the VJO with an imaginative and often harmonically adventurous variation on this role. He was first exposed to plunger techniques during a stint with the Ellington band (under the direction of Duke's son, Mercer) that began in 1981, the same year he joined Mel Lewis. At the time Art Baron was the plunger specialist in the Ellington band and Neumeister played Lawrence Brown's lead chair. After Baron left Neumeister dabbled with the plunger. He only "got serious about the plunger" later in the Mel Lewis band when Jerry Dodgion wrote "Butter," a piece in tribute to Quentin Jackson featuring Neumeister.

Rather than mimic Jackson and Nanton, Neumeister developed his own style:

> I started working on it, practicing it and studying it. Although I listened to recordings, at that point in my life and career I was not really into imitating anybody. There are influences, of course, but I just sort of explored my own path with it, playing and trying different things out. I never did transcribe or do any of that. It's just from what I heard and experimenting.

Neumeister's unique plunger work has become an important facet of his career, and his appearances more often than not feature unaccompanied free-form improvisations in this style. Chapter 6 contains an analysis of one of his solos from "Sticks," a concerto written for him by Jim McNeely.

In the Vanguard band the third trombone must play low notes that occasionally require the use of a "trigger" (a thumb-operated valve that lowers the pitch by a fourth, facilitating low pitches). For many years, before moving to the fourth chair after Earl McIntyre's departure in 1998, Douglas Purviance played a bass trombone in this chair. After this change Jason Jackson was hired to play third. Jackson improvises in a more extroverted, almost "gut-bucket" style, providing interesting contrast with Mosca's more technical playing and Neumeister's plunger work. Some players in the band feel that the section's blend improved after one of the bass trombones was dropped, changing the section to the more typical complement of three tenors and only one bass. "There was some natural competition down there with two basses," says one member, "and it could get a little bottom heavy down there at times."

Fourth or Bass Trombone. Because arrangers often assign the baritone sax inner parts (as discussed below), the bass trombone most frequently plays the bottom notes of the winds. A good sense of pitch is absolutely vital, as the other horns base their intonation on these fundamentals. Filling the bass trombone's tremendous bore requires huge quantities of air. When functioning independently from the rest of the trombone section, bass trombonists must play loudly and forcefully. Often the fourth player listens closely to the bassist, especially if they are playing a melodic line or vamp together, a practice that became particularly popular in rock, funk, and Latin arrangements (examples of bass and bass trombone doubling, Schneider's "Wyrgly" and Bley's "On the Stage in Cages," are discussed in chapter 6).

The Vanguard's fourth trombonist, Doug Purviance, is one of the few band members rarely spotlighted as a soloist. His deep tones can be heard buttressing many other New York bands as well as Broadway pit orchestras. A solid section player, he also acts as the VJO's business manager.

The Saxophone Section

The reed section is the most heterogeneous of the winds. Unlike the brass sections, which generally comprise exclusively trumpets and trombones, the reed section contains three or four different kinds of saxophones. Moreover, the saxophones have a wider range of inflection, articulation, and tone color than the brass. This expressive instrument is equally inclined to large legato leaps or biting attacks and bends notes fluidly—from subtle scoops to long, slow pitch modulations of a whole step or more. Arrayed in four vocal tessituras—soprano, alto. tenor, and baritone—the saxophone is the closest instrument to the human voice, capable of sweet singing or gruff rasps.

Compared to a symphony orchestra, the big band offers composers and arrangers relatively few instrumental resources. Writers depend on brass players' mutes and saxophonists' doubling for additional tone colors. Many saxophonists play other woodwinds: clarinet, bass clarinet, flute, and, more rarely, piccolo and double reeds. The entire section on flutes and clarinets offers a valuable contrasting texture to the orchestrator, yielding a pristine, almost classical timbre. In the VJO the two alto saxophonists double most often (on soprano sax, flute, and clarinet), and the tenors less frequently. First tenor Rich Perry plays flute occasionally but years ago received Jones's permission to play the clarinet parts on tenor (transposed up an octave). The other tenor, Ralph LaLama, plays clarinet and flute. Gary Smulyan, on baritone, almost never doubles, preferring to transpose occasional bass clarinet parts to baritone sax.

The saxophone section contributes a warm, reedy midrange to the band. Arrangers frequently use more open voicings, and in full ensemble sections the reeds occupy the vertical space between, and overlapping with, the trumpets and trombones, often doubling some of their notes. Considering saxophones nimble instruments capable of playing wide intervals, angular melodies, and fast runs, arrangers typically reserve their most intricate parts for them. "Of all the envelopes that Thad pushed," writes Mosca, "he expanded the parameters for the sax section more than any other. Naturally this placed great demands on the players, and the original section led by Jerome Richardson is one of the classic sounds of modern jazz."[25]

The setup of the saxophone section places the lead alto in the center, with the second alto and first tenor to his or her right. The second tenor and baritone sit to the lead alto's left, away from the rhythm section (see the standard big band seating arrangement in Figure 1). This configuration allows the baritone and the second tenor to hear each other (they are often voiced in parallel fifths) and the second alto to support the first and to play close harmonies with the first tenor.

Some contemporary jazz composers, such as Bob Mintzer and Maria

Schneider, avoid saxophone solis and other big band "clichés." Still, many saxophonists relish the opportunity to be featured as a section. Traditionally, saxophone players stand during a soli, so that their sounds project better over their music stands.[26] Jones wrote challenging solis, often using five-part harmony, that, in spite of their difficulty and occasional lapses in melodic voice leading in the inner voices, never lost their idiomatic saxophone quality. For his sax solis, Jones often replaced the lead alto with a soprano saxophone. Although historical precedent for using the soprano in big band arrangements existed in the music of Ellington and Charlie Barnet, Jones was probably more inspired by contemporary soprano players, such as Coltrane and his followers, who had rediscovered the instrument. According to Dodgion, for about the first year, most solis were written with alto lead. Knowing of lead alto player Jerome Richardson's facility on soprano, Jones experimented with a soprano lead. The result pleased Jones enough that he continued to write for the soprano, making it a salient instrument in many of his arrangements (e.g., "Don't Git Sassy," "The Groove Merchant," and "Fingers") and occasionally even putting both altos on soprano. Most contemporary big band composers and arrangers consider the soprano saxophone an essential alternate lead instrument for their saxophone sections.

Lead Alto. When fronting their sections, lead altos enjoy many of the same freedoms as the lead trumpets and trombones. Players make decisions regarding phrasing, breathing, note terminations, articulation, vibrato, laying back or pushing the time, swing feel, inflections, ornamentation, tone color, and dynamics. Like the lead trombone, however, the first alto must listen up to the lead trumpet in concerted ensemble passages such as shout choruses. Lead players must be able to produce a big sound, often involving a bright timbre, but they may also choose to play at a whisper, with a transparent, dark tone.

Of all the original members of the Thad Jones/Mel Lewis Orchestra, Jerry Dodgion had the longest tenure with the band, staying until 1979. He started as second alto and became lead when Jerome Richardson left in 1971. In the Carnegie Hall band Dodgion reversed this process, starting on lead and moving to second after Dick Oatts was hired. Dodgion is at home on either chair. Unlike many players, he moves easily from leadership to a strictly supportive role. For his lead playing, though he cites the influence of Marshal Royal and Willie Smith (both from the Basie band) and, of course, fellow TJ/ML member Jerome Richardson, he also has absorbed a wide range of styles from Johnny Hodges to Phil Woods. Until he started performing repertory with the American Jazz Orchestra in 1986, Dodgion says he never really tried to mimic other saxophonists. Dodgion and other highly regarded first altos in New York lead effectively because they instill a sense of confidence in the other players of their section. If section leaders make mistakes they quickly lose authority; musicians begin to concentrate on their own parts instead of listening to someone who could lead them astray.

Dick Oatts, lead alto with the Vanguard and Carnegie bands, has developed a dark, yet powerful sound that he says comes from playing a lot of small-group jazz. "I'm not looking to have brilliant sound," he says. "I'm looking to have it cover over the section with some depth and body." Even on soprano he does not like a "cutting, edgy sound." "I don't like soprano sounds generally," he explains, "so I try to get more of a deeper sound. I look at the soprano like it's an alto." When he first came with "Thad and Mel," Oatts concerned himself with getting the phrasing. He listened to the lead trumpeter, Earl Gardner, and to recordings of Snooky Young and Al Porcino with the band. But "the way Mel and Earl Gardner phrased together," following was not difficult.

Oatts came into the band on tenor in 1977, around the same time as the tenor saxophonist Rich Perry. After about three months he switched to second alto under Jerry Dodgion. Jones must have realized the importance of establishing a tradition in the band because when Dodgion left, Oatts offered to stay on second. "No way. You're playing lead," Jones insisted. As Oatts puts it, "I just stepped up to the plate. I followed Jerry's footsteps. Over the years, I started putting my own two cents in. It took me a while to evolve. . . . So I guess when you think there have only been three lead alto players in the band, I feel a deep kindred spirit to both of those guys." He has also played four of the five chairs in the section—every one except baritone.

Oatts has very concrete ideas about sectional blend within the saxophone section: "Play up to my volume and the way the harmony was written, I'm gonna sing over that anyway, at least on a sax soli. What I expect is the same volume as the second alto. I want everybody to blend." Oatts is not hesitant to say something, if necessary, in order to get the right balance: "Sometimes I might have a problem with the baritone getting a little edgy, so I have to say something, 'Just back off it.' You're gonna get a stronger punch if all the lines are equal than one guy extending a little bit too much or too little." When the section plays in unison Oatts likes to back off and "let the tenor saxophones carry it" in order to produce a deeper sound. Once in a while he tests the other players to see how carefully they are listening: "A lot of these guys have played this music for several years, and it's very easy to fall into a kind of 'same old thing,' so they stop listening. Once in a while I'll try something a little softer to see if they are [listening], and if they aren't, then I crank on them. 'Come on wake up, wake up.' " Even with intonation problems, he expects the others in the section to go with him, whether he is right or wrong.

In Oatts's view, the leadership comes more from the music than from himself: "If I put this much respect into the music, I expect everyone in the section to do the same." Although soloing is important in the band, the first consideration when hiring substitutes is their sensitivity to the needs of the section. If the sub is a good soloist but does not blend, it can be a difficult choice. Oatts says, "I don't mind a guy having a bright sound when he solos, but in the section I don't like that cutting edge unless it comes from me first and then I ask for it." Regular substitutes in the sax section in 1997–98 were respected section players active in many of the bands listed in the appendix: Steve Wilson, Steve Slagle, Walt Weiskopf, Pete Yellin, Tom Christiansen, Dave Pietro, Scott Robinson, Chuck Wilson, and Andy Fusco, as well as former members of the band such as Ted Nash and Ed Xiques. If Oatts must take a night off, usually the second alto, Billy Drewes, assumes the lead.

Second Alto. When the roles of section leaders and soloists were more distinct, the second alto was often considered a "jazz" chair, but today arrangers often assign solos to the lead alto. If arrangers are hoping to publish charts to sell on the lucrative school band market, they may assume that teachers will have only one good alto player (who will be expected to play lead and improvise). As a result, in some bands the second alto book has become boring. In the Vanguard and Carnegie bands, as in most professional bands, the second alto is featured on many arrangements. Many arrangers expect the second alto to also double on flute and clarinet.

In general, the second alto needs a darker sound than the lead. Many alto players (and saxophonists in general) use equipment designed to produce a bright sound because of the influence of popular music. R&B and fusion players (such as David Sanborn) prefer a cutting edge to their tone so that they can penetrate through electric guitar and synthesizer sounds. In the Vanguard Orchestra, because Oatts's sound is dark, he needs a second alto player with an even darker sound. In Billy Drewes he has found just that. "It's perfect for me," Oatts says.

Tenors. The tenor saxophonists are the soloists most often featured in many bands. The first tenor plays higher parts than the second, sometimes leading the section for short passages. In the 1930s Basie established a tradition of featuring two tenorists with contrasting styles as primary soloists in the band.[27] Lester Young's lighter tone and more "linear" approach contrasted starkly with Hershel Evans's heavier, vibrato-laden, Coleman Hawkins–inspired style. Although the VJO has not featured a tenor battle in many years,[28] its tenors, Rich Perry on first and Ralph LaLama on second, each pursue very different styles. Perry, who came into the band in 1977, explores adventurous harmonic substitutions with his distinctively dark tone. LaLama, who joined in 1983, plays more "inside" and with a brighter tone. According to Oatts, "It's the yin and yang, one compensates for the other. It gets a better blend, you're not getting all edgy sounds or all dark sounds. The difference creates a balance." Perhaps Oatts simply has become accustomed to this positioning, but he finds "it just seems to work." He explains, "I've been in sections where, or even subs come in where we've had brighter sounds to my right than mine or Ralph [LaLama]'s, and it hasn't worked as well as far as the blend." Perry takes a contrarian approach in general: "I consciously try to play differently. I would be doing it anyway even if Ralph wasn't there."[29] Of soloing, he says, "If someone is playing really incredible solo, with a lot of energy, instead of trying to start there, I will try to go somewhere else." He gives the example of "Eye of the Hurricane": "It's really fast, and Smulyan can play really fast, so when it's time to play after him I will have to start slowly and not try to start where he left off."

In the standard configuration the first tenor sits closest to the rhythm section. Because of the cramped conditions, Perry explains, "I sit right in the piano so I hear a lot of piano. I have a good seat though, I'll tell you, 'cause I'm right in front of the bass. But I do hear a bit too much trumpets in my left ear." The bass trombonist, on the other hand, though he sits directly behind him, does not seem to bother Perry. He has no problem hearing Oatts's lead alto because "he's got that sound that really projects."

Perry's primary objective is to play with a good sound: "For many years I used to try to compete with the brass section or something, and it really didn't sound good. I guess I just realized over time that the louder you try to play on almost any instrument, the worse it gets." Because Jones tended to favor harmonic over the melodic considerations in his inner voices, Perry tries to absorb his sound into the other horns, "to blend into the overall thing unless it's a moving part. That's it basically, not trying to overpower the instrument." The tenors and the baritone also must blend with the trombone section. Because they have similar ranges, arrangers routinely write unison parts for one or both of the tenors and one or more trombones. Blending is not only a matter of tone color, but also attack, as Oatts points out, "hittin' those hits," duplicating the "kind of pop they have."

When Perry left the band for several years in 1981, he was replaced by Joe Lovano. When Lovano's career started taking off in the late 1980s, Perry began subbing for him and eventually reclaimed the first tenor chair. Even with all his years in the band, Perry still finds the weekly gig challenging: "For me that music just doesn't get old. A lot of music, if you played it all the time, you might get tired of it. I really look forward to it. There's still stuff that I can't play as well as I'd like to."

Baritone. Baritone saxophonists must have multiple personalities; they are four players in one. In addition to playing with the saxophones, they sometimes function as an extra trombonist, especially in bands with fewer than four trombones. Occasionally the baritonist is called on to double bass lines with the bassist or bass trombonist. The only unique wind instrument in most big bands, the baritone offers a distinctive melodic resource. Ellington often featured his lush-toned baritonist, Harry Carney, with a prominent independent line.[30] Ellington's conception of this instrument illustrates an important trait of most baritone saxophonists: they are strong individualists, both in their sections and in the band.

Thad Jones and Mel Lewis's original baritonist, Park "Pepper" Adams, Jones's fellow Detroiter, was one of the most respected players of this instrument in modern jazz.[31] Adams was one of the longest lasting of the original members, staying until 1976. Known for his formidable intellect, phenomenal technique, big sound, and sense of humor, as evidenced in the occasional wacky musical quotes in his solos, he was featured on many tunes. Gary Smulyan, a player strongly influenced by the Adams style, inherited this chair in 1981.

In drop-2 voicings the baritone usually traces a path a ninth or tenth below the lead alto, producing a rich sonority between the outer voices. Stock arrangements were typically written in a less interesting four-part close harmony because dropping the second harmony note to the lowest saxophone would mean losing an important part if five saxophones were not present. In such arrangements the baritone could be considered expendable because it doubled the lead at the octave.

One of the most difficult decisions facing baritone players is choosing between an instrument with a low A or B♭. The low A extends the range to a particularly useful note, concert C_2, but not without a price. Many musicians insist that the low A baritone does not blend as well with the other saxophones because the lengthening of the instrument alters the entire overtone series. The Maynard Ferguson and Buddy Rich books required low A's; the Ellington, Jones/Lewis, and Woody Herman bands called for low B♭'s.

The Rhythm Section

The drums, bass, guitar, and piano, a close-knit, self-contained unit, provide a solid rhythmic foundation for the band. With the founding of the Count Basie Orchestra in 1935, Basie established the paradigm for intensely swinging, unified, and versatile rhythm sections. Dubbed the "All-American rhythm section," Jo Jones (drums), Walter Page (bass), Freddie Green (guitar), and Basie complemented each other's roles perfectly (Green joined in 1937).

Members of the rhythm section almost always improvise, as their parts are seldom fully notated. Bass players, pianists, and guitarists usually must create their own parts from an outline of the harmony. Drum parts are notoriously problematic because arrangers typically know the least about this instrument. Drummers often receive only the barest sketch describing the basic groove and indicating important figures. Other arrangers provide rhythmic notation for entire concerted ensemble passages, expecting that drummers will not play every note but rather simplify the parts by setting up and only playing the important accents. All the rhythm section parts must coalesce into an interlocking, coherent foundation for the band, an ideal best achieved by rehearsing apart from the rest of the band.[32] The full band easily obscures problems in the rhythm section. Troubleshooting becomes impossible as rhythmic confusion spreads throughout the band.

Thad Jones often started a gig with a tune that featured the rhythm section "out front," in Mosca's words, "a medium swinger that the rhythm section could really roll in on. This is a Basie thing as well." He remembers in particular a tour with Harold Danko (piano) and Ray Drummond (bass):

> They'd be six feet off the ground before we played one note. We'd come in with this brass ensemble, and the people would be screamin' after that ensemble as if we had just played the last tune of the night because they couldn't believe how good it felt. It got the rhythm section set up and warmed up. It made a lot of sense.

Musicians, educators, and leaders emphasize the importance of "keeping it simple" in the rhythm section during ensemble sections of the arrangement. Getting fifteen or more musicians into a common groove does not come easily, and complexity in the rhythm section makes this task even more difficult. In some small-group situations rhythm sections may intentionally obscure meter or form, but in a big band such obfuscation could result in disaster. The drummer, bassist, and guitarist must define a strong and unified sense of the basic pulse, the quarter note. Grooving together requires that the rhythm section—indeed, the entire band—feels the same subdivision. Throughout jazz history division of the beat has been variously interpreted, from dotted eighth and sixteenth (quadruple subdivision) to even eighth notes (duple subdivision). Since the bebop era the general tendency has been toward straighter eighth notes. In big band rhythm sections, however, the subdivision generally remains triplet (in effect, 12/8), leaving little room for subtler interpretation of eighth notes.[33] During ensemble playing, even if the lead trumpeter may cause the horns to "lay back," the rhythm section is expected to keep pushing.

One of the great achievements of the TJ/ML Orchestra was the ability of the rhythm section to move easily from a big band to a small group feel. In Mosca's words, "You could close your eyes during a solo and think there was just a quartet on stage, not a big band." Making this transition requires a drummer who "has to be able to adjust his textures, devices and sound to be a quartet drummer, and then be able to supply the amount of sound and weight to push the whole band." Mel Lewis, very active as a small-group drummer, unlike many "big band drummers," was as comfortable in a trio as a big band.[34]

Drums. The drummer, the central figure in the ensemble, defines the swing feel, determines the energy level (dynamic range), prepares ensemble figures with critical setup hits and fills, punctuates phrases, and both drives and responds to soloists. Lewis epitomized an almost understated style of big band drumming (in contrast to, say, Buddy Rich), which still managed to energize the group. "When Mel was there," says Glenn Drewes, "he set you up on everything. You didn't even have to read." According to Lewis, the drummer's primary duty is

> to hold the sections together, . . . to control three different lead players who have different conceptions of where the time should be and get them to put the time where the drummer wants it. In other words, the drummer should be working along with the lead trumpet player to set a whole concept for the rest of the sections, so that they will all follow that lead trumpet, who is following the drummer.[35]

Even when Lewis sent a sub, his drums remained at the club. Keeping a set at the Vanguard ensured continuity in sound (although different players will sound different on the same set). When he occasionally subbed for Lewis, the present-day drummer, John Riley, felt that playing on Lewis's drums helped him to "gain a better understanding about the way Mel blended with the band." "And to play his cymbals," Riley says, "they sounded good at a certain volume and not at other volumes, and that made me more aware of how to play." Like Lewis, Riley continues the tradition of leaving a set at the Vanguard.

Along with the bassist (and, depending on the style, the guitarist), the drummer supplies the fundamental quarter note. In traditional big band style, drummers play a steady stream of quarter notes on the bass drum. Many drummers abandoned this "four-on-the-floor" technique in small groups during the bebop era as they began to use the bass drum more for dropping "bombs" (accented hits, often in unexpected places).[36] A few modern players, notably Buddy Rich, continued to play loud and explicit quarter notes on the bass drum. Lewis executed his quarter notes more subtly, through a technique called "feathering" whereby the drum beater barely touches the bass drum head. Lewis was a fierce advocate of this technique, feeling that young drummers did not use the bass drum properly. These barely audible beats, more *felt* than *heard,* serve a very important function in building a unified sense of the beat and in giving the drummer, in Riley's words, "a feeling of internal stability." For Riley, "It's not so much an issue of small band or big band that I make a determination about whether to do that or not, it's really the vibe of a particular tune. Yes, I *do* do it, when I think it helps the music." This quarter note must lock in with the walking bass and "with the way that [bassist] Dennis Irwin plays." Riley continues, "I would say that I'm doing it maybe more than half the time, but hopefully only he and I are aware of it."

Tempo is an important factor. At faster tempos, as did Lewis before him, Riley frequently plays only the first and third beat on the bass drum.

The drummer more audibly sets the pulse through "tapping" a ride or hi-hat cymbal. In modern small-group jazz the bass drum's prominent role in time keeping was gradually supplanted by higher-frequency cymbals, liberating soloists from the oppressive, heavy four-on-the-floor bass drum. The "tap" is typically played on the ride cymbal or transferred to the hi-hat for variety, where it can be colored by opening and closing a pedal-operated pair of cymbals. In many Count Basie arrangements, the first few choruses were played on the hi-hat while Basie soloed. As the piece built, the drummer would switch to the ride cymbal.

Mel Lewis was capable of producing an enormously powerful sound within the band and yet not sounding loud. Mosca describes how he could be simultaneously sensitive and driving: "The way he would listen and play time and at the same time get a tremendous roll going. He could really get a lot of weight going at these big moments in these charts." Lewis gave a lot of thought to every aspect of playing. He could expound on arcane details concerning cymbals and was "famously fussy" (Mosca's words) in his use of calf-skin heads, which require constant care and tuning and are easily affected by the weather. He devised a specific sound for blending with each soloist in the band. Riley explains:

> Tone color is really important, blending but not covering is critical. You want to play with sympathetic sound but not one that obscures. There's sort of the classic thing that Mel always did, which was playing the Chinese cymbal behind the sax soli. It really works. If I didn't do it, somebody [in the band] would turn around.

When Riley sends a sub, "hopefully they know about the history of the band, but, if they miss it, that's when Earl Gardner might just yell out, 'Chinese cymbal!' "

In many ways Jones's partnership with Lewis helped to define the direction of Jones's writing. "I don't think that Thad would have written the things he did if he didn't have someone like Mel to play them," says Mosca, "because the demands on the drummer were extreme to get the band through this complex stuff. A traditional drummer couldn't have done it; you had to have ears like Mel. I think the two of them are inseparable in that regard." Lewis was not as showy or flashy a drummer as, say, Buddy Rich, and sometimes people overlooked his contribution. "I actually overheard someone say once, 'I'm not a big fan of Mel's, but the band sounds great,' " relates Mosca. "Isn't that hilarious! How can the band sound great if the drummer's not great?"

Bass. If a swinging jazz band can be considered an organism that lives through coordinated movement and breathing, then the bassist provides the heartbeat. A strong attack and deep tone serves to circulate the basic pulse throughout the band. A dark, bottomy sound stays out of the other instruments' range and will not muddy the already crowded sonic stream. Gut strings yield a darker sound than steel. Amplification should be kept at a minimum, so tones are less sustained and bassists are forced to pull the strings hard, resulting in more attack, or "thump." The bass player's walking lines must lock in with the drummer's tap and bass drum. Discrepancies here, even if not consciously recognized by the rest of the band, will probably be experienced as something vaguely unsettling. Ultimately, the bassist, drummer, and guitarist (if "chunking Freddie" as described below) should produce a fat, multitimbral quarter-note pulse under the band, as exemplified in the "All-American rhythm section" of Jo Jones, Walter Page, and Freddie Green.

Bass players also perform a crucial harmonic function. Their intonation must be accurate because the higher instruments derive their sense of pitch by building upward from this foundation. Also, voice leading in the improvised bass line gives the band a forward momentum through the chord changes.

While founding member Richard Davis was the TJ/ML Orchestra bassist (1966–72), the bass player assumed a prominent role in the ensemble. Renowned as a virtuoso soloist, Davis was equally at home in a symphony orchestra, big band, small combo, or drumless duo, and Jones featured him in a variety of contexts. Dennis Irwin, who began playing with Lewis in 1981, has been content to remain more in the background, concentrating on performing his vital duties with singular devotion.

Guitar. Guitarists perform two basic kinds of chording: "comping" and what has become known as "Freddie Green style" or "chunking Freddie."[37] "Comping," short for "accompanying," is a freer style of playing chords to accompany soloists or ensembles. When comping, guitarists and pianists set up rhythmic patterns and punctuate phrases while defining the harmonic flow. When both a pianist and a guitarist are present in a jazz group, usually they take turns comping so that they avoid clashes in chord voicings and rhythms, and, in general, do not create too busy a texture. In Freddie Green–style chording, the guitarist avoids potential conflicts with the pianist by softly playing chords on every beat, along with the bass drum and bass. As with the bass drum, the quarter notes are felt more than actually heard. Like the bass player, the guitarist strives for a strong attack, a dark tone, and a fairly short sustain. A large, hollow-body electric guitar that is barely amplified works best. (Green actually used no amplifier at all.) One arranger believes that the cheaper the guitar and the thicker its strings ("elevator cables"), the better it will produce this effect.[38] So that the chords will not sustain for too long, the guitarist dampens the strings by lifting his fingers off the fingerboard after each stroke. This style of guitar chording subtly fattens the quarter notes of the bassist by adding harmonic coloration. Bob Grillo, a guitarist with extensive big band experience, plays only the three or four bottom strings. In selecting these few notes, he concerns himself mainly with voice leading to the next chord, no easy task with chords frequently changing on every beat. Grillo says, however, that arrangers, in order to fit with the changing microharmonies of the horn voicings, often write overly complicated guitar parts. Recognizing most arrangers' limited knowledge of the guitar, he feels free to simplify the parts so that they make more sense for his instrument.

In some big bands, perhaps most notably that of the guitarist Sal Salvador in the 1980s, the guitar also had an important melodic function (Salvador's band had an additional guitar to play rhythm). Some contemporary big bands, such as Maria Schneider's, feature the guitar as a prominent timbral and solo resource. At times sustained and distorted rock guitar parts dominate the entire band. The Vanguard Jazz Orchestra has not had a guitarist since its earliest years, though in the beginning guitarists such as Sam Herman, Barry Galbraith, and David Spinozza performed and recorded with the band.

Piano. One of the most important and difficult things for a pianist to learn is *not* to play. In a big band fully concerted ensemble textures sufficiently define the harmony without additional chording from the rhythm section. Big band pianists would do well to study the examples of Ellington and Basie. As leaders and composers, these pianists understood the need to limit themselves to introductions, endings, punctuation, occasional solos, and a limited amount of comping behind soloists. In particular, during climactic shout choruses, according to Dave LaLama (a frequent sub in the VJO), the pianist should "sit on his hands."[39] By "laying out" or, at most, inserting sparse punctuation (often consisting of a single note or octaves) in the "holes" (rests), pianists will not interfere with the band's momentum. As with the guitar, piano parts require simplification because they usually contain many more chords than need to be played.

Beginning with the band's original pianist, Sir Roland Hanna, the piano has always had an important solo role in the VJO.[40] "It's almost like the piano player's own band, there are so many piano solos in the book," Mosca observes. The Basie band also featured its leader's piano, and charts often began with a piano solo (for example, the band's theme, "One O'Clock Jump"), but these solos rarely lasted more than a chorus or two. When he directed the TJ/ML Orchestra, Jones interjected long piano solos, often before strenuous shout choruses, in order to give the brass a chance to "reload" (rest their chops). He also wrote a number of piano features such as "A Child Is Born," "Que Pasa Bossa," and "Quietude."

Jim McNeely served as the band's pianist from 1978 to 1984 (beginning while Jones was still co-leader of the band) and returned in 1996 after being named resident composer. He is an accomplished soloist and a sensitive accompanist. He comps differently for each soloist in the band, sticking close to the original chord changes for an "inside" player like Gary Smulyan and venturing farther away from them for a "freer" musician like Billy Drewes.

BECOMING A *BAND*

A recent arranging textbook provides "a general synopsis of each instrument's function in the ensemble."[41] The descriptions of each chair are remarkably similar. The author lists the same responsibilities for nearly every horn: lead or section playing, ensemble playing, and soloing. He gives no hint of the contrasting personalities that go into making up a *band.* This small book, of course, was not intended to give a historical overview of the big band, but by removing the music from its context the author fails to communicate the richness of the big band tradition: the links between composers and players, contrasts in soloing styles, the variety of tone colors, and so forth.

A *band* has specific roles for all its members. Unfortunately, especially in school jazz programs, too often chairs are assigned on the basis of who the best players are, with little or no regard to building a group of musicians with highly differentiated roles. Other than section leaders (especially lead trumpets), who are required to have the requisite chops and reading skills, directors simply rank players according to their overall abilities and reward them with positions in the band. Often this approach results in a generic-sounding big band—the kind that many New York leaders take pains to avoid.

The musicians of the VJO choose from two basic blending styles that they understand to be dictated by the style of the writing. Centered, well-defined sounds are used in shout choruses and active melodic lines; more diffuse, or "spread," sounds are used in backgrounds or to create a "foggy" effect (Mosca's word). In this style the individual voices tend to become more washed out or indistinguishable. The saxophones use equipment designed to produce darker timbres that are better suited for denser styles of writing. In general, the players have developed sophisticated concepts of blend that, like so many of the elements of jazz interpretation, are not indicated in the music's notation and can only be acquired through working together.

During more than a thousand Monday nights at the Vanguard, a constantly shifting hierarchy of leading and following has evolved that is more or less tacitly understood by its members. Writers like to compare such tightly coordinated musical entities to precision-crafted machinery or highly trained military, but the VJO almost never sounds mechanical or regimented.[42] The band is more a living, breathing organism. Players usually nail their parts but occasionally crack or overshoot a high note. Figures are played way behind the beat; tone colors, richly varied. It is difficult to describe the excitement felt when Earl Gardner takes over the lead from the second trumpet in the shout chorus of "Don't Git Sassy," and the band climbs to a seemingly impossible higher level of energy. No words can replace the experience of sitting in front of the saxophone section during their soli in "Groove Merchant" and hearing every accent, inflection, and nuance coordinated in a rich reedy blend.

Still, understanding the complexity of the musical interrelationships among these sixteen individuals brings an even greater appreciation of their accomplishment. In the next chapter I explore how these individuals respond to leadership in becoming a *band.*

Chapter 5

Making It Work

Leaders and Musical Direction

Even with the Vanguard Jazz Orchestra's strong performance traditions, band members, section leaders in particular, enjoy substantial autonomy. As these same players move into other situations, the picture can change dramatically. "It depends on the leader how much freedom you have to play the way you want to play," says Jerry Dodgion. "He might have a stylistic thing that he does with all his stuff, then you're locked into something." The amount of control varies from band to band and derives as much from leaders' personalities as from their relationship to the music, their players' experience and authority, and the degree to which performance practices have been established in their bands.

Bandleaders shape the musical product on two levels—through selecting, rehearsing, and directing musicians and through editing and adapting the musical scores. The first task of any bandleader is choosing the right personnel; theoretically, at least, compatible musicians require less direction. Nevertheless, even with a hand-picked ensemble, some leaders attempt to shape every detail of performance. For such directors, choosing pliable and cooperative musicians may be the most important criterion. Scores are approached with a similar range of attitudes. Some leaders treat the written text as inviolable, whereas others adapt the scores to their stylistic conception, their musicians' abilities, or the performance occasion.

The number of big bands led by composers has grown with the rise of interest in jazz composition. But the Ellington paradigm of a composer working intimately with his or her band has not always been the dominant model. Throughout much of jazz's history, more often than not, leaders did not compose for their bands but commissioned material from outside arrangers or band members. Bands that worked steadily could generate enough revenue to support an "arranging staff."[1] Benny Goodman, Woody Herman, Chick Webb, Count Basie, Buddy Rich, Maynard Ferguson, and many others in effect acted as middlemen between composers and their musicians. Because they had commissioned the music, they felt free to adapt and edit it. This approach contrasts markedly with the Western classical tradition in which the composer's authorship is usually considered sacrosanct. Imagine the outcry if a classical conductor "fixed" the rhythms of a Beethoven passage to make them more comfortable for a violin section. In contemporary jazz, although fewer leaders commission arrangements, bands such as the Mingus Big Band, Diva, and, sometimes, the Lincoln Center Jazz Orchestra look to outside arrangers. One of the primary missions of the Carnegie Hall Jazz Band was producing new compositions as well as engaging arrangers to update classic scores.

Composers working with their own bands might be expected to be less flexible, to insist that their players realize every note and nuance of the work. In classical music, at least in the popular imagination, "the work" is often idealized as something fully formed in the composer's head that merely requires being fixed in notated score in order to communicate it to the performers. Jazz composers have been, in general, more content to work in the moment. A parallel might be drawn with film directors who remain open to the ideas and improvisations of their actors and the possibility of the "happy accident." A well-known story, perhaps apocryphal, has Ellington and Strayhorn asking musicians after each reading of a new score whether there were any notes they didn't like. Ellington's musicians contributed handily to his compositions, and arrangements continually evolved through performance. This approach, in which preconceptions remain contingent to the moment, seems essentially "jazz."

This chapter follows some of the players discussed in the previous chapter and compares the leadership traditions of the VJO with the style of musical direction in the Carnegie Hall Jazz Band. Believing that they are maintaining the hands-off policy of Jones and Lewis, members of the VJO claim, "The music is our leader!" By contrast, in the CHJB many of these same players found themselves meticulously rehearsed and directed by its trumpeter and leader, Jon Faddis, who does little composing and arranging but is intent on putting his personal stamp on the band's music.

Any comparison of the Thad Jones/Mel Lewis Orchestra and the Carnegie Hall Jazz Band must take into account that they were founded in very different eras. The CHJB emerged as the repertory movement finally gained a foothold in elite arts institutions and jazz won recognition as "legitimate" culture. The late 1960s and early 1970s were, of course, a period of experimentation, political upheaval, social license, and self-discovery. In this climate, the TJ/ML Orchestra flourished.

THAD JONES AND MEL LEWIS: "A-THAT'S FREEDOM"

When Thad Jones left the United States for Copenhagen to head the Danish Radio Big Band in 1979, orchestral jazz in America lost its most dynamic, engaging, and forward-looking exponent.[2] By all accounts Mel Lewis was devastated. Their extraordinary partnership had produced a band that was truly integrated both in its leadership and in its personnel. During much of this time, they even shared a room while on the road. Jones left behind his close friend and his band without a word of farewell.[3]

Even under Lewis's piloting and the dedicated cooperative leadership, Sixteen as One Music, Inc., that took over after the drummer's death in 1990, the Vanguard Jazz Orchestra has never reclaimed the level of recognition it had with Jones, despite the continued excellence of its performances and compositions. The public hungers for a recognizable name and personality in front of a band. Jones accomplished a rare balancing act: he satisfied desires for showmanship without distracting from the primacy of the music. He embodied the music in his conducting: every gesture, facial expression, and bodily movement conveyed to the players and the audience what he was trying to extract from the performance. According to his band members, he was not consciously trying to entertain the public; he *lived* the music.

Melding sixteen musicians in a unified musical vision and shared conception of swing is no easy task, not least because most jazz musicians instinctively want to be individuals. Count Basie and Duke Ellington managed to build tightly coordinated and grooving bands, even though they were directing largely from the piano bench. Their understated style of direction worked because they had personnel who stayed with them for many years. Though their leadership, they managed to achieve precision in ensemble performance without stifling the individual expressiveness of their band members. As several of his sidemen attest below, Jones was similarly gifted.

When Jones and Lewis formed the band in 1965 they assembled some of the most accomplished section players, distinctive soloists, and dynamic musical personalities of the day. Along with interpretive and expressive freedom, they also encouraged humor and farce. For example, one contemporary observer recalls a frequent routine in which the trumpeter Jimmy Nottingham and the saxophonist Jerome Richardson traded ribald insults by "speaking" through their horns. Although much of this insouciant spirit was retained, subsequent editions of the band never quite achieved the all-star quality of the early bands. In 1971–72 Snooky Young, Nottingham, and Richardson moved to California, following studio and television work. Players such as Richard Davis, Joe Henderson, Joe Farrell, and Roland Hanna found more lucrative work touring with small groups.

In their partnership, ostensibly Jones was the music director and Lewis the business manager, but, Mosca adds with wry humor, "neither one of them took care of much business." Much of Jones's effectiveness as a music director, says Dick Oatts, was a result of what he *did not* do: "He knew when to stay out of the way, and he knew when to come up and bring the most he could out of a shout chorus. He would give encouraging words in order for you to find your own voice. Thad wanted you to have your own voice so he could write for it." Mosca once asked him how to approach the trombone soli on "Mean What You Say." "I don't want you to play it the way Jimmy Knepper did," Jones replied. "I want you to play it the way you're gonna play it."

Oatts relates a story that illustrates not only Jones's nurturing qualities and ability to draw players out but also the intensity of his humor:

> Sometimes he would just look at you. And then everybody in the band would start looking at you. You didn't know what was going on. "Did I do something wrong?" Then he would just start laughing. Because sometimes the younger guys, well, they hadn't really found their voice yet, so they were trying to go any way but inside themselves to find it. He was the guy that would say, "Man, look inside yourself. That's where the answers are."

Mosca sees a connection with Basie's style of leadership. Both were effective without being confrontational.

> He led the band the way he had experienced leadership from other people, like Basie. There were signals that were subtle that guys wouldn't pick up until Mel would explain it to them. For instance, you were expected to dress decently. That may sound obvious, but remember in the seventies dressing down kind of became the thing to do. So guys were wondering why they weren't getting to solo. So, finally Mel would tell them, "Well, look at the way you look, you jerk." That lesson doesn't have to be taught twice. Whereas if you say to a guy, "Hey, man that stuff isn't cool," and everything else goes on as before, that's not going to change his behavior.[4]

Such an indirect manner of dealing with problems also has drawbacks. Players may take a while to get the message. Perhaps this facet of his personality also factored into Jones's inability to tell Lewis about his plans to leave the band and move to Europe.

Of all the original sidemen, Jerry Dodgion stayed the longest. Jones was his "musical guru," "his favorite musician even before they started the band." As Dodgion notes, Jones was "an unbelievable triple threat"—a player, composer-arranger, and conductor:

> His playing was unique, not like anybody else, and he never played the same thing twice, the writing still speaks for itself, and his conducting was unbelievable. Nobody seems to realize what a great conductor he was. A lot of guys can write arrangements, but they can't conduct. He did not study conducting, yet he was in total control of the tempo and dynamics. We'd start off a gig with eight subs in the band and we'd think, "Oh, this is going to be terrible." By the

> end of the first set the band started sounding like a *band.* It was for the love of the music. There was no ego, like with most bandleaders. That was never a factor—the quality of the music was the main objective. And it was fun! Some of it was difficult, but it was so fucking rewarding. If you even get *close* to playing it right it's rewarding. It's been my experience that there's not too much of that around. He had us all playing over our heads. We played better than we ever played.

In most big bands solos are jealously guarded. There simply are not many to go around. In the TJ/ML Orchestra, however, Jones's playing was so imaginative and spontaneous that band members used to ask Jones to take their solos so that they could get new ideas.

Jones also kept the band on its toes by doing the unexpected. At any moment he might have members of the rhythm section drop in or out behind a soloist, call for an extreme change in dynamics, or unexpectedly cue someone to solo. One night, in the middle of a three-month tour in Europe, the band was playing for an unappreciative audience, and the band members were tired and dispirited. Jones started the rhythm section on a blues and went through the band's ranks saying simply, "Sing." As each member scatted a chorus, the dark mood lifted. Says Oatts, "There wasn't a guy in the band that wouldn't have done anything for Thad musically. He was so dynamic. We couldn't wait for the gig, just to hear what Thad would do next or play next."

Jones loved to build performances gradually. On one of his blues arrangements, "Back Bone," Dodgion would begin alone for several choruses, before bassist Richard Davis entered, playing "in two." Eventually Davis broke into a walking bass line. After several more choruses, a two-bar break followed, Dodgion played a riff from Charlie Parker's "Bluebird," and the rhythm section entered with Lewis on brushes. After a few more choruses, Lewis changed to sticks. Finally Jones brought in the entire band.

After counting off a tempo, Jones's right leg might keep time while his hands shaped the melodic lines and cued sections, and his facial expressions conveyed the attitude. In a performance for Swedish television in 1969, the bassist Richard Davis decrescendos so radically during a solo that he becomes inaudible. With considerable humor, pretending to panic, Jones gestures for him to play louder. Pepper Adams, on baritone saxophone, was often given extended unaccompanied solos. On Latin numbers, such as "My Centennial," Jones played cowbell. Once in a while, Oatts says, he looked at you "like he was going to tear you apart." He was always intensely involved. "I never worked with anyone who was more dynamic," Oatts reports.

While keeping the band's attention focused, Jones drew in the audience. "That's a hard thing to do, especially when you consider that your back is turned to the audience," says Mosca, "but he'd always kind of be a little bit to the side, kind of three quarters to the audience, and he really got the people into it." The statements of his former band members make clear the love and respect they felt for their leader. Unfortunately, not much film footage was taken of Jones with the band.[5]

With Jones's departure, Lewis's less frenetic style of leadership became the norm. "Mel was the eternal sideman," says Mosca. "He had no interest in being a leader outside of the fact that that's what it took for him to play every night. He did as little real leading as possible, outside of his playing and talking to the audience." One immediate change was to remove most of the rock-flavored charts from the band's book. Although Jones's music still formed the core of the band's repertoire (which Jones continued to send from Europe), Lewis began to expand the band's repertoire in other directions, acquiring contributions from Brookmeyer, Dodgion, Bob Mintzer, Jim McNeely, Richard DeRosa, Kenny Werner, and others. While Lewis led the band from his drumset in the back of the band, he still could provide *musical* direction through aural cues: setups, fills, and dynamic contrasts. He also ceded considerable authority to his section leaders. "I decided that I should let each section leader run his musicians because I didn't play their instruments," he told Stanley Crouch. "Earl Gardner runs the trumpets, John Mosca and Earl McIntyre handle the trombones, Dick Oatts takes care of the reeds. Now we can play parts 10 different ways without anybody saying anything and make it work."[6]

Soon after Jones left Brookmeyer returned to act as music director. Unlike Jones, he was extremely particular in what he wanted in his own music. "Thad's music can withstand playing that's less meticulous," says Mosca. "You know, guys don't make dynamics, but it can still swing and still happen." Jones's music, despite its complexity, remained rooted in bop. When Brookmeyer borrowed twentieth-century compositional techniques from Western classical traditions—his excursions into atonality, his use of tone rows and unidiomatic voicings—he apparently also took something of the classical attitude. Mosca describes the different atmosphere:

> Brookmeyer's music really demands a high level of playing all the time. You really have to be on your game and consequently the best band that I played with was the band that Brookmeyer was leading. I think the band actually had to become better to play that music. Guys weren't that happy about it. A couple guys were fired. Mel actually did fire somebody, or he let Bob fire them.

Although he exercised tight control in the playing of his music, Brookmeyer had complete faith in Lewis. Mosca remembers an incident that brought home this contrast. After meticulously rehearsing a passage with the rest of the band, Brookmeyer simply turned to Mel and said, "Do something there." "Of course they had a relationship that went back years and years," Mosca explains.

"Mel's leadership style was really to be everybody's friend, which is a difficult way to do it," sums up Mosca. "But it worked for him, and it made the band tight like a family. We used to go over to his house and have small group sessions. He was the kind of guy if you were hung up somewhere at four in the morning you could call him and he would be there." In his dedication on a 1986 album, *The Mel Lewis Orchestra: 20 Years at the Village Vanguard,* Lewis said, "I can't believe I'm writing 'After twenty years!' I'm so happy now, I can't wait to write, 'After forty years!' To the band—I Love You." Just four years later he died at the age of sixty after fighting a losing battle with cancer. Gary Giddins eulogized, "[Mel] was fiercely loyal, especially to his family of musicians. It was always 'my band' and 'my guys.' "[7]

For the band members, "losing Mel was a deep family tragedy, for great bands invariably become families."[8] As Bill Kirchner writes in the liner notes to the VJO CD *Lickety Split,* "The band was at a crucial juncture. Few would have blamed them if they had decided to call it an era and disband." Still, they had the band book, their regular Monday gig, and, perhaps most important, a long tradition of musical performance. A year after Lewis's death, in February 1991, on the occasion of the band's twenty-fifth anniversary, the band was rechristened the Vanguard Jazz Orchestra.

The long precedent established by Jones of "putting the music first" facilitated the transition to a cooperatively led band. The "old pros" in the original band did not need to be told what to do. Jones and Lewis preserved this atmosphere in subsequent editions of the band and nurtured a new generation of jazz musicians. "That's why Thad and Mel were so revolutionary," says Oatts. "Thad's kind of leadership said, 'I want you guys to find your thing and I'll be just kind of an overseer with my music.' "

Instead of a leader, the VJO has a "president," an office held by John Mosca. He announces tunes, introduces the personnel, makes up the sets, and counts off the tunes. Sometimes he uses the second set of the Monday night gig for notifying band members about upcoming studio or concert dates. Regulars in the audience may know the band's schedule better than some of the players (who might have taken off that night). Decisions on musical matters are required only when learning new material and generally are made by the composer-arrangers, such as McNeely. From the musicians' viewpoint, the absence of a clear leader does not mean the band is without musical direction. "Even though we've gone through a lot of changes and the two leaders have died, it's basically the music that leads that band," says Oatts, who serves as vice president. "It's not Mosca or me or Purviance [secretary-treasurer], it's the *music.* That's the beauty of the Vanguard band."

Although much of the sense of freedom remains, the VJO operates in a changed climate. Band members typically wear jackets and ties on gigs; long gone are the green dashikis that were the band's uniform for a time during Thad's era. Blue jeans are seldom seen onstage at the Vanguard. The third set has been eliminated so that people can get home at a respectable hour. Many of their outside engagements are at schools instead of nightclubs and concert venues, and they often must conduct a clinic with students before the concert. Mosca exaggerates facetiously: "Every gig comes with a clinic nowadays. When you get a club date, they want you to come early and do a clinic before the cocktail hour." Because it is a not-for-profit organization, the VJO must compete for funding with similar entities. The leadership has set up educational and outreach programs and started printing a newsletter.

Jones's and Lewis's camaraderie and sheer love of playing that seemed to transcend racial barriers was reflected in the composition of the band. Over time, especially after Jones's departure, the number of African Americans in the band gradually decreased. Conscious of the band's history of racial balance, the leadership of the VJO has tried in recent years to fill rare vacancies in the band with minorities. Incorporation as a 203c nonprofit organization has created added incentive to diversify as the VJO looks for public and private funding. The gradual whitening of the band has not been lost on the public or the press. In a review of the band under Mel Lewis on the occasion of its twentieth anniversary, after noting that the "years have drained it of the stars it once had," Stanley Crouch wrote, "There are times when the band has the transparent weightlessness that disconnects so many white bands from idiomatic sonority." Still, he praised the band for showing "its stuff with such precision and passion that even those who might have dismissed it as no more than a largely white band lucky enough to have a great swinger at the drums, would have to back off, listen, and have a good time."[9] One band member glosses Crouch's statement as, "Basically, the band sounds good for a bunch of white guys." He complains, "I mean it was nice to get the compliment, but did he have to say *that?*"

Many of the alumni and current members of this Vanguard world have become accustomed to a looser style of leadership that they do not often find in other situations. Though they do not seem to resent competent musical direction, they may occasionally miss the freedom of "Thad and Mel's band."

JON FADDIS: "THE LEADER OF THE BAND"

The emphasis on original composition has resulted in many of New York City's big bands being led by composers, but nonwriting leaders still see themselves as fulfilling a historically and musically important role. Their distance from the compositional process, they believe, allows them greater objectivity in making editorial decisions. An often-told story concerning Neal Hefti's arrangement of "Li'l Darlin' " for Count Basie illustrates how a composition may benefit from a leader's fresh perspective. Hefti's arrangements helped to revitalize the band's repertoire, enabling the Count Basie Orchestra to survive the difficult years of the late 1950s. The Basie style, based on economy of gesture and clarity of orchestration, was well understood by Hefti. Nevertheless, Basie often made changes to material proffered by his arranging staff. In 1958 Hefti brought in "Li'l Darlin,'" a chart that he had conceived as an up-tempo "flag-waver" along the lines of "Whirly Bird" or "Kid from Red Bank" (both around ♩= 276). After a quick reading, Basie suggested drastically slowing the tempo (to about ♩ = 63). The tune became a classic and is still considered a paragon of laid-back, slow swing.[10] Like Basie, bandleaders who are not married to the material, especially if they commissioned it, often experiment with drastic changes. During the course of my playing career, I have seen numerous leaders, in bands as stylistically diverse as Lionel Hampton and Blood, Sweat and Tears, whittle away at charts until almost nothing remains of the original arrangement. This enforced austerity brings the distinguishing stamp of leaders to their bands.

The trumpeter Dean Pratt, along with his brother, Michael, a drummer, leads a band that plays charts by some of New York's outstanding arrangers. Dean believes his band benefits from his role as a leader who does not compose or arrange. In his liner notes for the Pratt Brothers Big Band 1997 recording, *Groovy Encounters,* he describes how he has taken "artistic license" with some of the arrangements. His work with "two of the greatest musicians and bandleaders of our time, Woody Herman and Buddy Rich," inspired Pratt to emphasize typical big band textures (high trumpets, call-and-response sectional writing, solis, etc.) and hard swinging figures. Because he is not trying to stake out new compositional territory, Pratt sees no need to apologize for pursuing what he sees as the essence of big band style: "interactions between the sections of the band, a groovy sax soli, swinging backgrounds, and a stomping shout chorus ending up with one of those wild last chords for which big bands are noted."[11]

These aesthetics were cultivated on a more public platform by Jon Faddis with the Carnegie Hall Jazz Band. Faddis did little writing for the band and functioned as music director, frontman, conductor, and occasional lead trumpeter. He allowed the players considerable freedom in their social interactions but remained fiercely committed to producing a tight and well-rehearsed ensemble. Although his band included some of the most highly regarded players in New York, Faddis rehearsed them with an obsessive attention to detail.

When he first began leading this ensemble, Faddis had little experience directing a big band. Although he had played in many (see chapter 3), actually running one was a different matter. As described by several band members, he grew gradually into his leadership role. One initial problem concerned personnel. The saxophone section, in particular, took time to gel. Players seemed to be hired more for their soloing than for their skills as section players. Some had little or no big band experience. Finally, Dick Oatts was hired to play lead, and Jerry Dodgion moved to second. When Basie veteran Frank Wess was unavailable, Ted Nash (formerly with the VJO and a member of the LCJO since 1998) was brought in to play tenor. Faddis immediately noticed a difference. "Now the saxes sound great," he said to Dodgion. The reason was clear to Dodgion: "Four of the five have been playing together for ten years. And three have been playing together for thirteen years. And I'm the only one who hasn't been playing with them all the time, so I'm the only one who had to make any adjustment." Except for Wess, the entire section (including Gary Smulyan and Ralph LaLama, in addition to Dodgion and Oatts) had long tenures in the Vanguard band.

The remarkable trumpet section of this band contained *four* renowned lead players. The principal lead, Lew Soloff, first came to prominence with Blood, Sweat and Tears in the late 1960s and has played with numerous big bands, from Gil Evans to the LCJO. The second trumpet chair was occupied by Earl Gardner, lead trumpeter with the VJO. The third trumpet, Byron Stripling, also a capable lead player, performed with Woody Herman, the VJO, and many other bands. Athough Faddis left most of the playing to this triumvirate of stellar trumpeters, with his legendary range and technique he is considered one of the most astounding lead players in contemporary jazz. Once in a while he would pick up his instrument and contribute a stratospheric climactic phrase. Faddis had three lead styles to choose from (besides his own). Dick Oatts observes, "They're constantly switching lead back there, depending on what Jon hears in a certain piece." The trombones were also an all-star section, featuring seasoned masters like Slide Hampton (whose experience extends all the way back to Maynard Ferguson's classic band of 1958) and longtime veterans of the Basie band or the VJO such as Dennis Wilson and Douglas Purviance.

Faddis was not intimidated by all this experience. According to one member, "Jon has a lot of definite ideas about what he wants. Sometimes it's hard because what you think is the right thing, he has his own idea about it. And he's the band leader so you have to go with him." Dodgion says, "Primarily he lets us do it the way we want to until he's decided that it should be another way 'cause the way we were doing it doesn't sound right." Some of the players expressed irritation about the level of control but were grateful that at least Faddis didn't waste time. Dodgion points out, "He's a good rehearser. He knows what needs to be worked on." Oatts concurs: "He rehearses the band incredibly well. He's really a stickler for consistency and I've learned a lot by playing in the Carnegie Band." Although the veterans of the TJ/ML Orchestra were accustomed to less control, they seemed confident in Faddis's musicianship.

One of Faddis's main concerns is balance, both within and among sections. In rehearsals he frequently asks for more or less of an individual part. He is especially conscious of the way the brass hold their horns. It may seem surprising that players at this level need to be reminded of something so rudimentary, but, according to one band member, "he's on them about that all the time. If one guy's holding his horn down and another guy straight up, you're missing a voice. Some guys play to the left or the right. He says, 'You may be playing your part OK, but I don't hear it in balance with the rest of the guys. The audience is out this way.' "

A chronic problem is getting the saxophone section to project through the brass during concerted ensemble passages. Perhaps as a trumpet player (and one who has an especially compact, focused sound), Faddis has difficulty appreciating the limitations of reed instruments in sound production. Watrous's criticism of the band being a "brass orchestra without much dynamic subtlety" was mentioned earlier.[12] The acoustics of Carnegie Hall (and other venues designed primarily for classical music) are too "live" for jazz. With the drums and brass reverberating around the hall and muddying the sound, "dynamic subtlety" was difficult to achieve. The band (and many of its arrangements) tended to emphasize the brass. As judges of big band festivals are well aware, one can usually tell what instrument the director plays by the sound of the ensemble. In the Carnegie Hall band's case, the trumpet players clearly received a lot of attention.

In his editorial role as music director, Faddis sought to bring greater coherence to arrangements. Says Dodgion, "Jon is really into the interpretation of the song. From beginning to end, the style not being schizophrenic." Occasionally, he made radical changes. For example, as originally conceived, McNeely's rearrangement of Ellington's "The Mooche" had many changes in dynamics. Faddis decided to make the whole arrangement soft so that it became more of a mood piece. After his editing only three loud ensemble notes remained in the entire piece, producing a clearer climax. For a January 1999 Ellington concert, Faddis cut large sections of McNeely's rearrangement of "Rockin' in Rhythm," extending solos while eliminating some of what he considered the arranger's digressions.

Faddis often adapted material to changing personnel in the band. "Sometimes we'll have a different rhythm section or a different brass section, or different soloists," says Oatts. "He makes it work because I think he knows the individuals. To me he got that from Thad. He really knows what's gonna make it work for the individual." Faddis also faced severe time constraints. Often there was simply not enough rehearsal time to put something together to his satisfaction. Oatts explains:

> When we're doin' these Carnegie Hall concerts, we don't have a lot of time. Four or five lengthy rehearsals. Two concerts, a lot of music to get through. Guest artists, guest conductors often. Jon to me is the perfect guy for that gig, he can pull something together in no time at all. He's got a gift. He's done major changes in a lot of things over the years. They generally work smoother for the amount of time that we have to rehearse it. I don't know if it's really fair for the composers and arrangers, but Jon gets that say.

Oatts "was kind of taken aback at first" the first time he witnessed Faddis make a change in an arrangement, but he has come to appreciate this role "because it brings clarity":

> Arrangers can get really inside themselves and forget that maybe this won't fit with this band. Maybe it's a concept you're hearing but you're not thinking of it from the band's angle. I think Jon does. I think it's really good to have a bandleader like that, that's pro-band, and everything that comes through the Carnegie Hall Band has to work.

Faddis may change a rhythm simply "because he doesn't hear it working." Arrangers might not be happy about his cuts and changes, but, as Oatts observes, "each time that you get something played by you at Carnegie Hall, that's pretty good."

Because the CHJB policy was to update or rearrange classic works, Faddis and his ensemble inevitably ran the risk of being compared to the originals. To purists in the repertory movement, no rearrangement will ever live up to the original. A 1999 concert celebrating the Ellington centennial featured rearrangements of the maestro's tunes in the first half and a spirited but somewhat shaky rendition of his extended work *Black, Brown and Beige (B,B&B)* in the second.[13] Watrous, though recognizing that "sometimes Carnegie Hall's rearrangements are admirable," noted that "in this case the result was a bad case of the Icarus syndrome; the proximity to Ellington burned the new works to the ground."[14] In some instances the new versions were not different enough from the originals. To my ear, Randy Sandke's arrangement of Ellington train tone-poems was little more than a medley of the originals. As Dodgion says, "Any time you do Duke Ellington you're in trouble 'cause it's already been done so perfectly. You should really come from some kind of totally contrasting approach."

Although Faddis kept a tight rein on the band's musical interpretation, like Jones, he stifled neither his own nor his sidemen's sense of playfulness. Faddis's reputation for superhuman chops is nearly exceeded by his reputation for incisive wit. The CHJB personnel clearly enjoyed themselves. Some of this pleasure was transmitted to the audience, even though the humor often consisted of inside jokes. With his back to the audience, Faddis somewhat surreptitiously entertained his band members with a quiet aside or gesture. Different racial, cultural, and educational backgrounds elicited comic episodes that demolished stereotypes by exaggerating them. For example, at a concert for the International Association of Jazz Educators (January 1998), the trumpeter Byron Stripling responded to a question from Faddis in a deep, rich gospel-style baritone, "Ooh Yeaaah!" Faddis then queried his bassist (who had recently completed a Ph.D.), "*Doctor* Todd Coolman," and the new doctor answered in the "whitest" precisely enunciated speech, "Oh yes." When the band members and the audience found this amusing, Faddis had them repeat it several times. In another instance of wordplay, after inquiring how long a break would be during a long, arduous rehearsal of *B,B&B,* Stripling stated, "I'll be right black." Coolman quickly responded, "I'll be white black." When I rehearsed and performed with many members of this band for a television appearance at the 1998 Essence awards at Madison Square Garden, I enjoyed working in a productive atmosphere of cutting humor tempered by a spirit of generosity and mutual respect.

LEADERSHIP

The relative values accorded freedom and direction, consciousness of different blending styles, the interdeterminacy of social networks and musical styles, efforts away from or toward racial and sexual integration, attitudes about competition, the authority of composers, and levels of collaboration between them and their players—all these issues resonate throughout this book. Relationships between players and their leaders need not be laced with tension. Jones and Faddis, despite the differences in their approaches to musical direction, created climates in which players felt considerable musical and social freedom.

Some of the contrasts between Jones and Faddis are attributable to the different social environments in which they operated. No figure such as Jones dominated the mainstream big band scene of the late 1990s. His openness to experimentation, his constant pursuit of the unexpected, the creative space he allowed his players, and his spontaneous and uninhibited style of conducting seem anachronistic in an age of repertory orchestras. Of course, differences between these two leaders must also be ascribed to their dissimilar backgrounds as players. Though each has a connection to Basie (Jones directly, Faddis indirectly through his involvement with Jones and the TJ/ML Orchestra), Jones remained fundamentally a soloist (on cornet and flugelhorn), whereas Faddis made his mark as a lead trumpeter. Faddis is accustomed to having the band follow his interpretation. But he also learned from Jones, in Oatts's words, "how to make it work for the individual." His broad strokes reflected a complete lack of timidity in facing composers, arrangers, and players.

As some of New York's busiest players, the musicians of the Vanguard jazz world are no strangers to competitive pressures. *Within* the band, however, the competitive spirit has faded over time. As Mosca says, "It's so old hat, we all know what each other can do and kind of build on that. That's what's nice about having a band together a long time." Competition among players, many musicians believe, frequently results in technical display and clashing egos rather than in musical expressiveness. In addition to competition, time pressure detracts from making "the music be the leader." Although many musicians would prefer to take their time with a piece of music and "just let it begin to find itself," often there are not enough rehearsals to permit this more relaxed approach.

Musicians are likely to complain when a composer or director asks them to do something different from what they are accustomed to. Not all composers care about pleasing their musicians. Charles Ives, as one extreme example, wrote in his *Memos,* "I began to feel more and more, after seances with nice musicians, that, if I wanted to write music that, to me, seemed worth while, I must keep away from musicians."[15] Because jazz composers are often closely linked to the players performing their works, one often observes more give-and-take between them than is typically found in the classical field.

With a renewed emphasis on original works, even in the repertory movement, the status of the composer-arranger in jazz is rising. Leaders seem less inclined to make changes in the music. Players' "shock" at Faddis's or other leaders' editing of an arrangement is symptomatic of this trend. The repertory movement, with its performance of meticulously researched music texts, also elevates the composer. Perhaps the growing preeminence of the composer over the performer is another reflection of the classicization of jazz. The possibility seems remote that VJO members would make radical changes in Jim McNeely's arrangements on their own, although they might occasionally complain about an awkward rhythm or chord change. But as the "composer-in-residence," when he rehearses the band he often edits his own arrangements.

In the end, what makes a band a *band* is not its precise performance of difficult arrangements or its exciting soloists, but its development of a distinct personality. The classic New York big band sound relies on three active ingredients: (1) composer-arrangers who understand the players and players who understand the writing, (2) variegated roles within the band and distinct playing styles featuring interesting timbral contrasts between players of like instruments, and (3) leadership that brings all this together, whether it comes alone or in combination from the composer, the leader, or the players.

Chapter 6

New Directions in Jazz Composition

Three Portraits

Since the 1930s most jazz has been based on repeating chorus structures such as the thirty-two-bar popular song or twelve-bar blues. An exposition of the theme followed by a series of individual solos leads into a climactic shout chorus or recapitulation of the theme. As solo improvisation received more emphasis in jazz, this "jam session" approach to large-scale form became the norm.[1] In a thoughtful analysis Travis Jackson has discussed the importance of these practices to African diasporic populations in the United States in terms of a ritualized blues aesthetic.[2] However, in much the same way that in modern Western societies "ritual" often takes on the negative connotation of "going through the motions," some artists have found these conventions musically confining. Orchestral jazz composers, in particular, because they work in a written medium, spend considerably more time planning and reflecting not only on how to develop their musical ideas but also on defining the improvisational parameters for their soloists and rhythm section. Written parts offer the potential of prescribing more complex and variegated structures than is possible in a strictly aural medium (at least without extensive rehearsal). This chapter explores three contemporary composers' approaches to structuring their musical creativity and the improvisational interactions of their performers.

Rather than look at the evolution of the composers' individual styles or general characteristics of their works, I wish to take a detailed look at one composition by each writer in an effort to get inside their musical thinking and understand better the creative processes behind their work. In addition, each piece is rich in details that illustrate more general trends in contemporary jazz composition.

The relationship of the composers to their works differs fundamentally in the three pieces I analyze. Maria Schneider writes intensely personal music requiring that her players understand the motivation for her work. Carla Bley, though she writes with a core group of players in mind, composes self-contained works meant to require little or no explanation. The third composition, by Jim McNeely, was commissioned by the VJO and is a jazz concerto, a vehicle for a specific performer.

All three composers have moved away from repeating chorus forms. Bley's piece combines a discrete series of different grooves, vamps, and short harmonic cycles. McNeely allows the soloist to develop his own separate musical narrative in dialogue with the band, leaving the musical structure of the solo section undefined except for tonal centers and tempo. Schneider also develops a dual narrative, but for the first solo she uses a repeating chorus structure, saving the more open sections for the later solos.

Sensitive performers, to some extent, will always base their improvised solos on the composition whether or not they have directly communicated with the composer. Most players recognize the importance, in Jerry Dodgion's words, of "playing the song," in other words, not simply "running the changes" or using the same ideas in every solo. "Playing the song" often entails fitting the mood or contributing to the dramatic development of the arrangement, not just taking melodic and rhythmic motives from the composition.

BEAUTY AND THE BEAST: MARIA SCHNEIDER'S "WYRGLY"

Perhaps no other jazz composer has created music as intimate as Maria Schneider's. Schneider builds on techniques passed down by her mentors, Bob Brookmeyer and Gil Evans, but she expresses her own intensely personal ideas. During live performances, she draws the audience into her musical narratives by relating the autobiographical content of a piece. Her music frequently concerns triumph over fears, from overcoming childhood anxieties to casting aside more rational fears surrounding the dangers of hang gliding.

As the least representational of the arts, music has lent itself to combination with film, probably the *most* representational of arts. Composers of film music manipulate conventional musical codes to enhance the affective and dramatic flow of the film. Still, music to varying degrees retains narrative qualities of its own, which are easily activated by the power of suggestion. Composers of "programmatic" music channel listeners' mental images by introducing a work with a few short descriptive phrases, relating an anecdote, or sometimes simply by affixing a title. Ultimately, a listener's understanding of such a work results from a combination of the composer's instructions, the listener's own experience, and performative characteristics of the moment.

Schneider discusses the feelings and experiences behind each piece with disarming frankness. For example, before performing the three-part suite *Scenes from Childhood* she tells the story behind each movement. The first, "Bombshelter Beast," resonates with baby boomer cold war anxieties. The

A Opening: sonorities	AB Transition to shuffle	B Boogie shuffle
mm. 1–66	mm. 67–91	mm. 92–105

A Central theme (3×)	A Tenor solo	A Double time interlude
mm. 106–126	mm. 127–160 open, backgrounds enter 143	mm. 161–169

B Boogie—trombone solo	B Boogie—guitar solo	B(A) Ending Boogie, sonorities
mm. 170–189 Open, backgrounds enter 174	mm. 190–223	mm. 224–fade

Figure 3. "Wyrgly" formal structure (Maria Schneider, 1989).

second movement, "Night Watchman," concerns "awakening sexuality" and her feelings—of "repulsion and attraction"—toward a security guard at her father's plant. The third part, "Coming About," evokes memories of sailing with her parents and reflects her growing optimism, self-confidence, and maturity. Another important element of the live performance is Schneider's unique conducting style. Instead of beating out the tempo, dramatically enacting punctuations in the brass, and other histrionics, Schneider's dignified conducting seems more spatial than temporal; she emphasizes shapes, gestures, and dynamics.

Schneider's odyssey from the small midwestern town of Windom, Minnesota, to recognition as perhaps the leading contemporary orchestral jazz composer began at the University of Minnesota, where she studied composition and theory.[3] In 1983 she began graduate study at the University of Miami. After transferring to Eastman and finishing her master's degree in 1985, she came immediately to New York. Here she worked as Gil Evans's assistant for several years, studied with Bob Brookmeyer, and led a band with her husband, John Fedchock. Eventually she and Fedchock parted, and Schneider and her orchestra began a long residency at Visiones, a now-defunct Village bistro.

Monsters frequently inhabit Schneider's works, especially her earlier ones, Pieces such as "Bombshelter Beast," "Dance You Monster to My Soft Song," and "Wyrgly" reflect this fascination.[4] In "Wyrgly," composed in 1989, and ap-

EXAMPLE 3. "Wyrgly," tone row (Maria Schneider).

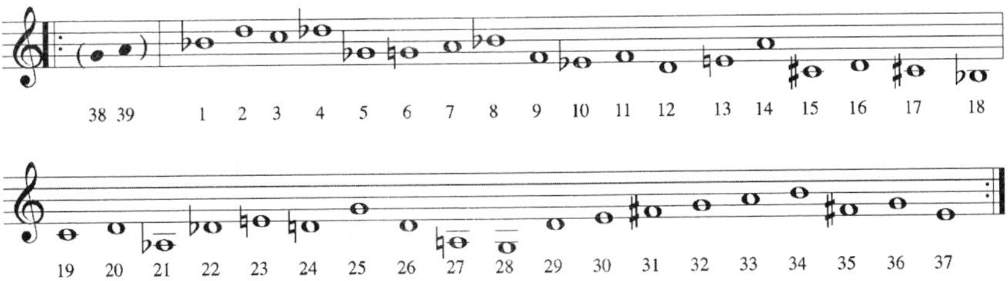

pearing as the opening track on her debut album, *Evanescence,* in 1994, Schneider juxtaposes and overlays two musical streams, as she explains in her liner notes, to portray the "metamorphosis" of a monster "from a mesmerizing vapor to an embodiment characterized by a dramatic display of multiple flailing limbs."[5] These two distinct musical ideas, or what Schneider calls "embodiments," contrast in melodic style, harmonic structure, chord voicings, and, most important, time feels. The first musical stream, which I have labeled A in Figure 3, is more lyrical and more harmonically complex and played with a lighter swing feel. The second theme, labeled B, is a short, hard-driving, eight-to-the-bar boogie shuffle figure.

In composing "Wyrgly" Schneider began with the lyrical middle section and worked outward. She explains, "I knew gesturally what I wanted the different sections to feel like, but couldn't figure out the material until I realized I could use the reed line of the slow section as a tone row for the beginning and later in the piece again."[6] I have extracted the thirty-nine pitches of her tone row in Example 3. The first eighteen pitches work their way down an octave from $b^{\flat}$ to $B^{\flat}$ and the following twenty-one back to the original starting point of $b^{\flat}$ again. The most common pitch class, D, is repeated seven times. The second most reiterated pitch class is G. A and $C^{\sharp}$ ($D^{\flat}$) occur the next most frequently, with four appearances each. The aggregate (all twelve tones) is not sounded until the B in pitch 34.

Example 4 shows five different melodies composed by Schneider from this tone row. I have placed the melody from mm. 109–16 on top because it is the melody from which Schneider derived her tone row and because it is the embodiment in which the entire tone cycle can be heard most clearly as a distinct melody. Because of the difficulty of aligning melodies of such different lengths, I have omitted the bar lines. The broken vertical lines indicate measures of rests of variable duration that also have been omitted. In the piece's opening, because of the different articulations, rhythms, and contours, it is not easy to hear that the same ordering of pitches is used. Schneider varies the lines by octave displacement, rhythmic variation, and altered

EXAMPLE 4. "Wyrgly," tone row melodies (Maria Schneider).

phrasing. Moreover, Schneider's use of space to separate the phrases in the opening section further obscures the pitch order. In her original melody (mm. 109–26) Schneider breaks the row into two distinct phrases, one three bars long and the other four bars long. The first phrase ends at pitch 12 (d), and, as she often does, Schneider begins the next phrase by repeating the same pitch, a habit that lends smoothness and continuity to the phrases. Example 5 illustrates an interesting transformation of a stepwise ascending line in mm. 114–15 (pitches 29–34) into an angular figuration in mm. 26–28.

EXAMPLE 5. "Wyrgly," octave displacement (Maria Schneider).

Despite the differences between the five melodies in Example 4, they have more in common than merely the tones. For example, the contour of the first four notes is always preserved (except for the $b^{\flat 1}$ to d^1 in mm. 49–52), as it is in the phrase ending on pitches 9, 10, 11, and 12 (F–E♭–F–D). Tone 12 (D) retains an important structural function in every treatment of the row.

The opening section (mm. 1–67) conveys the wispy, ethereal character of the gestating monster through light, scattered phrases of two or three measures, described by Schneider as "sonorities shooting around."[7] There is no contrary motion, and much of the movement is parallel, at times sounding more like block chords on a synthesizer than a big band. These short phrases are separated by two or three measures of breathing space filled only by the drummer's brushwork. The brushes and the trumpets playing in cup mutes contribute to the subdued atmosphere. All of the horns are voiced in close harmonies, with the saxophones generally doubling the bottom two trumpets and top three trombones (Example 6). Only the bass trombone is silent, waiting to become part of the monster's next manifestation.

No tonality is established until the section beginning at m. 67, contributing to the disorientation of this section. The harmony is dense: most chords contain six different pitch classes. The first five chords are major sevenths with added sixths and ninths and have the third in the lowest voice. Each contains the interval of a minor ninth by having the root as the top voice and the major seventh below. These voicings suggest Brookmeyer more than Jones (who usually avoided minor ninth intervals in his voicings). Other harmony consists of major seventh (#11) and suspended fourth chords. Much of the harmony could be considered "synthetic," that is, harmony that is not identifiable as an idiomatic jazz chord. Although the chords avoid some of Brookmeyer's dissonance, the influence of her teacher is clear (for example, in measure 6, the B♭$^{\text{sus}4}$ contains a major third).

Schneider's rhythms further add to the textural and tonal disorientation of this opening section. The first phrase suggests four measures of 3/4, and the second phrase enters on the offbeats in the ninth bar. In the rhythm section

EXAMPLE 6. "Wyrgly," opening voicings (Maria Schneider).

the bass "lays out" and the piano and guitar have the option of playing the top voice only with the brass. As this section builds, the phrases, while remaining irregular, grow longer. The dense voicings continue until the final measures, where Schneider sustains several chords, finally coming to rest on a $G^{minor11}$.

In her transition to the heavy, "monstrous" shuffle boogie in half-time (mm. 67–106) Schneider makes her most strikingly original innovation. During this remarkable passage, she maintains two different time feels simultaneously until, as the various sections of the band change over, gradually a new, earthy, half-time shuffle groove takes over. While the drummer and still-muted brass maintain the light, fast swing of the opening (although the drummer switches to sticks, subtly changing the feel), the bass begins playing a weighty, ominous-sounding chromatic walking line in 4/4 doubled by the bass trombone and pianist's left hand. Example 7 gives the basic pattern.

EXAMPLE 7. "Wyrgly," "monster boogie," bass line (Maria Schneider).

As the saxophones leave the brass to join in on this new "boogie-woogie" theme in half-time, their notes are not missed because their parts had been doubling the midbrass, as is common practice in jazz arranging (Example 8). Schneider has taken a conventional voicing procedure and adapted it to her programmatic aims. The saxes become part of the emerging "monster" while the opening figures continue without the loss of any part. The brass, still at the faster tempo, play nearly the entire tone row, repeating the opening section of the piece up to m. 21, but now, in its final chord, pitch 28 (G) is raised a half-step to G♯. The trombones enter with the boogie figure at m. 84 and are joined by the trumpets, without their mutes, at m. 87. At this point everyone in the band has succumbed to the heavy eight-to-the-bar shuffle, except for the drummer: the only holdout, he clings to the double time feel until, finally, at m. 92, he breaks into a full-fledged shuffle. The boogie figure, which has been thrashing about wildly through many keys, finally comes to rest momentarily in D. Four bars later, at m. 96, with the single word "BIG!" Schneider instructs the drummer to play loud and forcefully. The monster has reached its first incarnation and the arrangement its first climax. This section abruptly winds down on an $E^{\flat\,\text{major}\,7\,(\flat 5)}$, which is sustained for two measures (104–5), and Schneider instructs the drummer to "ease down" and "free up."

A short vamp by the rhythm section forms an interlude and introduces a new open texture (Example 9) that will become an important part of the upcoming tenor sax solo at m. 127. These chords are related to the "sonorities shooting around" at the beginning of "Wyrgly," but they have been pared down and opened up. The first chord, B♭/D, is the same as the opening chord of the piece in m. 3 (Example 6), minus the added sixth, ninth, and major seventh. Three solos dominate the remainder of the piece: first tenor saxophone, followed by trombone and, finally, guitar.

The other part of the harmonic structure of what will be the first solo is outlined during the main theme of the piece, which finally makes its appearance at m. 109. The saxes repeat this eight-bar theme in unison three times while the trombones and third and fourth trumpets (now on flugelhorns) state the underlying harmony in smooth four-bar phrases. The first chord is once again the now-familiar $B^{\flat\,\text{major}\,9}$/D. On the last repeat, the muted first and second trumpets play a lyrical, highly dynamic line voiced in perfect fifths.

EXAMPLE 8. "Wyrgly," "monster boogie" saxophones (Maria Schneider).

The tenor solo by Rick Margitza grows out of the final sustained chord at m. 127. Margitza begins his solo by holding a *b*♭ that "grinds" against the lead trumpet's *a* before descending into the next chord. Though the piece is still in the slower 4/4, this solo evokes the ethereal "mesmerizing vapor" mood of the opening. The solo is structured around the chord changes to the lyrical middle section, with their durations doubled, and the three-chord vamp of Example 9. Background figures borrow motives from the tone cycle. The rhythm section, led by drummer Dennis Mackrel, gradually builds behind Margitza's solo. As the backgrounds begin to sneak in at m. 143, Margitza's solo builds to the second climax of the piece at m. 159.

After the tenor solo, a brief double-time transition based on the tone row leads to the monster's next incarnation.[8] For the remainder of the piece, the boogie shuffle predominates. During solos by the trombone and guitar, Schneider builds to the ultimate climax by overlayering increasingly dense boogie figures. At m. 170 Schneider instructs the drummer to "slam into [a] shuffle" for trombonist John Fedchock's solo. The bassist, Tony Scherr, returns to the monster boogie of mm. 67–95 (as in Example 7), but now the harmony remains stationary—the harmonic language provided the soloist and rhythm section says simply "'E'-ish." As the solo builds, backgrounds enter at m. 174. After this point the solo sections are no longer open-ended, and Schneider brings in the other horns until the end of the piece.

The piece reaches a third climax sixteen measures later at m. 189. Here the solo shifts seamlessly from the trombone to the guitar. The "monster" is fully incarnate as the guitarist Ben Monder takes over the soloing with a distorted, rock sound. Schneider's instructions read, "'D'-ish WILD OVER TOP." Monder's demonic guitar solo continues to build to the piece's frenzied fourth and final climax, ending at m. 224, where he joins the horns in a figure culminating in another E♭ major7(♭5) chord at mm. 225–26 (as in mm. 104–5, Schneider tells the drummer to "ease down").

The "monster" begins to vanish as the shuffle figure returns at the end (mm. 227–29), twice interrupted by the vaporous sonorities of the opening

EXAMPLE 9. "Wyrgly," chord progression (Maria Schneider).

section. The B♭/D chord reappears, with its major seventh and ninth restored, but this time without the trumpets. The monster slowly recedes into the distance as the vamp fades away at the very end.

Although she finds that "assigning too much responsibility to the soloists can be risky," Schneider often depends on improvisers to carry "the piece to a contrasting place. The soloist needs to help that arrival feel inevitable." In "Wyrgly" the tenor saxophonist Rick Margitza constructs a solo setting up the double-time interlude at m. 161. Leading to the final climax of the piece, Ben Monder's guitar solo grows out of John Fedchock's trombone solo. As with the Vanguard band, competition between soloists is not a key element of performance. In fact, Schneider does not "like the idea of each soloist being compared in some way to the person before. It draws the listener out of the musical experience."[9]

In realizing this work, Schneider found it essential that the musicians understand her intentions. "At first it wasn't easy to divulge my personal motivation behind the music," she says. "But in the case of 'Wyrgly,' for example, it's necessary in order to explain why the approach of that solo shouldn't be bluesy or anything traditional. It should be monsteristic and atmospheric."[10] In October 1997 I observed Schneider leading the band at her regular Monday gig at Visiones. The trombonist on "Wyrgly" that evening, Bruce Eidem, took a wild solo unlike anything I had ever heard him play. When I talked to him later, he explained that Schneider had described that part of the tune to him "as a nightmare going on in her head."

The interplay of the binary structuring components I have labeled A and B invite comparison to sonata form. In its classic form the more active and forceful theme on the tonic precedes the more lyrical and unsettled, often on the dominant, contrasting section. Traditional music theory discourse describes the opening theme as masculine and the secondary as feminine. In *Feminine Endings: Music, Gender, and Sexuality,* Susan McClary described how classical music narratives reproduce hegemonic relationships that conflate race, sex, and class distinctions as "Others." Although allowing that the "paradigms of tonality and sonata . . . can be read in a variety of ways," her analysis of sonata form in Bizet's *Carmen* and Tchaikovsky's Fourth Symphony links the secondary "feminine" theme, the exploration of distant and unstable key centers, and their eventual resolution to fascination with and, ultimately, subjugation of the Other.[11] Marcia Citron has pointed out the paucity of compositions in sonata form by female composers. Paradigms that "symbolized women's subordination in society" failed to speak to female composers.[12] In the following discussion we must keep in mind Citron's distinction between gendered elements and gendered strategies. Gendered elements are socially constructed musical codes such as characterizations of the lyrical or unsettled as "feminine" and the active and tonal as "masculine." Composers, consciously or not, may strategically reaffirm, realign, or subvert such codes.

Schneider has reversed the elements of the conventional classical music narrative. First, material based on the gentler, more lyrical A idea opens the piece. The hard-driving boogie shuffle figure intrudes on this space by imposing its meter and eventually, near the end, by establishing the most tonal section of the piece.[13] This reversal is not entirely obvious, however. The opening, lyrical theme is not clearly stated until the middle of the piece, the spot where Schneider began composing. The elements of the musical narrative do not unfold in a traditional linear sense. Even the tone row could be considered more of a tone cycle. It repeats and cycles back on itself after tracing a downward path and meandering back up to its initial tone. The harmonic progression underlying this central section remains tonally ambiguous, although by the end of the sax solo most of the winds have settled on A as a central pitch. The A and B ideas also remain separate; unlike the developmental strategies common in European art music, one theme does not establish its dominance over the other through motivic transformation or tonal resolution.

In addition to analysis of sonata form, McClary offers a close reading of Madonna's "Live to Tell." Describing Madonna's oscillation between "two tonal poles on D and A," McClary writes that "this extraordinary song is not about unambiguous triumph, [which is] what tonal pieces conventionally do." Like "Live to Tell," "Wyrgly" can be seen as "resisting closure" and insisting on "flexibility in identity."[14] In "Wyrgly" it is hard to describe either the "boogie beast" or the ethereal "vapors" as "triumphant." The development of the dual narrative and the ambiguous ending, in which the boogie fades as the wispy chords twice reappear, suggest that both ideas can coexist. A close reading of "Wyrgly" must also mention its strong allusions to sexual fantasy. The thrusting figurations of the boogie monster, the ebb and flow of musical styles, the dueling grooves, the piece's multiple climaxes (mm. 92–105, mm. 161–69, and trombone/guitar solos), and the ending's fade—all suggest female eroticism.

Jazz discourse provides another important meaning for "monster." One of the highest compliments a jazz musician can receive, a "monster" is a musician of consummate skill. In music a "boogie monster" could be Albert Ammons, Meade Lux Lewis, or Mary Lou Williams. "Wyrgly" can also be heard as a portrait of the artist as a young woman. In 1989, the year "Wyrgly" was composed, shortly after Gil Evans's death, Schneider was studying with Bob Brookmeyer. When she had received a grant to study with him, several years earlier, she described her feelings with characteristic honesty: "I felt lucky—and scared. I could see how much he demanded of himself to keep moving and growing and felt nervous to open up those demands in myself, but I wanted to grow and find more of myself in my music. I guess I feared going inside myself and not finding much." Brookmeyer helped her rein in her creative forces: "As he helped me focus my ideas, I started to feel that my compositions became more uniquely mine."[15] A performance context exists for "Wyrgly" even when listening to the CD. As the first track on her debut recording, the piece not only announces her arrival as a composer; it tells the story of her personal growth. At a conference in which she appeared as a respondent, Schneider confided, "I have a lot of fears. . . . I was afraid of sounding too girlie. My music has become more feminine as I've become less uptight. I like pretty." She also offered two different perspectives on her role. During a performance, she is focused on the music and the musicians. Only when seeing a video, she states, do "I realize I am a woman."[16]

Although we know that the composer began "Wyrgly" in the middle and worked outward, we experience the music temporally as a move from disorder to order. This process is acted out physically through the transformation of the wispy opening sonorities into a coherent harmonized melody after the monster's first intervention. The first solo, over these changes, is more careful and bounded by the harmonies. The monster's return in the trombone and guitar solos brings abandonment. Even though the boogie vamps are the most tonal sections of the piece, the soloists are harmonically freer. Schneider simply instructs the soloists to play over a vague tonality and the drummer to go "over the top." Bruce Eidem, who played trombone that night at Visiones, recalls, "I'd never heard the chart before, or anyone else play it. It was actually a very liberating moment, I had a chance to express myself without having to play hip jazz licks." He confesses that he feels somewhat intimidated by the players in her band: "They have an unbelievable grasp of the jazz language. That solo gave me a chance to just play without a lot of pressure." So for the soloists too "Wyrgly" can be about liberation from fears.

Any work of art that finds resonance among audiences is not reducible to a single reading. Although Maria Schneider sutures the audience and her musicians to her musical narratives by relating the personal motivations behind them, her works remain open to appreciation and interpretation on a variety of levels. Close readings of musical texts better capture the polysemous nature of music by engaging in a sort of "thick description," in Clifford Geertz's phrase, rather than by promoting a single interpretation. Schneider has described her compositions somewhat maternally, thinking of them as "little personalities," "like my kids." Compositions, like children, eventually have lives of their own. Though in her liner notes to *Evanescence,* she stated that "her feminine side" is something she was learning to "value rather than hide," a feminist reading is but one, albeit important, way of hearing "Wyrgly." What is certain is that Maria Schneider, in the predominantly male universe of jazz, has found a distinctive and original voice, which she expresses with refreshing openness.

Jazz has been male-dominated for its entire history, and few people would describe it as embracing the open expression of femininity as practiced by Schneider. Still, she has no explicit agenda to fight for women in jazz. The personnel of her band has been nearly entirely male (except for the trumpeters Laurie Frink and, more recently, Ingrid Jensen). Despite her exploration of femininity, she insists on being accepted on her own terms as a composer, without any gender qualifier as in "*woman* composer." Speaking to a nightclub audience about a commission for a "women in jazz" concert at Carnegie Hall in 1994, she said with thinly veiled sarcasm, "Don't you just love that."

"ON THE STAGE IN CAGES": CARLA BLEY'S VERY BIG BAND

Carla Bley, older and with less formal training than Schneider and McNeeley, takes pride in her distance from the contemporary jazz scene. Having retreated to the artsy upstate community of Woodstock, New York, with her partner, bassist Steve Swallow, Bley rarely ventures into the city except to "visit the dentist" or for other necessities. Her cloistered existence is in stark contrast to her earlier years, during her twenties: "I worked at all the New York clubs as a cigarette girl, or a hat check or cloakroom girl, or a photographer girl [carrying] a tray of stuffed animals around my neck. I got my education at Birdland, Basin Street, the Five Spot, Jazz Gallery, etcetera, and I got paid to do it. I just worked there for maybe eight years, and that's where I learned everything."

With the encouragement of her first husband, pianist Paul Bley (whom she married in 1957), she began contributing compositions and musical themes to him and other experimentally minded musicians such as Jimmy Guiffre and George Russell.[17] In the mid-1960s, with her second husband, trumpeter Mike Mantler, she helped found the Jazz Composer's Orchestra and received critical acclaim for her compositions for Gary Burton *(A Genuine Tong Funeral)* and Charlie Haden's Liberation Music Orchestra. Because of these early collaborations, Bley often is associated with avant-gardism. "I got in somebody's long-term memory for that," she explains, "but that was so many years ago I can't believe it. That was before I learned chord changes, that was before I was with Steve Swallow who of course turned me into a very conservative person." She quickly points out, as anyone familiar with her work would know, that her conservatism is strictly musical, not political. As she sees it now, her involvement in avant-garde jazz resulted more from necessity than choice: "When I first got to New York, and before I really knew how to play the piano or write music, I fell into the free camp because I couldn't do anything else." Realizing that her characterization of free jazz could easily be construed as criticism, she hastily adds, "I don't wanna talk about other people who are still doing that, good heavens no, I take that back." But, she continues, "I like a lot of rules, and I like to know the grammar of everything, I like to know where the words came from and where the notes came from, and I just sort of enjoy that."

Like many composers, Bley begins at the piano. Facing a blank score armed only with a pencil and a cup of coffee is the most difficult part of composing. "I don't like it at the piano," she admits. "I can't wait to get to the desk [where] you don't need your imagination anymore. It's just math from then on, you know. Sitting at the piano you're just at a loss. You just don't remember what music is and why the notes are put together in any way whatsoever, you have no ideas, and that's just the most horrible part, or you have a great piece and you don't know what the ending could possibly be, it just won't end."

Her first big band arrangements arose from a visit to Harvard in 1986. Tom Everett, Harvard's band director, "kept bugging me to come up there and do a concert," Bley recalls. At the time she was leading a ten-piece band, and Bley demurred: "I can't because I've never written for a big band and you have a big band." Everett offered to give five of her pieces to Jeff Friedman, a composition teacher at Berklee, who would expand them to traditional big band instrumentation. After the concert at Harvard she asked herself, "How hard can that be? Am I really gonna not be able to write for big band because it's got three more horns?" When she was invited to perform in Berlin with Alex von Schlippenbach's big band she decided to adapt her compositions herself. In 1989 she began leading her own big band and in 1990 released her first big band album, *The Very Big Carla Bley Band.*

From her experience in Boston she had seen how Friedman added "color notes. You can get away with a note that just provides a color, it's a little clash, it just makes it sound thicker." She summarizes her arranging technique succinctly: "I give the high notes to the little horns and the low notes to the big horns." Recognizing her oversimplification, she adds, "You have to figure out who plays the chords, what section plays behind that solo. The rhythm section is difficult too, figuring out who plays what, but all the notes are there, and then afterwards it's just little things like phrase marks, the dynamics. It's really not that creative. The last seven months I haven't written a single original note, I've been an arranger, and it's a lot easier than composing." Her arrangements are painstakingly conceived and continually revised until she arrives at the final product. Bley explains, "We [Swallow and Bley] just figured out that I wrote seventy minutes of arrangements, over seven months, so I can write about ten minutes of arrangements a month. And that's working all day long, every day. So I'm really slow." She expects her soloists also to adopt something of this reflective attitude: "You're supposed to think. In music, you're not just supposed to put your horn in your mouth and blow. I guess maybe some people do, but . . ." Having made her point, her voice trails off.

"On the Stage in Cages" appeared on Bley's second big band CD, *Big Band Theory*. The title derives from lyrics Bley had written for another song, "Ups and Downs."

> They used to take us on the stage in cages,
> The journalists would say we were outrageous,
> Now all we do is sit and turn our pages.

Although Bley claims to have chosen the title simply because the line "just appealed to [her] because stage and cages sound good together," the title and lyrics suggest how sitting in a big band and reading parts can feel confining. On another level the words evoke Bley's transition from "avant-garde" to "conservative" musician. She explains, "We used to be crazy, but now I just sit and turn my pages and I'm totally normal." In this piece Bley displays her collection of favorite soloists in a series of vividly contrasting musical contexts, or "cages." Bley characterizes "Cages" as "almost like a review rather than a piece in one style." Figure 4 gives a sense of the piece's continually shifting grooves.

"Cages" begins with a series of sparse, stabbing single notes or widely spaced pairs of notes passed around the horns. As the only rhythm section accompaniment, the drummer Dennis Mackrel ties together these parts not only by accenting some of the horns' rhythms but by supplying counterbalancing rhythms in the empty spaces of his written part. Even though the band swings, Mackrel refrains from defining the groove overtly (by playing a ride cymbal pattern, for example). Similarly, although the opening D's in the first trumpet and bass bone and subsequent F's in the soprano sax and baritone imply D minor, a sense of tonality is not firmly established. Monkish leaps and dissonant simultaneities of major and minor sevenths and ninths hint at chromaticism. Section A2 is a slightly truncated reprise of A with the horn lines thickened and the bass joining in. The A sections use every pitch class except B and B♭. The vagueness of this opening leaves open the possibilities of moving freely between different grooves and tonalities.

The ambiguities of Sections A and A2 give way to the more explicit swing

Rehearsal letter	Length (measures)	Groove	Description
A	12	sparse	pointillistic, angular, "Monkish"
A2	10	sparse	"A" repeats, bass enters, figures thickened
B	16	swing	swing; 8 bars, B♭ min; 8 bars, D♭ minor
C	8	Latin	chromatic, angular "montuno"
D	16	swing	Mingus flavor
E	8	Latin	Soloff (tpt 2) solos over "C" boogaloo
F	16	swing	solo (cont.) over "D" changes
G	16	Latin	solo (cont.); 8 bars F; 8 bars A♭
H	32	swing	Puschnig (alto 2) solos
I	16	swing	solo (cont.) smooth sax bkgrds
J	16	swing	solo (cont.) rhythmic bkgrds brass & saxes
K	8	slow ½ time	Valente (tbn 2) minor third motive
L	8	shuffle	Valente improvisation
M	8	rubato	Valente plays and conducts
N	6	shuffle	brass, bluesy figures
N2	8	shuffle	"climb" to sustained chord
N3	5	conducted	transition to ballad
O	16	ballad	Sheppard (ten 1) solo
P	16	Latin	chromatic, angular "montuno" from "C"
Q	16	Latin	boogaloo acc. and more lyrical melody
R	8	gospel ½ time	Valente; motive (now major third)
S	8	shuffle march	Valente solos
T	24	sparse	trades between soloists
U	20	sparse	trades continue
V	16	swing	Sheppard tenor solo
V2	16	swing	Puschnig alto solo
W	20	Latin, big ritard	Ten & alto trade; ending ens. unison tritone
X	6	shuffle	brass plungers à la Ellington
X2	8	shuffle	climb to sustained chord
Y	3	conducted	transition to ballad
Z	7	ballad	Sheppard tenor

Figure 4. Form of "On the Stage in Cages" (Carla Bley, 1993).

and tonality of rehearsal letter B. This section introduces the two remaining pitch classes, B and B♭. As seen in Example 11, on the last beat of A1 two trombones, a tenor, the baritone, and Swallow on bass play the root and seventh of a B7 chord to lead into B♭ minor. The tenorist Andy Sheppard, one of Bley's favored soloists, contributes full-throated bluesy improvisations over eight bars of B♭ minor before moving to eight bars of D♭ minor. The interval of the minor third, which is reminiscent of the first two pitch classes of the piece (D and F) and becomes an important melodic motive in section K, is used harmonically repeatedly by Bley in "Cages" (for example, the section

EXAMPLE 10. "Cages," section A (Carla Bley).

EXAMPLE 10. (continued)

EXAMPLE 11. "Cages," section B (Carla Bley).

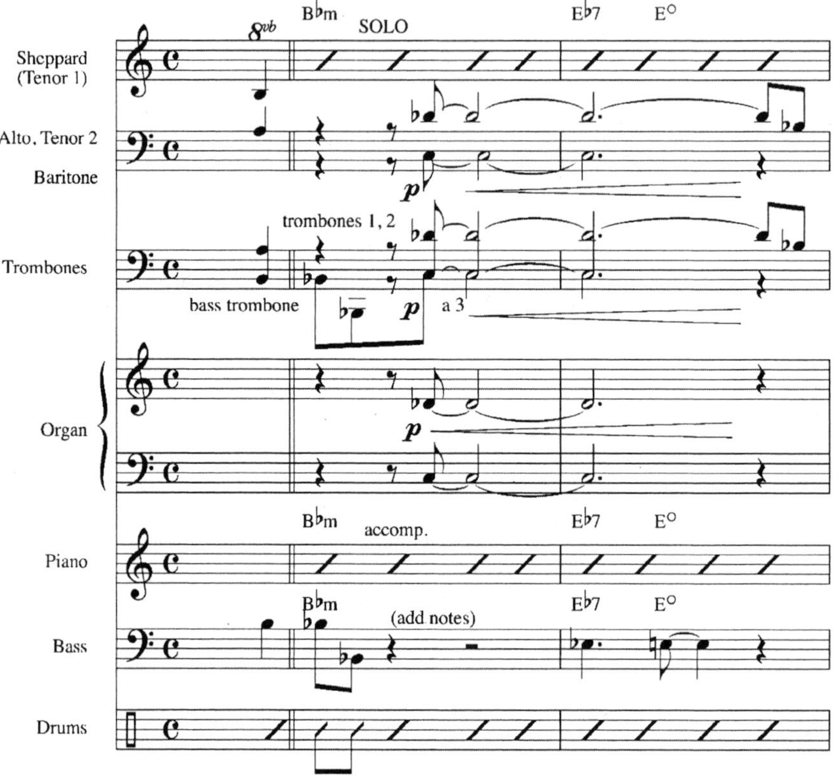

beginning at rehearsal letter G shifts between F and A♭; in sections H–J the chord cycle begins with D7 to F7). In section B Bley's sparse voicings feature the second and the minor third of each chord voiced in highly dissonant minor ninths.

After a one-measure break the second soloist, Lew Soloff's trumpet pick-ups lead into an extremely angular Latin montuno in section C (Example 12). This section heightens the chromaticism of section A as the flute and first trumpet play acute major seventh and minor ninth intervals. The wide intervals in the bass part are exceptionally difficult, and Bley mentions problems that bass players, especially on upright, have playing it: "Even Steve Swallow can hardly play it—he has to memorize those notes because he can't look at the page and at his instrument."

Soloff's solo leads into a hearty bop-flavored swing section (Example 13) based on the tetrachordal idea in m. 8 of section A. These melodic figures,

EXAMPLE 12. "Cages," section C (Carla Bley).

comprising major triads with added sixths, are placed in a descending series from B♭ to F before passing through A and reprising their appearance on C as in section A. For the second eight bars of section D most of the remaining horns join in stating this line, their boisterous octave unison adding to the Mingusian flavor.

After this section most of the remainder of the chart features Bley's soloists. Returning to the montuno section of letter C for eight bars, Soloff begins soloing in earnest. His solo continues over sixteen measures of the changes from rehearsal letter D, ending after another sixteen bars of "boogaloo," this time following the modulation up a minor third from F to A♭. Puschnig contributes some hard-edged Sanbornesque alto improvisations over a series of dominant chords moving from D to F to C to G before his solo abruptly ends.

EXAMPLE 13. "Cages," section D (Carla Bley).

In a striking shift to a slower half-time swing, the concerted ensemble interrupts the alto solo with the minor-third figures (C–A) in Example 14. Trombonist Gary Valente then leads the band through four more heavy gospel-infused iterations of this motive before temporarily settling on an amen-like cadence in A minor.

Valente begins to solo for eight measures over a heavy A minor shuffle (section L). Continuing to play, he conducts the band through an eight-bar rubato section (M) before going into a short shuffle section reminiscent of an Ellington train tone poem (N). This section leads into the first climax of the work—the long slow climb to the sustained chord in Example 15. A short conducted transition (section N3) introduces a ballad tempo featuring tenorist Andy

EXAMPLE 14. "Cages," section K (Carla Bley).

Sheppard. After yet another shift back to Latin, Valente reenters playing the motive in section K but now with a major instead of a minor third. Valente solos once again over a marchlike shuffle (S) before the piece returns to a sparse open groove much like the opening of the work (section T).

The remainder of the piece recaps the main sections of the work but with the soloists dominating the proceedings. In sections T and U the main soloists, occasionally joined by other members of the band, trade phrases back and forth. These trades eventually give way to back-to-back solos by Sheppard and Puschnig that evolve into another series of trades over the Latin boogaloo (this time between only the two of them). A big ritard leads into the Ellingtonesque shuffle with muted brass, once again setting up the final climb to the sustained chord. A short transition sets up the ballad tempo over which Sheppard contributes some soulful figurations. The piece ends as it began with concerted unison D's, this time played by nearly the entire band.

One of the most remarkable aspects of "Cages" is Bley's ability to maintain coherence throughout all these shifts in tempo and groove. Dramatic

EXAMPLE 15. "Cages," section N2 (Carla Bley).

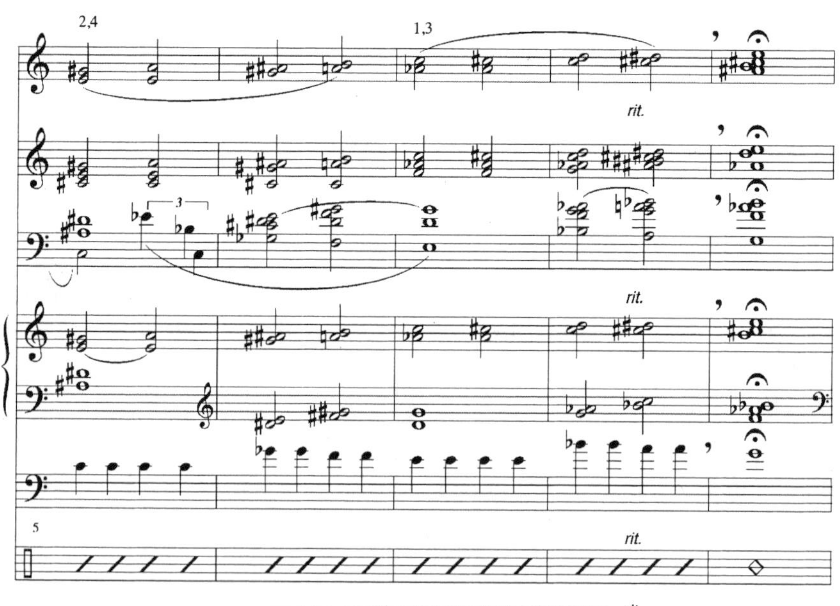

temporal changes are unusual in jazz and can be difficult to execute in larger ensembles. In this regard, Bley's work seems indebted to Mingus, and, as discussed in the next chapter, the Mingus Big Band is similarly adept at negotiating frequently shifting grooves. In "Cages" Bley links the different time feels by various motivic devices such as the wide dissonant intervals, the minor third relationship, and various melodic fragments such as the four-note figure in letter D. Such devices may not achieve "unity" in a classical sense, but they create interesting interrelationships between different parts.

A consistency within this work arises from Bley's reliance on a core group of soloists. Unlike Schneider, who is reluctant to place too much responsibility on the soloists, Bley depends on her soloists for much of her development. Rather than rework the melodic material from the opening sections of the piece, each reappearance of the various sections (such as the sparse opening groove, swing, Latin, shuffle, and ballad sections) features improvisations from one of her hand-picked soloists.

In fact, one of the first impressions on any listener of Bley's music is the extremely robust style of all her soloists. Since his emergence with Blood, Sweat and Tears, Lew Soloff has been known for his range and huge sound. Wolfgang Puschnig's hard-edged alto saxophone tone evokes David Sanborn's R&B stylings. Gary Valente's gigantic, overblown, gutbucket sound is immediately recognizable. Bley explains:

> I just like that better. I would start with the trombone. My first trombone player that I wrote for was Roswell Rudd, and he was definitely a robust stylist. He wasn't like a J. J. [Johnson]-type or something. He was playing out of Dixieland. Then when I got Gary, it was an extension of that. Not so much out of Dixieland, but an extension of overblowing, you know, every note is huge. I also like people that I don't even use for that same reason. I like alto players like Dave Sanborn who really blows so hard that the muscles on his face turn into Arnold Schwarzenegger or something. I like a hard, strong sound on a horn. I like a violin player that can rock the rafters. I like loud players, and I don't like soft romantic things, even, I mean sometimes I'll do it for a minute to show the guys I have a soft side or something, but only for a minute.

Recognizing the "masculinist" tenor of her music and discourse, Bley adds, "I think maybe because I'm a woman I don't wanna sound like all pink and frilly, maybe I just want to go in the opposite way because I just don't like doing what's expected of me, and I don't like doing the obvious." Unlike Schneider, Gil Evans's music never appealed to Bley "because it was too pretty. The chords were too beautiful." Bley also preferred stronger soloists than often appeared on Evans's recordings: "I don't wanna come down on Gil, but that was not an influence." As can be seen in "Cages," Bley has emulated Monk, Ellington, and especially Mingus. She explains, "Paul Bley was in Mingus's band for a year and I used to go every night as though it were a gig and sit in the audience and listen to every single note. So that's another way I got in free because my husband was in the band. I would sit there and just absorb." While Schneider has become more comfortable with exploring her "feminine" side, Bley says, with obvious sarcasm, "I don't think I have that side, but maybe I do, maybe some day I'll be liberated and go back to writing frilly pink waltzes or something."

Despite her hypermasculinist rhetoric, Bley recognizes the constructed nature of gender and that gender roles are something of a game: "It doesn't even matter if you're a man or a woman. There can be a masculine woman and a feminine man. So nowadays everything goes and you can use those words, it's no big deal." From her perspective, she and her partner, Steve Swallow, complement each other's gender roles:

> Steve has a more feminine side than I do musically. When he plays a ballad he'll put a lot more expression into it, and if we're playing a duet, I'll be saying, "Oh come on let's get over this section, it's too slow, it's too romantic, don't hold that note so long," and then he's the opposite, he's holding me back and saying, "Wait a minute, relax. Give this note its worth. Sing it out." And I'll say, "Nah, nah, nah, nah." So, you know, that's the two of us, he's the man and I'm the woman and we do the opposite when we play.

Bley's husbands facilitated her initial entry into the jazz scene. She remains unapologetic about her reliance on Swallow, especially for his strong sense of time: "I still sort of lean on Steve. You know, I always play with Steve. I mean a big band or small band I've got Steve there . . ." As is common with many successful artists (especially female), Bley's appearance has also been an essential characteristic of her success. She is a striking figure. Her Andy Warhol-like image—slender and pale, with a bleached, perfectly straight coiffure—has graced many album covers. Her daughter, Karen Mantler, who cultivates a similar appearance, remains the only other steady female musician in the band. When I asked whether she has attempted to hire other women for the band, Bley seemed surprised at the question—as if she had never given the idea any thought. As for the soloists, she responded, "I haven't heard anyone of any gender that can play better than Gary, Lew, Wolfie, and Andy, I don't know, but if I did I'd sure hire them." When I inquired about the other chairs, she responded, "I've never even thought of it before. . . . I should get some women in there." Like most bandleaders, she relies on recommendations to fill her band. Since she seldom ventures into the city to hear music, she claims to be unaware of any qualified female musicians.

Although "pink" and "frilly" themes seldom appear in Bley's music, children's songs frequently are used. Her first big band composition was based on "All Fall Down." Songs such as "Old MacDonald" have received extended treatment. Bley explains, "I think everything in your past is fair game, and it lives in some sort of like really swampy part of your brain, and when it comes out I always let it out." Unlike Schneider, Bley totally rejects any maternal instinct toward her compositions. "Oh god, no. When my daughter was a baby I made her wear rubber pants made out of black umbrellas. I just, really was not the motherly type."

THE JAZZ CONCERTO AS COLLABORATIVE WORK: JIM MCNEELY'S "STICKS"

Both "Wyrgly" and "Cages" illustrate the skillful intertwining of composition and improvisation. Schneider and Bley write for and depend on sympathetic players. The third piece, "Sticks," differs from the previous two in being a concerto—intended to showcase a particular soloist or group of soloists.[18] In the case of a jazz concerto, the composer's primary aim is to develop some facet of a player's musical personality in an orchestral setting.

Ellington, the most prolific and enthusiastic patron of this genre in jazz, seems a logical place to begin the discussion. In a few of Ellington's early self-described concertos, for example, "Yearning for Love" (subtitled "Lawrence's Concerto" and written for his lead trombonist, Lawrence Brown), the role of the orchestra is minimal. In many of his most interesting concertos the roles of the orchestra and the soloist counterbalance each other, something like the "friendly competition" expected in a classical concerto. Ellington often left room for virtuosic display, especially in a climactic cadenza. Table 1 lists many of the concertos that Ellington and Strayhorn wrote for their band members.

A jazz concerto can be considered "collaborative" in the sense that the soloist makes a substantial contribution, whether in the form of original improvisations or melodic, timbral, and rhythmic variation. Pertinent issues are the degree of freedom accorded the soloist; the structural relationship of ensemble to soloist, that is, alternating passages or background accompaniment; and relative emphasis on the individual styles of the writer and the player.

Undoubtedly, the best-known concerto in jazz is Ellington's 1940 work featuring the growling, mute-inflected playing of his trumpeter, Cootie Williams, "Concerto for Cootie." André Hodeir, in his important 1954 work, *Jazz: Its Evolution and Essence,* concluded that "Concerto for Cootie" was a "masterpiece . . . because what the orchestra says is the indispensable complement to what the soloist says; because nothing is out of place or superfluous in it; and because the composition thus attains unity[, the] . . . cardinal virtue of any work of art."[19] This unity, however, does not come without a price. For Hodeir, "one of the essential characteristics of 'Concerto for Cootie' is the elimination of improvisation." The approach of Hodeir and other classically trained analysts such as Gunther Schuller[20] has increasingly come under attack by scholars such as Lawrence Gushee in a 1970 review, "Musicology Rhymes with Ideology" and, more recently, Robert Walser in the article "Deep Jazz: Notes on Interiority, Race, and Criticism." Researchers frequently are blind to everything except what they have been trained to

TABLE 1 Ellington and Strayhorn Concertos

Tune	*Year*	*Soloist(s)*
"Yearning for Love (Lawrence's Concerto)"	1936	Lawrence Brown, trombone
"Trumpet in Spades (Rex's Concerto)"	1936	Rex Stewart, trumpet
"Clarinet Lament (Barney's Concerto)"	1936	Barney Bigard, clarinet
"Echoes of Harlem (Cootie's Concerto)"	1936	Cootie Williams, trumpet
"Boy Meets Horn"	1938	Rex Stewart, trumpet
"Battle of Swing"	1939	Barney Bigard, clarinet; Rex Stewart, trumpet; Juan Tizol, trombone
"Concerto for Cootie"	1940	Cootie Williams, trumpet
"Jam-A-Ditty (Concerto for a Jam Band)"	1946	Taft Jordan, trumpet; Lawrence Brown, trombone; Jimmy Hamilton, clarinet; Harry Carney, baritone sax
"Flippant Flurry"	1946	Jimmy Hamilton, clarinet
"Launching Pad"	1959	Clark Terry, trumpet; Britt Woodman, trombone; Jimmy Hamilton, clarinet; Paul Gonsalves, tenor sax; (Ray Nance, trumpet solo)
"The Eighth Veil"	1962	Cat Anderson, trumpet
"Charpoy"	1967	Cat Anderson, trumpet

look for, and as Walser notes, Hodeir and Schuller "studied in an analytical tradition that prized organic unity."[21]

But what happens when improvisation is not "suppressed" and the soloist chooses to take a path quite different from what the composer may have intended? If "thematic coherence" of soloist and orchestra is not the goal, is it possible to identify some other governing aesthetic that is less tied to the notion of "organic unity"? I examine these issues in Jim McNeely's "Sticks," a jazz concerto commissioned by the Vanguard Jazz Orchestra and featuring its trombonist, Ed Neumeister. Despite his own clear interest in motivic development, McNeely has not created a vehicle for Neumeister that ensures any degree of thematic unity between soloist and orchestra.

As we have seen, the performance traditions in the Vanguard Jazz Orchestra run deep, with some of its members' tenures dating to the early 1970s when the band was still led by its founders, Thad Jones and Mel Lewis. McNeely's long association with the TJ/ML Orchestra began in 1978, three years after the Chicago-born pianist arrived in New York. He continued as a featured soloist when Brookmeyer became musical director after Jones's departure. After touring with such major jazz artists as Stan Getz and Phil Woods, he returned to the VJO as pianist and resident composer in 1996. In April 1997 the VJO recorded *Lickety Split,* an album of McNeely's works.

When composing a new piece McNeely likes to begin by posing hypothetical questions. As he sees it, "the essential job of a composer, jazz or otherwise, is *speculation:* to ask 'What if?' " At the 1998 International Association of Jazz Educators convention, he gave a few sample questions of the kind he says "keep [him] up at night":

> What if a "shout chorus" reaches its peak, but just when the listener thinks it's peaked, it keeps on peaking for another 16 bars?
>
> What if a *great* be-bop saxophonist walks into a post–Wayne Shorter whirlpool?
>
> What if a tonal center gradually dissolved into a chromatic swamp?
>
> What if a three-note cell kept developing, or splitting (mitosis?), and gradually grew into a scale, which then spit out another three-note cell?
>
> What would it sound like if a big band fell down a flight of stairs together?[22]

To "get past the standard 'arrangement' format" the composer must think about larger concepts and begin to "value the planning process." He advises writers to "sketch things out. Make a time line and indicate where and when you want things to happen, and who will play them." Perhaps most important, composition requires "belief and courage[,] . . . the belief in your gut, heart, and soul that [your] ideas are valid and worth pursuing *because they are yours;* and the courage to express them in the face of possible criticism, misunderstanding, and/or rejection. We can all learn from Thelonious Monk."[23]

For the liner notes to *Lickety Split,* New World Records took the unusual step of asking the composer to provide some analysis of his own work. Although McNeely modestly questioned whether he is "equipped with real analytical tools," his insights inform the analysis that follows.[24] Almost all the music on this CD was written for the VJO and with specific soloists in mind. For example, McNeely's arrangement of "In the Wee Small Hours of the Morning" was inspired by Dick Oatts's alto playing. "Absolution," writes McNeely, "is another instance in which the sound of the major soloist (Rich Perry this time) served as an impetus for the piece" (7). The title track, "Lickety Split," could be an illustration of a "great be-bop saxophonist" (Gary Smulyan) walking into "a post–Wayne Shorter whirlpool." Other pieces are tributes to Jones ("Thad") and Lewis ("Mel"). VJO's second trombonist, Ed Neumeister, who joined the band in 1981, is known for his growling, plunger mute–inflected trombone solos, a dissonant or atonal version of Bubber Miley and Joe "Tricky Sam" Nanton in the Ellington band. In "Sticks" McNeely wanted to give Neumeister "a darker, more dissonant harmonic palette to work with" (8). This "mini-concerto" (McNeely's term) illustrates prominent features of the composer's style: motivic and thematic free development, departures from idiomatic harmony, unusual integration of soloist and ensemble, orchestrational skill, and creative use of the rhythm section. Like his mentor, Bob Brookmeyer, and many of his contemporaries (such as Maria Schneider and Bill Warfield), McNeely tries to get beyond the standard arranging form of "head—solos—shout—head." Abandoning the chorus structure liberates the composer from lockstep chord changes and allows for freer development.

As can be seen in the graphic representation in Figure 5, McNeely repeatedly alternates between the soloist and the ensemble in almost a ritornello format. Neumeister has four different spaces for improvisation, besides his statements of the theme. This structure allows for greater development of ideas by both the soloist and the composer.

In writing this piece McNeely faced a dilemma. Plunger features are usually on ballads, but McNeely did not want to write another slow tempo tune for the CD. The challenge in an up-tempo piece would be to maintain the lower dynamic level in the ensemble required by Neumeister's use of mutes. McNeely solved this problem in two ways. First, other than a short segment of backgrounds by a clarinet trio and trumpets in harmon mutes, nowhere in the piece do the solo and ensemble playing overlap. Second, the work maintains a subdued atmosphere by making use of flutes, clarinets, and soprano sax in the reed section and cup, harmon, straight and tight plunger mutes, as well as flugelhorns, in the brass.

In essence, "Sticks" is a study of the third degree of the scale: major, minor, and "raised" (sus 4). The main theme of "Sticks" is derived from the melodic cell in Example 16. In addition to playing around with the upper third, this cell offers the sixth degree of the scale as a lower neighbor to the tonic, in a kind of "ladder of thirds."[25]

The piece opens with the bass and the pianist's left hand playing what is essentially a four-bar vamp derived from the pitches of the melodic cell. The drummer also plays these figures with his mallets on his tom-toms, which McNeely says "add to the mystery of the piece." During the recording, they found it necessary to tune the drums to an F minor triad, "otherwise the tonal center of the bass line would be obscured."[26]

The ladder of thirds, at least in van der Merwe's view, is the basis of the blues mode. But McNeely has reversed the usual melodic flow in the blues by going from the major to minor third (see Examples 17 and 18), somewhat reminiscent of Milhaud's decidedly unidiomatic use of the blue third in *La Création du Monde*.[27] Measure 16 introduces a melodic minor or "blue" seventh, a scale degree that is also slated for further development as the piece proceeds. Another notable characteristic of this cell is the total avoidance of the fifth degree.

mm. 1–8 (2×) rhythm section intro 16 F	mm. 9–24 trombone theme "a" 16 F	mm. 25–44 ensemble theme "a" 20 F	mm. 45–60 trombone: 1st solo improvisation 16 F	mm. 61–80 ensemble theme "a" 20 F

mm. 81–96 trombone: 2nd solo improvisation 16 F	mm. 97–111 reeds "bridge" new theme 15 G	mm. 112–156 ensemble development of theme "a" 45 free transposition of theme G A B♭ C D E♭	m. 157 final 3 chords 1 F F# G

trombone: main solo section			
mm. 158–173 (poss. open) 32 (16) C (16) G	mm. 174–183 clarinet background 17 C	mm. 184–202 add brass 19 G	mm. 203–208 piano accom. 16 F

ensemble "shout"	
mm. 209–216 (4x) "fugue" 32 D pedal	mm. 217–252 counterpoint-climax 42 free transposition upward to F

m. 253 trombone cadenza (open) 41 seconds (5:49–6:30) approximately 33 bars

mm. 254–269 trombone cue 16 G	mm. 270–286 (2×) reeds "bridge" 2nd x add brass 32 G	mm. 287–297 trombone final statement 11 (8) E ped (4) F ped	m. 298 final 3 chords 1 F F# G

Figure 5. Form of "Sticks" (Jim McNeely, 1995). (The measure numbers in McNeely's original score have been changed to reflect several cuts he made before recording the work.)

EXAMPLE 16. "Sticks," melodic cell (Jim McNeely).

EXAMPLE 17. "Sticks," bass line (Jim McNeely).

This opening section is the closest Neumeister comes to a literal statement of the theme. Entering after sixteen bars of funky bass doubled by the pianist's left hand, he freely incorporates plunger and other effects all his own. The thirds are almost always smeared (using the slide), whether descending from major to minor or ascending to the fourth degree (as in mm. 12–13). In the second half of the sixteen-bar passage, Neumeister takes a few rhythmic liberties with the melody.

After this exposition the ensemble plays nearly the same melody but with the two halves separated by a few measures of drummer John Riley's malletwork. The line is thickened with nonfunctional harmony in a way that is similar to Schneider's "sonorities shooting around" in "Wyrgly." McNeely, however, limits himself to only four voices, the top three of which are either major or minor triads or seventh$^{\text{sus4}}$ chords (these sus 4 chords actually sound like major triads with an added second and the third in the bass; that is, the first chord in Example 19 could be heard as A$^{\text{add2}}$/C$^{\sharp}$).[28] In this texture the close position triads (ignoring for a moment the flute doubling the lead at the octave) sound distinct from the bass notes by virtue of the wide interval separating them. They are further disjoined orchestrationally, by McNeely's placement of the winds on the upper triads and only the string bass and left hand of the piano on the bass line. His choice of harmony for the triads is related directly to the three kinds of "thirds" in the melodic cell (major, minor, and "raised" or sus 4).

McNeely almost entirely eschews idiomatic jazz chords in this work. Combined with the bass notes, these triads create interesting sonorities while

EXAMPLE 18. "Sticks," theme (Jim McNeely).

avoiding the underlying harmony of fuller voicings and the limitations that functionality imposes. To keep the weight of these voicings consistent, he must select four different pitches and steer clear of root position seventh chords (except for 7^{sus4}). For example, when using major triads, he is free to put any note in the bass, except, of course, the three notes already in the triad and the sixth (which would make the chord a simple, root position minor seventhh chord, i.e., F/D = D^{minor7}). Still, the chords are not without any suggestion of more traditional jazz harmony; for example, F/F$^{\sharp}$ sounds like D7$^{\sharp}$9 and D/E is a stock voicing for $E7^{sus4\ add9}$.

Table 2 gives the frequency with which McNeely uses the various bass notes available for the major triads in the two theme statements. As can be seen, the most favored is 2 (e.g., D/E), with a total of sixteen occurrences, followed by $^{\flat}$2 (e.g., F/F$^{\sharp}$), with eight, and $^{\flat}$7 (e.g., B$^{\flat}$/G$^{\sharp}$) and $^{\flat}$6 (e.g., D$^{\flat}$/A),

TABLE 2 Occurrence of Available Major Triad/Bass Note Combinations in "Sticks"

bass note	*mm. 25–44*	*mm. 61–80*
7	1	0
♭7	3	2
♭6	4	1
♭5	3	0
4	2	2
♭3	1	0
2	7	9
♭2	5	3

with five each. Another frequently occurring sonority is 7^{sus4}/2 (with ten appearances) and, in the second statement, minor/2 (e.g., F^{minor}/G; with five occurrences). Each statement of the theme by the concerted ensemble (mm. 25–44 and 61–80) is harmonized quite differently.

In Example 19 I have added chord symbols to the first eight bars of the opening ensemble statement. By using triads with "altered" bass notes, some jazz composers have explored sounds that get away from familiar seventh chords. Furthermore, unlike some of the dense, complex structures earlier used by Brookmeyer and others, these harmonies are reducible to concise chord symbols that can easily be used for comping and soloing (although they are not put to that purpose here).

McNeely has also "thickened" the first two ensemble presentations of the theme (mm. 25–44 and 61–80) by orchestrating the melody with two flutes, one clarinet, a flugelhorn, and two trumpets (one with harmon mute, the other with cup mute). The first flute plays the melody an octave higher. The second part is played by tenor sax, flugelhorn, and trombone with a tight plunger, and the third part is played by baritone sax and two trombones similarly muted. The result is a rich, yet not overbearing, orchestration featuring the full ensemble.

McNeely sandwiches two sixteen-bar improvisation sections for Neumeister between ensemble sections of approximately equal length (refer to Figure 5). Accompanied only by the drums, Neumeister abandons McNeely's thematic material (he never once uses the major to minor third motive) and does not confine himself to the pitch collection provided to him by the composer (essentially the notes of the melodic cell in Example 16). Tonally, his ideas fit more within traditional blues modes; thirds and sevenths are always minor (A♭ and E♭).

In mm. 97–111 (Example 20) the reeds introduce material that provides melodic, harmonic, and textural contrast with the A theme (see Example

EXAMPLE 19. "Sticks," theme harmonization (Jim McNeely).

18). McNeely refers to this section as a "bridge," perhaps because it leads to a restatement of the theme in a new key. But unlike the bridges in most jazz tunes, this section has been deferred until well into the tune and does not form part of an underlying chorus structure. Despite the extreme chromaticism of the harmony, this segment is strongly suggestive of the key of G (for one thing, the bass line begins on G). This theme uses some of the scale degrees that were avoided in the earlier cell, notably the fifth, minor seventh, and second. It also incorporates the two remaining kinds of triads that were not used in the winds in the earlier harmonization: augmented and diminished. Indeed, McNeely stacks these two triads on top of each other. He is limited to five pitches (the number of players in the reed section), so the two triads must share one note. The first chord is $D^{aug}/E^{\flat\ dim}$, the triads sharing a common central tone, $F^{\sharp}$. Despite the differences in the triads, the harmony is related to both the pitches in Example 16 and the harmonization of the first tonic occurring in the melody in Example 19 ($D^{\flat}/A$). Transposed up a semitone these pitches yield nearly the same pitches used in the bridge harmonization ($B^{\flat\ aug}/E^{\flat\ dim}$). The voices move in parallel harmony (used sparingly until now—earlier harmony used much contrary and oblique motion) containing dissonant major seventh and minor ninth intervals. As he does often, McNeely concocts interesting orchestrational colors: two clarinets (one on the lead voice) and soprano, tenor, and baritone saxes.

This "bridge" leads directly into an extended development (mm. 112–57) of the melodic cell, beginning with the unmuted brass, who are joined in m.

EXAMPLE 20. "Sticks," "bridge" harmonization (Jim McNeely) and analysis.

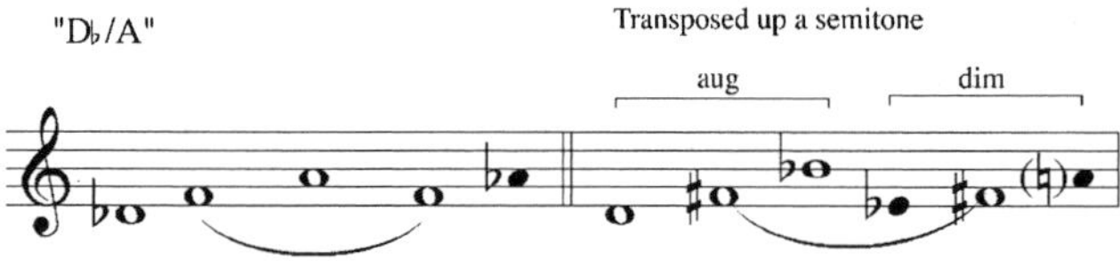

125 by the reeds. McNeely transposes the cell upward by steps, starting in G and gradually moving through A, B♭, C, D, E♭. Finally in mm. 155–57 the movement becomes chromatic, culminating in the figure in Example 21. The last three chords are extremely dense. The first contains eleven pitches: every note of the chromatic scale but G (which is withheld until the final chord). Because these chords are short they are heard more as percussive hits than as dissonant chords.

The next section is the main solo of the piece. McNeely offers Neumeister the pitch collection in Example 22, which is derived from the melodic cell in Example 16 (the tetrachord on F). The pitches have been transposed to C for the bottom tetrachord, and a second symmetrical disjunct tetrachord has been placed on top. Neumeister solos over a repeating bass line containing every note of this scale, which particularly exploits the "cross relation" between the major and minor third and major and minor seventh (Example 23).

The band performed the piece for about six months before entering the studio to record it. This gave the band and the soloist, in Neumeister's words, a chance "to settle into it [and] experiment with the tempos and feels." In the beginning he practiced and "worked off the scale" but gradually took the improvisation in his own direction. He no longer thinks much about the chord changes—in fact, during our conversation in April 1999 he had trouble remembering them (there are only two). The chords given in the

EXAMPLE 21. "Sticks," three final chords (Jim McNeely).

EXAMPLE 22. "Sticks," solo pitch collection (Jim McNeely).

part (C major seventh ♯9 ♯6) are extremely unusual. In the beginning Neumeister sought guidance from the composer:

> [McNeely's] changes were really kind of open. C major 7 with a raised thirteen. I asked him, "What do you have in mind here?" He said to just play whatever you want. So I think about it more as chromatic over a pedal. That's sort of the way he was thinking about it too, I think. And I like that sound anyway, the dominant and the major together. I think of it more like an extension. A dominant

EXAMPLE 23. "Sticks," bass vamp (Jim McNeely).

> chord and then extend up and the upper extensions include the major seventh. Minor third and major third is more normal—a sharp nine kind of thing. I use the changes as pedal points and play over the tonality. That particular chord, I just kind of think "C-ish."

Though he has sometimes "explored themes from the piece," Neumeister says that he tries to play different things every time he performs. On the recording he develops his own ideas and has used D, A, F♯, C♯ and other notes outside the pitch collection (see Example 24). This contrasting melodic material makes his solos seem even more disjunct from the written composition. In general, he seems most concerned with exploring the sonic possibilities of his mute setup, as the composer intended.

In the overall arrangement, Neumeister's improvisations are also set in relief by their sparse accompaniment. Because this discussion is concerned mostly with his melodic ideas, little attempt has been made in Example 24 to represent the special effects such as the opening and closing of the plunger, the speechlike sounds and growls (which are difficult to capture in notation), and his interactions with the rhythm section.

After some backgrounds by the clarinets and the trumpets (with harmon mutes), Neumeister's solo winds down as the vamp repeats for sixteen measures. At m. 209 a long section of polyphony begins, leading to a climactic finish and trombone cadenza in m. 252. An eight-measure segment (Example 25) repeats four times, each time with a new voice entering in fugue-like imitation. This highly chromatic "additive" section is based on alteration of the third and seventh, this time in the key center of D. The entrance of the first voice on G♭ (F♯) and F (the thirds) begins the chromaticism, which keeps growing until all twelve pitches have been used by the time the second voice enters at m. 209 on D♭ (C♯) and C (the sevenths).

McNeely again orchestrates the band across sections, dividing the horns into three groups. Group one (the top voice) consists of flute, soprano sax, and the first three trumpets in harmon mutes. The second group consists of baritone and tenor saxes and third and fourth trombones in cup mutes. The third part to enter is played by the second alto saxophone and fourth trumpet and first trombone also in cups. The piano joins the bass in m. 225 in a highly chromatic line.

Out of this counterpoint, or what McNeely might call a "chromatic

EXAMPLE 24. "Sticks," beginning of main trombone solo (Jim McNeely). Transcription by the author.

swamp," the main melodic cell emerges once again, now in the key of E (mm. 217–24). After sixteen measures (2 × 8), the figures move down to E♭ for eight bars then up to F at m. 233 (Example 26). The cross relation of the thirds (A and A♭) intensifies as they are constantly switched back and forth in the first and second voices while a third voice works its way down chromatically from the minor seventh.

These polyphonic strands converge at m. 241 (Example 27) as the entire band (minus soloist) plays the opening motive voiced in dense harmony, first on the tetrachord centered on E♭ and then on A♭. This phrase ends with the first idiomatic jazz chords to appear in the score: $E^{\text{major7}(\flat 5)}$–$D^{\text{major7}(\flat 5)}$–$C7^{\sharp 9\flat 13}$, one of the few spots (other than the two chords in the solo section) in which chord symbols are used in the entire piece. These figures are repeated in the tetrachords of C and F, and in octave unison in E♭ and B♭, finally coming to rest on an $E^{6/9\ (\flat 5)}$ for the trombone cadenza.

In m. 252 Neumeister begins a 41-second cadenza that leads to a return

EXAMPLE 25. "Sticks," "fugal" polyphony (Jim McNeely).

of the "bridge" section. McNeely's score calls for the soloist to begin on the pitches B and B♭ (continuing the idea from the backgrounds in mm. 189–200). Instead, Neumeister starts his cadenza by oscillating between C♯ and C. After this opening figure, his improvisations are more closely related to his previous solos than to the primary motive of the piece, which has been relentlessly developed by the ensemble. Neumeister concludes the cadenza and cues in the band by playing a loose paraphrase of a rhythmic figure on the repeated note G provided by the composer.

A second appearance of the bridge, this time played with a calypso beat and supplemented with a simple chromatic riff in the brass, is followed by Neumeister's restatement of the main theme, now reduced to its most basic form: 3–♭3–1. This motive is transposed down in whole steps from E♭ to A over a D-pedal before one final statement in E. The piece closes with three dense chords, as in the end of the fugal section at m. 157 (see Example 21).

Many instances of McNeely's creative use of the rhythm section can be found in this piece. Pianistic devices are sprinkled liberally throughout, for

EXAMPLE 26. "Sticks," polyphony (Jim McNeely).

EXAMPLE 27. "Sticks," convergence (Jim McNeely).

example, the "shimmering" tinkling in the piano's uppermost register at the beginning of the central polyphonic section (mm. 209–52), the low drones in perfect fifths during the final statement of the theme, and the strange chords constructed from the pitch collection (see Example 22) near the end of the main solo section. The rhythm section explores a wide range of rhythmic feels, from funky bass vamps and calypso marches to straight-ahead swing. McNeely also relies on the creativity of his bassist, Dennis Erwin, and drummer, John Riley, to fill out certain sections. Instructions such as "light broken time" (m. 209), "colors, light time" (m. 287), and "broken walk" (m. 33) leave plenty of room for creative interpretation.

Other than his opening and closing statements Neumeister improvises freely in his allotted space. Within this austere framework McNeely has presented Neumeister with a wide variety of textures, ranging from no accompaniment (the cadenza) to drums alone, drums and bass only, rhythm section alone, and backgrounds of clarinets and muted brass. Even though McNeely has voiced the ensemble in softer colors in order not to overpower the soloist, transitions between the opening sections are more abrupt because the soloist is accompanied only by the drummer.

Neumeister accentuates this built-in contrast between solo and ensemble by staying away from the 3–♭3–1 motive during most of his soloing. Perhaps this recording illustrates some of the difficulty composers encounter when they encourage jazz soloists to improvise with unusual materials. McNeely's scales featuring major *and* minor thirds and major *and* minor sevenths are extremely unidiomatic. The VJO's long tradition of encouraging individual growth has been absorbed by McNeely in his more than twenty-five years of involvement with the band, and he raised no objections as Neumeister's soloing increasingly departed from the pitch sets and thematic material he had provided.

By Hodeir's standards, "Sticks" surely fails to achieve the degree of thematic coherence to qualify as a "masterpiece." Nevertheless, "Sticks" maintains an important element of the concerto: balance between soloist and orchestra. As shown in the above analysis, McNeely's liberation from chord progressions and chorus structures has allowed him to develop freely the melodic cell. Because of the stringent thematic coherence of the writing, the soloist might been encouraged to proceed similarly, but McNeely has freed the soloist from any such constraints. He gives Neumeister free rein to develop his own ideas. The contributions of composer and soloist, though roughly equal, are fixed in one case and frequently changing in the other. With its unusual structure, harmony, and compositional techniques (at least in jazz), "Sticks" contrasts individual freedom with highly coordinated group activity. The highly segmented structure of "Sticks" seems analogous to the technique of cross-cutting in film. Two distinct narratives alternately unfold. While Schneider's "Wyrgly" seems to follow a similar method, the improvisations of her soloists are carefully integrated into the structure and narrative of her work. Neumeister's collaborative relationship with McNeely is dialogic rather than assimilated. As a verb, rather than a noun, the title "Sticks" has implications, obvious and otherwise. By *sticking* in his solo in the improvisational sections, much as he *sticks* in his mute, Neumeister asserts the masculinist, individualistic ethos of jazz.[29]

Early in summer 1999 Neumeister left New York and the Vanguard Jazz Orchestra to take a teaching position in Austria. During the time the band searched for a replacement, "Sticks" was seldom performed. Since hiring another plunger specialist, Luis Bonilla, fellow trombonist and leader of the VJO, John Mosca, has on several occasions included "Sticks" in the Monday night set list.

Some of Ellington's and Strayhorn's concertos continue to be performed by repertory orchestras. Today players active in the repertory movement often try to faithfully reproduce their solos, if not note for note, at least in spirit. No one expects Bonilla to copy or mimic Neumeister. Though McNeely's composed portions, originally inspired by the playing of Ed Neumeister, will continue to be played with precision by the VJO, the piece eventually may move in a very different direction as Bonilla finds his own improvisational path.[30]

FORM AND IDEAS

Decisions regarding form and structure shape the development and, ultimately, the musical meaning of these works. Many composers believe that freedom from restricting chorus structures remains a vital step in the liberation of their musical thinking. Experimentation with form in jazz composition is nothing new, of course. In 1957 Gunther Schuller, mentioning Mingus, George Russell, and John Lewis, noted that "*forming* of tonal material on a larger scale [original emphasis]" had become a main concern of the younger generation.[31]

McNeely often conceptualizes the formal structure of a piece before actually composing by constructing a "time line," sometimes even determining the location of climaxes by mathematical formulas.[32] The complex form of "Sticks" involves alternating sections between the band and the soloist. In the recorded version the soloist has chosen to accentuate this built-in contrast further by developing his own ideas rather than the composer's. In "Wyrgly" Schneider also conceived of the formal structure of the piece before she decided on its musical content. Of the three pieces analyzed here, the form of "Wyrgly" is the most difficult to map because of its overlapping ideas and time feels. She has spoken often about her struggle to free herself from the confining expectations and conservatism of jazz musicians and teachers. Much of her breakthrough involved liberating herself from the head-solo-head structure that has dominated jazz composition:

> To realize I can reinvent form every time I write is daunting. But often what I want is to open up and tell a story. I want people to feel like my music takes them on a journey, brings them to different places, enticing them or surprising them. I develop the form based on my dramatic needs.[33]

Both she and McNeely acknowledge Bob Brookmeyer as a pioneering influence in developing freer concepts of form.

Schneider has used obvious forms of development such as transposition of the "monster boogie" motive, as well as subtler techniques such as manipulation of the tone row and variation of chord voicings (e.g., the opening B♭/D chord). McNeely's conceptual approach ("What if . . ?") and imaginative musical thinking have led him to develop his ideas on many levels:

harmonic (e.g., the harmony derived from the melodic cell and the different kinds of triads between the theme and the "bridge"), textural (homophony to fugal polyphony in the concerted ensemble and, for the soloist, virtually every possible combination of accompaniment except the full ensemble), orchestrational (various cross-sectional combinations of instruments), and melodic (free transposition of ideas).

Because "Cages" is more of a "review" (Bley's term) than a linear musical narrative, development is better understood in terms of the relationships between different sections: common elements such as the dissonant wide intervals, melodic motives, and the harmonic shifts of a minor third, or the shift from minor to major in sections K and R. Bley's piece seems more a series of vessels into which her soloists pour their improvisations. Much of the development of "Cages" depends on their contributions.

As a self-taught composer, Bley arrived at her style empirically through a process of trial and error. Throughout her career she benefited from the encouragement of her partners and, especially in her earlier years, by immersing herself in the jazz scene. Although such osmosis is vital to any composer, Schneider's and McNeely's compositions show the influence of years of formal training. In addition to taking advantage of the freer development less rigid harmonic architecture permits, these composers have borrowed from classical music such techniques as manipulation of tone rows and melodic cells. Within their complex macrostructures they have retained the use of more traditional, cyclical jazz forms such as the bass vamps in "Sticks" and the choruses during the tenor solo in "Wyrgly."

Each composer has found distinctive ways to convey improvisational parameters to the players. Bley works more traditionally by providing idiomatic chord changes to the soloist and rhythm section. Some of Schneider's solo sections in "Wyrgly" leave a lot more room for the improviser harmonically. Her instructions may simply indicate "E-ish" or "D-ish," without specifying major or minor. For his soloing on "Sticks," Neumeister has taken McNeely's unidiomatic chord symbol $\text{C}^{\text{major7}(\sharp 9)(\sharp 13)}$ and mentally converted it to "C-ish." In addition to sharing her personal feelings about a piece, Schneider tries to shape the dramatic contours of an improvisation by using unconventional instructions on her parts, like "over the top" and "ease up."

Bley and Schneider are part of a long tradition of female composers in jazz—Lil Hardin Armstrong, Mary Lou Williams, and Toshiko Akiyoshi. Like Bley, most have been keyboardists as well as composer-arrangers. As Lucy Green has suggested, because, "in jazz, improvisation has more status than notated composition," women have felt less discouraged from pursuing composition. Moreover, composition occurs in the private sphere, permitting less public display of creativity, more in keeping with traditional notions of femininity.[34] As a male composer working in a male-dominated idiom in a patriarchal society, McNeely may be less conscious of gendered codes and strategies. It is doubtful that he is often forced to think of himself as a "male composer." Of course, this unawareness does not mean that such gendered elements are not at play, however unconsciously, in his compositional style.

Bley and Schneider have reacted to gender pressures in very different ways. Their different strategies may reflect generational differences. As Schneider's confidence has grown, she has become less concerned with proving something. Rather than compete in traditional masculinist terms, Schneider plays with gendered musical conventions in highly personal ways. While keeping a similarly playful attitude, Bley's hypermasculinist musical discourse becomes part of a strategy to challenge dominant power structures on their own terms. At the time of my interview, in summer 2004, she was busy composing music for an upcoming tour of Charlie Haden's Liberation Music Orchestra. Song titles on her recent album *Looking for America* (2003) ask "OG Can UC?" and "Whose Broad Stripes?" The next chapter looks closely at the music of another composer whose hypermasculinist discourse embraced class and racial struggles in the United States.

Chapter 7

On the Edge

Sue Mingus and the Mingus Big Band

"I felt like I was being flung by a huge human slingshot way out into the universe," says Alex Norris about the first time he played trumpet with the Mingus Big Band. "And things were flying by me, like trees and people and buildings. I had no idea what was happening. It kind of shocked me at first. But then I realized, this is Mingus's music—this is actually the way he did his music." The trombonist Clark Gayton adds, "Anything you learned in any other big band does not apply here. Throw all that out the window. In other bands you can basically follow the chart and make it through the gig. In this band you have to be always on your toes and be aware of where you are at all times. You can never really sit back and chill and listen to the music."

The Mingus band is not for musicians who play it safe. Soloists screech and honk, trying to outdo one another. The legions of young fans who gather on Thursday nights at the band's home base, the Time Café,[1] spur the musicians on by shouting and cheering, rewarding those who have played the loudest, highest, or fastest. Sue Mingus, emulating her late husband, Charles, encourages players to take chances even if they sometimes miss their marks. Critical reception of the band typically emphasizes these centrifugal forces (summed up in the title of one review, "Mingus Lives! New Adventures in Big-Band Chaos Theory"). Like her late husband, Sue Mingus urges the musicians to "play themselves"—to find their own voices rather than imitate someone else.[2] To many listeners, Mingus's presence is palpable: his spirit seems to hover over the proceedings.[3]

Ironically, for most of his career Charles Mingus was frustrated in his desire to lead a big band playing his compositions.[4] Though his virtuosic bass playing and forceful leadership received more attention, Mingus's first and foremost interest was composing. Inspired by classical composers and his lifelong adulation of Ellington, Mingus could stake out more clearly the ownership of his creations as a composer. His music, like his personal relationships, disrupted complacency. This desire to put musicians "on edge" can be understood, along with his cultivation of the "angry man of jazz" image, as critical interventions in a society that restricted black men's ability to control their destinies and denied their manhood.[5] Much of Mingus's rage stemmed from the powerlessness he felt in the face of white control of the music industry. While his anger often found expression through an exaggerated machismo, most forcefully articulated in his fictionalized autobiography, *Beneath the Underdog*, he also craved close, intimate relationships. Mingus depended on his domestic partners for emotional and professional support, and his wives, Celia and Sue, performed vital roles in his career. Ultimately, Mingus's hypermasculinist discourse not only challenged other musicians and dominant racist power structures but also turned inward, as reflected in his relentless drive for mastery and spiritual fulfillment.

In the critically acclaimed and economically successful Mingus Big Band, Susan Graham Mingus has brought to life her late husband's dream of establishing a standing orchestra. Finding herself in a role she "could scarcely have imagined" when Charles was alive, she supervises all aspects of the music, even to the point of "occasionally storming the stage."[6] Her recruiting of "one hundred of the best musicians in New York" throws together a diverse assortment of jazz musicians, many of whom rarely encounter one another in other bands. Although very few women pass through the band, the musicians vary greatly in terms of ethnic background, style, and experience. Gayton says of the band's personnel, "There's no rhyme or reason to it. . . . [Some chairs] are ten deep. Some people will get a tour and they will take that and then the rotation will change. It changes constantly." Even with this flux, Gayton observes, "there is a common thread through all of it. Some people kind of anchor it. [Tenor saxophonist] John Stubblefield is a major component in anchoring the band. There's a lot of qualities that the musicians must have, so a lot of things are constant, yet they're changing all the time."

But the unsettled atmosphere and intensity are not only a product of this constant change. At a deeper level the musicians believe that these qualities reside in the music itself. In Stubblefield's words, "That vibe is in the notes that Mingus wrote, that vibe is in there. It just keeps you on the edge." After examining how Sue Mingus's personnel policies and style of management help to maintain Charles's presence in the band, I seek to explain how, even with their beauty, "the notes" keep musicians "on the edge."

LEADERSHIP AND DOMESTICITY

Despite the difficulty of maintaining domestic relationships in the jazz universe—musicians' time away from home on the road, temptations to infidelity, and the closed homosocial fraternity of many jazz scenes—domestic partnerships have been crucial to more than a few jazz musicians' careers. Sometimes these roles have been quite public—for example, Gladys Hampton's management of her husband Lionel's business or Alice Coltrane's musical collaboration with her husband, John. More often women's contributions have gone on behind the scenes. In the subcultural and often chaotic existence that characterizes many jazz musicians' lives, women brought a modicum of stability, not only through maintaining a home, but also, often, through employment that provided steady income and benefits. Nicole Rustin credits many jazz musicians' domestic relationships with helping them to achieve "middle-class respectability." Policing of interracial relationships in the United States left this avenue less open to racially mixed couples. As Mingus discloses in his memoirs, he and his partners often were forced to conceal their relationships.[7]

Even without outside pressures, life with Mingus was not easy. Like some Romantic artists, he seemed intent on blurring the categories of genius and madness. In *Beneath the Underdog* Mingus describes himself as split between an angry firebrand, a trusting, almost naive innocent, and an outside observer caught helplessly in between (3). His memoirs depict a misguided self-imposed hospitalization at Bellevue, as well as his fascination and eventual disillusionment with psychoanalysis. *Underdog* also describes Mingus's troubled relationship with his father, an authoritarian military man whose attitude toward his own mixed racial heritage reproduced both inter- and intraracial hierarchies based on skin color (26). With his light complexion, the younger Mingus was occasionally able to "pass" (181–82). Of course, if his racial background was discovered, the dominant white society considered him black. At the same time, as a youngster he experienced rejection from his black schoolmates (52). For Mingus, his outsider status, as the title of his memoirs suggests, could be a source of unfathomable bitterness.[8]

When after years of struggle *Beneath the Underdog* finally saw print, jazz fans and critics reacted in horror or disgust to his unbridled machismo and detailed sexual exploits. As recent scholarly discourse has suggested, Mingus's sexual braggadocio and fascination with pimpdom can be understood as allegorical responses to what he saw as the "whoring" and exploitation of black jazz musicians.[9] As a bandleader he felt complicit in the "pimping" of his stable of sidemen. Throughout the text machismo constantly vacillates with obvious sympathy for women as fellow "underdogs."[10] In stark juxtaposition to its crude and graphic language, *Underdog* also chronicles Mingus's need for intimacy and determined quest for spiritual enlightenment. All these conflicting emotions and desires found expression in his music, as evidenced in such introspective titles as "Myself When I Am Real," "Self-Portrait in Three Colors," and "Passions of a Man" and heartfelt tributes to partners, such as "Celia" and "Sue's Changes."

In 1952, in an effort to escape white domination of the music industry, in partnership with Max Roach, Mingus and his second wife, Celia, founded Debut Records. Celia continued to work various day jobs as she managed Debut's affairs, until in 1957 the label folded and Celia and Charles separated in 1958 (198). As she later described the situation to Brian Priestley, "I . . . found it difficult to function as his wife and manager . . . because he didn't want his wife telling him what to do." Their relationship could have survived, she felt, only if she had "completely sacrificed" everything she wanted. "And I couldn't do that," she said.[11] Though Mingus felt betrayed, they remained on mostly friendly terms. Several years later when Celia went to work for Fantasy records, Mingus gave Fantasy the entire Debut catalog. Ironically, after the demise of their record company, Mingus's career began an upward trajectory. A fertile relationship with the producer Neshui Ertegun led to a series of enduringly popular LPs on Atlantic. In the early 1960s Mingus forged ahead in innovative work with musicians such as Eric Dolphy and Jaki Byard and began an association with the musician-friendly Impulse label.

Mingus first met Susan Ungaro Graham at a gig at the Five Spot in July 1964 as she was in the throes of the breakup of her first marriage. Sue has provided an intimate account of their stormy relationship in *Tonight at Noon: A Love Story.* Despite an instant attraction, their relationship started slowly. As they became more involved she managed to avoid moving in with him for nearly a decade, despite his persistent entreaties. Nevertheless, early in their relationship Mingus managed to enlist Sue in his efforts to start another business, Charles Mingus Enterprises. As she describes it, "[B]usiness with Mingus was a blend of theatrical derring-do, frequent time-outs, fits of brilliant imagination, and constant creative trouble" (42). In his dealings with musicians, she noted he was often "more concerned with conviction than accuracy" (47). She also observed his "impromptu firings and rehirings of band members; his explanations of their flaws ('mental tardiness'); fiery lectures to the band; and the familiar full spectrum of soaring composition, personality clashes, musical ruptures, and, finally, resolution" (45). Despite his domineering personality, in their rather frequent arguments Sue held her ground, at one point warning him, "I'm not a sideman reading your notes" (47). As the record company declined and Mingus's fortunes along with it, he gradually withdrew from the music scene. His eviction from his Manhattan loft and subsequent arrest in November 1966 was captured in Thomas Reichman's documentary *Mingus.* In this now cult-classic footage, while cradling a shotgun, Mingus lashes out at the United States ("My country 'tis of thee, sweet land of slavery"), muses over the desirability of finding an ideal mate, ponders conspiracy theories surrounding the assassination of Kennedy, and fulminates on other subjects before finally blasting a round into the wall. This action is not so much an act of rage or defiance, as he takes obvious pleasure in its sheer audacity. Similarly Mingus's music often mixed anger and frustration with scathing humor and political farce as can be heard in songs such as "Oh Lord, Don't Let Them Drop That Atomic Bomb on Me," "Eat That Chicken," and "Fables of Faubus."[12]

After a turbulent period marked by Mingus's frequent outbursts and tender reconciliations, Sue and Charles parted in 1968. Mingus's career accelerated its decline.[13] A "chance" encounter brought them back together the following year, and Sue once again became active in his career. She helped to set up an extensive European tour for fall 1970 that led to the release of his first new albums in five years. By printing excerpts of his controversial autobiography in her "alternative" periodical *Changes,* she managed to interest Knopf in publishing *Beneath the Underdog.* A Guggenheim fellowship in composition in 1971 also boosted his spirits. They finally "gave their love an address" by establishing a common domicile in 1973 (111) and married two years later. They lived as a "bona fide couple" for "five happy years" (118) until Charles's health began to deteriorate. In 1977 he was diagnosed with amyotrophic lateral sclerosis, Lou Gehrig's disease.

After Mingus's death in 1979 Sue's experiences as Mingus's domestic partner and ostensible manager were to prove useful. She was asked to assemble a band for a two-night tribute at Carnegie Hall. Calling on some of his old sidemen, such as John Handy, Jimmy Knepper, and Dannie Richmond, she used the same instrumentation Mingus had used in the late fifties: four horns with a rhythm section.

It was instantly clear to her that it was possible to capture "the spirit, energy, and intent of Mingus' music":

> It was really quite astonishing. No one had anticipated a Mingus band without Mingus himself. Particularly in Europe the notion was inconceivable. His personality was too large, his presence on the bandstand too powerful for his music to be played by anyone else. Other musicians played Monk and Duke; they did not play Mingus. The composer overshadowed his own compositions.[14]

Mingus's band was reincarnated on a more regular basis as the Mingus Dynasty in the 1980s. In 1989, with Gunther Schuller conducting, a thirty-one-piece ensemble performed his two-hour monumental opus, *Epitaph.* As her confidence grew Sue abandoned her practice of hiring only musicians who had played with Mingus. She formed a big band in 1991 to play Thursday nights at the Time Café. Though Mingus had left one of the largest compositional legacies in jazz, very little was scored for big band. Almost immediately the leader, trombonist Sam Burtis, and other band members were put to work transcribing and reorchestrating his works for the expanded instrumentation. The band did not start touring until summer 1994, when it went on the European jazz festival circuit. Enduring interest in Mingus's music along with the band's eclectic approach brought critical and popular acclaim and numerous awards for best big band in 1997.[15]

Sue Mingus brings a nurturing spirit to the Mingus Big Band, as evidenced in her constant search for young, talented players. She is involved in every aspect of the band, though she "considers her role to be primarily spiritual and administrative," as she told one reporter. "She looks for lost saxophone screws, gives feedback to the soundman, handles bookings, holds court with visiting jazz fans and dignitaries, arranges the play lists and even chooses the order of soloists."[16]

Over the years Sue Mingus has grown in her leadership role. In the beginning, not only were musicians unaccustomed to following orders from a woman, but many questioned her musical qualifications. While she might possess intimate knowledge of Charles's personality and career, Sue's musical background was limited (her mother had been a harpist; Sue studied piano as a child). One of her early musical directors, complaining that a "nonmusician" was making "musical decisions," disagreed with her "on almost everything." Another member, commenting on her lack of experience, remembers bringing in arrangement and asking who would be on lead trumpet:

> "Oh, Jack Walrath leads the band." I said, "*Sue,* I'm not talking about who *leads* the band, who's playing the *lead trumpet.*" "Oh, who hits the highest notes? I think so-and-so can play high notes." She didn't know what a lead trumpet was. She didn't have a lead trombone player for many years, she'd call different guys every night. That became very frustrating for me as an arranger.

Without a consistent lead player, the section cannot arrive at uniform phrasing, articulation, and dynamics. Of course, this lack of consistency also accentuated the looser, more chaotic ensemble blend for which the band is known.

Handling such criticisms was not easy, and Sue was occasionally reduced to tears. Her memoirs recall an episode in which she over-heard several musicians in the bands discussing her leadership: " 'Hey, man,' one of them said. 'She doesn't know the first thing about what she's doing.' I couldn't believe what I was hearing. The speaker was the same musician who had helped me and advised me from the start, the one I thought was in my corner the most."

Meanwhile, other musicians offered support, assuring her that she would "become a trouper." Indeed, "after two decades on the road as 'one of the guys,' " she has "come to feel a part of the Mingus music and a kinship with the extraordinary musicians who keep it alive."[17] While admitting that she is "not a professional musician and do[es] not perform on stage," she remains the ultimate authority. Going against her instructions risks incurring her wrath, and everyone knows other musicians are waiting in the wings. In a *New York Post* column an unnamed band member is quoted, "I think I understand what Mingus was talking about when he wrote the tune 'The Eye of Hurricane Sue.' "[18]

A certain friction, among the players and between them and the leader, is inevitable in any large group. Running the band might be easier if the players had similar backgrounds. As Steve Slagle, lead alto saxophonist, points out, "When you have different people, you do have to deal with more than one kind of personality, and some guys that aren't as punctual in their time, or guys that dress differently. As a leader it can create more problems, more headaches, for you." Different backgrounds contribute to disagreements over musical issues (tempos, blending, dynamics, etc.), which in Slagle's view is not necessarily a bad thing:

> I think some of that friction is what makes the music happen. That's the legacy of Mingus too. He could hardly do anything without punching somebody. I'm not for that, but I find that a little healthy argument, in my own bands, some of my closest friends, we also argue over things, not to the point of pulling a knife on anyone, but a little bit of that is OK. I think it makes for a good product in the end.

Stubblefield believes that this attitude is also important to the audience. After all, people came to see Mingus never knowing what to expect. He might get in an argument with a musician, deliver a tirade to the audience, or stop a tune abruptly. Stubblefield explains, "We're not saying that people are going to pay to see us at the Time Café start throwing music at each other if something's not right, but we'll carry on the tradition; if something's not right about the music, we might stop it, because that honesty was not found a lot in people that were performing in Mingus's time or thereafter."

The following account relies heavily on information and observations supplied by two performers and arrangers who have worked closely with Sue Mingus. Steve Slagle, who worked with Carla Bley, Charlie Haden, and Ray Barretto throughout much of the 1980s, began playing in the band about six months after it was formed in 1991. In addition to contributing arrangements, he eventually became the band's musical director and front man until a disagreement with Sue Mingus led to an extended "sabbatical" beginning in 1999. Michael Philip Mossman has played a wide range of musical styles and idioms, from Latin to mainstream and avant-garde jazz. Though he frequently performs in the band, his primary involvement has been providing arrangements for the band and for Sue's latest project, the Mingus Orchestra. Interviews with the tenor saxophonist John Stubblefield provided valuable insights because of his central role in the band and his long association with the music, dating back to a stint with the bassist himself in 1971.

PERSONNEL

Most jazz orchestras grow organically out of existing social networks. In the Mingus band, however, instead of being musician directed, the flow of personnel is closely overseen by Sue Mingus. While players may on rare occasions (such as a last-minute emergency) call their own replacements, the general procedure is to notify Mingus so that she can cover the position. According to band members, she prefers to try out musicians whom she has discovered or heard about on her own.

Though she follows her own instincts for bringing people in, a prospective member must still meet the approval of the rest of the band. The Russian bassist Boris Kozlov recalls, "Sue called me, and I just did this gig at the Time Café." Sue didn't make it to the club that night, but "the next day she calls me and says, 'Would you like to go on this tour?' And I'm sayin', 'Wait a second, you haven't heard me.' She says, 'Well, I called fourteen other guys.' "

Being an accomplished musician does not guarantee that a player will be called back either. The pianist David Kikoski recalls that it took a while for Sue to accept him: "I guess she just started hearin' my name around. I was workin' with Randy Brecker. I just got a call from Sue and I went down to play and she said something like, 'You play great, we're not really sure if you're right for the band.' She kept callin' me and eventually she sort of settled for me."

In Stubblefield's words:

> Sue will not call the average player. She'll call those people who are on the edge. On that musical edge. That's what Mingus was like, he was always on the edge, walkin' the tightrope. We've had some great people that have come through, and it worked well and sometimes it didn't. It's basically a vibe. If they have the vibe of playin' Mingus's music, we know it and that's what we go with.

Although Sue continued to employ seasoned elders such as the late Britt Woodman (who grew up in Los Angeles with her husband) and consummate professionals such as Randy Brecker (who participated in Mingus's last recordings),[19] she also has been attracted to uncompromising firebrands (Ku-umba Frank Lacy) and young "discoveries" (Seamus Blake). Stubblefield confirms: "That's the thing that we try to keep going as Mingus did; he would bring in musicians who were not known and give them a shot and find what they have to say."

Unlike many of the leaders in New York, Sue Mingus has constructed a jazz world that remains ethnically, racially, and stylistically diverse. In a sense, the band reflects her late husband's multiracial background and hiring practices. He regularly employed white musicians, from the trombonist Jimmy Knepper and the tenor saxophonist Bobby Jones to the trumpeter Jack Walrath. For the Mingus Big Band, Sue has hired both white and black musicians and has included Europeans (especially Russians, for example, bassist Kozlov and trumpeter Alex Sipiagin), Latinos, and others.

Slagle, former lead alto player and sometime music director, believes that the diversity in the band is one of its greatest strengths:

> That's the one thing that people should learn from the Mingus band, and I would hand this to Sue Mingus, as the person who contracts the band. She doesn't draw her players just from one clique or one source. We all can be guilty of this, but as a big band leader it's more obvious 'cause you got, let's say, sixteen people. . . .
>
> They tend to be too similar [and] sound too much alike. . . . There are little groups within communities and sometimes these bands are drawn from just one group and I find that to be boring. Sue Mingus tends to draw from a very large spectrum of people, whether it be total studio musicians, to total outcast, kind of avant-garde guys that would never get a studio gig, and she puts them all together and creates something that works out of that. I think to audiences it's more interesting and to the music it's often more interesting.

Despite her commitments to diversity and nonconformity, on one of the band's first tours Sue tried to coordinate the band's clothing and provided everyone with white T-shirts that featured a picture of Mingus. Her efforts met resistance. Slagle recalls:

> One concert, somewhere big like Berlin, we all came in the T-shirts and Stubblefield, God bless him, came backstage with a real slick, pin-striped three-piece suit and tie on. Sue commented, and John said, in a totally positive spirit, "Sue, this is my vance [thing], and this is what I want to wear." Sue is not that thick, and the rest of the tour we all wore what we wanted—from T-shirts to three-piece suits.

Like their varied styles of dress, players display contrasting musical personalities on the bandstand. The bass trombonist Earl McIntyre, a veteran of the Thad Jones/Mel Lewis Orchestra and many other bands, says, "One of the things that's really different about *this* big band is the amount of individuality that you're able to bring to the music as a player. There's not as much latitude in terms of interpretation with other big bands." One tenor saxophonist who played with the band describes it as "full of good players, but the looseness of the approach can be haphazard—it can go either way." This player was not called back to perform with the band again and felt that Sue Mingus probably thought he "played it too safe." He confirmed the perception of the masculinist ethos of the band by his choice of metaphors: "She wants somebody who will pull his dick out, extroverts like __________."

Because Sue Mingus casts such a wide net, the Mingus Big Band is unusual in that its players have vastly different concepts of ensemble blend, a fact that guarantees the group will sound less regimented and more raucous than other bands. Individuated styles of ensemble playing grate against the sensibilities of many musicians and listeners accustomed to more homogeneous or "refined" (in their view) ensemble blends. As Michael Mossman puts it:

> Some people *hate* that music. Some people can't stand it. A good conductor can spend fifteen or twenty minutes fine tuning or balancing one chord in the

woodwinds—working on that and elevating that to a very high art. It's just one form of art though. A musician who spends much of the time focusing on that, that's what they look for. When they hear something that's not that, they're gonna be thinking about how they would fix it. But that's not the point, it doesn't *need* fixing. It's a different thing.

To Mossman, it's a matter of a fundamental difference in philosophy: "Some people think that the whole thing is subjugating your personality for the greater good. What the Mingus band is about is that the greater good is when everyone goes for it."

ARRANGERS

Widely considered the first modern jazz composer to exploit the full breadth of historical resources in jazz, Charles Mingus absorbed influences from early New Orleans jazz and mainstream swing to bebop modernism and beyond. Drawing from his own experiences, which included playing with New Orleans trombonist Kid Ory, Louis Armstrong, Lionel Hampton's big band, Charlie Parker, and, eventually, young "radicals" such as Eric Dolphy, from an early age Mingus also explored classical music while absorbing black popular and gospel styles from his surroundings.

In the Mingus Big Band the involvement of many different arrangers adds another element to this eclectic mix. Contributions from Chico O'Farrill are more traditional. Arrangements by band members such as Slagle and Ronnie Cuber tend to remain faithful to the original recordings. Walrath writes more adventurous arrangements. Mossman specializes in Latin charts, and on some pieces the entire band works collectively, in the spirit of Mingus's Jazz Workshop. Occasionally the connections with Mingus are more direct. Transcriptions of early arrangements by Mingus himself have been donated to the band by Lincoln Center,[20] and Mingus's chief arranger, Sy Johnson, continues to write for the band. Working from confusing and sometimes contradictory scores in Mingus's hand, Gunther Schuller and Andrew Homzy have reassembled an important but never entirely performed work, *Epitaph,*[21] and adapted parts of it for the big band.

Even though he wrote works of great complexity and length (as in some of his through-composed pieces and *Epitaph*), Mingus at times expressed dissatisfaction with notated music. In the liner notes to one of his best-selling albums, *Mingus Ah Um* (recorded in May 1959), he wrote, "My present working methods use very little written material. I 'write' compositions on mental score paper, then lay out the composition part by part to the musicians."[22] The Mingus Big Band's size and constant need for subs largely preclude such methods. Many of Mingus's "head charts" have been written out.[23] However, Sue Mingus and the band still try to maintain much of the "jazz workshop" atmosphere. On tunes that are worked out together, arranging credits are given to "the Mingus Big Band Collective" (e.g., "Dizzy Moods" on *¡Que Viva Mingus!*) rather than to an individual.

In his liner notes to *Mingus Dynasty* (recorded in November 1959), Mingus criticized the typical big band for "playing arrangements as though there were only three instruments in the world: a trumpet, a trombone, and a saxophone, with the other three or four trumpets, three or four trombones, and four or five saxophones there just to make the arrangement sound louder by playing harmonic support to the leading trumpet, trombone, and saxophone." His plan for a larger ensemble called for "thinking out the form that each instrument as an individual is going to play in relation to all the others in the composition. This would replace the old hat system of passing the melody from section to section, for example from trumpet to reed section while the trombones run through their tired routine of French horn chordal sounds."[24]

As a way to get beyond some of the clichés of big band arranging and in order to focus on individual players, Mingus emphasized linear composing. "I think it's time to discard these tired arrangements," he wrote, "and save only the big Hollywood production introduction and ending which uses a ten or more note chord. If these ten notes were used as a starting point for several melodies and finished as a linear composition—with parallel or simultaneous and juxtaposed musical thoughts—we might come up with some creative big band jazz."[25]

As much as Sue Mingus and her arrangers try to put these principles into practice, it is not easy to be creative in expanding to the big band format while preserving their original character, arrangements designed for only three or four horns. The obvious solution is simply to pile the players on each part in unison or in harmony: the trombone part is given to the trombone section, the trumpet part to the trumpet section, and so on. Generally, the Mingus arrangers have resisted the temptation to thicken his lines with harmony.

Mossman explains the difficulty arrangers face as they try to balance the requirement to retain a clear Mingus identity with the desire to develop their own ideas:

> The problem we've had with arranging the Mingus things is that if you get too much into arranging, then you lose "the Mingus." When I first started working with Sue arranging, I had all these ideas. She said, "Well, we tried that and it started getting too far away from Charles." It became more *them,* which is natural, than *Mingus.* You know, shout choruses, solis, and the kinds of things that arrangers use to develop. What Sue was saying was that she wanted to preserve Charles's thing. It put somewhat of a limitation on how far you could go with the material. But at the same time you didn't want to just have it be just a tran-

scription. You wanted to add some things, first to add some length to the arrangements and add some variety.

By avoiding some of the standard devices of big band writing and focusing on melodic lines rather than complex harmony, Mossman and other Mingus Big Band arrangers have found ways to keep the distinctive Mingus qualities at the forefront of the music. "It's not like Thad Jones's band or the Basie band," says Mossman. "It's somewhat like the Ellington band. In the Ellington band, the secret was voices, individual voices. That's the thing we found with Mingus: if you're going to have a lot of harmony, generally it's the sum total of a lot of moving voices."

The discussion that follows is organized around characteristics of Mingus's composing that were vital to his music and help to keep musicians "on the edge" in the Mingus Big Band. Five procedures have remained important to the Mingus band arrangers: preserving unison voicings, foregrounding dissonance, additive composition, collective improvisation, and pushing instruments to their limits.

Unisons

Somewhat paradoxically, jazz worlds that favor heterogeneous sound, despite the emphasis on individuality, maintain a high incidence of unisons. One might expect composers to allot as many different pitches as possible to the players, but in practice more complicated voicings require more careful blending. The players of the Mingus Big Band tend to play unisons in a way that preserves the individual identity of each musician.

In more traditional settings the usual idea is for players to sound as one. Even when several different timbres are involved, they should be combined so that no one obtrudes. Players often use darker, drier sounds, and composers avoid extremes in range that can create intonation problems. Many section players "take the edge off" their sounds and play underneath the lead player. By emphasizing the fundamental, they can avoid harsh grating between the overtones emitted by the different instruments. One handbook for jazz band directors states unequivocally that "no one should use vibrato during unisons."[26]

The Mingus Big Band approaches unisons differently. Unisons are often played loud, even abrasively, and vibrato is applied liberally. Composers and players do not shy away from registral extremes. Their sense of a unison is "not what it would be with the Carnegie band or the Mintzer band," notes Mossman (who has played in all three bands).

In "Ecclusiastics" (from *Mingus Big Band 93*) the arranger, Sy Johnson, has given the two tenors, John Stubblefield and Craig Handy, the main theme of

EXAMPLE 28. "Ecclusiastics" (Charles Mingus).

EXAMPLE 29. "Jump Monk" (Charles Mingus).

the piece in unison. They begin on their lowest note, $G^{\sharp 1}$, which is a difficult note to blend. Stubblefield and Handy do not hold back; each plays with a full, distinctly individual sound. The long, slow bend in the second and third measures (shown in Example 28), difficult to execute by one tenor, must be coordinated by two (the original on the 1961 release *Mingus, Oh Yeah,* Atlantic 1377, included a trombone on this line, which, with its slide, can easily make this bend). Both tenors make little effort to coordinate the rate and depth of their vibrato or to sound like only one saxophone.

On "Jump Monk" *(Gunslinging Birds)* the entire band plays the melody in unison (Example 29). Because the three-and-one-half-octave range is beyond the capability of most instruments, octave displacement must be used. At one point or another almost all the instruments in the band will be at an extreme end of their range when playing this line, a requirement that does not encourage timidity in playing.

Dissonance and Harmony

Charles Mingus's compositions range from simple gospel and blues-based riff charts (e.g., "Work Song") to lush, harmonically intricate ballads ("Celia") and lengthy through-composed pieces containing little idiomatic harmony ("Children's Hour of Dream" from *Epitaph*). Sometimes all these levels of harmonic complexity may be combined in a single work ("Open Letter to Duke").

During most of his career, Mingus's options as a composer were limited by the size of his groups—usually two to four horns plus rhythm section. In expanding his works most of the Mingus Big Band arrangers seem to heed Mingus's dictum and harmonize sparingly, thereby retaining the clarity of the original recordings. In "Nostalgia in Times Square" the stark beauty of

EXAMPLE 30. "The Man Who Never Sleeps" (Charles Mingus).

Mingus's exposed major seconds could easily be lost in expanding the harmony into full-fledged chords. The Mingus Big Band arrangement by Ronnie Cuber on *Mingus Big Band 93* keeps the seconds in the foreground of the orchestration, retaining much of the dissonance of the original.

One compositional texture that works well with individualized instrumental timbres is melody and countermelody. Very often one or both melodies are played in unison. Mingus had a penchant for writing melodies consisting of two-bar cells that have a binary structure—one bar of motion and another of stasis. Some of the tunes containing these cells are "Farewell Farwell," "Reincarnation of a Lovebird," "Work Song," "Self-Portrait in Three Colors" and the swinging section of "Cumbia and Jazz Fusion." As can be seen in Example 30, in the first eight bars of the last chorus of "The Man Who Never Sleeps," Mingus has written two melodies that have this cell structure. He has offset them so that the moving part of one occurs while the other is sustaining a note.

Sometimes Mingus used shorter cells, in ballads in particular, of only one measure that were divided into two beats each. "Duke Ellington's Sound of Love," "Celia," "Diane" (Example 31), and "Us Is Two" are four examples of such tunes.

Mingus also wrote polyphonic compositions in which the lines move concurrently. "Self-Portrait in Three Colors" uses additive procedures to introduce, one at a time, a melody and two countermelodies. In combination with the first and second parts, the third part produces some dissonant grinds (half-steps and minor ninths) that seem to express Mingus's inner conflict.[27] The dissonance is all the more striking with each voice kept in unison, undiluted by harmony.

EXAMPLE 31. "Diane" (Charles Mingus).

Michael Mossman's arrangement of "Tijuana Gift Shop" preserves the unison of Mingus's original in the first chorus of the theme's opening statement. In the second chorus Mossman adds some harmony and counterlines in several spots. He has also contributed a long, sinewy background line played in unison and octaves by all the winds, part of which is included in Example 32. In the last four measures the line bifurcates into two-part harmony, consisting only of the root and the seventh, that is at once mildly dissonant and very open. "One of the things that is a hallmark of Mingus, and especially the big band," Mossman says, "is these real bombastic kinds of unison lines that maybe go into harmony at the end." Both the background line, with its recurring motive of a triplet moving to a stationary note, and the thin harmony are in keeping with the Mingus style. The harmony on the head and this background are about the only things Mossman has added to the original.

Mossman typically begins the process of arranging a Mingus tune by transcribing several versions from recordings and comparing them. In "Tijuana Gift Shop" he did not "just want to have a head and solos and the head out, which is what the original was." Realizing that he "needed something to go in between there," he came up with the idea of using a background—"but a very Mingus background." He wanted to "make it sound like Mingus but have it do the job: a bridging element to get from one place to another."

The two-note harmony at the end is also something that Mossman thought sounded like Mingus. "It's extremely spare," he says. More "like shells" than full harmony.

EXAMPLE 32. "Tijuana Gift Shop" (Charles Mingus; Michael Mossman, arr.).

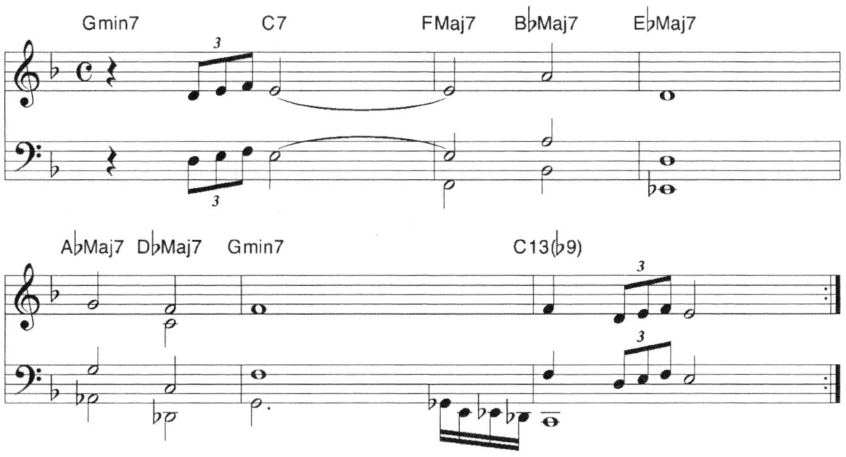

> Mingus was a very contrapuntal writer. So it's not so much a thing about heavy chord voicings. I think it's much more the melodic line and just hinting at what the harmony is (which is basically what that background line is) just enough underneath it to show when the changes start coming faster.

Additive Composition

In his interviews with Alan Lomax for the Library of Congress in 1938, Jelly Roll Morton explains the importance of riffs—short, repeated phrases—in New Orleans jazz. Riffs, a defining characteristic of the jazz that emerged from Kansas City and the Southwest in the 1920s and 1930s, were often created by musicians on the bandstand during public performance. Each section of the band invented different riffs. As the arrangement neared its climax, interlocking riffs were piled on top of each other. Tunes such as the Basie theme song, "One O'Clock Jump," were built from such cumulative rhythmic/melodic ideas.[28] Riff-based arrangements became the basis of much big band dance music during the swing era.

Additive procedures work well with heterogeneous ensemble styles because the parts are introduced one at a time. The listener's attention focuses on each new riff, relieving the performer of some responsibility for preserving the intelligibility of the separate melodic strands. Instead of striving for precise, uniform execution, the players on each line are freer to revel in the rhythm and in their own individual sounds.

In his arrangement of "E's Flat Ah's Flat Too" (*Live in Time,* 1996), Sy John-

EXAMPLE 33. "E's Flat Ah's Flat Too" (Charles Mingus; Sy Johnson, arr.).

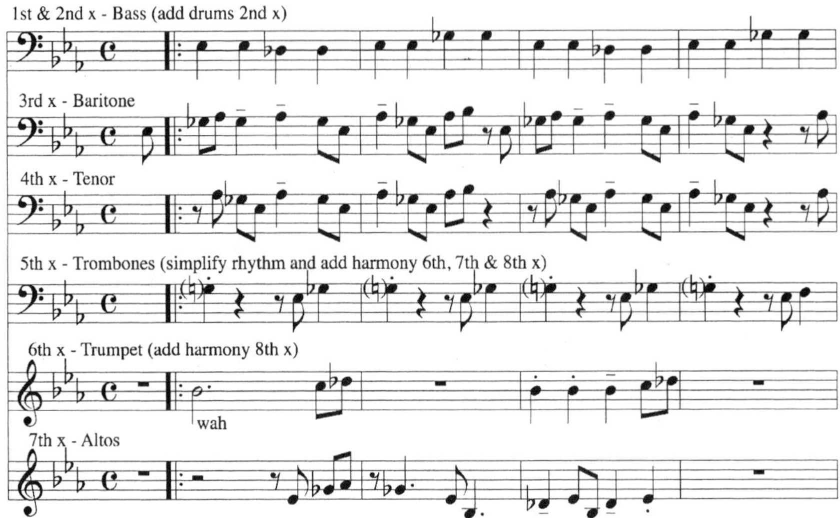

son preserved most of the composer's ideas when he expanded the original arrangement for six horns to the big band format (recorded in 1959; released in 1960 on *Blues and Roots,* Atlantic SD-1305). Beginning with unaccompanied bass, Johnson gradually layers instruments (drums, piano, baritone and tenor saxophones, trombones, trumpets, and, finally, alto saxophones) until, by the seventh and eighth choruses, the twelve-bar blues reaches an even higher level of density than the original version.

Additive techniques and riffing are also important to salsa, in sections called *moñas,* a similarity that has enhanced the compatibility of Mingus's compositions with Latin music. Often the rhythm section will spontaneously go into a Latin groove, surprising the rest of the band. Such unexpected turns keep the music fresh and interesting.

When he arranged "Los Mariachis" Mossman contributed some additional backgrounds, which enter one at a time. As they combine with the improvisations of the three soloists, these backgrounds heighten the level of density beyond Mingus's original version on *Tijuana Moods.* Mossman explains, "Mingus's music is dense, he was not afraid to push that level of density. With a larger ensemble we can really go far with that."

Collective Improvisation

The Mingus Big Band exalts collective improvisation to a degree surpassed perhaps only in early jazz and a few avant-garde ensembles. In traditional

New Orleans or Dixieland styles, jazz players kept from intruding on each other's sonic space by using different phrasing, tessitura, and timbres. The trumpet extemporized on the melody, the clarinet played obbligato figures, and the trombone outlined the harmony in "tailgate" fashion. In the Mingus band collective improvisation is less codified and may occur anywhere in the arrangement. It may involve any number of players and often includes the entire band.

Of the sixty-five tracks in the recorded repertoire of the Mingus Big Band as of 2005, twenty-five display some form of collective improvisation (see Table 3). Although occasionally resembling a noisy argument, these sections commonly sound more like a boisterous party, prayer meeting, or, in one instance, a hog-calling contest. "Tijuana Gift Shop" and "Los Mariachis" suggest the sound of a wild "south of the border" excursion as numerous members of the band improvise over extended additive vamps.[29] "Ecclusiastics" builds to a frenzied climax as John Stubblefield "preaches" on his tenor and members of his "congregation" join in. On "Hog Callin' Blues" various players contribute shrieking hog calls and piglike squeals.

The Mingus Big Band and its arrangers have found many creative ways to weave collective improvisation into the musical fabric. Used to great advantage at the beginning of a piece, collective improvisation has the effect of making the tune seem to emerge from chaos. At the start of "Don't Be Afraid, the Clown's Afraid, Too" the band ad-libs strange sounds using instruments (or parts of them) and whistles to suggest a circus. "Nostalgia in Times Square" begins with the rhythm section vamping while the baritone saxophonist, Ronnie Cuber, relates the story, in a sort of beatnik patois, of his first encounter with Mingus at Birdland. The horns improvise various sounds to accompany his narration, including traffic noises and a fragment of Charlie Parker's "Ko Ko."

Other arrangements end with collective improvisation. The final minute and a half of "Moanin' Mambo" features the entire band blowing over the four-bar chord pattern of the tune. Riffs played by some of the band members periodically emerge only to disappear once again into this festive chaos. The mambo ending of "Open Letter to Duke" goes into a New Orleans second line–flavored free-for-all over a two-bar bass pattern before suddenly ending on three notes played in unison: 1–5–1.

One of the most common means of introducing collective improvisation, similar to additive composition, brings in soloists one at a time, gradually weaving a dense polyphonic web of improvisation. After an opening bass solo on "Los Mariachis," the trumpeter Randy Brecker improvises over a two-chord vamp in 6/8, $B^{\flat\,\mathrm{minor}7}$–$E^{\flat\,7}$. Another horn enters every four measures until almost the entire band blows. On "Cumbia and Jazz Fusion" about a third of the way through (5:18) Brecker and the soprano saxophonist trade a few ideas back and forth. Gradually, as their playing begins

TABLE 3 Mingus Big Band Arrangements with Collective Improvisation

Mingus Big Band 93 (1993)
"Moanin' "
"Ecclusiastics"
"Nostalgia in Times Square"
"Don't Be Afraid, the Clown's Afraid, Too"
"Weird Nightmare"
"Open Letter to Duke"

Gunslinging Birds (1995)
"Hog Callin' Blues"
"Fables of Faubus"
"Jump Monk"
"O.P."

Live in Time (1996)
"Moanin' Mambo"
"Sue's Changes"
"The Man Who Never Sleeps/East Coasting"

¡Que Viva Mingus! (1997)
"Tijuana Gift Shop"
"Love Chant"
"Ysabel's Table Dance"
"Los Mariachis"
"Cumbia and Jazz Fusion"
"Far Wells Mill Valley"

Blues and Politics (1999)
"Haitian Fight Song"
"Meditations for a Pair of Wire Cutters"
"Pussy Cat Dues" (cadenza)

Tonight at Noon: Three or Four Shades of Love (2002)*
"Passions of a Woman Loved"
"Black Saint and Sinner Lady"

I Am Three (2005)*
"Song with Orange"
"Paris in Blue" (voice and tenor saxophone)
"Tensions"

* These two compact discs also contain recordings of the Mingus Orchestra and Dynasty, which are not included in this analysis.

to overlap, they are joined by a trombonist and, eventually, several other horns.

On "Fables of Faubus" the reverse process takes place: the arrangement gradually subtracts players during a section featuring collective improvisation. At the six-and-one-half-minute mark, the ensemble suddenly dissolves into a chaotic jumble of sounds as each player plays free. After about thirty seconds of this "noise" all the instruments drop out except for the two main soloists who were featured earlier in the piece, the trumpet and alto. Eventually (at 7:05) the trumpet soloist, Philip Harper, is left alone and begins an extended unaccompanied gospel- and blues-flavored cadenza. Band members punctuate his short phrases with shouts of encouragement as in a revival meeting.

In the Mingus band group improvisation can also be totally unplanned and has evolved during performance. According to Mossman, collective improvisation often begins when "two guys will start soloing at the same time and neither one will back down." Although Sue Mingus usually dictates who will solo on any given piece, in the actual performance anything may happen. "She may get mad, but they still do it. Guys get fired and then a month later they're back again," says Mossman. "Some guys would know that they were going to get fired, and they would do it just to get fired. That's a sick band," he laughs.

> There are certain guys in that band that are really into that, Ronnie Cuber is one. Ronnie is really quintessentially a Mingus kind of player. He's been fired more than anyone else in the band. It's real with him. He really lives that music. Stubblefield is another guy that just doesn't care about other stuff. He's not gonna stand up there and try to sound like John Coltrane. He just wants to stand there and go wild. Talk about excess, now there's a guy who knows how to do that.

Approaches to collective improvisation range from carefully organized to totally chaotic, programmatic to spontaneous. In its freest forms the composer-arranger relinquishes all control over the ensemble. At this extreme musicians play anything they wish, resulting in probably the most heterogeneous style of ensemble playing found in any music anywhere. "That's another thing people have trouble stomaching," says Mossman, "because when it starts to get really dense people start to get freaked out. It's too much for them. Mingus's whole thing was excess, just pure excess."

Playability

Mingus also challenged his musicians by refusing to accept what he called the "classically defined" limitations of instruments: "There are many . . . instruments . . . which jazz musicians have made to do the impossible. And they can play, for hours on end, technical, involved, difficult, educated lines that have melodic sense. They are all virtuosi."[30] Mingus's competitiveness with classical musicians was probably fed by his experiences as a youth, when he had been discouraged from pursuing classical music.[31] Undoubtedly, his prodigious facility and innovative techniques on the bass encouraged him to expect more from players of other instruments as well.

One piece that was explicitly composed to challenge his musicians is "Number 29" (1972). According to the arranger, Sy Johnson, it was "written without restriction, free of the normal constraints required to make it playable. . . . Mingus's ambition was simply to frustrate the best trumpet players in town."[32] Jon Faddis recalled:

> One day I went to see him and he told me he wanted to write this piece for trumpet that went from the very bottom—and I mean bottom—to the very top. He wanted to know if it was possible what he had in mind. I said sure it's *possible.* Then he asked if I could do it, and I said nope. But he wrote it out anyway.[33]

Rescored by Johnson to feature alto, tenor, and trumpet, the piece contains difficult high notes, fast, convoluted runs, and obtuse, angular melodies. The octave leaps in Example 34 are not easy to play at this brisk tempo, but what makes them especially difficult is the requirement that they swing.

Mingus would not be bound by "classically defined" ranges. As was seen in Example 29, the three-and-one-half-octave melody of "Jump Monk" is not playable by any wind instrument without using octave displacement. In the Mingus Big Band extremely high trumpet notes are often strained and sometimes missed. The musicians do not seem overly concerned—why try to play something with a classical tone that few classical musicians would even attempt to play? In the most homogeneous ensembles, ideally, even a very difficult passage should sound effortless. By contrast, arrangers for the Mingus Big Band may intentionally seek the musical effect of musicians struggling. When Mossman added the accompanying parts in Example 35, which were not part of the original arrangement of "Tijuana Gift Shop," he wanted something "on the edge":

> There are some other things in that arrangement that are *extraordinarily* difficult. I would never write that kind of stuff for a band that was supposed to play that accurately. At that tempo? No way. . . . It's not supposed to happen. It's supposed to sound like they're goin' for it, this wild kind of a tumbling-all-over-the-place effect. On the recording they had to rehearse it and get so they could do it, . . . but it gives you that sound of "Oh my God!" Sometimes you push people beyond so that you get the sound of people pushing beyond.

Mingus's unusual formal structures also challenged musicians. The seventeen-bar blowing section of "Los Mariachis," in addition to its chordal

EXAMPLE 34. "Number 29" (Charles Mingus; Sy Johnson, arr.).

EXAMPLE 35. "Tijuana Gift Shop," mm. D6–7 (Charles Mingus; Michael Mossman, arr.).

obstacle course, presents improvisers with one extra measure over the standard sixteen. The Mingus Big Band has revived difficult works (some of which remained unrecorded during their composer's lifetime). In one such piece, "O.P.," the A section is fourteen measures. Instead of the usual eight, the tenors trade solos on odd numbers of bars at a very fast tempo (♩ = 276).

Mingus prevented musicians from settling into comfortable grooves by changing time feels and meters within tunes, sometimes for only a few measures at a time, creating a sort of musical montage. In "Los Mariachis" (1957) he switches repeatedly from Latin to rubato to swing sections. "Open Letter to Duke" (1959) begins with up-tempo swing, moves to twelve measures of Latin, and slows to a ballad. In a later tune, "Sue's Changes" (1974), Mingus incorporated numerous tempo changes, portraying his wife's changeable moods. Most jazz musicians are not accustomed to changing tempos and meters within tunes: the count-off usually establishes the pulse for the entire piece. The Mingus Big Band, however, makes sudden and frequent changes. Like a circus elephant, the Mingus band impresses by displaying nimbleness unexpected from such a large creature.

GUNSLINGING BIRDS

In a remarkable triumph, especially for a woman in the male-dominated jazz universe, Sue Mingus presides over an unruly, masculinist jazz scene of her own creation. She has assumed a very public role as artistic director, entrepreneur, manager, and proprietor through her publications, website, and appearances in the media. But during performance, despite her most careful planning, she must recede to the background, letting the performance traditions, the dynamic personalities of the musicians, and "the notes" take over. The five procedures outlined above: rich unisons, foregrounding dissonance, additive composition, collective improvisation, and challenging of musicians' limitations, reinforce the masculinist individualism of Mingus's musical discourse, keeping the musicians on edge, even without any clear authority onstage.

In the course of a videotaped interview I conducted with Earl McIntyre, Stubblefield, and several other band members, before a live audience in Burlington, Vermont, McIntyre described the Mingus band as "the only band [he] know[s] of in existence where the bandleader is not on the bandstand." Though she may be present in the club, Sue Mingus's lack of hands-on musical direction "changes the whole dynamic of what happens on the bandstand; sometimes it's benign dictatorship, sometimes it's very subtle democracy and sometimes it's anarchy." At McIntyre's mention of the word *anarchy,* Stubblefield and a few of his bandmates shouted, "Amen!"

In her role as artistic director Sue Mingus determines set lists and the order of soloists. Many leaders, in keeping with the spirit of improvisation, prefer to call tunes according to the mood of the musicians or audience. Because she is not onstage with the band, she must prepare such lists in advance. Stubblefield recalled:

> [Early on,] dependin' on the vibe of the festival or the club, we would put the music together right there on the spot, or right before we hit the stage. Then things changed. . . . She would send faxes to the musical director what we were going to play. We said, "Sue, it don't really work like that. Most musicians will not sit at home the day before and say I'm goin' to play this and this and that. It's based on more than that. It's based on the feeling of how you feel right at that moment before you go onstage."

In any event, enforcing the order of the tunes and soloists is not easy from the back of the club or from home if the band goes on a tour without her.

Onstage, the musical director, most often the lead alto player because of his central position in front of the orchestra, gives the cut-offs and cues to the band. Despite this direction, entrances and endings can be ragged, as can be heard on the double CD *Live in Time.* "It's really hard to record a big band. I learned that after years with this band," says Slagle. "I mixed that particular record—it took days. Believe me, I was aware of every little part that was off and learned to live with it." As he listened with me to the opening rubato sections of "The Shoes of the Fisherman's Wife," Slagle pointed out several instances of sloppy entrances and suggested that a conductor might have helped, though it is not clear that the musicians would have followed his direction. As a former music director of the band, Slagle notes, "You have a lot of renegades in there and guys that aren't ensemble players. So they don't really go for that [following a conductor]." Mossman, describing several bad experiences trying to conduct the band through his arrangements, vows never to get in front of them again:

> Conducting the Mingus Band is like, did you ever see the guy at the carnival, you know they throw the ball at him and he gets dunked, it's like being the guy who gets dunked! You're gonna stand up there in front of this band, nobody wants you to be there, and they don't watch you anyway, they're still gonna screw up and you're gonna be up there flailing around. It's the stupidest feeling in the world to conduct that band.

Mossman's ordeals in front of the band grew out of his involvement in arranging much of the material for the Latin-flavored CD, *Que Viva Mingus!* The band rehearsed for the upcoming record date on their regular Thursday night gigs at Time Café. The audience did not know what to make of it. Mossman describes the scene:

> The whole night would be us rehearsing these parts, stopping in the middle of tunes and Sue would say, "Oh yeah, this is the Mingus workshop. Charles always did that, and they're just going to have to like it," but people started wanting their money back.

Eventually, Sue reluctantly admitted defeat and scheduled private rehearsals.

Musical direction would certainly be easier with fewer changes in personnel. Slagle recalls recording *Live in Time:*

> We recorded three or four nights, and she would have different combinations of guys every night with the core of seven of us who were the same the whole recording. The other seven will be different. It's terribly hard to do, especially when you're an arranger and you say like, "No, I want Earl Gardner to play the lead trumpet on this and you're not calling him tonight? You're having someone else who's never played it?" And she says, "Mingus did that all the time." Well, to hell with "Mingus did that all the time." He didn't write this arrangement. I want Earl Gardner to play lead trumpet.

On the *¡Que Viva Mingus!* recording Slagle continues, "There were people who were *sight*-reading because the guy that had made ten rehearsals she didn't call to do the record."

Many of the regular band members dispute Sue Mingus's contention that the band is a flexible entity drawn from a pool of players. One of them says:

> There's a core of maybe less than ten people that have been there for a long time who are most responsible for the band being what it is. That might not be something that Sue Mingus will admit in interviews. She likes to say, "It's a hundred musicians, and they're all equally good." That's not true. I know that the people that contributed the most to that band are very few, a group of really strong players. The good thing about New York is that you do have more than a pool of a hundred musicians that you can call on. But that doesn't make a *band.* That just makes a group of good musicians. A *band* is made by a core of people that really know what the music is that you're doing.

A glance at the personnel of the band's recorded output confirms that the roster has remained fairly constant. Core players have tended to appear with some regularity for several years at a time, a few for nearly its entire lifetime.

Some musicians and listeners grow tired of the masculinist individualism—a rugged, "Wild West" approach to improvisation and ensemble playing as confirmed in the title to their 1995 CD, *Gunslinging Birds* (which takes its name from Mingus's tune, "If Charlie Parker Was a Gunslinger, There'd Be a Whole Lot of Dead Copycats"). Recalling her experience in the audience at Time Cafe one night in 2004, a woman jazz musician confessed to me, "Man, the last time I saw them I had to leave, I felt like there was just too much testosterone in this room. I couldn't handle it. And I can handle high levels, you know, I'm not squeamish." In Slagle's view, the band and jazz in general have been too "macho." "Loud, aggressive shouting and competitiveness tends to be more male-oriented," he says, rather than "on the side that would be lyrical." "Mingus as a composer had both sides," he points out, "but the Mingus Big Band emphasizes the macho side." The band remains, in Slagle's words, "male-oriented": "The fact is there aren't enough women coming to see the music and there aren't enough in the band. Look at the audiences, the problem has to be confronted." One of Slagle's former students, the baritone saxophonist Lauren Sevian, started working with the band somewhat regularly beginning in 2002. She describes her experience: "I expected to feel this huge macho vibe from them and maybe not feel very welcome, but they all are such incredible musicians and really took me in with open arms, so to speak. At least at face value, from what I can tell, they all really *like* having a female in the band. I never got any strange vibes from anybody." Of course, women's greater presence will not necessarily tame the macho approach. Sevian, who has played a lot of funk as well as jazz, says, "Well, honestly, I feel most like myself when I'm playing with that band because I've always loved Mingus's music and I've always been into that high-energy feel."

With income generated from the publishing rights and the reissue of recordings on CDs, Sue Mingus has invested heavily in the Charles Mingus Orchestra, a project intended to explore another side of Mingus's music. "Charles was very lyrical in his compositions," she says. "People tend to think of him as writing boisterous and explosive music—aggressive bebop and blues—but they don't understand the breadth and width of his repertory. He was oriented toward classical music and wrote many through-composed works. There were ballads, but there was so much more." The Charles Mingus Orchestra appears on an album of Mingus's love songs, *Tonight at Noon,* that was timed to be released concurrently with Sue's memoirs of the same name.[34]

Mossman, who has done a lot of arranging for this group, says, "I give Sue a lot of credit for her commitment to that music. I mean going into Birdland [with the orchestra], she's takin' a real bath, just financially. She pays the arrangers; she pays the band." He believes in her good intentions and applauds her achievements: "Sue's straight ahead. She's a strong person very much like Mingus, and she really believes in that music and she really wants to do the right thing. And she's constantly calling me up, calling Sy Johnson up, and calling everyone else up to ask them what they think the right thing is. She's deep into that."

Despite her intimate association with Charles, it is not easy for Sue Mingus to make decisions based on the composer's surmised intentions. One night at Birdland, while discussing some of the problems in the orchestra's performance, Sue and Sy Johnson pondered over "what Charles would have done." A major difficulty of trying to do "what Charles would have done" is that the mercurial bassist, composer, and bandleader was so capricious. Like his wide swings in body weight, different styles of dress, musical eclecticism, and changing grooves, many of his priorities and goals were constantly shifting. Mingus recognized his complex and often contradictory impulses. One could easily come to the conclusion that even if the impulsive composer could be consulted, he might not know what he *would* have done.

Sue Mingus's navigation between public and private spheres raises the question, What would happen without Mingus family involvement? On the 1999 CD, *Blues and Politics,* Mingus's son, Eric, recites his father's words on "Freedom" and "Oh Lord, Don't Let Them Drop That Atomic Bomb on Me." Could someone outside the family succeed in this role or as leader of the band? If a band member were to take charge of hiring, personnel almost certainly would begin to be less diverse and would begin to be drawn more from a single network. Musical direction might become more careful and consistent.

Perhaps the ultimate irony in the Mingus Big Band's success is that the group began its life and held court every Thursday at the Time Café, only a few doors away from the loft where Mingus spent some of the bleakest days of his career and fired off his notorious shotgun blast. Says Stubblefield,

"Where we're performin' right now is right across the street from 5 Great Jones Street. There's an artist livin' in that place now, and that hole is still in the wall. Since that period there's no one has touched that hole." The irony is not lost on the musicians that during this period, Mingus could not even get a gig. Now Sue Mingus and the Mingus Big Band play his music for enthusiastic audiences, and, like the artist in that loft, pay homage to his audacious spirit.

Chapter 8

"In the Crack" to "Totally Outside"

Avant-Garde Bands

A common trope in writing on jazz has been celebration of improvisation as an expression of human freedom. Indeed, some writers have interpreted the entire span of jazz history as an ongoing struggle of the individual against musical constraints. In his book on avant-garde jazz, *The Freedom Principle,* John Litweiler proclaims, "The quest for freedom . . . appears at the very beginning of jazz and reappears at every growing point in the music's history."[1] Others have traced this quest to much earlier African American musical expression. Amiri Baraka notes that in the "pre-church worship of the Black slaves, the songs were about freedom," however camouflaged in biblical metaphor.[2] In the evolution of jazz the pursuit of freedom has been seen to take various forms—liberation from slavery to written parts; from confinement within chords, harmony, and meter; from the control of leaders, especially in large ensembles; from the tyranny of the marketplace or tradition; even from all forms of preconception and habit. Desires for musical freedom naturally were linked to struggles for political liberty, civil and economic rights, and dignity for African Americans, especially during the political and social upheaval of the 1960s. In one of the first books chronicling the avant-garde scene (1977), Valerie Wilmer wrote, "The music itself describes the political position of Blacks in America just as their position dictates their day-to-day life, the instruments they play and the places where their music can be heard."[3] Musicians as stylistically diverse as Charles Mingus, Max Roach, and Archie Shepp recognized that musical and political liberation would only come when African Americans exercised more control over the means of production and dissemination—record companies, performance venues, and media.

Given the extent to which avant-garde musicians extolled political and musical freedom and the discourse that has seen large groups and arrangements as suppressing individual liberty, one might expect big bands and avant-garde jazz to be diametrically opposed. That one of the earliest and longest-lived avant-garde ensembles, Sun Ra's Arkestra, was essentially a big band counters this premise. According to Sun Ra (1914–93), who came of age during the big band era, "The big band and the hard work that lies behind its precision, epitomized all that is fine and heroic in Black music." As Wilmer points out, Sun Ra admired "the sheer professionalism of an organisation like Ellington's, Lucky Millinder's or Jimmy Lunceford's." Instead of seeing the demise of the big bands and the rise of small groups as "progress" toward greater freedom, Sun Ra lamented the fact that "Black people lost their determining factor as to what was really natural or really sort of the master type of music for them." Sacrificing the collective expression of the large ensemble, musicians sought individual glory. "Instead of holding their units together to play for their people in an organised way with the big bands, they moved down to trios and combos. They moved down to duos and the ego, they moved down to all of that."[4] In his definitive book on Sun Ra, John Szwed explains, "He demanded precision and discipline, but the kind that comes from a natural affinity for music rather than from an impulse to suppress individuality." To reconcile these two seemingly polar opposites—discipline and individuality—Sun Ra "sought to make his musicians his friends, his community, a community he would recruit and train, who would live together and devote themselves entirely to his music and teaching."[5]

Along with the desires for economic autonomy of many black artists (particularly in the political climate of the 1960s and 1970s), the somewhat lower expectations of financial reward of many avant-garde musicians aided leaders such as Sun Ra in their recruitment efforts. Moreover, the entrepreneurial spirit characteristic of Charles Mingus and many other jazz musicians seems even more intense in the avant-garde. Oliver Lake, who has participated in the founding of many groups, could be speaking for many in the avant-garde movement(s) when he says, "My whole career has been based on me doing what I do rather than me doin' it with someone else. It's always been like that." The sense of individuality, the celebration of the "maverick" artist is so vital that many musicians prefer to form their own groups rather than join existing ensembles.

Broadening individual freedom in large ensembles requires more flexible and open compositional models. Here, after looking a bit further into Sun Ra's methods, I compare and contrast two approaches that intentionally blur the boundaries between composition and improvisation. Andrew Hill dwells in this twilight region. His big band compositions—often fragmentary and mutable—remain recognizable mainly as a series of ensemble passages, layered figurations, or backdrops for improvisations. At its most extreme, the "composition" as a metaphysical entity can hardly be said to exist except as a title, a performance, or a recording. William Parker rarely repeats works but records nearly every performance, sometimes only naming them afterward. Such open-ended techniques enhance the possibility that a performance might fail to meet audience or musicians' expectations. Many musicians cite the tension resulting from this experimental attitude as a central experience of the performance.

Andrew Hill (b. 1937) began to explore "the crack" between composition and improvisation in his earliest recordings as a leader in the 1960s. Hill also works stylistic and social boundaries, bringing together experimental musicians such as Eric Dolphy and more traditional modernists such as Kenny Dorham in such albums as the aptly named *Point of Departure* (1964). In his more recent groups he has continued to seek diversity by hiring young black and white musicians. William Parker (b. 1952), though of a later generation, was attracted to the radical avant-gardism of the Black Arts movement of the 1960s.[6] As a youthful bassist coming up in the early 1970s, he participated in Jazzmobile classes and workshops in Harlem and eventually went to work with the pianist Cecil Taylor. Parker's works for his large ensemble—the Little Huey Creative Music Orchestra—show the influence of Taylor as well as his own eclecticism and openness to all musical possibilities.

INDETERMINACY

Western culture has tended to romanticize the composer as a "genius" wielding almost Promethean power to create new works out of thin air. A favorite image depicts the composer as a solitary figure hunched over a keyboard furiously jotting down ideas, using as raw materials the sounds of nature, life, or "pure inspiration." These notions are inextricably linked to the fixing of sounds in text. Encoding the music in notation allows the composer to reflect on and edit the work, supposedly yielding a more refined product. Despite the gradual disappearance of improvisation from the Western classical tradition and the increasing control that composers asserted over performances of their works, musical notation cannot possibly prescribe every nuance of performance. Dynamic, mensural, rhythmic, intonational, and timbral subtleties are impossible to convey except in relative and often crude encryption. Performances of the same piece may vary greatly.

In the mid-twentieth century some Western art music composers began to interrogate aspects of composerly authority by leaving elements of the composition open, or "indeterminate." Initially, at least in the works of John Cage, these experiments were not intended to allow more freedom to performers. In pieces such as *Music of Changes* (1951) performers were compelled to follow a set of instructions that were no less binding because they were rendered through random acts such as tossing dice or coins. In later works Cage and his protégés Morton Feldman and Earle Brown, and European composers, such as Stockhausen, permitted greater agency on the part of performers by allowing them to take part in the decision-making process. Composers experimented with "open forms" in which they left out barlines and clefs or permitted the performers to rearrange the order of the pages. Other pieces utilized nontraditional notation such as drawings and graphic and conceptual representations that permitted more open interpretation.

In a trenchant analysis George Lewis points out that, despite disavowals of interest in jazz, Cage (and his colleagues) were influenced by the reemergence of improvisation in Western musics such as jazz.[7] By the same token, although indeterminacy already played a central role in jazz in the form of the "jazz solo," like classical art music composers, some jazz composers sought to raise the level of indeterminacy in their compositions. Seeing indeterminacy as a subset of improvisation, Lewis uses the terms *Afrological* and *Eurological* to distinguish between jazz and classical improvisatory systems. Lewis recognized the socially constructed nature of these categories and describes them as "historically emergent rather than ethnically essential" (93). The absence of improvisatory pedagogical systems in Eurological music education required composers to provide ad hoc rules to their performers (116). Moreover, unlike Afrological musical practices, in which performers seek a distinctive individual sound and their improvisations usually "tell a story," Eurological improvisation tends to distance personal narrative. Lewis sees this as part of a larger tendency in Western culture to see art as "autonomous significant structure[s]," citing an analysis of Subotnik, regarded as "complete and meaningful within themselves" (118). Lewis calls for "a more nuanced view of improvised music [that] might identify as more salient differentiating characteristics its welcoming of agency, social necessity, personality, and difference, as well as its strong relationship to popular and folk cultures" (110). One vital difference is that in jazz, composers typically participate in the performance and collaborate directly with performers.

The role of composers as performers and collaborators has facilitated compositional and performance strategies that rely less, or not at all, on notation. Many of their techniques conflate composition, arranging, and improvisation. Sun Ra claimed, "If I write an orchestration, I want the solos to sound as if I'd written them too, as if it is a continuum."[8] Sam Rivers considers his big band compositions little more than "background colors for improvisers, interspersed with interludes and free improvisation."[9] One of his musicians, the altoist Steve Coleman, explains:

> Improvisation is a major part of the compositional structure, and being inseparable from it, also shows the music's cultural connection to Africa. There is improvisation virtually at all moments in the music, sometimes up front, many times within a maze of predetermined melodies and rhythms. It is rarely possible for the uninitiated to hear the difference between composed and improvised material.[10]

To merge composition and improvisation, composers must relinquish much of the control that they traditionally exert over performance. Although Andrew Hill uses standard notation, his works maintain a high degree of flexibility from performance to performance. William Parker has found even less prescriptive ways to communicate his musical thinking to his performers. Many of these composers' procedures were anticipated in the work of Sun Ra.

SUN RA

Although he claimed to belong to a race of extraterrestrial angels who came to Earth to spread cosmic truth, according to biographers and family members, Sun Ra's earthly life began as Herman Blount in Birmingham, Alabama, in 1914. After touring the South and Midwest with a series of lesser-known groups and surviving a harrowing stint in the U.S. Army, "Sonny" Blount, as he was known then, settled in Chicago. In the years immediately after the war he played with the blues singer Wynonie Harris, worked in strip clubs, and played piano and provided arrangements for Fletcher Henderson's orchestra. In the late 1940s he became a devoted student of Egyptology and joined a secret society dedicated to a heady mix of the occult, Black Nationalism, and outer space. He changed his name legally to Le Suny'r Ra, which he simplified to Sun Ra for the stage, and founded the orchestra commonly known as the Arkestra. Like his music, his name and the name of his orchestra were subject to a bewildering array of variants.

By claiming to be from Saturn, Sun Ra distanced himself from the limiting racial categorizations prevalent in the United States while opening himself to the most extreme eclecticism. Freed from stylistic sectarianism, his repertoire ran the gamut from swing era charts to the most far-out free jazz; from serious, mythological works to camp tributes to pop culture. He deployed a wide range of compositional strategies—from more traditional, fully arranged thirty-two-bar forms to seemingly unstructured group cacophony. Sun Ra's relentless rehearsals belied the apparent looseness of his ensemble. One of the musicians estimated that they practiced one hundred eighty hours for every hour that they played in public.[11] Sun Ra explained, "In rehearsal we do just like a football team. I give them their little exercises, strict disciplined rhythms." But such regimentation was not intended to stifle spontaneity once they were on the gig: "When you get on the field you don't do exercises. Then it's part of the game, and you do what you have to do."[12] Even with the rigorous rehearsals, the meticulously notated music was seldom played as written. Sun Ra's longtime trombonist, Julian Priester, explained that the written parts were "only a sketch of what he really wanted." By the third or fourth rehearsal, "there was nothing familiar on that paper." Sun Ra's goal was to make them "work harder, put more of themselves into it. That way even the written ensembles sound like solos."[13]

His compulsion for change kept the musicians on edge. According to Lucious Randolph, "We rehearsed one way on paper and then played another way on the gig. It was frustrating. When you complained, Sun Ra said, 'If you're a musician you'll follow me.' "[14] Indeterminacy was integral to his compositional style. Pieces were always "works in progress." As he succinctly stated his philosophy, "Something that's perfect is something that's finished, and if it sounds finished, it doesn't have any spontaneity left, and then it isn't jazz." According to Priester, "Sun Ra was a genius at it, he sort of directed us and kept us in the dark at the same time."[15]

Sun Ra oversaw their living as well as their musical arrangements. Anticipating the jazz collectives of the 1960s, he circumvented many of the economic difficulties of supporting a large ensemble by organizing the Arkestra communally (which did not mean band members were necessarily paid equal, or even regular, set amounts). After spending much of the 1960s in New York, the band finally settled in a large house in Philadelphia in 1968. Living together also compensated for their inconstant touring schedule. In some ways their intense communal lifestyle approximated the environment of the swing era in which big band musicians spent much of their lives traveling, playing, and living in close quarters. Many of his band members, such as Charles Davis, Julian Priester, and James Spaulding, established their reputations in the Arkestra, and several, most notably John Gilmore and Marshall Allen, remained with Sun Ra for most of their careers.

In addition to the constant changes in the music, the haphazardness by which Sun Ra recruited band members guaranteed a certain heterogeneity in the sound of the ensemble. If he liked a musician he would invite him to join the band, regardless of his musical background. At any given time, as Szwed describes it, the band could "include musicians from the very best music schools and amateurs; intellectuals and comedians; those who had given up otherwise lucrative careers and those who had never held a job; and sociopaths whom only their mothers, the army or prison might be able to restrain." Band members frequently could not understand what he saw in these players. But, in the words of James Jacson, "Sun Ra sensed who would have the will power to give up everything and start a new life. He knew who would be able to subordinate himself to him in order to play his music."[16] The musicians' close quarters allowed Sun Ra to control and discipline them, to work on them from the inside out. From his pulpit behind the keyboard Sun Ra controlled the band with the subtlest gestures and musical cues, often invisible to the outsider. Over time his players' ability to sense his unspoken directives almost seemed telepathic.

Few big band leaders and composers, other than perhaps Ellington, have been able to establish long-term relationships with their band members on the order of Sun Ra. Without the rapport, intimacy, and instinctive interaction that comes from constantly living and working together, composer-leaders wishing to experiment with more open forms must remain flexible in their expectations.

ANDREW HILL AND WILLIAM PARKER

Taken together, the music of Andrew Hill and William Parker illustrates many of the approaches to orchestral composition characteristic of avant-garde jazz scenes. Their works also display some of the serendipity as well as occasional frustrations that come from taking chances with open composition. Differences in their methods to some extent reflect their different backgrounds. Hill came of age on the cusp of the hard bop and avant-garde movements. While following his progressive instincts, he kept one foot in each camp. Fifteen years his junior, though respectful of the more traditional masters he was exposed to both at home and in school in the South Bronx, Parker was drawn irresistibly to the adventurous sounds he heard on the cutting edge of jazz.

As a teenager in Chicago during the early 1950s, Hill took piano lessons and studied composition with Paul Hindemith. His first important gigs were with rhythm and blues bands and backing up visiting jazz musicians such as Charlie Parker, Miles Davis, and Johnny Griffin. After coming to New York in 1961, he worked with Dinah Washington and played and recorded with Roland Kirk.[17] His series of five albums for Alfred Lion's Blue Note label, all recorded within an eight-month period beginning in November 1963, established Hill as a unique voice. The most famous of these albums, *Point of Departure,* exemplifies Hill's delicate maneuvering between the freer styles of jazz then unsettling the jazz universe and the mainstream styles commonly recorded in Rudy Van Gelder's legendary studios. Through his leadership and compositions, Hill encouraged his band to express "a wide diversity of emotions within a single piece." In his liner notes to the original release, Nat Hentoff described the organization of the music as flexible enough to permit the "quality of the solos [to] reveal new values on each replaying." The music still was based on harmonic structures. But as Hill explained to Hentoff, "The way I set up the tunes, it was more possible for the musicians to get away from chord patterns and work around tonal centers."[18] Without abandoning metric pulse, some pieces shifted between 4/4, 3/4, and 5/4. Hill also sought stylistic diversity among his band members by featuring the trumpeter Kenny Dorham, known for his hard bop work with Horace Silver and Art Blakey, alongside technically advanced and innovative musicians such as Joe Henderson, Ron Carter, and Eric Dolphy. The drummer Tony Williams (just eighteen years old) was selected "for his extremely free sense of time." Hill cites "the personalities of the musicians themselves" as producing "a freer interaction between quite different kinds of people."[19]

William Parker's career followed a different trajectory. His earliest musical recollections at the age of five or six were listening to his father's records of Count Basie, Duke Ellington, Ben Webster, and Coleman Hawkins. Every night his father sponsored dance contests to Ellington's "Diminuendo and Crescendo in Blue" for William and his brother. They each received a quarter, Parker remembers, regardless of who won or lost. The boys also made up other games with the music, such as pretending that their toy guns were horns. Parker didn't "get serious about music" until he discovered Ornette Coleman and John Coltrane: "I guess around '67, I was already deep into what you call avant-garde jazz and free music, so that was what I really wanted to do." He chose the bass because he wanted to "get into the heavy-duty spiritual aspects of the music, and really get underneath it." Through Jazzmobile's classes offered in Harlem, he was able to receive instruction from more traditional mentors such as Jimmy Heath and the bassists Milt Hinton, Richard Davis, Art Davis, and Paul West. Though he recognized the need to build a foundation in technique and theory, his heart was pulling him in a different direction. He tried to talk to his teachers about the adventurous sounds he was hearing from Albert Ayler, Archie Shepp, "and things like that, and they weren't really into that." He remembers in particular approaching Joe Newman, who responded, "Oh, no. We don't do that here." Their closed-mindedness turned off the young bassist. He believes things might have worked out differently "if they had said to me: 'Well William, we're going to get to that stuff later,' or 'You can get to that stuff, but right now why don't we learn this and later on we'll talk about Shepp and them other guys.' "

Parker felt that "everything was boiling up." "I wanted to blow and play and get out there," he explains. "I needed both, and there was no school that was teaching that music at the time." He started going downtown where he found kindred spirits in James DuBois and Wilbur Ware at Studio We and in the thriving loft scene of the 1970s. "I wasn't trying to do something new, just to do something new," he explains. "I mean, what I liked about the music was that there was an aesthetic behind it as far as spirituality and politics that I liked." Unlike his more traditional mentors, who rejected avant-garde music, Parker remained open to all styles, "everything from what Jackie McLean and those guys did, all the way to the furthest out music you could hear."

Eventually Parker became one of the most active bassists on the free-jazz scene, performing with Cecil Taylor, Sam Rivers, Don Cherry, Butch Morris, Wayne Horvitz, Rashied Ali, Roscoe Mitchell, David S. Ware, and many others. Parker was also an important catalyst on the scene, helping to initiate the Sound Unity Festival, the Vision Festival, the Improviser's Collective, and other free-jazz projects in New York.

Big Bands

Parker's interest in orchestral jazz culminated in his forming his own big band, the Little Huey Creative Music Orchestra, in January 1994.[20] He named the group in honor of Huey Jackson, "an aspiring poet who grew up in the housing projects of the South Bronx." According to Parker, Jackson, who was influenced by the work of Samuel Beckett, "envisioned a world where anything was possible." Tragically, the young poet died just before his eighteenth birthday. Parker dedicates the Little Huey Creative Music Orchestra to "all those who are told not to dream. We exist for those who have had the flame of hope put out in their lives. All those torn apart by war, poverty, madness, loneliness, and hate." Parker hopes to instill a sense of empowerment among his musicians: "One of my dreams is for the music to eventually evolve to the point of limitless possibility. Where each player would have complete freedom to go wherever he or she wanted in the music. Freedom to use any sound or color to create something beautiful."[21]

As discussed in chapter 1, although the instrumentation for Parker's orchestra is similar to a conventional big band, he has organized it differently. Rather than the four standard sections (reeds, trumpets, trombones, rhythm), the Little Huey orchestra is divided into seven stations, which are free to contribute to the unfolding musical narrative in any way they see fit.

Over the course of his career, most of Andrew Hill's recordings have featured the pianist alone or with small bands that include two or three horns. His big band album *A Beautiful Day* (2002) was a product of his close collaboration with trumpeter and arranger, Ron Horton. Horton first explored Hill's music in a quintet he organized in 1996, before he began playing with the pianist's sextet in 1998. In May 2000 Horton put together a big band and arranged Hill's music for a concert at the New School.[22] Horton describes his own arrangements as "more in the conventional mode," an approach he characterizes as "very writer oriented—the writer writes the intro, the head, the space for the soloist, dictates who the soloist is, writes the backgrounds, the shout chorus, the coda." Hill had attended the rehearsals and the concert, but his response was typically muted. "He was very quiet, didn't say anything about anything, except, you know, 'Oh, sounds good.' " Perhaps hearing Horton's more conventional arrangements convinced Hill he should start his own big band project. While retaining traditional big band instrumentation and structure and using many of Horton's musicians as a starting nucleus, Hill brought in several players from his small groups. Collaborating closely with Horton, he became directly involved in the arranging process and the direction of the ensemble.

Personnel

Parker recognizes that working together intuitively requires players who have experience performing with each other: "I've got a lot of people who are over twenty years playing with me. And playing with each other. People like Alex Lodico who's been playing with me since 1977 and Lewis Barnes who's been playing with me since 1980." Like most big bands, the Little Huey orchestra grew naturally out of existing social networks as players recommended other players. Parker had little involvement in selecting people for the band, especially in the early days: "When I started the big band at first it was like, 'Who wants to play? You know a drummer, bring down a drummer. You know a saxophone player, bring down a saxophone player.' " Because "a big band is totally a pain in the neck to travel with, to get funding," the formation of his band was based on "economics, of course, and then it was about who was interested in playing the music rather than who was interested in getting paid for a gig. So who would stay, who would come down and learn the music and learn the systems" determined who was in the band.

Despite this long relationship with many of his musicians, Parker notes that, compared to Sun Ra and Ellington, he actually spends very little time with his musicians:

> Sun Ra had the luxury of living with his big band. "WAKE UP! GET UP! TIME TO REHEARSE! Come on, I got a new tune." Or Duke could say "All right, come on, going to rehearse." I can't do that. I mean, I could, because people are very loyal and they say, "Don't worry about the money, I just want to play the music. We understand about the money." Which is really great.

But even if he wanted to take advantage of their dedication, Parker's time is limited because he is busy with other projects both at home and on the road:

> The fact is I'm running around quite a bit, I've been on the road a lot. I haven't really had time to devote to the large ensemble. But I have to because to me it's like a company and they've invested their time so I've got to make sure I get some work for them and really keep them together in some fashion.

In contrast, Hill has not attempted to maintain a standing ensemble for extended periods, preferring to bring together a diverse group of players for specific projects. As Hill became more involved in Horton's big band project, he suggested adding some of the players he regularly worked with in his smaller groups. Horton recalls:

> Some of the people I had at my concert were kind of standard, kind of more big band, studio, Broadway show–type players and I had pulled them in because they're old friends of mine. They can read anything, and they sound great the first time down. Andrew pulled them along into his ensemble, but a few of them had not really played free improv kind of stuff before and certainly not the way Andrew did and, man, it was liberating.

More like the Mingus Big Band than the Little Huey orchestra, many of his musicians operate in different social networks and would be unlikely to play with each other under normal circumstances

To some extent their coming together reflects differences in Horton's and

Hill's generational and racial backgrounds. Horton believes that "it was a very conscious decision on [Hill's] part," noting that "Andrew digs putting together these people that would normally not see each other."

> [He could easily perform with] musicians of his generation, and he's been offered a lot of money to go out and tour with Jackie McLean or James Spaulding or any number of great players that he played with over the last forty years. But I think he doesn't like to play with them because, this is just my take on it, I think he likes to initiate younger players to his world. He could be still playing with Joe Chambers or Bobby Hutcherson or all those people, but he's made a conscious decision to break out of it. He's like "Yeah, I want to play with some younger people, I want to play with some of these white guys. I want to play with some . . ."

Horton's voice trails off as he reflects on the situation. Obviously, discussing race is not a comfortable topic for many musicians, but the unusualness of the situation stands out. He continues by comparing social networks:

> I think sometimes it comes out in a racial kind of way. Like Andrew could be comfortable playing with older black guys. And primarily, the group of people that I've played with in New York are my generation of white guys. But it's not that we plan that, it's not like "That's who I'm going to play with." It's just kind of who you play with. Unfortunately, I'm a little self-conscious of the fact that when I called all my friends to play my music it kind of had an all-white vibe to it, and I know Andrew didn't want to go that way.

Ultimately the band turned out to be "kind of a mix of half of my band and half his idea of players," Horton observes. "The leaders could, if they wanted to, play with all these different people. I could pick up the phone and call them. I think that's what it takes. I think people have to step out and make an effort." Just bringing them together is not enough: "You really have to work to find your common musical ground and have confidence that, if you put together a diverse kind of band, it's going to come off."

Arranging and Musical Direction

Rather than score his material for big band himself, Hill preferred to work closely with Horton. "The whole first year he gave me little scraps of stuff in pencil," Horton recalls.

> When he started presenting me with musical ideas they seemed very short except for one piece that looked like he wanted to write something very long, like a suite or something. And everything else was just in dribs and drabs except for one long thing that seemed very unfinished, like forty-nine or fifty bars and then it just stopped. His handwriting is very unclear and he tried to write things out on score paper and it was hard to read and that was the first snippets of what I saw. Some of it I would just copy out as he wanted it and I would think to my-

> self, "You know, I don't see anything as far as big band arranging or orchestration here, it just looks like a smattering of ideas and it doesn't seem cohesive." I was just thinking to myself, "You know, I'll write it out but I don't really know if this is going to come off." But if I'm hired to do something, I'll try to help it along as well as I can.

The music did not lend itself to conventional arranging practices. Rather than change Hill's ideas, Horton decided to leave the music mostly intact, fixing only things that he thought were obvious mistakes. In the process he began to adopt a more experimental attitude toward the music:

> He was writing trumpet, alto, and tenor and I would see the melody of the trumpet would be dah-dee-dah-dee-dah, very scalar, and then he would have the tenor jumping in like ninths [sings]. Boop-beep-baap-beep-boop. I was like wow, that's kind of different to have the third voice just leapfrogging up and down over everybody else's parts, but that's what he hears or that's what he's trying out. I'm not going to change that to conform to sort of my preconceived arrangement habits. I would say, you know, I'm game. I want to hear what it sounds like too. So a lot of times I wrote things out thinking, like jeez, I don't know if this is going to work. Let's find out. And it was a great journey for me.

After Hill acquired the computer music notation programs Freestyle and Sibelius, he began to send Horton scores in which he had layered ideas over one another, sometimes offsetting the phrases by several beats or measures. Horton's job was to sort through these figurations, which were sometimes scored for as many as thirty instruments, and create a coherent big band arrangement, a job he found "tricky" to say the least, especially while trying to remain true to Hill's intentions. Music notation software lends itself to a postmodern, pastiche aesthetic. Such "cut and paste" techniques came naturally to Hill. Even before he acquired the software, during rehearsal he frequently instructed the musicians to jump around in the arrangement or even between different pieces.

In his Little Huey orchestra Parker relied much less on written music. Parker is less concerned with specific notes and rhythms than with capturing musical gestures and feelings and exploring timbral resources. Some of his musicians are not adept readers. He uses the colorful term "spirit catchers" for these musicians "because they were people who you couldn't really write for." He has worked with many of his musicians for many years; they understand his use of colors, numbers, and aural and visual cues in lieu of musical notation. He explains:

> You had other people who were reading some music but also could improvise and other people who sort of played ensemble or textural parts because we used a color system, a number system. The color system would be where you play colors like brown, which is the earth, which means you play low tones, or light blue, which is the sky, you play higher pitches. Red colors mean you play

music with very hot or intense energy, orange might be not as bright, yellow might be up-tempo but not as bright.

John Coltrane's playing during his "late period" suggested to Parker the idea of using numbers to indicate pitches.[23]

Like many experimental bandleaders, Parker also considered "conduction" techniques such as those used by Lawrence "Butch" Morris. Morris, best known for his big band collaborations with David Murray since the late 1970s, communicates instructions to the performers visually through the use of onomatopoeic signals that signify musical gestures, such as trills, glissandos, "blips and bleeps," and other figures. Although Morris has become the leading practitioner of this art, Oliver Lake notes, "In the Black Artists Group in St. Louis and in Chicago in the Art Ensemble, the AACM, we have been doin' that kind of thing with big bands for years and years before Butch Morris got a name to put on to that."[24] Lake describes some of his own techniques while also noting some of the difficulties and limitations:

> As my band is playin' I'll walk up to the brass section and say, "Play a chord." Or I have a signal I'll make with my hand which means I want them to play a chord. It could be any note or any chord. Sometime I'll say play D $^{\text{minor7}}$ and then they'll pick a note and play that. Or I'll give them a rhythm to play and they'll play that. You point them in and you take them out. They really have to watch me a lot when I'm doin' that kind of thing. I'm just trying to create some stuff on the spot with an entire sixteen- or seventeen-piece group.

As a bassist performing in the ensemble, Parker found such conduction techniques impractical. The idea in Little Huey was "to have the players learn the systems that we were using and to develop with the main thrust being to have a orchestra that works like a quartet or a trio." Just as a small group would not have a conductor cueing the ensemble, Parker says:

> I wanted the trumpet section to bring themselves in and out, the trombone section bring themselves in and out, the altos bring themselves in and out when they want to, and I just play free and bring myself in and, you know, when I play something they go with it. . . . I can sort of get in front of the band and conduct but I really don't like to do that anymore. I mean, I did a little bit of that to take us through pieces and but I'm saying we wanted to get to another area and the only way we can get to this area is by this process.

Over time, Parker notes, "we used fewer and fewer charts."

> You can always pull out a chart and say, "Boom, boom, boom let's play this." But I wanted to see if we could do the same kind of openness you do with a small group. And so it's beginning to work.

Performance

Unlike Parker, Hill and Horton rehearsed their band frequently in the days leading up to their first gig at the Jazz Standard in February 2001. But, as in Sun Ra's Arkestra, these rehearsals were not intended to make the musicians more comfortable with the music or the convoluted arrangements. Pieces were seldom rehearsed the same way twice. Solos occurred in different spots and could be taken by different players. Horton explains:

> The music for the whole evening just seemed to be made up of a ten-bar phrase and a solo, a fourteen-bar phrase then another solo, or an eighteen-bar phrase and then all the saxophones solo. But he never dictated at the rehearsals who would solo and at every rehearsal he would say something different. "I think at this place, we'll have just trombones play." And everyone would write in, "trombones play." And at the next rehearsal we'd get to that same spot he would say "Oh, maybe just drums." And everybody would erase or scratch it out, "OK, just drums." And at the next rehearsal it would be all different.

Little in Horton's substantial experience of leading ensembles prepared him for Hill's approach to musical direction. Hill's rehearsal style mirrored his noncommital approach to composition. Horton frequently felt that he was not getting the ensemble to do what Hill wanted, but he received little in the way of guidance from the composer. When asked about the tempos, Hill would respond, "Oh, you know, whatever you think." Horton would count off a tempo, and the band would play rather metrically. Hill suggested, "ever so nicely," that Horton "conduct it in phrases," but Horton remained confused. "Well, the whole phrase is eighteen bars long how do you want me to . . . ?" Horton asked. Finally, Hill started a piece without counting or indicating the tempo in any way:

> He just put up his hands, everybody put up their instruments, and then he just kind of like dropped his hands, you know, like not in tempo, he just kind of went whommp and then the whole band just kind of went "Warraowwaowh." And just kind of played through the music like not in tempo. It sounded real weird like an LSD kind of inspired moment or something. And everybody laughed, including Andrew, because it sounded so weird compared to the way we had played it two minutes before.

In classical music the conductor does not count off pieces, instead conveying the tempo to his orchestra through a two-part continuous motion by raising (the "preparation") and lowering his hand (the "downbeat"). By not combining these movements, by holding his hands in a raised position and, without warning, simply dropping them, Hill imparts little sense of tempo to his players. Hill's approach almost seems like anticonduction; he purposely tries to communicate as little as possible in his conducting.

By the time of the gig at the Jazz Standard, Horton realized that Hill wanted nothing "set in stone." The more conventional players in the band, who had never experienced anything like this, probably felt the most insecure. Their parts were full of directions they had dutifully marked in and scratched out during rehearsals. Their very different backgrounds ensured that the musicians still "didn't really know each other as a band. Everybody was just trying to figure out what Andrew wanted."

The first night, just moments before they were to begin playing, Hill presented Horton with instructions (the "road map") for the first set. Once again, many things were changed from the last rehearsal.

> He wanted to go from one part of one piece, play the first nine bars, then go to like the last few bars of another piece and then he wanted to skip back to the first piece and play thirteen bars between bar 39 and 52 and then he wanted to play backwards from bar 36 of this other tune back to bar 33, play it over and over again and while they're playing that backwards, he wanted trumpets to make up a background and he wanted tenor to solo over top of that. And then the lights dimmed and [the announcer said,] "OK, everybody put your hands together for Andrew Hill Big Band." And it was like "Oh, man." Everybody was just sweating. He just wanted everybody to be totally off guard.

Another of Hill's tactics that contributed to the band's uneasiness was the composer's tendency not to play during rehearsals. Horton describes a trip to England for which they had to hire numerous local players for a big band concert. Over the course of several days of rehearsals, "Andrew played no more than two notes":

> They were even asking me [imitating English accent], "Oi, y'know is Andrew going to play, y'know? You think he's going to play a little more piano?" I was like, "Well, I don't know."

The band's nervousness was compounded by Hill's tendency to speak very little. Feeling intensely scrutinized, many players interpreted his silence as disapproval. Just as at the Jazz Standard engagement in New York, the musicians began to wonder, "Man, what's going to happen at the gig? Is it going to suck?"

> And sure enough, when we get to the first concert . . . Andrew becomes very generous when he performs and it puts everyone at ease. . . . A lot of people who play with him in a big band setting have never even really heard him or checked him out. They don't really know what he's about. Andrew starts playing everybody starts opening up. It's a very bonding kind of feeling; it's like we're up here in front of people trying the shit out for the first time.

Like his compositions, Hill's sets remain flexible, not necessarily following a preordained order, sometimes ending abruptly. Many musicians, like those in the Mingus Big Band, after carefully gauging the mood of the band and the audience, prefer to call out tunes as the set progresses. Hill, however, does not seem especially concerned with audience response. Horton says:

> He doesn't adhere to the formula of a set. He doesn't have a flag-waving kind of an ending, necessarily. He may, but he may end with a ballad, and so audience reaction sometimes is different from set to set because if we're supposed to play for an hour, well, when an hour comes up if we're in the middle of a ballad he's just going to close with the ballad. It may be an awkward moment, you know. I think that's another thing I admire about him is that he is just not concerned whether people walk away like stomping and clapping and "Wow, that was success." I think he always told me that he considers a lot of stuff a "work in progress." I'm sure he's not happy if things kind of fall flat, but I don't think he worries about it because he always looks forward to the next thing

On both the New York and London opening nights, by the time the bands broke for their first intermissions, the members felt more than just relieved to have averted a train wreck. Their joy in discovering the beauty of Hill's music for the first time also was communicated to the audience: "Jeez, the break is just like, people, their eyes are bugging out, the audience is like, wow. And the musicians are like, wow, I've never played music like this before."

The greater the indeterminacy in the composition the more the players need to listen to the progression of the piece and respond to each other. Getting through the gig requires communal effort. Like Hill, Parker's instructions are intentionally vague:

> So instead of saying, like, "Play it this way, play it that way." I say, "OK. Now guys, you can play that soft if you want now, soft as you can. And you can play it loud." "But how do you want us to play it?" "Well, you'll see. Fit it in the context." This way, you tell them ideas but have them make their own decisions by what they hear. So it's that kind of sort of intuitive training where you're giving them the options, giving them the vocabulary and having them blend their own vocabulary and then trust. Trust is running through the whole thing.

Even in works with few specific compositional instructions, Parker still sees a narrative thread extending through the performance: "I always like to have some sort of mythical or political or some kind of message or shape in the music whether it's through titles, stories, whether it's through the music itself. So I don't want just let it go yet." These concepts, however nebulous, give each performance the aura of being a "piece" as opposed to a totally free performance in which absolutely nothing is predetermined. Although little difference may be apparent to an outside listener, Parker distinguishes between these works and performances in which such concepts are absent and no one is leading the ensemble. Extending traditional jazz terminology, he calls such free performances "jams." As much as he values the freedom in these encounters, Parker voices his frustrations at musicians' limited understandings of interactive possibilities:

> With the jams there were just certain things that people, I felt, needed more training. Just a pure raw energy thing is OK. But it really takes a gifted player to make that happen. . . . They weren't thinking on their feet as far as the possibilities of the music. This is where the training comes in, where OK, now, if I'm playing fast you can play slow, if I'm playing slow you can play fast, if I'm playing in 3 you can play in 5. If I'm playing in 2 you can play in 3.

Such contrarian strategies can be discomfiting. Parker remembers the first time he played with the British saxophonist Derek Bailey:

> The first set I thought, "This guy isn't listening to one note I'm playing. Everything I play he's just playing his own thing." And the second set I played my own thing, and it worked. Because we were together by being apart. It's like a strange concept, but sometimes when you play, like opposites you attract and it works. In music they'll tell you that you have to be together, but sometimes you can be apart.

Instead of working off each other, exploring contrasting or complementary strategies, members of the group tend toward entropy. Parker explains:

> Mostly people try to congeal and to try to find a groove, and I'm saying, well we have to see if there's a different kind of groove, people might call it antigroove. But it's polyphony, it's a groove where the lockings are just different, it might lock in every 94 bars or every 136 bars, or you might change a rhythm every bar.

As is apparent in the Mingus band, the big band offers tremendous potential for layering parts. In discussing layering techniques in the Sam Rivers big band, John Murphy describes an aesthetic similar to Parker's of "playing apart and playing together." Likening Rivers's ensemble to an "African big band," one of its members, the tuba player Bob Stewart, explained to Murphy, "I mean you have all these individual lines kind of going off and then every once in a while the lines will kind of match each other and do something in a semi-unison fashion. But then at the end of a phrase the whole band would come together playing the same rhythm, either in unison or in harmony, and it would just be so *extremely powerful,* particularly when everybody kind of landed together, the way it's supposed to be."[25] Steve Coleman, who played alto in Rivers's big band, describes his big band compositions as being "closer to the Ancient West African concept than what may be apparent. There is the remarkable cyclic nature of the music and the layering of melodies leading to creative rhythmic relationships."[26] Murphy says that other band members also view these layering techniques as "African" and connects these practices to West African drumming ensembles and large Afro-beat ensembles such as Fela Kuti's Afrika 70.[27]

Parker feels that his asymmetrical patterns, densely layered textures, and musical noises mirror sounds in the natural universe:

> I mean there's all these kinds of things, and nobody can say it doesn't exist. I mean, listen to nature, listen to the wind. I mean there's patterns the birds are singing. So there's all kinds of possibilities which, if you investigate them and do them and really look into, you can make them work.

Because they are based largely on precomposed ideas, Hill's layerings have a different quality. By familiarizing the band with the material during rehearsals, Horton found that Hill "managed to instill a lot of energy and focus" even when there were "just a lot of layering things going on":

> He wanted one section to be doing one thing and another section to be doing something else. One section of this tune played while another section of another tune would be playing by another group of people. I think he really likes that layering thing because when somebody listens to it as a texture you don't really know what's going on in there. You're just kind of listening and going like, wow, are these people lost? You don't know.

Hill's conducting, with its lack of a count-off or even a preparation to suggest a tempo, produces layering of another sort. According to Horton, the phrase may or may not come out the way Hill wanted: "It kind of comes out, you know, haphazard. And sometimes I think he likes that and sometimes, well, jeez it didn't come out the way he liked." Such pitfalls are simply the cost of maintaining Hill's open attitude.

The solos in Hill's arrangements can be planned in advance, cued, or simply occur spontaneously. Horton explains:

> Out of all this density comes simplicity. Andrew doesn't put his hands up and say, "OK, that's enough, bass solo." It's just like his small group it just kind of evolves. Everybody maybe is tired of playing this riff over for fifteen minutes or group improv for five minutes and then it just kind of evolves into a solo.

Hill's openness to the moment means that he remains flexible, whatever happens during the performance. If he feels that a piece has reached its conclusion, he may not even play the entire arrangement: "He did one thing on the album *[A Beautiful Day]*, the bari solo with J. D. Parron wasn't dictated and it just kept on going. Live at least, it might have just ended with solo bari. Andrew might not bring in the rest of the arrangement." Less experimentally minded jazz composers and arrangers tend to be less willing to relinquish their control or abandon any of their "precious" precomposed material.

The solo section itself may be over a vamp, a set of chord changes, a tonal center, or totally unaccompanied. Horton characterizes Hill's "dialect of writing changes" as kind of "old school." His chord notation tends to be rudimentary and "may not correlate with what he's playing 'cause he uses some interesting voices that are hard to write as a chord symbol." Unlike many pianists who try to avoid playing low notes for fear of clashing with the bassist, Hill encourages his bass players to stay away from lower roots and play higher on their instruments so that, as Horton reports, he can "play the bottom end of the piano. . . . He wants the bass to be up in another register, out of the way." Chord changes may not have fixed durations. As in Hill's small groups, tonalities often seem to shift imperceptibly as members of the rhythm section and the soloists try to follow Hill's playing.

Because members of the Little Huey ensemble are free to contribute musical ideas whenever they wish during a performance, players often work in tandem with other members of their section or respond freely to one another. Parker is able to set much of the underlying feel of the musical activity through his bass playing:

> This is one of those things I learned from playing this music all these years, as the bass player, who's the navigator in these things, many times, I can use any rhythm I want, any time signature, anything I want. I just have to place it at the right time. And that is the intuitive thing—when to play fast, when to play slow, when to play a little Latin, when to push it, when to take it back, when to use the bow, when to use this, when to use that. When the music is flowing you just know when to do it and that's kind of what you're going for without really worrying about style, because you're really not worried about style here. Because I think it's really beyond style or even beyond category.

For Parker, the essence of "free" music is that it sets no limitations on the player. Unfortunately, many players limit themselves in terms of what they feel is acceptable to play. Parker says:

> That's a problem that some people have, that improvisers have, is that they're playing and here comes the melody. "Oh, we're not supposed to play a melody." Well, why not? "If we play a melody we're not avant-garde." Well, who says you got to be avant-garde? "But, we, we, we're supposed to be avant." Why? Play a melody. Play a rhythm.

Though he is reluctant to criticize his musicians, Parker admits to occasional feelings of frustration during performances, as my following exchange with him illustrates.

WP: In my head sometimes I'm like yelling out, "Oh, man, all this stuff is going on and you want someone to play a nice pretty melody over all that cacophony," and no one is. "Come on, come on, play that melody now!" I mean, that's what it's there for.

AS: You're thinking this. You're not telling them.

WP: Yeah. "Come on, come on. Hear it." And that's what I'm getting to so that people can hear the contrast when all of this is going on and play that nice slow melody over that.

AS: Does somebody sometimes do that?

WP: Yes, every once in a while somebody makes a mistake and plays it. No, I'm just kidding guys.

Parker's final comment reveals his obvious desire not to offend his band members. But it also confirms his reluctance to make judgments about their musical decisions. After all, Little Huey has been dedicated to empowering musicians and reaffirming their individual freedom. Although he still believes "it works best when you don't have to say anything," he has decided that once in a while "it's OK to say some things." "And," he adds, "I'm really beginning to know how to articulate this stuff more clearly."

In his view avant-garde musicians who limit themselves to playing "avant-garde" ideas are no better than "straight-ahead" players who dismiss free jazz: "It's the same with the guys that's playing rhythms and melodies all the time. 'Well we ain't supposed to play that, it's just noise.' Who says it's noise? You know music's all these things." Parker does not equate "freedom" in jazz with freedom from musical structure. In fact, he feels that such preconceptions only foreclose harmonic, melodic, or metric possibilities. In his words: "The idea of free music is that you're free to play what you want to play. That is the definition of it."

Recording

When Hill recorded a live CD at Birdland the compositional process did not end with the performance. After a series of evenings beginning on Thursday, 24 January 2002, were recorded, Hill worked closely with Matt Balitsaris, a guitar player and engineer as well as the owner of Palmetto Records. Together they edited the over six hours of music. Many of the pieces were twenty-five or thirty minutes long and needed to be shortened so that more tunes could be fitted on the CD. Tunes were cut and spliced, long solos were shortened, and some solos were eliminated altogether. Interestingly, during the live performance Hill played very little, barely even comping. As in the rehearsals, the musicians began to wonder what was going on. Horton relates his conversation with Hill:

> [I asked,] "Are you going to play more the next set, or tomorrow night or whatever?" I think he made a comment to me, "Oh, maybe I'll just overdub my parts." And I was thinking, "Hmmm. A little difficult to do." Because in a live big band situation you don't have much room to overdub. You're not isolated. What he did was he played very little on the gig and Matt has a great piano out at his studio and from what I understand, they played back some stuff and An-

> drew did actually overdub onto the big band tapes. So that made it easier, he didn't have to match his sound with two different pianos because he was playing very little live.

Although it removed an important source of inspiration and musical direction from the rest of the band, Hill's decision not to play during the performance allowed him more flexibility during the editing. With the benefit of hindsight and time to reflect, he reshaped not only the "raw" materials gathered at Birdland over the three nights but also almost his entire contribution as a performer.

Parker's recordings, on the other hand, are meant to capture the essence of spontaneous composition. Nearly every performance of Little Huey is recorded, and many are released on Parker's AUM label. A "Sessionography and Gigography" available on the internet lists many hundreds of Parker's performances, a great many of which have been recorded.[28] A recent CD, appropriately named *Spontaneous* (2003), recorded at CBGB's, the punk rock and alternative music establishment on the Bowery, contains just two tracks, "Spontaneous Flowers" and "Spontaneous Mingus." As Parker describes the second piece, it began as "just about eight notes" that grew into a nearly thirty-three-minute work. He decided to call it "Spontaneous Mingus" after it was performed because it ended up sounding like "something, perhaps, that Mingus could have written. But it just is spontaneous." Parker seldom repeats works except occasionally when the band travels. He notes, "Every time we play we do a new composition. We don't repeat any of the compositions we play. Actually when we went to Europe we repeated the piece we did in Paris when we went to Italy. But generally in New York we do a different piece every time we play."

Because Parker's compositions are so thoroughly connected to performance, the "same" work might bear little resemblance to itself from performance to performance. In another sense, as spontaneous improvised works by a fairly consistent band membership, all the pieces could be seen as part of a larger, never-ending work-in-progress. Even if people in the band or the audience ask him to repeat a work, Parker demurs. He worries, "If we play the same tune over and over, we'll only get better, and we might develop a repertoire." But he quickly adds, laughing, "I figure in a way we're doing the same tune. I mean it's different, but it's the same process and the same idea."

FREEDOM AND THE JAZZ COMPOSER

One might expect that since "indeterminacy" in the form of solo improvisation was already an important part of jazz, more open conceptions of composition would be welcome in the jazz universe. However, the absence of a clearly defined musical narrative unsettles many musicians. Most avant-garde or experimental jazz composers cultivate this tension in their works. Musicians from mainstream jazz worlds prefer clearer distinctions between composition and improvisation. Each role leaves a clearer trail of agency: the composition expresses the writer's intentions, while sharply defined improvisational sections reflect those of the soloist.

Mingus saw himself as a composer in a more traditional sense. Although, like Ellington, he exploited his musicians' individual sounds and tried to spur them to new soloistic heights (practices that practically have been fetishized under Sue Mingus's leadership), his tendency to dominate the musical proceedings left little room for indeterminacy in the composition itself. Many of the techniques championed by Mingus—additive composition or layering, collective improvisation, lack of concern with playability, rich unisons—form the core practices of the experimental or avant-garde composer. Although Mingus often disparaged the avant-garde movement, many avant-garde musicians continue to cite Mingus as a prime influence. Interestingly, Sun Ra is mentioned much less often, despite his obvious importance in maintaining a standing jazz orchestra and establishing an economic model of independent production and communal living. Perhaps this obvious omission reflects the higher esteem in which Mingus is held as a composer and a tendency for experimentally oriented musicians to emphasize their connections with more traditional masters.

Traditional and experimental bands differ in their attitudes toward composition. In the former, the composition functions as a safety net, holding everyone together, providing continuity and a predictable sequence of events. As Horton describes it, "Before I worked with Andrew I would go into the rehearsals or whatever and have everything mapped out so everybody knows where the beginning is, the middle and the end. And if somebody clams or somebody misses the coda, then, you know, then there's sixteen other guys to cover up for somebody's flub."

Parker's and Hill's devotion to musical freedom does not necessarily encompass abandoning all musical constraints. In discussing his music Parker emphasizes the need for musicians' training—training that sensitizes musicians and opens them to new possibilities of interaction. Clearly, the musicians in Hill's bands feel a greater obligation to fulfill the composer's wishes—no easy task with a composer so reluctant to communicate. The combination of Hill's reputation as a first-rank composer and the deference to composerly authority by the musicians, especially those with mainstream backgrounds, fed the players' obsessive concern with trying to discover what he wanted.

Despite his interest in keeping his compositions flexible and encouraging "a freer interaction" between his musicians, Hill seems determined to retain some of the composer's traditional prerogatives. His collaboration with Horton ensured that the music would be properly scored and copied (especially important to the more mainstream players in the band), with any obvious mistakes excised. Hill's active role in the editing and overdubbing of the recording allowed him to maintain a composerly attitude of reflection. At the same time, his minimal direction and penchant for change kept the musicians on edge and open to the moment. According to Horton, Hill likes it when "none of us knows what's happening . . . because everybody has to stick together. The only way you're going to get through it is if you all stick together. You just feel each other's vibe." Unlike the Mingus band, the feeling of being on the musical edge is not exacerbated by frictions among the musicians and the leadership. In Horton's words, "You can't have this contentious thing happening, because if you're not working with other people to get through the chart or the gig, then it's definitely going to not happen." On the Jazz Standard, Birdland, and London gigs "everyone really wanted it to work."

Throughout his career Hill has challenged musicians—young and old, black and white, and traditional and experimental. Hill's music is perfectly suited for bringing together such diverse musicians. In Horton's words, "It's not totally out, I mean you can hear that, true. And then you can hear something really inside, but Andrew's kind of in that crack, and he can ride that crack. He gets a little out at times, gets a little in at times, but not for too long." Like Sam Rivers and other composers who "ride the crack," Hill maintains some of the traditional structure of featuring individual players in extended solos with the rhythm section. Despite this and other fundamental similarities, Hill favors certain soloists whereas Rivers prefers to let every member of the band solo on every tune.[29]

Although Hill and Parker may begin works with distinct musical ideas, the haphazardness of their direction and openness to taking chances means things do not always work out as planned. Their experimental attitude keeps them open to different potential outcomes, even a less than satisfying result. Still, one senses occasional frustrations. While Parker has clear expectations about the musical interactions he would like to hear in his works, his devotion to the ideals of freedom limits his ability to communicate these ideas to his players. Some of his musicians seem to grasp better than others what he is striving for. He seems to yearn for a telepathic power to communicate to his musicians during a performance. Despite his unshakable belief in their individual freedom, he wants them somehow to make the "right" choices. He wants them to leave behind preconceptions about what an "avant-garde" musician should play. But, short of total immersion in their lives, he has not found a way to work on them from the inside out, as did Sun Ra.

In the bands studied in this chapter, as in most of the avant-garde, despite the experimentation with more open forms of composition, the composer's role remains central. Hill's personality, though much less forceful than Mingus's or Sun Ra's, runs throughout his work. His withdrawn attitude only serves to make his musicians even more sensitive to his desires (real or imagined). Parker has loosened the compositional reins still further, yet his central role in the Little Huey ensemble is undeniable. By sheer force of personality and his dynamic bass playing, he dominates the proceedings. He suggests ideas, themes, and feelings. Whether they "ride the crack" or go "totally outside," their presence as composers and performers ensures that these composers' personal narratives influence the musical flow even as they maintain open attitudes.

The frustrations and the limited reception for experimental music, compounded by the difficulties of keeping a large orchestra together, beg the questions, Why keep playing music that attracts such a minuscule audience? Is this music an exercise in self-indulgence? Are Hill, Parker, Rivers, and Lake and their musicians playing mainly for themselves? Perhaps the answers are to be found not in the musical product but in the processes described above. Like Sun Ra, these composers see creative potential within the greater social responsibility demanded by the large group. They pursue freedom not simply for its own sake. While not divorced from ongoing political and economic struggles, their compositional challenge goes deeper, inspired by desires to bring about change within the musicians themselves. Idealistic anarchists, they imagine a world not only in which people see the full range of possibilities open to them and are empowered to make choices, but also in which they make the *right* choices—the moral, artistic, and socially responsible ones. Perhaps these musician-leaders are best understood not merely as composers, but as teachers, nurturers, or even prophets.

Chapter 9

Jazz and Clave

Latin Big Bands

A Sunday, 1998. I receive a last-minute call to substitute in a rehearsal with the Chico O'Farrill Afro-Cuban Jazz Orchestra. The band rehearses uptown, on the edge of El Barrio, in the space at Boys Harbor where another Latin big band, led by Ray Santos, also meets regularly. I arrive a little late, but much of the band is still not there. Hoping to meet Chico, I am a little disappointed to learn that he rarely attends rehearsals because of his advanced age. Instead, his son, the pianist Arturo O'Farrill Jr., leads the rehearsal. Although I have not been very active on the Latin scene in New York, I notice many players with whom I have become acquainted in various "straight" jazz situations over the years. As we begin, the mix of African Americans, Anglos, and Latinos barely registers—this is, after all, Latin jazz. Arturo calls "Undercurrent Blues," an original arrangement his father had written for Benny Goodman when the latter flirted briefly with bebop in the late 1940s. We rehearse several other charts, including O'Farrill's most famous work, *Afro-Cuban Jazz Suite.*

Since fall 1997 the Afro-Cuban Jazz Orchestra has been performing O'Farrill's classic repertoire Sunday nights at Birdland. Since I only filled in for the rehearsal, I am not on the gig that night. With a friend, I decide to head down to Birdland anyway. When we arrive the band is already playing, and the club is full of attentive listeners. A vintage poster on the wall of the club reminds them that O'Farrill headlined at the original Birdland in the 1950s. Chico, who seems quite frail, conducts several tunes in an extremely low-key manner before turning over the band to his son. Arturo introduces a tune he describes as a "psychedelic bugalú," appropriately titled "Algo de Fumar" (Something to Smoke).

Despite the importance of Latin and Caribbean musical influence during the entire history of jazz, recognition of this contribution—Jelly Roll Morton's "Spanish tinge"—has been largely absent from jazz histories, recorded anthologies, and documentaries such as Ken Burns's *Jazz*. In a cogent analysis, the trombonist and scholar Christopher Washburne has described this ongoing marginalization, even as "straight" jazz benefited from its consecration as both an American and an African American art form worthy of public and private support.[1]

During the 1990s, after years of obscurity, O'Farrill and Ray Santos, two of the leading figures in orchestral Latin jazz, finally reappeared in the limelight. Returning from a long "exile" in Puerto Rico, Santos found himself once again in demand as a composer and arranger. Instead of commercial sound bites, O'Farrill received commissions to compose for films, records, and concerts. Perhaps most satisfying, after decades of performing in or writing for other leaders' bands, both Santos and O'Farrill finally heard their music played by their own standing orchestras. Santos's band rehearsed regularly and performed occasional gigs around town. O'Farrill recorded three CDs, including the first new recording in more than forty years of *Afro-Cuban Jazz Suite*. On 10–12 September 1998 Santos and the elder O'Farrill (with his son on piano) were honored in a Jazz at Lincoln Center concert titled "Con Alma—The Latin Tinge in Big Band Jazz." Each maestro conducted the LCJO through several compositions.

Coming of age during the height of the swing era, O'Farrill and Santos initially were drawn to jazz through their love of big bands. The ebb and flow of their careers not only illustrate the vagaries of the Latin big band business in New York, Cuba, and Puerto Rico but also shed light on differences between the social networks involved in performance of Latin jazz and those involved in other types of jazz performance. Arguably the most multicultural genre within the already multicultural idiom, Latin jazz brings together musicians from diverse backgrounds. In the NEA-sponsored study conducted in 2000 only 3.1 percent of the jazz musicians in New York identified themselves as "Hispanic or Latino."[2] Still, based on the study's estimate of the large population of jazz musicians in New York, this rather small percentage amounts to more than a thousand Latino jazz musicians. Despite their relatively small number and the participation of players with widely varying ethnicities, from Japanese to Israeli, Latin jazz has functioned as an important symbol of Latino identity, especially among Puerto Ricans living in New York ("Nuyoricans").[3]

Above all, the story of Latin jazz concerns movement and contact—transmigration of musicians and musical practices. Santos grew up in East Harlem (El Barrio) and the Bronx, nexuses of fertile exchange between Latinos and African Americans. His musical activity oscillated on the San Juan/New York axis. O'Farrill, born in Cuba, traveled between Havana and New York, with detours to Los Angeles and Mexico City, before eventually settling permanently in New York. Despite the transnational nature of the music, the development of Latin jazz centered in New York. Here the existence of a large Puerto Rican population provided a fertile base for the influx of Cuban, Dominican, Panamanian, Venezuelan, and other Latino musicians. Latino and black musicians, usually confined to living in the same neighborhoods or in close proximity often worked together and performed for each other. Many white jazz musicians also found work in the burgeoning mambo scene as the swing era came to a close.

A music of the feet, as well as the heart and mind, Latin jazz, unlike most modern straight jazz, blurs the boundary between dance and listening music. A union of Afro-Latino and African American diasporic traditions, Latin jazz challenges both experienced salseros and seasoned jazz musicians. Latin dance musicians must learn to improvise fluently over sophisticated jazz harmonies. Jazz players must acquire sensitivity to the underlying rhythmic matrices of Latin music, especially the Afro-Cuban principle of clave. These challenges lead to complex discursive exchanges in which competence and "authenticity" variously hinge on place of birth, ethnic background, and musical training and experience. As Washburne writes, "The Latin presence in jazz history complicates the black/white dichotomy of racial politics in the United States jazz scene."[4] Historical comparison of racial discourse in Latin musical cultures, particularly Cuban, with straight jazz scenes sheds light on the articulation and contestation of jazz as "black music" in the United States.

I have benefited from the experience and insights of several key figures of Latin jazz. Ray Santos, who has participated in Latin jazz orchestras as player, arranger, and leader, generously shared his ideas in a series of interviews and e-mail communications. Because Chico O'Farrill grew increasingly frail in the years before his death in 2001, he depended increasingly on his son, Arturo Jr., to manage his affairs. I too have relied on Arturo Jr., both for a sense of the elder O'Farrill's viewpoint and for his own insights into the Latin jazz scene. To avoid confusion, like most of the musicians who worked with them, I refer to the elder O'Farrill as "Chico" and to his son as "Arturo." An accomplished jazz pianist, Arturo assumed a leading role in the establishment of the first Latin repertory orchestra, Lincoln Center's Afro-Latin Jazz Orchestra. A discussion of the compositions of Ray Santos and Chico O'Farrill leads naturally to the roles of the performers as I look at the Latin jazz scene from the perspectives of two prominent players: the trumpeter Ray Vega and the trombonist Rick Davies.

BIG BAND CLAVE

Despite Cuban musicians' ongoing interest in jazz since its earliest years,[5] recognition for the first important fusion of modern jazz and Latin music went to musicians in New York, not Havana. Leonardo Acosta suggests that the greater renown of the performers in New York gave them higher visibility. Moreover, the media had not been interested in recording Cubans playing jazz, believing they "should stick to playing their own music." Perhaps most important, in New York the musicians were more aware of their groundbreaking work. In Cuba musicians naturally absorbed the sounds of their giant neighbor to the north. Acosta writes, "Nobody seemed to realize it or give it any thought, except for a few musicians who mastered both and were drawn to experimentation and fusion."[6]

Although Dizzy Gillespie, Stan Kenton, and other Anglo musicians received the most attention, Bauzá along with another Cuban expatriate in New York, Frank "Machito" Grillo, initiated the Latin jazz movement by uniting the separate conjunto and bebop streams in the big band format.[7] Bauzá came to New York in 1930 and almost immediately became active in African American big bands, working with Noble Sissle (1932) and Chick Webb (1933–38). After performing and recording with Don Redman (1939–41), he joined Cab Calloway's band and was responsible for bringing in Dizzy Gillespie. In 1937 Bauzá's brother-in-law, Machito, arrived from Cuba, and in 1940 he formed the seminal group the Afro-Cubans. Bauzá soon joined him, bringing all his years of experience in black jazz bands to fruition in his position as music director. The instrumentation consisted of three saxophones, two trumpets, piano, bass, bongó, and timbales. According to John Storm Roberts, "From the start, Bauzá included non-Latins in his wind sections, partly because he wanted jazz-oriented players, and because there were relatively few top rank Latin hornmen in New York."[8] The group incorporated big band voicings and jazz solo styles in Latin musical forms, rhythms, and harmonic patterns. As Bauzá described it, "Our idea was to bring Latin music up to the standard of the American orchestras. So I brought a couple of the guys that arranged for Calloway and Chick Webb to write for me. I wanted them to give me the sound—to orchestrate it."[9]

Gillespie's first direct involvement in Latin music came in his performances with the Cuban flutist Alberto Socarrás in 1938 at the Savoy Ballroom and the Cotton Club.[10] Socarrás, who immigrated to New York in the 1920s, established his band playing opposite Glenn Miller at the Glen Island Casino in 1940. Gillespie's early efforts to fuse big band jazz and Afro-Cuban music produced mixed results. At the recommendation of Bauzá, Gillespie hired the Cuban *conguero* Chano Pozo. Though it produced some interesting compositions (e.g., "Manteca"), this experiment often resulted in unsettled and chaotic grooves. In a live recording from the Pasadena Civic Auditorium in 1948 (GNPD 23), abrupt changes from Latin to swing and back, the American drummer's obvious lack of experience with Latin rhythms, and Pozo's busy playing during the swing sections detract from the performance. At one point in "Manteca" the clave is even "turned around"—the mortal sin of Latin music. The clave pattern consists of a two-stroke measure and a three-stroke measure either of which may come first (2–3 or 3–2 clave). Once the

EXAMPLE 36. 2–3 clave percussion patterns.

pattern is established, it must be maintained throughout the entire piece and rhythms that suggest the reverse pattern must be avoided. Players inexperienced in Latin music often violate these principles. A complex matrix of interlocking rhythms are built around the clave. Example 36 gives the basic percussion patterns, which, true to principles of much African music, create a cohesive, satisfying whole while maintaining the individuality of the players through distinctive timbre and pitch.

It would take time for U.S. jazz musicians to understand and become proficient in these rhythms. In the meantime, the most successful fusion of Afro-Cuban music and jazz came from the Latino side.

Chico O'Farrill

Arturo "Chico" O'Farrill arrived in New York at precisely the right moment to participate in the confluence of modern jazz and Latin music. "This was the cradle of bebop," he later said. "For me it was a miracle to be here." For O'Farrill, who took his Cuban musical heritage for granted, and whose interest in jazz and classical music always outweighed his interest in Latin music, being in New York was a chance to pursue his dream. Shortly before his death in 2001 he confided to a reporter, "I feel more like a New Yorker than Cuban because the city has the music I love."[11] O'Farrill, as Acosta points out, was the only arranger to figure prominently in both Cuba and the United States.[12] He traveled frequently between the two countries, and established a reputation in Cuba before permanently departing. Unlike other important Cuban big band arrangers and leaders such as Armando Romeu,

EXAMPLE 37. *Afro-Cuban Jazz Suite*, opening chords, m.1, and melodic theme (mm.11–17) (Arturo "Chico" O'Farrill).

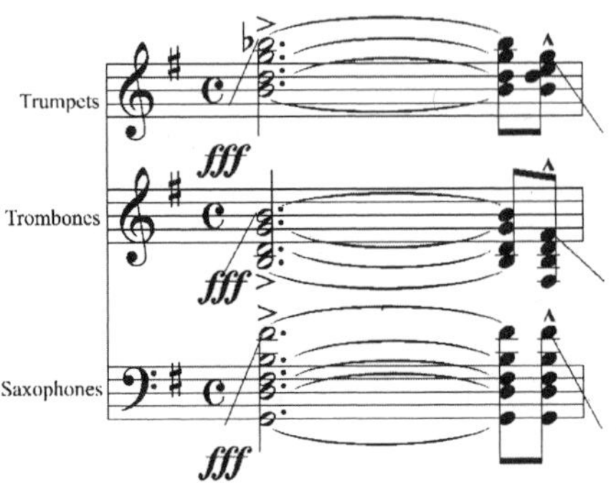

who was little known outside the island, O'Farrill established himself as an important force in jazz through his work for Goodman, Kenton, and later Machito, Gillespie, and Basie.

O'Farrill was born on 28 October 1921 in Havana into an upper-middle-class family; his father was a lawyer of Irish descent. According to Arturo, Chico spent his earliest years in the rural area around San José de las Lajas, about an hour outside Havana on the road to the port city of Matanzas. As a teenager he attended Riverside Military Academy in Gainesville, Georgia (1936–39), where he picked up the trumpet and discovered swing bands.[13] After returning to Havana, his parents, dismayed by his fascination with black jazz and hoping to draw him away from this scene, arranged for him to study with the Cuban composer Félix Guerrero. Nevertheless, he became active as a jazz soloist in the bands of René Touzet (1938) and the Tropicana (1942) and in several smaller groups such as the Swing Racketeers (1945) and Los Beboppers (1947), one of the first bop groups in Havana. He also began supplying big band arrangements for Romeu and other leaders, many of which reflected his growing interest in bebop and modern jazz. In 1948 he arrived in New York, eager to enter the jazz scene. He studied with the classical composer Stephan Wolpe and composed "Undercurrent Blues" and other commissions for Benny Goodman. Although he had previously shown little interest in Afro-Cuban music, which he found harmonically simple and repetitive, he fell into the burgeoning Afro-Cuban jazz, or cubop, movement. In 1950 he wrote "Cuban Episode" for the Kenton Orchestra and his classic extended work, *Afro-Cuban Jazz Suite (ACJS)*, for Machito and His Orchestra, featuring Charlie Parker, Harry "Sweets" Edison, Flip Phillips, and Buddy Rich.

EXAMPLE 38. *Afro-Cuban Jazz Suite,* melodic theme, mm. 11–17 (Arturo "Chico" O'Farrill).

ACJS, a four-movement suite, reveals many facets of O'Farrill's art, in particular his natural integration of classical techniques with jazz and Cuban musical resources. Starting as a bolero, the suite moves through an assortment of grooves including mambo, fast swing, Afro 6/8 (or bembé), and other Afro-Latin grooves. Structurally, most of the divisions between movements occur seamlessly and do not necessarily follow changes in groove.

Two important musical ideas shape the piece from the outset: a highly dissonant chord at the beginning and the main melodic theme (Examples 37 and 38). Both motives appear often throughout the work. The brash opening chord forcefully announces O'Farrill's complete lack of timidity in exploiting the sonic resources of the big band. The trumpets sound a symmetrical simultaneity containing both major and minor thirds, one of the most important "source chords" of twentieth-century composers; similar vertical structures appear in numerous works by Webern, Schoenberg, Stravinsky, Bartók, and Debussy.[14] The mixture of thirds also expresses a blues feeling. By combining this chord with a major-seventh chord in the saxophones, a decidedly unbluesy but heavily favored chord of the bop musicians, O'Farrill unites classical, blues, and modern jazz harmony.

Nestled between five iterations of this chord is the highly lyrical melodic theme in Example 38. First appearing as a bolero, this melody goes through several transformations before its final statement in a climactic mambo section. After restating the opening chords, *ACJS* ends on the bolero vamp, exploiting the cross-relation of minor and major thirds, this time between the saxophones and piano as well as through alteration of melodic fragments taken from the theme.

As Machito's band consisted of only trumpets, saxophones, and rhythm section, O'Farrill later added trombones for full big band versions, such as the recording on *Carambola* (2000). In this expanded orchestration, rather than recompose *ACJS,* O'Farrill has retained the essential character of the piece.

The added trombones almost never venture out separately. Instead, they double or add harmony to saxes or trumpets, as can be seen in Example 37. Since the saxes originally covered the lower range, O'Farrill places the trombones in a higher register, between and overlapping the saxes and trumpets.

True to jazz conventions, most of the solos follow a thirty-two-bar form. The long solos in D minor during the fast swing section adapt a set of chord changes popular at the time (e.g., Gillespie's "Bebop" and Parker's "Diverse"). In his compelling union of Afro-Cuban rhythms and riffs, blues tonality, jazz harmonic structure and improvisation, and classical techniques, O'Farrill established a reputation as an ambitious and thoroughly rounded composer.

During the 1950s, his career thrived. He toured with his own big band and recorded an album, *Jazz,* for Clef Records. He ghost-wrote arrangements for Walter (Gil) Fuller, Quincy Jones, and Billy Byers and contributed "Manteca Suite" to the Gillespie band. Fleeing marital and legal entanglements, he briefly went back to Cuba in 1955, then on to Los Angeles. In 1957 he moved to Mexico City, where he continued to work, composing "The Aztec Suite" for the trumpeter Art Farmer, as well as "Six Jazz Moods," a twelve-tone piece. In 1965 he returned to New York and over the next several years arranged a series of pop albums for the Basie orchestra and an album's worth of Latin jazz (*Spanish Rice,* 1966) for Clark Terry. In 1967 he recorded two albums under his own name for the Verve label, *Married Well* and *Inolvidables.*

During the 1970s, O'Farrill entered a difficult period. Salsa had brought the smaller conjunto back to the forefront of Latin music, and, except for Tito Puente's large group, the Latin big band, along with other jazz orchestras, had become virtually extinct, at least in terms of providing arrangers with commercially viable work. There were a few bright spots during this time: O'Farrill rejoined Machito and Gillespie for an album, *Afro-Cuban Jazz Moods* (1975), and collaborated with the Argentine saxophonist Gato Barbieri (1974). But for the next twenty years his only recordings were jingles and other commercial projects. Refusing to compromise, he rejected offers to record with smaller ensembles at insultingly low budgets.[15]

During this extended fallow period, O'Farrill's significant contribution to orchestral jazz was virtually forgotten. He supported his family in New York by writing commercial music on the periphery of the jazz and Latin scenes. Ray Santos, whose career was always more directly linked to the mambo big bands, found a different path to survival as he followed the dwindling Latin big band work to Puerto Rico. Although both came to Latin music with a love of jazz, O'Farrill remained primarily a composer of concert music that incorporated Afro-Latin elements in the jazz idiom. Santos, while integrating jazz harmonies and melodies into his work, made his mark playing and writing for mambo dance bands, especially the "big three": Machito and the two Titos—Puente and Rodriguez.

Ray Santos

One night in 1948, while listening to his favorite jazz programs on the radio, a young saxophonist from the Bronx heard Symphony Sid announce: "Now here's 'Bird,' Charlie Parker, soloing with Machito and His Afro-Cubans." To a teenaged musician of Puerto Rican descent living in New York, the sounds coming over the airwaves that night brought together everything in his life—big bands, jazz, and his Latino heritage. "WOW, this is it!" Ray Santos remembers thinking. "This is the real meeting between Jazz and Afro-Cuban Music."[16]

Santos was born on 28 December 1928 on 113th Street and Lexington Avenue and remained in El Barrio until about 1942, when his family moved across the Harlem River to the Bronx. His home was roughly divided into Latin and American musical zones. "On the Spanish language radio in the kitchen," he remembers, "my mother would listen to recorded music from Puerto Rico by such artists as Canario y su Grupo, Ramito, Daniel Santos, Pedro Flores, Cuarteto Marcano, Trío San Juan, Noro Morales, Machito, Bobby Capo and many others." Meanwhile, his "father liked to listen to English-language radio in the living room."

The 1930s were a fertile period for Latin music in New York. Many Puerto Ricans came to New York looking for work, and they became the largest ethnic group in New York's Latino population.[17] The Great Depression, which devastated the island's economy, fed the huge influx. As one Puerto Rican musician described the situation, "When there's a depression there [in the United States], here there's a depression and a half."[18]

Growing up in El Barrio, Santos was surrounded by music. As he describes the scene:

> The Park Plaza was on 110th Street and 5th Avenue. There is a church there now. That was where Machito's band started. Noro Morales would be at the Odd Fellow's Temple on 106th Street between Park and Lexington. There was another club on 102nd Street and Madison Avenue by the name of El Club Obrero. On Saturday nights I would hear the bands playing there on the second floor. Since I lived on 102nd Street and Park Avenue I would just walk up the block and listen to the bands play when I was about 10 years old. There were a lot of places in El Barrio where you would hear live music on a Saturday night. Since there was no air-conditioning you would hear the music wafting out onto the streets. You would also hear the music coming from house parties because people really didn't start going out until later on when the Palladium started up in the late 40's and 50's.[19]

Since his early teens Santos also had enjoyed listening to big band music. He recalls hearing on the radio and buying "records by Duke Ellington, Count Basie, Stan Kenton, Woody Herman, Gene Krupa, Lionel Hampton,

Benny Goodman, Artie Shaw, and the list goes on and on." Around 1945 Santos started playing the saxophone. He studied at a school of music in the Strand Building on Broadway, where, for $40, he received the loan of a saxophone and twenty lessons. He started frequenting Times Square in order to hear the bands he had been listening to: "There were a lot of theaters that had shows and in between the movies they'd have bands. I saw everybody down there. Visually it was very impressive because the band would come out of the pit. The pit stage would rise up, and they would be playing their theme songs as they came up."

Unlike O'Farrill, who found dance forms confining, Santos was fascinated with all the material the arrangers could get into three minutes. He played jazz arrangements in his high school band and in local bands from his neighborhood that played for dances. In 1948 he began studies at Juilliard while continuing to play at night. His bands often shared the bill with more prominent bands, such as those led by Machito and the Puerto Rican pianist Noro Morales. By hanging around and looking over the shoulders of the musicians "to see what was going on musically," Santos became acquainted with Morales and Machito, as well as Mario Bauzá, Tito Rodriguez, and Tito Puente. As he became more involved, his interest in harmony and arranging grew.

His first big break came in 1953, a year after graduating from Juilliard, when he joined Morales's band. Although the pianist's stardom had faded, Santos remembers that during the 1940s, "he was bigger than Puente and Rodriguez, he was *the* band here in New York City." Like many Latino bandleaders in the 1930s and 1940s, Morales had added saxophones to his band: "Noro loved the saxophones, so he, sometimes he would actually sacrifice one of the trumpets and just use two trumpets so he could get the five saxophones 'cause he liked the sound of five saxophones, and he had a nice book for five reeds, really well written."

The demand for saxophone and other wind players in the Latin bands came at the right time for many Anglo musicians. By the late 1940s swing bands were in serious decline, and many players were looking for work. Santos remembers:

> New York was crawling with good saxophone players from the bands, and brass players, and they were all looking for a job, so there were many Anglo players in the band. In fact, Doc Severinsen was a steady player in his working band for a while because he was on the road with Charlie Barnet, or one of those good bands, and the band broke up. He was here in New York and he stayed around looking for a job and his first job was as lead trumpet with Noro Morales. Bernie Glow also, who was a top studio player.

For Santos, sitting next to a seasoned saxophone player like Jerry Sanfino was "a beautiful experience," since "he'd played with Goodman and everything."

Santos was impressed with the Anglo players' ability to learn the rhythmic phrasing of Latin music; "Puente or Rodriguez would more or less sing the phrasing to them, and they would adapt immediately. They were such good readers and had such beautiful tones; they made the band sound good."

Soloists also needed to be able to improvise without contradicting the underlying clave patterns. Santos says that "the mambo beat of the fifties was kind of attractive to the jazz players," especially when it was in 2–3 clave (which was more common). "Almost every hip jazz phrase that you can play fits in pretty good with the 2–3 clave." The 3–2 clave, on the other hand, which Santos describes as "more Cuban oriented" presented more difficulties for jazz players: "There you gotta be a little more careful, 'cause I've heard a lot of jazz players, they go in and play against the 3–2 clave, but they're playing 2–3 phrases. Something about the 2–3 clave and jazz phrasing—they kind of gel together. I guess that's why the mambo was so popular with the jazz players."

The rhythm sections naturally remained predominantly Latino. Not only was it rare to find Anglos who were trained in Latin percussion instruments, but few pianists and bass players had acquired specialized skills in playing *guajeos, tumbaos,* and other specific rhythmic patterns required in *sones, guarachas, boleros,* and other Latin genres. The presence of Anglo horn players caused some tension with the younger Latinos trying to break into the scene, but Santos remembers that "the leaders like Puente or Machito and Rodriguez, they'd always go out of their way to give a competent Latino player a chance—to get him into the band." Santos also notes that in Machito's band, despite the leader's desire to play with "a predominantly black band, a lot of white players would come in to play, and Mario [Bauzá] would hire a lot of white players." Whatever frictions might exist between Latino and non-Latino players, race was not a central issue. Echoing the observations of scholars such as Ruth Glasser,[20] Santos observes, "The different races get along pretty good in the Caribbean countries 'cause of the racial mixtures. The discriminations there in the Caribbean are more class than racial. The makeup of the bands is that way also. From the first time I went to Puerto Rico, I noticed that the bands were pretty mixed."

In 1956 Santos began a four-year stint with Machito, playing saxophone and contributing arrangements. Despite its emphasis on jazz harmonies and soloing, Machito's band played essentially Latin dance music. "Sunny Ray," composed in 1958, illustrates Santos's ability not only to integrate harmonic and melodic elements of jazz and Latin music but also to retain rhythmic principles fundamental to each. Machito and his music director, Bauzá, "were always very heavy on jazz instrumentals." Santos estimates that "half their repertory at that time—the late forties and all throughout the fifties—was instrumental, with lots of soloing." "Sunny Ray" was commissioned as an instrumental dance tune for Machito's book.

EXAMPLE 39. "Sunny Ray," introduction, mm. 1–4 (Ray Santos).

"Sunny Ray" begins with a ten-measure introduction, its two-measure pattern rhythmically reminiscent of the "do-wah do-wahs" of Ellington's "It Don't Mean a Thing." This rhythmic motive (which has antecedents in ragtime and even earlier) superimposes a three-beat pattern on top of the regular 4/4 time. Santos's use of this motive illustrates some of the differences between swing and clave-based music. Unlike Ellington, who sets the pattern on the second beat, Santos begins the pattern on the first beat of the measure. Because of this placement, Santos must begin the piece in 3–2 clave. By the fifth "do-wah," the pattern has reset on the third beat of the second measure or the second stroke of the two-stroke measure of 3–2 clave. Example 40 compares this figure with both 2–3 and 3–2 clave patterns. In the four measures only two notes fall on 2–3 clave strokes, whereas in 3–2 clave nine of the eighteen attacks land on a clave stroke. The "do-wahs" of "It Don't Mean a Thing," by beginning on the second beat, conform to 2–3 clave and support Santos's thesis that jazz musicians' phrasing fits 2–3 clave better than 3–2 clave.

For the theme of "Sunny Ray," Santos has written a melody that explicitly states the underlying 3–2 clave (Example 41). Based on a thirty-two-bar AABA structure in which the "A" section is reminiscent of "Bernie's Tune,"[21] the harmony of "Sunny Ray" uses ii7– V7 progressions common in modern jazz.

Like many pieces of clave-based Cuban music (e.g., the *bolero-son* "Lágrimas Negras"), "Sunny Ray" shifts clave as a means of building excitement. Santos probably decided that the soloists, especially the jazz players, would be more comfortable improvising in 2–3 clave. Because the underlying clave must never change, composers shift clave by inserting a phrase or section containing an odd number of measures. Santos's transition from 3–2 to 2–3 clave features an interesting amalgamation of Cuban and jazz elements. After a seven-bar section that sets up the clave shift, Santos combines a

EXAMPLE 40. "Sunny Ray," introduction with 2–3 and 3–2 clave comparison, mm. 1–4 (Ray Santos).

EXAMPLE 41. "Sunny Ray" theme, mm.11–14 (Ray Santos).

EXAMPLE 42. "Sunny Ray," transition, mm. 56–59 (Ray Santos).

melody strongly suggestive of 2–3 clave with a heavy jazz-flavored backbeat on the second and fourth beats (Example 42). After four measures the rhythm section begins restating the clave, now in 2–3 because of the uneven number of measures in the transitional section.

Santos's interest in modern jazz harmony is evident throughout. In addition to the typical ii7–V7 progressions, Santos favors upper chordal extensions such as thirteenths, raised elevenths, and minor chords with major sevenths. When the trumpets enter in the last eight measures of the transition

EXAMPLE 43. "Sunny Ray," interlude, mm. 48–51 (Ray Santos).

section, major sevenths and flatted fifths, favored devices of bebop, are prominent melodic features. (See Example 43.) To help jazz musicians and players less familiar with Latin music, Santos carefully indicates all the articulations and accents. Santos explains:

> It's not like Latin players where you just give 'em a piece of paper with no phrasing or accents and they know exactly what to do. When you write for a band of students or non-Latino players you have to put the articulations in carefully and try and get the phrasing as close as possible.

Santos stayed with Machito until 1960, when he rejoined Noro Morales's band to play an engagement in Puerto Rico at the Hotel La Concha. After the Cuban Revolution in 1959 and the consequent U.S.-led embargo, Puerto Rico became a leading destination for tourists. Resorts, hotels, and casinos proliferated. When Santos returned to New York two years later he noticed that profound developments in jazz had occurred during his absence: "When I came back, I put on the radio and I started to hear things, the harmonic things, like the modal things Miles was doing. I heard the harmonic structures were tending to get a little simpler, and I actually went to a teacher because some of my friends had studied with him, Hall Overton." Overton, who had recorded big band arrangements with Thelonious Monk at Town Hall a few years earlier, told Santos to buy *Kind of Blue* and transcribe solos by Davis and pianist Wynton Kelly. Santos recalls:

> I extracted the whole harmonic structure from "Freddie the Freeloader." That was like a whole lesson or course in the blues—of the contemporary blues they were doing at that time. So when Mario and Machito asked me to bring in an instrumental, I wrote "Azulito" and I brought it into the studio.

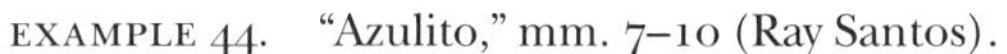
EXAMPLE 44. "Azulito," mm. 7–10 (Ray Santos).

In "Azulito" ("A Little Blue"), Santos transformed the simple triadic textures and modal vamps of *Kind of Blue*'s "Freddie the Freeloader" into a jazz mambo (Example 44). The bass plays the standard tumbao or anticipated figures while the rest of the rhythm section supplies the underlying groove in 2–3 clave.[22]

In 1963 Santos returned to Puerto Rico with Tito Puente. There he met a woman whom he married and eventually "brought back to New York to start a family." On 22 February 1965, a day he remembers clearly because it was the morning after Malcolm X was assassinated, Santos left for Argentina with Tito Rodriguez's band. The New York scene in which Santos had thrived was rapidly changing. The mambo big bands that had supported him as a player and arranger were giving way to new styles of Latin dance music, boogaloo, and, later, salsa. A year later Rodriguez notified his musicians that he would break up his band when they returned from a trip to Venezuela.

The year 1966 brought the end of an era. The Palladium Ballroom, where the mambo kings and their big bands had held court since the early 1950s, closed its doors. Serving as a kind of bridge between mambo and salsa, the boogaloo dance movement briefly brought together Latino and African American audiences. Some older Latin musicians saw boogaloo as a dumbing down of Latin rhythms, arranging skills, and jazz harmonies. But this process merely paralleled the simplification occurring in jazz, as it too absorbed influence from rhythm and blues. Latin musicians who had already shared neighborhoods and nightclubs with African Americans for several generations absorbed the funky backbeat and rhythms of soul music.[23]

The boogaloo fad was short-lived but helped to pave the way for a new generation of Latin musicians. Salsa was a product of New York, created mostly by musicians of Puerto Rican descent. The Cuban connection, which had been central to New York's Latin music scene for decades, was cut off by the embargo. Puerto Rican musicians at last came out from under the shadow of Cuban musicians and took undisputed leadership of New York's Latin scene. Although they were quick to adopt classic Cuban repertoire, in particular the *conjunto* format of Arsenio Rodríguez, the *salseros* modified the instrumentation and introduced distinctly Puerto Rican and Nuyorican subject matter as well as elements of such Puerto Rican genres as *aguinaldo, plena,* and *danza.*[24] But, where the mambo bands had featured saxophones, the new salsa bandleaders, Mon Rivera, Willie Colón, and Eddie Palmieri, emphasized the trombone. Santos explains:

> These were not bands like Rodriguez, Puente, and Machito always had—four trumpets and four or five saxophones. On recordings we used to use trombones also, even though the working bands didn't always have trombones. . . . Now they had two trombones and two trumpets or three trumpets tops, and maybe a baritone saxophone. They came to be more brass ensembles and saxophones got shunted out.

In Santos's view the change was mostly a matter of economics: "There wasn't that money, and even Puente and Machito were having problems with just keeping up their bands." The emphasis on brass compensated for having fewer horns: "They always wanted the brassy sound, so, we can get a smaller band, just use the brass, because the sound has always been very brassy. To cut through all that percussion, the heavy percussion, you need the brassy sound." Despite the many changes in the scene, Santos does not believe that there were significant generational divisions between the young *salseros* and the older Latin musicians. Nothing about the big band format itself made it "out of date." Unlike the burning controversies between swing musicians and beboppers in jazz twenty years earlier (stoked by the jazz press), *salseros* found much to admire in the previous generations. According to Santos, "They had been listening to everything that we did in the fifties and the sixties, only the money wasn't there for them to make a big band. As a matter of fact, they admired it, and whenever they got a chance to make a band just a little bigger they would do it."

Just before leaving for Venezuela with Rodriguez, Santos bought a home in Puerto Rico. Not only had the music scene changed in New York, but urban life had deteriorated significantly because of drugs, unemployment, and other social ills. Feeling that New York had become "very lawless," he decided to move to the island and raise his children "down there." Moreover, the big band scene in Puerto Rico remained alive due to the thriving tourist industry. The hotels maintained bands to play the shows of visiting artists such as the Supremes, Tony Bennett, and Nat Cole. These bands retained the mambo big band format—mostly trumpets and saxophones, with the number of trombones varying depending on the visiting act.

Santos remained busy playing and arranging music for television shows, commercials, and local bands on the island. The scene grew as many of Puente's and Rodriguez's best players also fled the mainland. Santos wrote salsa arrangements for some of the younger bands. After the hotel gigs he hung out with renowned musicians such as Cortijo and Ismael Rivera. By the late 1970s the work began to dry up, especially in the hotel bands. Competition with resorts on other islands and, eventually, Atlantic City and other gambling centers in the United States took its toll. A costly dispute with the musicians' union on the island led to further reductions in the hotel bands. "Yeah, it got really bad down there, so I decided to come back," Santos recalls.

Redemption

"I guess, if the music business doesn't kill you, it will ignore you." Arturo's words sum up his feelings about his father's two decades of virtual obscurity. With the fierce competition in New York, Arturo remembers that his and his sister's use of the phone was restricted because their father was afraid he might miss a call to do a jingle or some other date.[25] Although recognition came almost too late (especially for O'Farrill), O'Farrill's and Santos's perseverance eventually paid off.

O'Farrill's path to rediscovery began with his arrangements for David Bowie's 1993 album, *Black Tie, White Noise.* The following year, with the encouragement of the Cuban filmmaker Jorge Ulla, for whose 1984 film, *Guaguasi,* he had composed music, Chico put together a band for an engagement at the Blue Note. With the support of Ulla and the record producer Todd Barkan, O'Farrill recorded three albums over the next five years: *Pure Emotion* (1995), *Heart of a Legend* (1999), and *Carambola* (2000). Throughout this period Arturo became more and more involved in his father's affairs by contracting musicians, leading rehearsals, and leading the band on its weekly gigs at Birdland. Over the years, Chico's career intertwined with those of many studio musicians. In fact, the earlier albums had been recorded by studio bands, which, in Arturo's opinion, "didn't always make for the best interpreters of that music." Chico often delegated the role of hiring musicians to contractors, who, as is common practice, hired their cronies. Arturo says, "One of the biggest contributions I made to Chico's music was having an orchestra that was truly his, that wasn't put together for the moment." With "their expertise in the field" and "commitment to the music that was beyond just the date," the ensemble for the weekly gigs at Birdland began to sound more like a *band,* especially by the time they recorded *Carambola* in 2000: "I think that in order to play Latin music you really have to have a lot of years of playing clave-centered music, and a lot of the studio guys just didn't. I mean they were very good musicians and they would be the first ones to tell you that they weren't specialists in that field." Arturo allows that the playing on the earlier recordings is precise but complains that "there's no fire." He can only speculate whether having his own band earlier would have changed the course of his father's career but believes that even though the recognition came "toward the end of his life, he was very moved."

The founding of the Chico O'Farrill Afro-Cuban Jazz Orchestra was an important turning point in Arturo's life as well. As a child Arturo did not hear much Latin music at home. His father listened to jazz and classical music: "On Chico's stereo system you would hear a lot of Oscar Peterson, Count Basie, Bill Evans, Beethoven, Dvořák, Luigi Nono, [and] he loved contemporary composers, Messiaen. He listened to a lot of straight-ahead jazz. I never heard him play a Latin record as long as I've known him." In his teen years Arturo listened obsessively to Bud Powell and, later, Chick Corea. After graduating from LaGuardia High School for Music and Art, Arturo gravitated toward the avant-garde scene: "My first formative experiences in jazz were playing in as far opposite musically as you can get from Chico. I was playing with Carla Bley, and Rashied Ali, and Oliver Lake." Although he had "a Latin gig here and there," he now feels that his playing in that idiom was superficial, that he "was just going through the motions" because he had not studied the music.

His Latin jazz epiphany came through the mentoring of the bassist Andy Gonzalez, one of New York's most articulate and knowledgeable figures in Latin music and, with his brother, Jerry, leader of the groundbreaking Fort Apache Latin jazz band. In the course of recording a Latin jingle, somebody suggested that Arturo hire Andy Gonzalez:

> I called Andy, and I was very moved, actually. He had been following my career as meager as it was, and he was very warm and engaging and very generous with his knowledge. He invited me to his house and he literally took me through the history of Latin piano. That was '94, maybe '93, and I had just finished a three-year stint with Harry Belafonte, and I was kind of a little desperate for work and Andy just came into my life and really took that opportunity to show me a lot about music.

Arturo also began subbing for the regular pianist in the Fort Apache band, Larry Willis.

As Arturo and his father brought the Chico O'Farrill Afro-Cuban Jazz Orchestra to life in the latter half of the 1990s, long-delayed recognition finally came to Chico. In 1995 Wynton Marsalis commissioned a trumpet concerto, "Trumpet Fantasy," which was performed a year later at Lincoln Center. The Chico O'Farrill Afro-Cuban Jazz Orchestra appeared in Fernando Trueba's acclaimed film on Latin jazz, *Calle 54* (2000). Chico toured Spain and just before his death was working on a Broadway musical.[26]

O'Farrill's redemption was both dramatic and bittersweet. A December 2000 *New York Times* article that appeared only six months before his death compared O'Farrill to the recently "rediscovered" heroes of *The Buena Vista*

Social Club and proclaimed him the "Duke Ellington of Latin jazz." Despite "his accomplishments and the reverence of his peers," the article reported, O'Farrill had remained "the most invisible of the Latin jazz innovators."[27] Unfortunately, much of this acclaim came when Chico was so frail and infirm that he could barely stand in front of his band. Arturo reluctantly assumed the leadership of the band. He explains: "He just became slower, and weaker, and he would just impede the process of rehearsal. So sometimes, you know, just to get the job done, I would rehearse without him." Arturo is pleased, of course, that his father "got his due," but he struggles with the sense that "it was too little, too late." Because of his illness Chico was not able to really enjoy the resurgence in his career.

Although less heralded in the press than O'Farrill's, the revival of Ray Santos's career has been no less dramatic. With the depth and breadth of New York's music scene, any void left by a departing musician is quickly filled. Yet the often-close bonds formed in jazz networks allow returning prodigals to rekindle old relationships and, with a little luck, eventually reestablish themselves. While Santos had been away, he had done little writing for New York bandleaders. When they learned he was back, Puente, Machito, and Bauzá soon were calling for arrangements, and he was offered a teaching position at City College. His role as chief arranger for the 1992 film *Mambo Kings* led to a recording session in California with Linda Ronstadt.

Some of the musicians with whom he had been involved over the years began to ask why he did not start a band of his own. Like many jazz composers, he liked the idea of being able to hear his works-in-progress. But he was fully aware of the responsibilities of trying to keep a band together. "I don't want the headaches of calling people up and everything," he told them. When the musicians offered to take over these duties, he relented. The band began rehearsing in the Bronx on Monday nights, but, after a short time, moved to Boys Harbor, a more convenient location for many of the musicians. Santos has assembled a huge roster of players who are familiar with his music. "My address book is full," he says. "I think I have around two hundred guys that have come and played with me at one time or the other, either rehearsed or done the gigs." Santos's book has grown to more than one hundred charts—including originals, big band arrangements of *conjunto* pieces, and swing standards. Ninety percent of the material is Latin; Santos keeps a few swing charts on hand "just to cover any requests." "In my case they usually want more Latin than American," he explains.

Both Santos's band and the Chico O'Farrill Afro-Cuban Jazz Orchestra play dances on occasion. Santos says, "If it's a dance, I have plenty of dance charts like from the fifties and sixties, a lot of the Machito dance charts. It all depends on the venue." Although more oriented to concert repertoire, according to Arturo, Chico "would do dances if called upon to." "All I really do to modify the book," Arturo says about taking a dance gig, "is I open up sections where the rhythm just chugs along. It's all danceable—it's Latin music, but it's eminently listenable because it's Chico."

Arturo is alluding to Latin jazz's continuing connection to dance. Transforming a jazz standard into Latin jazz usually means changing the groove from swing into a mambo, bolero, chachachá, or other Latin dance style and adapting the melodic and harmonic rhythms to clave. Coming at Latin jazz from the other side, Latin repertoire is "jazzed up" through reharmonization and opening up the structure for extended solos. These differing rhythmic, melodic, and harmonic matrices give rise to claims and counterclaims of "authenticity" and competence.

JAZZ AND CLAVE: SOIL, BLOOD, AND LIVED EXPERIENCE

Latin jazz networks stand apart from other jazz networks for reasons that might be considered strictly musical—such as the requirement that musicians be schooled in clave. By the same token, to play Latin jazz, musicians proficient in Latin dance music are expected to improvise fluidly, even over difficult chord progressions. Latin jazz is distinguished from other forms of jazz primarily by its rhythms, which have retained their connection to dance and bodily movement. Practice theorists describe the body as "a mnemonic device upon and in which the very basics of culture are imprinted and encoded in a socializing or learning process which commences during early childhood."[28] Musical interaction, as socially scripted sound and movement, is a primary medium for the bodily inscription of culture. Cultural insiders consider such bodily knowledge a birthright. For most people who were not born surrounded by them, the feel for Latin rhythms is not acquired easily.

The primacy of rhythm produces a hierarchy in which relationships to the sources of these rhythms are prioritized. The most direct connection, through birthplace, or "soil," supports the strongest claims of "authenticity." Next ranks familial ties, or "blood." Although distanced from the homeland, musicians who grew up in diasporic communities can cite their immersion in these rhythms from earliest childhood. Finally, musicians without direct connections through soil or blood emphasize the importance of their apprenticeships, mentoring, and performance experience.[29]

In his listening habits and statements, Chico O'Farrill evidenced little interest in traditional Cuban music. Nevertheless, Arturo insists that his father "had an intimate knowledge of these very sacred Afro-Cuban rhythms." His father's earliest years were spent in the rural area outside Havana, where, Arturo speculates, "he grew up hearing the chants, right outside his window probably." Although he was raised in an upper-middle-class Irish-German household, Chico absorbed Afro-Cuban culture directly through his contact with black housekeepers and other domestic workers. By emphasizing his father's island roots, Arturo provides a powerful counterclaim to his father's lack of interest in strictly Cuban musical forms.

The striking image of Ray Santos's childhood home illustrates the dual birthright of diasporic communities. His mother's Spanish radio in the kitchen provided not only a culinary but also a musical link to Puerto Rico, while his father's English-language radio in the living room suggested the lure of the larger Anglo-American living space outside the barrio. Still, island roots trump familial ties. Even with all the years Santos spent in Puerto Rico, as a musician and after he married and raised his family "down there," he never felt accepted. "They look on us Nuyoricans as assimilated Americans," he explains, "and we're not the real Puerto Ricans."

Ray Vega agrees. A lifelong Nuyorican resident of the South Bronx, who played trumpet with many of the leading groups in Latin music and jazz (such as those led by Tito Puente, Mongo Santamaría, Mario Bauzá, Joe Henderson, and many others), Vega visits the island regularly. Despite the fact that his parents hail from Ponce on the southern shore of Puerto Rico, known as a center for the island's African culture, he finds that he has "a very difficult time getting to 'point A' with the people of Puerto Rico." "If you're from Puerto Rico they're gonna bend over backwards for you," he elaborates. "If you're an outsider, even if your parents are from there, they're not. I've just found that to be the way that it is. I mean, they're just not very accommodating." Vega's feelings to a certain extent sum up what it is to be a Nuyorican—the sense of not thoroughly belonging to either scene. His parents moved back to Puerto Rico when his father retired in 1986. On his visits he remembers, "[There were] times where they would say, 'Oh, there's Lucy'—my mother's name was Lucy—'there's Lucy's son, the American.' You know, pretty corny shit, and then you'd come back here and it's like, 'Well, there's that Puerto Rican,' you know, so it's kind of like a man with no nation."

Nuyorican musicians in Puerto Rico were seen as interlopers or, in Santos's words, "kind of like a carpetbagger thing": "They looked at me like, 'What is this guy doing now? Why doesn't he stay up there? He comes down here to take our jobs.' " As a first-generation New York–born Puerto Rican, the island was "the most logical place to go": "I knew people down there and people were always offering me jobs. And I wanted to raise my kids out of New York City. But they adopted the attitude of, 'Well, he couldn't make it up there so he had to come down here.' Yeah, that type of thing I always resented."

Anglo musicians had an even tougher time in Puerto Rico. Santos remembers a trombone player whom Tito Rodriguez had brought from New York: "He was a really nice person, a very good trombone player, and he went down there and when he was playing with Tito he met a nice girl down there and he stayed in Puerto Rico and got married." Despite a shortage of good trombonists and his obvious qualifications, "he was always shunted aside by the local players." Santos heard many complaints about using him.

Anglo horn players have found greater acceptance in the mainland Latin music scene. The trombonist Rick Davies began playing in Latin bands in the 1970s in his native Albuquerque. After his arrival in New York in 1977, salsa bands on the "cuchifrito circuit" quickly became his main source of work.[30] For club dates and other commercial situations, trombones were often the last horns to be hired, only after trumpets and saxophones. Even the mambo big bands, such as Machito's and Puente's, tended to hire trombones only for record dates. Mon Rivera was one of the first leaders regularly to feature a trombone section, but Eddie Palmieri's group, La Perfecta, in Davies's words, "really put it on the map." Featuring the arrangements and powerful sound of the trombonist Barry Rogers, La Perfecta combined trombones and flute in a style that became dubbed "trombanga," in reference to its obvious debt to traditional Cuban *charanga* music. Soon Willie Colón and other leaders followed suit, and, as Davies notes, "it started a trend. All of a sudden everybody's got trombones." The mambo bands gave way to the classic salsa lineup: two trumpets, two trombones, and a baritone sax. Far from being treated as an expendable item, Davies felt almost like a "star," especially on his trips to the islands:

> You know Americans, they look at a trombone and they say, "Well, a little color or something." But you go down there and audiences really appreciate you. It's almost like a trombone player or a trumpet player in Puerto Rico or Haiti, or wherever, it's almost like a guitar player in a rock band.

Popularity with audiences did not help to relieve tensions between Anglo and island musicians. Davies recalls a time he "got closed out" of a recording session in New York: "I was the only gringo there. I ended up having to leave, and they got somebody else." Davies, whose Spanish is minimal, knew it was time to leave when "they didn't talk to [him] in English": "It was just a bad scene, you know. I wasn't welcome. The producer didn't want to deal with me. And it wasn't Nuyoricans, it was a lot of guys from Puerto Rico." Davies has built a successful career playing and composing for mainland Latin bands, in which he rarely faces such hostility. Like Vega, he has encountered the most friction "in some scenes where it's all people from 'down there'—Puerto Rican born and raised." Given the upheaval that colonialism wreaked on the economic and cultural life of the island, especially in music, such lingering resentments should come as no surprise.[31] However, for the musicians involved in these day-to-day struggles, maintaining historical perspective is not easy.

Unable to claim a connection to Latin music as a birthright, non-Latino players compensate by emphasizing their extensive experience playing with Latino musicians. When reading parts as a member of a horn section, rhythmic issues arise less often than during improvisation. At first, learning the ins and outs of clave isn't so important. Davies explains:

> Horn players get away with it, especially if they don't play solos. You can usually play the chart right as long as you start right, but it really shows in the soloing. Boy, guys can get dark real fast. [Laughter] You start messin' up the clave. I feel like I probably played on that scene for fifteen years before I really felt comfortable.

A breakthrough came when Davies worked with a fellow trombonist, Jimmy Bosch. Bosch grew up in the Puerto Rican community in Jersey City and had played in Latin bands from a very early age. Praising Bosch as "probably the most natural sounding trombone player in that style," Davies expresses gratitude for his generosity with his knowledge. Between sets, when they were in the back room, Bosch would invent little exercise routines by playing a riff or *moña.* In Davies's words, "[Bosch would] rake me over the clave coals."

> We'd start doin' *moñas* and he had this thing. He said when he was a kid they used to make him do it. One guy would start a clave, a *moña* pattern and the other guy would come in. The first guy would drop out and the second guy would change into a different *moña.* You know, back and forth like that. Nowadays I can hold my own, but at that time I just felt like a total idiot. You know, I'd come in with something and it wouldn't be—it would cross over or whatever. I'd have to make one up and it would be bullshit. If it was bad enough, sometimes it would break down. Then I started becoming more aware of it. I was lucky 'cause he's one of the masters.

One of the most important things Davies learned was to "keep it simple." More complicated *moñas* were less effective:

> That's the worst thing, if you get into a band and they're makin' up *moñas* and some guy, usually an American guy, starts gettin' fancy on a *moña,* some of the stuff stops swingin'. And then you see some guy like that [Bosch]. Everything's very simple, nothing complex, just pure swing, that's all that matters.

Davies entered the Latin scene already proficient as a jazz player. But, as Ray Vega points out, players whose only experience has been in Latin dance music are ill prepared to face the challenges of soloing, especially the more complex harmonies often found in jazz: "Latin jazz or anything that has to do with improvising in a style based on the modern jazz, that's American experience. Because to me, when I think of improvising over Latin jazz I just think of bebop."

As a Nuyorican, Vega has a foot in each camp and can claim a birthright in jazz as well as Latin music. Musicians in Puerto Rico, on the other hand, have little exposure to jazz and even fewer opportunities to play it. Vega points out, "Puerto Rico, first of all, is not a mecca of jazz. Puerto Rico is a good place to go if you want to play with a merengue band, if you wanna do some TV jingles, if you wanna pack on some pop band." Even Latin percussionists have difficulty adjusting to jazz because of its much simpler rhythmic structure. Arturo explains the difference:

> Swing is like a really good boxer, just kind of jabbing and keeping a clean, spare style. The really good boxers, in my opinion, are the ones that do the least work. 'Cause they tire the opponent out, that's good boxing. And to me swing, straight ahead swing, is a very lean, muscular kind of groove that requires very little except just a real drive.

Compared to jazz, Arturo finds Latin music "cluttered," explaining that "in the Latin rhythm section each instrument plays a specific role that fits in with the other one, but they don't play the same thing so it tends to sound very busy." The greater freedom that characterizes the jazz rhythm section means that players have less clearly defined roles. Traditionally, congas have been the most commonly added instruments to swing rhythm sections. Prominent *congueros* in jazz such as Candido Camero and Ray Barretto have limited themselves to playing a simple tumbao (𝄽♪♪𝄽♩) that accentuates the backbeat. Arturo explains "that do-do *bop* locks it in." When his band does a straight-ahead number, he finds that the easiest solution is simply to have the percussionists leave the stage.

In theory at least, although ethnically diverse groups of musicians coming together in the field should be on a more or less equal footing, clearly Latino musicians hold a dominant position in Latin jazz. The primary creators of Latin jazz have been Latino. Most important, Latin music has figured prominently in the formation of Latino identity. In particular, since the 1960s what Wilson Valentin has described as the "working class avant-garde" aesthetic of Latin jazz played a vital role in Nuyorican and other Latino communities' struggle for political, economic, and cultural capital.[32]

RACE AND ETHNICITY IN LATIN JAZZ

Although often portrayed in monolithic terms ("Hispanics"), Latino diasporic populations in the United States actually comprise a wide range of distinctive national heritages. Juan Flores reminds us that "this is an ethnicity of ethnicities, an 'ethnic group' that does not exist but for the existence of its constituent 'subgroups.' " Despite important commonalites of language and culture, and some convergence of political interest resulting from being lumped together and "racialized" by census takers and demographers, successive waves of immigration from the Dominican Republic, Cuba, South American countries, and, especially in recent years, Mexico have brought distinct musical traditions and largely separate communities to the New York area. Many Latino communities in the United States have maintained close contact with their compatriots as well as with specific communities in their homelands. In New York, as the oldest and largest group, Puerto Ricans continue to outnumber other Latino groups, but their presence declined from 80 percent in 1960 to less than 37 percent by 2000.[33] In the Latino diaspora Puerto Ricans are unique in that their homeland is neither state nor independent nation. Their status as U.S. citizens (since 1917) has not come without cost. Unlike other members of the Latino diaspora, Puerto Ricans lack cultural capital available through the institutional support of embassies, consulates, and autonomous governments.[34] With their loyalties torn between homeland and mainland, divisions between island-born Puerto Ricans and those born in the United States remain deeper than among other nationalities of the Latino diaspora.

In contrast, divisions among Cuban musicians are more likely to be the result of politics than place of birth. Many Cuban "exiles" are bitter and outspokenly hostile to the Castro regime. For its part, the socialist government has been unwavering in living up to its dictum, "Sin cultura, no hay revolucíon" (Without culture, there is no revolution). Cuba's cradle-to-grave support for the arts has produced no shortage of great musicians, many of whom, to the dismay of the Cuban government, eventually have defected, whether in search of greater artistic freedom or tempted by monetary gain. Because he left the island well before the 1959 Revolution, Chico O'Farrill mostly avoided this conflict. In Cuba today, instead of being seen as traitor or defector, he is held in great regard as a composer, even in official circles.

Although non-Latino blacks and whites faced similar challenges in Latin jazz—they had to master a new rhythmic vocabulary—they did not come with the same viewpoint. For many African Americans, judging from the comments of musicians and artists such as Dizzy Gillespie and Katherine Dunham,[35] Caribbean music and dance represented a step closer to Africa, and African Americans felt a greater solidarity with their black counterparts in Latino culture. Rather than identify with Afro-Caribbean culture, many Anglos undoubtedly were attracted by its "exoticness." Despite these differences, for many U.S. musicians, the Latin jazz scene has offered a welcome refuge from the racially charged atmosphere in straight jazz.

Why then did Latin music escape the degree of racial tension that has characterized jazz during much of its history? Racism and discrimination were certainly as prevalent in Cuba as in the United States. People of color, scorned and despised by many of the white upper classes, formed a distinct underclass. White leagues, similar to the Ku Klux Klan in the United States, oppressed the huge black underclass. In music influential writers such as Eduardo Sánchez de Fuentes attempted to whitewash Cuban music history by denying or underplaying the influence of African culture in Cuban music.[36]

Despite these prejudices by the dominant white classes, a crucial difference between Cuba and the United States was the articulation of a vital counterdiscourse that combined nationalism and pride in creole or mulatto culture. While jazz, in its earliest years, was seen by many in the United States as a distinct subcultural form to be feared for its "primitive" sexual content,[37] in Cuba and elsewhere in the Caribbean, despite similar phobias, an intellectual movement took root that rearticulated mulatto and creole cultural forms as emblematic of national identity. In Cuba, where it received official recognition after the Revolution, Afro-Cuban culture was articulated as representative of Cubanness, not just a marginalized minority.[38] No similar movement occurred in the United States, where, despite its enormous contribution, black culture continued to be feared, denied, detested, exploited, exoticized, or appropriated. In contrast, the Harlem Renaissance, which happened more or less concurrently with the *negritud* movements in the Caribbean,[39] was viewed mainly as a subcultural phenomenon, not as a movement to redefine the overall identity of the United States.

The much smaller percentage of blacks in the United States and the long, concerted repression of African cultural forms made ignoring their contribution easier than in Cuba. Perhaps even more important, as noted by Antonio Benítez-Rojo, since the sixteenth century a fertile creole crescent blending African, European, and, to a much lesser extent, Native American forms had been allowed to flourish in eastern Cuba, outside the watchful gaze of colonial authority that was centered in Havana.[40] Despite endemic oppression, exacerbated by the large-scale importation of African slaves to work in the sugar industry in the early nineteenth century, this nascent creole culture was to lay the foundation for subsequent hybrid cultural forms.

Because clearly African-derived forms such as rumba and sacred music (Santaría, Palo Monte, Abakuá, etc.), as well as more European-descended forms like *punto* and *décima,* coexisted with syncretic musical genres, popular Cuban dance music such as *son* was more easily interpreted as jointly owned. Despite the existence of segregation, many more opportunities for integrated musical performance existed in Cuba than in the United States. As Acosta observes, "We see black and mulatto musicians from the very beginning and even more in the Thirties, in the capital and in the provinces, as well as black orchestras and others in which integration was a very normal thing, something still quite uncommon in the United States at the time."[41] For blacks in the United States, jazz became an important symbol of cultural achievement. Although it was performed by both blacks and whites from its earliest years, jazz remained contested territory not only because of segregation in its performance and the larger profits gained by whites in its marketing but also because of the virtual absence of unquestionably African cultural forms that had not been appropriated by or shared with whites.[42]

Frictions in the Latin jazz scene are more likely to result from the continuing legacy of colonialism than from racism. Despite the importance of

Latin jazz to Latino identity, it has continued to attract an international following. Latin big bands, because of the larger number of players involved, require leaders to reach out to diverse musicians, reaffirming Latin jazz as a transnational music. Ray Vega articulates an inclusive vision of Latin jazz, one that celebrates universalist aspirations without dismissing the ethnically particular:

> I think history is the great equalizer. . . . I think as long as people keep a historical perspective as to what's going on, it doesn't matter where the hell you're from. In order for you to have some shit to say, don't forget the fact that you are black, or Jewish, or whatever. That's the reason why the music of the Palladium was as special as it was. Because those bands were all intermixed. But was the black trumpet player trying to play Latino style? No, he was playing jazz, he was playing himself, you dig what I'm saying? Retain your own identity, but go forward with the music. And the only way to do that, you have to study. In this music it's a double-edged sword because, not only do you have to know who Benny Moré and Tito Puente and Machito are, but you're gonna have to know who Count Basie is and Fletcher Henderson, and Jimmie Lunceford and Bird and Coltrane. You gotta know all that stuff. So it's a double-edged sword. If you're gonna do it for real, it's a question of historical perspective.

CODA—THE LINCOLN CENTER AFRO-LATIN JAZZ ORCHESTRA

The rediscovery of Ray Santos and Chico O'Farrill set the stage for the revival of Latin big bands and, true to the 1990s spirit of "neoclassicism" in jazz, soon led to efforts to create a standing repertory orchestra exclusively devoted to Latin jazz.[43] As Arturo relates the story, after the 1995 performance of O'Farrill's "Trumpet Fantasy" by the Lincoln Center Jazz Orchestra, he called Marsalis's assistant, April Smith, with a proposal:

> I have a great idea. I would love to start a repertory orchestra for *our* music, and I would like to get Wynton's suggestions on how to go about doing that. About securing funding and who we should approach. She said, "Well, I'll talk to Wynton about that and we'll set up a meeting." And apparently she talked about it with Wynton and, you know, Wynton's the busiest human being I've ever known. He's so busy running around doing things, you know, writing and playing, that it's hard to lock him down for two minutes.

Over the next several years, whenever Marsalis and Arturo occasionally met on gigs, although the subject would come up, they did not pursue it further. One evening in 2001 after a performance, Wynton approached him and said, "I've decided to do your idea." "By this time I had completely forgotten about it," says Arturo, "so I asked, 'What are you talking about?' 'I want to start an Afro-Cuban orchestra and I want you to be the director.' " Although the band has started out slowly, Arturo states proudly, "We started actually with more gigs than the Lincoln Center Jazz Orchestra did in their first year. I think they had three gigs. And we had five."

As with all things connected to Jazz at Lincoln Center, Arturo and Marsalis's founding of the ALJO has not occurred without controversy. In a move that stirred up resentment in the Chico O'Farrill Orchestra, Arturo assembled a new band rather than simply hire the regulars from the Birdland gig. Recognizing the dedication of the musicians who had stuck with him through rehearsals and low-paying gigs (like the Sunday nights at Birdland), Arturo maintains he "struggled over" the decision. "The main reason I did it," he explains,

> is because I didn't want there to be confusion between the two orchestras. One was created for one purpose, the other was created for another. Wynton did not say to me, "Can you install the Chico O'Farrill Orchestra in-residence at Lincoln Center?" He said to me, "I want you to *start*." And, if you think about it, what's inherent in that is that you should *start* a new orchestra. Also, I feel that, there's a vibe and a specialness in the Chico O'Farrill Orchestra that pertains to it being the Chico O'Farrill Orchestra. I think it's a unique and special group of people and I didn't want to mess with the essential identity of that orchestra by dressing it up in another guise.

One member of the O'Farrill band, describing the disappointment felt by bandmembers, disputes this explanation: "But, the thing is that a lot of the guys were drug, man, because they were figuring, 'Now this is our big payoff.' And he can't say, 'Well, I need to keep two separate bands,' because he picked his friends . . . to come into the other band. He hand-chose his buddies."

Arturo acknowledges that the members of the Chico O'Farrill Orchestra were justified to feel unhappy with his decision but suggests it was not a matter of them "being passed over" for the other players:

> I really see it as a different mission. A repertory orchestra is different than an orchestra that's designed to play exclusively in one genre or school. Because a repertory orchestra has to be able to transcend a lot of styles and a lot of different things. I mean it's hard to articulate, let me see if I can say this. The Chico O'Farrill Afro-Cuban Jazz Orchestra is a very sweet, supple, flexible animal. It has a lot of nuance, and it has a lot of style. The Afro-Latin Jazz Orchestra needs to be different. It needs to be brasher, to be more of a *proclaiming* kind of orchestra. Because it's devoted to the performance of repertoire that is canonical, it has to be very rigid in that sense, and it also has to be conducive to performing new repertoire. I felt that confusing the two would be a tragic mistake much to the detriment of either one.

Some members of Chico's band suggest that Jazz at Lincoln Center pressured Arturo to hire musicians "with Spanish surnames" for the new band. Unlike Chico's band, the majority of the members of the Afro-Latin Jazz Orchestra are Latino. Such controversies raise the question: Will increased recognition of Latin jazz be accompanied by rising "protectionism" within the idiom—exclusion of non-Latino(a)s from "nuestra música"? As in the Latin jazz scene in general, racial balance seems less of an issue. Unlike Marsalis, O'Farrill hired a woman as a full-time member of the orchestra, the young saxophonist Erica von Kleist.[44]

As was done for the LCJO, Arturo has begun collecting music for the band's library. One obvious source has been his father's music, although he has been careful to keep some of his father's material exclusively for the Chico O'Farrill Orchestra. He also has gathered classic arrangements from René Hernández, Machito, Tito Puente, and Mario Bauzá: "Ray Santos is represented, I mean to me, to take the major composers of this genre, arrangers, and have them be represented, I couldn't do that with the Chico O'Farrill Orchestra. You know, that's an orchestra devoted to Chico's music and/or music that is inspired or directly related to Chico's style of writing." Commissions have gone out to Tom Harrell, Michael Mossman, and, in another move reminiscent of Marsalis, Arturo himself.

Although Jazz at Lincoln Center has raised millions of dollars, musicians point out that the management often tries to cut corners at their expense. Some composers complain that they have been offered insultingly low sums for their arrangements. One Latino musician, who played with the orchestra at its inception, feels particularly incensed at the treatment of the Afro-Latin Jazz Orchestra:

> I find it completely insulting when the Latin Jazz Orchestra from Lincoln Center gets paid considerably less than the Lincoln Center Jazz Orchestra. Here I am, I gotta be slumming my ass, you know, so that we can be the good house niggers and get paid and why? They're giving us an opportunity. Man, I did that already, I really don't [need this], you know. You've got masters like Bobby Porcelli and Mario Rivera in the band, and they're getting paid less than the guys at Lincoln Center jazz band who have no experience playing what they're playing.

While this musician's frustration with Jazz at Lincoln Center is palpable, his inflammatory racial imagery perhaps should be viewed as a strategic response to the historical marginalization of Latin jazz in comparison to other forms of jazz.

Economic and personnel disputes aside, the Latin jazz orchestra fits into Marsalis's vision of reinvigorating jazz as dance and popular music. Even as bebop moved jazz away from mass popularity, its Latin stepchildren, cubop and Latin jazz, at least for Latino audiences, have continued to blur the boundaries of "popular" and "art" music. Marsalis also needs more than one resident ensemble to fill the stages of the ambitious new complex at Columbus Circle. His occasional forays into Latin music with the LCJO brought the realization that he needed a specialist ensemble devoted to that repertoire.

Guest conductors and soloists could not atone for his band's lack of schooling and experience in clave and Latin jazz. Perhaps he saw in O'Farrill a reflection of himself, a second-generation jazz musician, not from New Orleans, the "birthplace of jazz," but from New York, the "birthplace of Latin jazz." And as O'Farrill has not only led the ALJO but also conducted master classes and clinics, lectured on Latin jazz appreciation, and handled other Jazz at Lincoln Center assignments, he has staked out a more prominent role distinct from his father—as a musician in his own right and as a leading spokesman for Latin jazz.

Chapter 10

Going for It

All-Women Bands

"You are what you are," groans the baritone saxophonist Claire Daly after learning that the purpose of my call is not to ask her to sub on a gig or a rehearsal but to interview her for a chapter on all-women bands. Still, despite having been interviewed innumerable times about "women in jazz," she good-naturedly fields my questions. "Ultimately, what most women musicians would like to see," she explains patiently, "is that they don't have to be in a separate chapter." Like most women in the workforce, professional women who are musicians would like to erase distinctions based on biology. Rather than be identified as "woman musicians," they would prefer to be recognized simply as "musicians." Unfortunately, one drawback to performing in all-women bands (unlike all-men bands) is that it draws even more attention to the performer's sex. Nevertheless, as long they remain marketable to the public, providing jobs and valuable experience, all-women bands continue to form an important part of the musical landscape. As a socially distinct network (with fairly obvious boundaries), for analytic reasons, I study all-women bands separately, much as I have other jazz scenes.

The number of female musicians may have grown significantly in the past two decades, but the pool of female players remains somewhat small in comparison to the jazz field at large (about 20 percent across the three cities examined in the NEA study, somewhat higher in New York; among union jazz musicians only 15.6 percent are women).[1] Still, newcomers continue to trickle in, adding to the ranks of the women's jazz scene in New York. The larger number of female jazz musicians in New York has allowed independent male and female music scenes to flourish. In San Francisco, by contrast, the NEA study showed a much lower rate of homophily among women jazz musicians, suggesting that in San Francisco "females interact indirectly, through males."[2] The flow of personnel through the bands studied here, Diva and the Kit McClure Band, resembles that in other "mainstream" bands in New York (such as the Vanguard or Schneider orchestras), that is, musician initiated. Though the leaders (McClure and, in the case of Diva, Sherrie Maricle and Stanley Kay) make the final decisions, most players come into the bands through recommendations or through making themselves known to the leaders. As Diva's reputation has spread, women have sent audition tapes hoping for a chance to play with the band.

Musicians who become identified with networks outside established mainstream jazz scenes (as we have seen in the avant-garde) risk being considered lower caliber. Even when praised, these players often are marginalized by comments such as, "Well, so and so sounds good but would never make it in a regular band." While a few successful contemporary female musicians (Maria Schneider, Carla Bley, pianist Renee Rosnes, and trumpeter Laurie Frink, to name a few) have resisted identification with other female players and all-women groups, many others have found a space in all-women bands, where they can gain valuable experience as they compete for a foothold in the music business.

In this chapter I explore the issues raised by the formation of all-women bands. How have women used the relative safety of this space to grow musically? How have the presentation of these groups and the expectations of the public affected musical style? Has joining together in all-women bands helped or hindered women's prospects for entering mainstream networks? These issues lead into a more wide-ranging discussion of gender representation and performance in the predominantly male jazz universe. How has gender inflected musical performance in jazz? Through their dominant position, have male musicians experienced greater freedom to construct variable and varied musical identities? Most important, has progress been made in the integration of the sexes in jazz, as many believe? Or is this optimistic view simply wishful thinking, or worse, a pernicious cover-up of the continuing exclusion of women?

The principal voices heard here are those of Daly and her close friend, the trombonist Deborah Weisz. Each has long experience in mostly male as well as all-women bands. Despite their similar backgrounds, each has a different attitude toward Diva and the Kit McClure Band. Daly, because she arrived in New York earlier, was involved with the McClure band sooner, and with Diva from its inception. At the time of our first interview, she had recently left Diva. Weisz, who came to New York several years later than Daly (in 1993), was still performing in both as of November 1999.[3] My discussion also is informed by numerous conversations with other female musicians on club dates and in rehearsal bands and by published interviews in magazines and books.[4]

Originally from Chicago, Weisz grew up in the late sixties and early seventies and was inspired by the horn sections of groups like Chicago and

Blood, Sweat and Tears. She explains, "I kind of fell in love with the music, I was exposed to it through some wonderful band directors who really played us a lot of stuff. I thought, 'I like this.' So I just started playing trombone." She was "especially attracted to improvisation." Before coming to New York, she spent a number of years in Las Vegas playing with various bands, including Frank Sinatra's.

Daly discovered jazz at the age of twelve, when her father took her to see the Buddy Rich Orchestra at the Westchester County, New York, municipal arena. "It was the seventies and no one was there. They were doing *Beatles* songs, like 'Norwegian Wood,' " she states incredulously. "I was standing on my chair screaming. I had been playing saxophone for about three months. I said to my father I would do anything to be on that bus. I wanted to get autographs. It was the most unbelievable thing I had ever heard in my life." After attending school in Boston, she toured with several all-women rock groups, before returning to New York in the late 1980s.

"NO MAN'S BAND"

Diva is owned and managed by a single promoter, Stanley Kay. A former drummer with Patty Page, Frankie Laine, and other entertainers, Kay had become involved in the business side of the music industry as Buddy Rich's manager and occasional relief drummer. The idea of an all-women band first occurred to him in 1990 when he conducted a band in which Sherrie Maricle played drums. Kay "wondered if there were other women musicians with a similar caliber of musicianship."[5] Discovering their mutual love of the Buddy Rich Orchestra and its leader's style of drumming, Kay and Maricle auditioned female players from all over the United States, hoping to put together a first-rate band that would prove that "playing like a girl [could] mean with passion, strength and serious musicianship."[6] Casting as wide a net as possible, Kay and Maricle held open auditions, a procedure hardly seen since the big bands' heyday during the swing era. But then Kay's project was already exceptional: since the 1940s few show business entrepreneurs have viewed big bands as an exciting business opportunity. The promise of fairly steady work and good pay for playing jazz stimulated interest among many female musicians and assisted Kay and Maricle in their goal of building an "all-star band." In March 1993 Diva gave its first concert.

Although Kay had worked closely with Buddy Rich, he did not share the drummer's attitude about women musicians. Rich's statement on the *Tonight Show* in 1979 ("No chick will ever play in my band.") is "kind of a famous quote around most of the [women] musicians," reports Daly. She continues:

> Stanley was not really coming from *that* place, but that's who he managed for years. It wasn't even considered that a woman would be taken seriously, and

> Stanley started to realize this because he was behind it. It enraged him. It really made him mad. I think it became his cause. I think that Diva is Stanley's reason to live.

Daly describes the initial enthusiasm surrounding the project:

> It started out, we're gonna have a really hip band, great charts, great players, we're gonna take this top of the line, so that nobody can say it's just a gimmick, that it's got women in it. They really picked the A team. They picked a great band.

For the first couple of years, there was little turnover in personnel. Daly felt that the band started to gel as the players became accustomed to playing together.

Determined that the women be treated with respect, Kay lavished the band with "first class accommodations, . . . paid airfare and free limo service[,] . . . not everyday occurrences for the average big band."[7] Daly reports:

> Stanley really wanted to do this thing in a big way. We were treated very respectfully. It felt like an honor to be in the band. We were making more money than almost anybody else (being somebody who does the other big bands around town). The pay was at least $200 a gig. Often a gig would pay $250. They were kind of high-profile gigs. It really was a first-class operation. Meanwhile, Stanley is shoveling money into this to try and get it off the ground. He's calling in every favor. He's hustling. This became a greater cause for Stanley.

After this auspicious beginning, the economic realities of maintaining a touring big band forced Kay to retreat somewhat from his original plans. As expenses mounted, Kay dipped further into his own assets. To keep the band afloat, pay and quality of accommodations declined, and younger and less experienced players were brought in.

Kay was probably unprepared for the resistance he encountered from his associates within the entertainment industry. Daly continues:

> My take on it was, when Stanley experienced sexism for the first time in his life he saw it in a way that he saw racism in the fifties and sixties. See Stanley is, in a way, one of the good ol' boys and I think the other good ol' boys weren't taking him seriously on this. So what became of this idea for a big band that would be a loud, fast, Buddy Rich–style big band, it turned into something else for him. It turned into this greater cause. It ruffled his feathers that women were not taken seriously or given a chance in a lot of ways, 'cause he experienced it. He was tryin' to get his good ol' boys to come down and hear the band or to get a deal for the band.

His expectations that the band would be able to get a recording contract with a major label and generate the necessary revenues to continue as a "first-class" operation proved unrealistic.

The band's presentation also began to change. In an interview, the saxophonist Virginia Mayhew described the shift in the band's direction:

> When DIVA started out it was *very* exciting. We understood that the all-female angle was a necessary hook to get work, but the original mission was about this band playing great jazz. . . . Now it seems like the female part, the show business aspect, is getting the emphasis instead of the jazz part. The musicians in the band are still good, but the music the band is playing is more "commercial" jazz.[8]

Daly believes that "as time went on and Stanley met up with different forms of resistance and, for whatever reason, not being able to get a deal for the band," he fell back on his long experience in the entertainment business. "All of a sudden it started to take a little more of a show-biz turn, and I think it's gone more in that direction."

A performance at Birdland in spring 1999 seemed to confirm their observations. A Scott Whitfield arrangement harmonized Armstrong's solo on "West End Blues." In a takeoff on the trumpeter's famous prolonged note, all the trumpet players held a pitch indefinitely. One by one the players pretended to pass out until only the lead trumpeter, Liesl Whitaker, was left standing. In another instance, the saxophone section fooled the audience by standing as if to play a soli but only played a single note before returning to their chairs. On a feature for the trombone section, the bass trombonist played an unaccompanied cadenza in which she kept playing lower and lower, until finally the band members stopped her. At Birdland the New York audience (always a tough crowd) did not seem particularly amused by these antics. Looking around the club, I saw few familiar faces. Many of the musicians who "hang" regularly on big band nights (Sundays, Mondays, and Tuesdays) stayed away that evening, perhaps indicating the unwillingness of many jazz musicians to give an all-women band a chance.

Some of the band's routines have evolved spontaneously after many nights of performance. On "Three Sisters and a Cousin,"[9] which features a four-way saxophone "battle," the saxophone section goes into a little dance. Weisz says, "The rest of us would just kind of sit there and play and have fun, and now over the years it has evolved, and we all get in on the dance. On the road, people get a little crazy. It's all in a good way, which is nice."

One thing that Kay especially disliked, however, particularly in the beginning, was when the *audience* danced. Daly illustrates this point with an amusing anecdote: "Early on in the band, if people got up and started dancing, he would tell them not to. In his mind, a dance band and a jazz band were different things. It was really funny, he would ask them to sit down and tell them, '*This* is not a dance band.' He'd walk right up to them and interrupt and say, 'This is a concert, this is a show, this is not for dancing.' "

On the rare occasions, however, when Diva performs for dances, Kay and

Maricle pull out some stock arrangements. Still, Kay is adamantly opposed to managing a "club date" or a "dance" band. One way he maintains Diva as a "concert band" has been a move into the expanding jazz education arena. Maricle, who recently completed a doctorate in jazz performance and composition, is active in the International Association of Jazz Educators. Not everyone appreciated the change of direction. To some players, it was a step down from the higher-class venues where they had started. Says one veteran player, with slight annoyance, "We started having to do clinics . . . in high school auditoriums and stuff." Diva seemed to follow the course of the Buddy Rich band in ways that Kay and Maricle had not anticipated. As it began to feel less like an all-star band, Diva, much like the later Rich bands, provided work for budding musicians looking for a chance to play.

In our first conversation (1998), Daly confessed that the time might not have been the best for her to talk about her experience because she had just left Diva. She explained, "I'm not in my cheeriest space about Diva. I burned out on it. . . . I think what they're gonna end up with is sort of like the Buddy Rich story but in drag. *Some Like It Hot* all over again." Recalling her moment of musical epiphany when she first saw Rich's band, she noted, "If that's the case, the Buddy Rich band was good experience for a lot of people. Look at us who were little twelve-year-olds freakin' out." Over the years Daly has remained on good terms with Diva and its leaders and occasionally subs in the band. In a more recent interview (2004), Daly praised the band and especially Kay and Maricle for their devotion to keeping the band alive. Weisz, who chose to stay on, retains much of her initial enthusiasm: "It's an amazing ensemble, . . . not just a band of musicians who are women. It's a band of musicians who are wonderful players, who are definitely soloists, who are brought together in a unique situation."

Not surprisingly, the players in all-women big bands echo much of the discourse heard in New York's jazz community. Like the musicians in other bands, they aim for a distinctive sound and an ensemble style—to sound like a *band.* Weisz states that the band's primary goal is "to have an identity as Diva, like Ellington's band had an identity, Basie's has an identity, and to be recognized for that." To prove that all the members are accomplished (as might be expected in an all-star band), almost every player is featured at least once during an evening's performance.

Unlike most prominent New York bands—for example, those led by Maria Schneider, Bob Mintzer, Carla Bley, Frank Foster, and Arturo O'Farrill—Diva has no central figure arranging and composing for the band. But Diva members emphasize the "custom" quality of their arrangements—all of which are commissioned specifically for the band. As Weisz points out, the band's arrangers, John LaBarbera, Mike Abene, Tommy Newsom, and others, are "writing for individual soloists, they're writing for individual players who play with Diva—so they're taking in those considerations." While it is most often compared to the Buddy Rich band, which produced a kind of lingua franca big band style, Weisz believes that Diva is gradually evolving "into something that is identifiable as the Diva sound." She acknowledges that "the leader of the band, Sherrie Maricle, is very influenced by Buddy Rich." "When these commissions are given out," she says, "I do believe a lot of consideration is given to that particular style. That's Stanley Kay and Sherrie. Stanley has a lot of input into how these arrangements are done. He talks with the arrangers and composers, tells them what he is thinking about and they try to re-create that for him." This brash, Buddy Rich style of the arrangements feeds the competitive spirit within the band.

An article written for *Windplayer* magazine in 1996 by Diva's former bass trombonist, Lee Kavanaugh, focused on the intense competition between band members. According to Daly, "It really was the best article most of us had ever seen about being in an all-woman band. She lived in Kansas, and she heard about this band, she had preconceived ideas about it, because it was an all-female band, so she wrote honestly about that." Kavanaugh, buying into the usual stereotypes, had envisioned "a group of giggly, air-headed girls who knew more about makeup than they did about Duke Ellington. Or alternatively, they were femi-Nazis, women with tattoos, hairy armpits and a real hatred for men." When she watched a video sent her by Maricle, she wrote, in "fifteen seconds . . . 15 years of gender biases were blown away."

> Out of my speakers came a wall of sound, accompanied by electronic images of women leaning into bop licks and playing with the strength and power I had witnessed in the bands of Stan Kenton, Woody Herman and Buddy Rich. . . . "The players look so masculine," I caught myself thinking. Then again, I had rarely seen other women playing, let alone myself. And it occurred to me that, of course these women looked masculine—there is no dainty way to pump out pedal tones. Or soaring high notes. Playing music requires you to make a statement with soul and body, and that doesn't depend on gender.[10]

In her description of the intensity of the band, Kavanaugh quotes the lead trumpeter, Liesl Whitaker: "Diva is more competitive than any other band I've worked with. . . . I, too, was used to that 'Wow, you're incredible for a girl' reaction, but in auditions when I heard all these other women who were really good, I was so jealous. . . . With women, I feel like we have to be better than each other to get back to that level of being a novelty." In mixed bands female players might receive some encouragement from their male colleagues, even if it sometimes seems condescending. The saxophonist Laura Dreyer notes, "You are treated special when you're the only woman in a band. In a way, though, that works against you: you become self-conscious about being different, or you start thinking you're better than you really are."[11]

As described in the *Windplayer* article, three of the five saxophonists and a majority of the brass players use mouthpieces designed to cut through loud ensemble textures. These choices of equipment are seldom heard in mainstream bands, such as the Vanguard, in which players strive for a big, yet darker, more easily blended sound. Competitiveness within the band augments the hypermasculinst Buddy Rich style on which it is modeled. Daly says, without a trace of irony, "I would call it macho. The loud/fast factor. Being here to prove something rather than let's all listen to each other and *blend.*" The emphasis is on the technical attainments of the players. Through their relentless ensemble style and aggressive soloing, members of Diva seem to be saying make room for us.

Even with this competitiveness, band members demonstrate deep levels of collegiality and mutual support. In their Birdland gig the musicians listened attentively to one another's solos. Rather than appear bored or distracted, as often happens in big bands during periods of protracted soloing, players frequently turned to watch the soloist, occasionally punctuating the improvised phrases with shouts of encouragement. In New York's competitive environment men tend to be less supportive of other men. During my long experience observing and participating in big band performances, I have learned that only something musically extraordinary turns the heads of New York's more blasé jazzmen.

The other major all-women big band in New York turned heads in another way. McClure, who founded her band in 1982, gained notoriety in a 1986 international tour with the rock star Robert Palmer. Palmer's "Addicted to Love" video that appeared around this time surrounded him with several scantily dressed professional models holding instruments and pretending to play. Through their robotic manner and nearly identical appearance, their presence suggested their only value was as sexual objects. On the tour, although McClure's band members wore their trademark black miniskirts and high heels, they actually accompanied the rock star on several numbers. McClure "admits that, superficially at least, there would appear to be a contradiction between her concern that the members of her band be accepted on their merits as musicians and the sexy presentation."[12] Perhaps agreeing that such concessions to the male gaze were "superficial," many writers chose to focus on the sexual politics. For example, for an article on McClure's big band, the Oakland, California, magazine *Jazz Now* proudly heralded on its cover "Kit McClure: Fighting Sexism, Playing Jazz." "I worked in a lot of male groups before I had my own band," McClure explains, "and I think the patronizing comments were one of the main motivating factors of my starting my own band." McClure feels these contradictions are only on the surface: "I think this probably goes through people's minds when they see a sexy photo with everybody posing. But when we get on stage and the people see the band in action, they quickly see that we are serious musicians."[13]

Despite McClure's claims that music is her priority, former members complain that appearance came first. Musicians were often subjected to makeup checks before performances. One accomplished musician described repeated attempts by McClure to get her to lose weight. Says another, "It has basically turned into a club date band." Some players are troubled by the unabashed appeal to male images of female sexuality. "She is blatantly exploiting the fact that the band is women," says one. Another compares it to the "cheesecake" bands of the 1940s (she mentions Irma Rae Hutton, "the Blonde Bombshell," and the Melodears): "They were babes. They dyed their hair blonde and bobbed it," explains this player. "In Kit's band, people weren't allowed to wear eyeglasses on stage. If you had your average musician body, it wasn't good enough. She would replace people with other people who looked better." Still, many women hesitate to condemn McClure totally. One of them says, "It infuriated me sometimes when it was happening. Speaking on my highest levels of integrity I could get all mad about it. But that's just what she's doing to make a living." Being exploited by another woman is no worse than being exploited by men: "People are exploited in many ways, and that's just the way that she's doing it."

Diva presents an emphatically different image. In the words of one player, "Certainly with Diva it was 'anti-little-black-dresses.' " The band has experimented with uniforms that look more like sports jerseys. Around 1997, perhaps following the model of Diva, McClure began to tone down the sexy image of her group. The tight miniskirt rule was relaxed. Weisz connects this change to McClure's growing interest in jazz: "When she started moving into more of the jazz realm, I noticed on the bandstand it wasn't such a big thing. And actually some girls wear pants, and I prefer to wear a long skirt or pants because when I play I don't sit like a girl." Instead of adapting music written for other bands, McClure has begun to perform music specifically written for her group. Weisz continues, "Close to two or three years ago, she started to do more creative jazz types of gigs; it was more like concert jazz, with a smaller band, music written for the band to play. We did a couple of tours with that kind of stuff. It was nice."

Many women fall somewhat reluctantly into the all-women bands. Describing her arrival in New York, the trumpeter Ingrid Jensen, explains that, besides club dates and day jobs and other work she really did not want to do, she "got pretty involved in the all-women band scene. It's almost like New York causes people to create their own networks so certain groups can support one another's survival."[14] One former player in both Diva and the McClure band suggests that "if they really wanted to help women, they would form a band that was comprised of women and men." Unfortunately, robbed of their most valuable promotional device, the bands would face more difficulty finding work. Although this player recognizes the bind in which many women are trapped, she confessed that she too had formed an all-women club date band.

After their 1995 CD, the Diva logo usually appeared with the words "No

Man's Band." Daly was not thrilled by this sobriquet: "It used to just be Diva, and now they say 'Diva, No Man's Band.' For a while it was 'Sherrie Maricle and Diva,' and I'm just not sure what's going on. It kind of seems like 'No Man's Band' has squeezed its way in there, which frankly, I found offensive." Promotional material such as jackets and other gear began to incorporate this phrase. Daly says, "I bought one of these jackets a couple years ago, a nice, good bomber jacket, and it says, 'Diva: No Man's Band,' and I blacked out all the letters so it would just say 'a band.' "

"WOMEN IN JAZZ"

In the early decades of the twentieth century, female classical musicians in the United States formed their own orchestras during a period of "great expansion" in American musical life, when "symphony orchestras—the hallmark of cultural respectability in the United States—increased dramatically in number."[15] The phenomenon of all-women orchestras in the classical field ultimately turned out to be transitory. By the early 1940s most had disappeared. The onset of World War II, which depleted the ranks of male musicians, facilitated the move of women into formerly all-male orchestras. After the war, with most all-women orchestras gone, a few of the women managed to retain their new positions. Despite intense sexism, the classical field slowly began to become more integrated.[16] Women's participation in big bands followed a very different trajectory. During the war, even with the shortage of musicians, very few women were hired for established male bands. Instead, demand for entertainment expanded the number of "all-girl" bands. Although attitudes in the classical universe probably were as patriarchal as in jazz, as "high" culture rather than mass entertainment (in jazz, often with a racial stigma as well) classical music evidently seemed a safer site for integration of the sexes. As big bands waned in the postwar years, all-girl big bands also faded. Like many of their male counterparts, female musicians struggled to find work in small groups, became active in music education, or left music altogether.[17]

One obvious difference between big bands and classical orchestras is their instrumentation. In the late nineteenth century American women took up the violin and other orchestral strings that had previously been thought of as male instruments. As Judith Tick notes, traditionally "the piano, harp, and guitar were deemed appropriate feminine instruments. They were instruments for domestic entertainment and required no facial exertions or body movements that interfered with the portrait of grace the lady musician was to emanate." These instruments also could be used primarily in supportive roles for accompanying. The shift to solo instruments such as the violin, in Tick's words, "marked a significant change from the past."[18]

A half century later, when all-girl bands were at their height, women increasingly turned to brass and other instruments favored in jazz. Ironically, some writers called for women to return to strings and instruments, which were "more in keeping with their temperament." Horns, even more than the violin and other orchestral instruments, demand "un-ladylike" postures and facial exertions. "They do NOT shine on wind instruments," continued an anonymous writer in *Down Beat,* "nor do they make good percussionists. If more girl drummers had cradle rocking experience before their musical endeavors they might come closer to getting the beat." He attributed female horn players' weak tone production and reticence in "blowing it out" to overconcern with appearance. "Gals are conscious of the facial contortions," he wrote condescendingly, "and limit their power for fear of appearing silly in the eyes of men. Milady's dimples take an awful beating when reaching for the high notes and dearie, was my face red on that last high note!"[19]

While evidence suggests that the magnitude of gender associations of specific instruments has diminished (slightly) among music students, at least since the 1970s, instruments' positions on the masculine-feminine continuum have remained relatively constant. Drums and lower brass are considered the most masculine; flute, violin, and clarinet, the most feminine.[20] Certain instruments, however, enjoy wide popularity among both genders, as reflected in the choices of fourth-grade students. Drums rose to first choice among boys and became the second choice among girls. Another study showed that although raw numbers of women taking up "masculine" instruments such as trombone increased, this could be attributed largely to greater participation of girls in school music programs, band in particular. While crediting societal factors such as more female role models, the depiction of women in popular culture (films, television, etc.), changes in employment patterns, more single-parent homes, and greater awareness of legal issues, music education researchers highlight the importance of Title IX laws that prohibit discrimination on the basis of sex in federally assisted education programs. Since these laws were passed in 1972, as described by music education researchers, teachers have made significant efforts to eliminate gender stereotyping from their curricula and music programs.[21] Even with these gains, gender stereotyping of instruments among children remains strong, with boys less likely than before to take up an instrument considered feminine, such as flute. Despite implementation of blind auditions and a substantial increase of female members over the past three decades, in an informal survey of five leading orchestras in 2004, I found only one female brass player (French horn). Since most of the instruments traditionally used in jazz carry strong associations with masculinity, overcoming instrument gender stereotypes in children remains critical to women's participation in jazz.

One significant development for jazz is that young women's interest in improvisation is growing. Much like their counterparts in classical music who aspired to compose, female jazz musicians have been discouraged from improvising. While jazz may have been more open to women composers, as Lucy Green has observed, "The woman jazz improviser cannot be concealed . . . because she not only composes but performs: not only uses her mind but displays her body."[22] Stepping away from the written page to spontaneously create music under the critical gaze of one's peers requires self-confidence. At least playing in sections limited women's participation to supportive roles more in keeping with accepted notions of femininity and domesticity. According to Marian McPartland, in one of the premier woman jazz orchestras of the swing era, the International Sweethearts of Rhythm, because few of the women improvised, at least in the early years, solos often were written out.[23] A *Down Beat* article that appeared at about this time attributed women's inability to play "hot jazz" to their banishment from the "jazz classroom," described as "a dimly-lighted gin joint in any city where the price . . . for learning to play . . . is a salary of maybe one meal a night or whatever the kitty can squeeze out at dawn when the work is done." "Is it any wonder," the writer reckoned, "that, excluded (as of course she should have been) from this environment, . . . she should be so barren of any appreciation of the finer points of playing jazz on an instrument?"[24]

As recently as 1996, the lead trombonist with Diva, Lolly Bienenfeld, estimated that probably fewer than a dozen women brass players in New York could improvise a blues solo.[25] However, the shift of the "jazz classroom" from the "gin joint" to the public school and university has helped to swell the ranks of female jazz musicians who make improvisation central to their playing. Weisz says, "Because of the way the music scene is now, there are more players that are women coming up through college." Like Weisz, most contemporary female jazz musicians, from an early age, find improvisation especially attractive. But in her study of public music education in England, Green found that girls continue to identify more with classical than with jazz and popular music performance and express discomfort more often than boys when asked to improvise in school jazz bands.[26]

Whether contemporary all-women jazz orchestras will be a transitory phenomenon, like the all-women classical orchestras of the prewar years, remains to be seen. Regardless of the eventual outcome, Weisz thinks "everyone has to be honest and say that Diva does exist for a very important reason and that hopefully some day it won't be necessary." Pursuing this logic, Weisz imagines a utopian universe in which female musicians are no longer identified primarily by their difference: "It will be, 'Oh, Diva, what a wonderful band,' not necessarily 'a band made up of all women.' Of course, that's an obvious factor, but nobody says, 'Oh, the Basie band, what a wonderful band, a band made up of only men.' " When Weisz uses the word *nobody,* she refers to the dominant discourse. Among female musicians, all-male bands *are* noticed and commented on.[27]

But all-women bands provoke strong reactions from every quarter. Says

Daly, "I've seen women be so blown away by seeing this group of women playing this music that it's an emotional experience. I've seen women start sobbing." When she was touring Japan with Kit McClure, some men in the audience walked out, but the women who stayed just started "going crazy. They got up and they were dancing. They probably had never seen women being strong." Weisz states proudly that after concerts someone always comes up to express appreciation: "You know [that] we spoke to them, in other words. They got it. They heard us."

More important, the band inspires young women musicians. The supportive atmosphere in Diva extends to players they meet on the road. With obvious pride, Weisz relates the following story:

> We were playing up at SUNY Potsdam, and a young trombonist came up to me and she said, "Until you, my favorite trombone player was Glenn Miller." I said, "Well, thank you, that's quite an honor." We were out in the lobby talking, and she was just glowing, she was so blown away by the experience. "I'm in trombone heaven, I'm in woman heaven. You guys are the Spice Girls of jazz." So I told that to Stanley because I think that kind of says it right there, for a young trombonist, for a young musician who happens to be a woman, it's probably pretty mind-blowing to see us. Or to see any band of professional musicians out there doing this who happen to be women. And I've met her since. I was a guest artist at the international trombone festival this past summer and she was there.

These contacts sometimes lead to lasting professional relationships. Weisz is especially inclined to help young women. "All my peers when I was growing up were men," she explains. "We didn't have that many role models that were women. . . . I'm always on the lookout for young trombonists who happen to be women who can play."

Although they may long for the day when they are not identified as "women musicians," many women are resigned to that categorization if it means they can get work playing the music they love. As a veteran of the music business, Daly feels extremely mixed emotions: "I'm forty, and I've been in all-female bands for twenty years, not exclusively, but I always sort of end up in all-female bands. On any different day I can feel radically different about that. But basically, I guess it's a necessary evil." Like most of the women who have performed in Diva, Daly feels that Kay deserves a great deal of credit for forming an all-women band in which the emphasis is on playing rather than on visual attraction:

> If Stanley Kay can get that band work, then so be it. The big band seems like such a dinosaur in this day and age, and such a huge thing to be carting around the country. Stanley's an interesting guy and he sort of reinvented the wheel. I mean there have been plenty of all-women bands, and most of us in town, women players, have been in lots of women bands because you get clumped there. Sometimes people are looking for "a female sax player," or "a female

> drummer," or a whatever, and if you're qualified for the job, you just end up there anyway, whether you want to or not. Sometimes I'm really disgusted by that, and sometimes I just figure, "Oh, whatever, at least it's work."

Daly has realized that making a living in jazz is not easy for anyone, male or female: "The music business is just a minefield of obstacles, and I pretty much put on my blinders and do what I can see to do. I didn't go into music to have a cause. I didn't go in to be a *woman* in music."

While they hope that gender barriers disappear, many women enjoy working in all-women bands. "In Diva, we're in this for the music," states Mayhew. "But a great side benefit is the fact that we girls get to hang out together. And that's something we didn't get to do very often until Diva."[28] Weisz, who also has extensive experience playing in groups made up mostly of men, agrees: "It's just different. I've done what I call the 'boy hang' on the road. I've done that, been the only woman in the band. And I've done the girl hang on the road, and I like them both. They're just different because men and women are different." Disagreements and frictions may lead to occasional clashes among members, but musicians who travel together must learn to live in close quarters. Musicians with similar backgrounds tend to get along more easily.

For Weisz, differences between male and female bands are difficult to pin down. They are simply "the difference between men and women." She shares an anecdote to illustrate: "We were just in Austria and Diane Schuur's music got held up in customs and she was a little upset and I'm sure anyone would have been understanding, but she didn't hide it from us that she was upset." Weisz wonders if Schuur would have displayed her emotions so openly "if it were, you know, the Basie band or something." When Weisz toured with bands in which she was the only woman, or one of only a few women, she was friendly with many of the male band members: "It's just a different hang. What can I say? It's a girl thing [laughs]. There are things that you talk about with women that you don't talk about with men, but musicians will talk about the same things, period. We all talk about music."

GENDER AND IDENTITY IN JAZZ

Although they may select, rework, and frame their materials in very different ways, musicians, like other artists, have inherited socially constructed and historically contingent conventions of gender representation. While for the most part remaining unconscious and unrecognized (especially by men because of their dominant position), gender constantly inflects performances as well as interpersonal relationships. Gender also informs critical and public reception of performance. Study of women's homosocial networks can help us to understand better how gender operates in male homosocial networks, where it tends to be ignored or denied. Individuals' senses of relative freedom or constraint within conventions of gender and sexuality vary historically, across fields of activity, and according to their positions in other social categories such as race, class, and nation. Although jazz musicians have shared certain gender conventions with their classical counterparts, as an African American cultural form, jazz has offered to its participants (practitioners and listeners) a set of musical codes and practices unique to itself.

A comparison of gendered musical traits and terms in classical music and jazz reveals that the two idioms share many of the same oppositions. Playing fast, loud, and rhythmically vigorous are widely perceived as masculine. Lyrical, soft, and gentle styles are viewed as feminine or "not masculine." But gender adheres differently to other musical elements in the two fields. Centuries of musical practice in the Western art tradition have resulted in elaborate and highly conventionalized methods of treating dissonance and its resolution. While acknowledging that music can be interpreted in a variety of ways, in her own close readings of classical music texts, much of McClary's study of gender representations focuses on harmonic practice. Supporting her interpretations with examples of gendered discursive terms in music criticism and theory (e.g., "masculine" and "feminine" cadences) and women's roles in dramatic musical works such as opera, she concludes that diatonic passages, tonic harmony, and stability typically are associated with maleness; chromaticism, nontonic harmony, and instability often are linked with femininity.[29] Compared to classical music (at least up to the Romantic era), the tonal resolutions of jazz are less codified and frequently less distinct. Standard harmonic structures are almost exclusively cyclical (vamps, blues, and popular song formats). Harmony most often contains extensions, or "emancipated dissonances," which remain unresolved in the classical sense.[30] Since the 1940s jazz has favored the tonic major seventh chord in final cadences, which includes the leading tone as part of its own resolution. The blues typically starts and ends on tonic dominant seventh chords. As regards harmonic practice, in modern jazz improvisers' ability to negotiate difficult chord progressions often became a test of mastery. In jam sessions players competed to demonstrate their superiority in "making the changes." David Ake has discussed how Ornette Coleman's abandonment of "harmonic structure left him open to the charge that he 'couldn't make the changes,' or was, quite simply, 'faking it.' " Ake sees Coleman's efforts as an attempt to "re-masculate" jazz, especially in light of Coleman's desire to desexualize performance, his contemplation of castration, and his nonconformist lifestyle (vegetarianism, long hair, and beard).[31] Jazz musicians have also defined masculinity in opposition to classical music, as demonstrated in Mingus's desire to explore beyond classically defined instrumental ranges and ideals of tone production.[32] Musical qualities associated with gender in jazz discourse, such as penetrating/spread, high range/moderate range, and big sound/soft sound, often involve timbre and tessitura. As an indication of their relative valorization, musical traits that are highly prioritized in each idiom tend to be gendered masculine.

Gender's inflection by race in jazz has been viewed differently from different vantage points. Dominant white discourse, according to Sherrie Tucker, "constructed African-descended men as masculine (violent, powerful, virile) in some ways, and as feminine (irrational, intuitive, physical) in others." Such discourse intersected with views of African Americans as "primitive," and white admirers of jazz often valorized black musicians as "intuitive, sexual, and uninhibited."[33] At the same time, facing this stereotyping and dehumanization, African American men found in jazz a space in which to define themselves as men. Monique Guillory writes that "constructs of masculinity in jazz sought to correct and overwrite the history of slavery, lynchings, and discrimination that spawned the music." Because she focuses on hypermasculinist discourse in "historical chronicles and biographies" of musicians such as Mingus and Davis, Guillory finds that the "cloak of masculinity" fashioned by jazzmen "reified the patriarchy, misogyny, and sexism of the white mainstream."[34] Rather than emphasize reproduction of white patriarchal values, Rustin characterizes the experiences of black jazz musicians as "interventions in the dominant constructions of race, masculinity, sexuality, and creativity."[35] Similarly, for Herman Gray, "jazzmen articulated a different way of knowing ourselves and seeing the world through the very 'structures of feeling' they assumed, articulated, and enacted—from the defiantly cool pose and fine vines of Miles to the black and third world internationalism that framed the ceaseless spiritual and musical quest of Coltrane."[36] As DeVeaux documents in *The Birth of Bebop,* African American jazz musicians saw modern jazz as a triumph of *intellectual* achievement. Moreover, concepts of black masculinity embracing soulful expression could be found in traditional African American idioms such as spirituals, gospel, and blues that often foregrounded themes of loneliness, abandonment, and redemption. By celebrating individual strength in the face of obstacles, the blues conveyed a rich spectrum of masculine (and feminine) expressivity. These liberating subjectivities also found their way into jazz, where they were available to white as well as black, female as well as male musicians.[37]

Though so-called hot jazz may have received more attention, lyrical and less aggressive styles also flourished. Jelly Roll Morton contrasted jazz with "hot style" ragtime and extolled the virtues of playing "sweet, soft, [with] plenty rhythm."[38] Instrumentalists such as Joe Henderson and Clark Terry cultivated dark tones, which, though centered, could hardly be considered "penetrating." The flugelhornist Art Farmer played at an extremely soft volume. Lester Young (who referred to fellow musicians as "lady" instead of the more traditional "man") played with a lighter tone, despite the vogue of Coleman Hawkins's heavier tenor sound. Many jazz musicians (e.g., Dexter Gordon) have played in a laid-back style, lagging behind the beat. Miles

Davis's playing revealed a legendary tenderness and vulnerability (through missed and cracked notes, etc.), especially in ballads. "Cool" or "West Coast" jazz offered an alternative to the bluesier and harder rhythms of bebop, although to the degree that it was associated with white musicians, it was sometimes disparaged as unmasculine.[39] Hard bop has been historicized as "the black musician's reaction to the West Coast 'cool,' a predominantly white musicians' thing that had sucked its blood from Lester Young and Miles Davis."[40] The relative "blackness" perceived in a player's style could become an index of masculinity.

Given the valorization of blackness and masculinity in jazz, white female jazz musicians would seem to have two strikes against them. Virginia Mayhew feels somewhat overwhelmed with what she sees as an "infestation" of white male tenor players who, although they may not get that many "good gigs" either, crowd the scene. Ingrid Jensen says, "As a white woman, there are many gigs that I would never, ever even be called to audition for." Some of the severest resistance she has encountered has come from African American musicians. Jensen notes, "The negative experiences *I've* had in my life . . . are when musicians of both colors, but unfortunately more black, will refuse to acknowledge my presence because it is such an unnatural thing for them to accept in their world."[41] The drummer Terri Lyn Carrington, who grew up in the African American jazz scene in Boston (her father played saxophone), feels that she has met less resistance than "a lot of other women": "Because I feel respected. . . . Not only do I not invite it [disrespect], I don't accept it." Hearing occasional grumblings from other musicians as she competes for work ("Why did they call her for the *Arsenio Hall Show?* There are a lot of brothers that need the work"),[42] as an African American, Carrington seems less challenged as a legitimate jazz musician.[43] However, the vast majority of female instrumentalists in New York big bands are white. During the entire span of my research, the number of African American women playing saxophone and brass in New York big bands that I have observed could be counted on one hand.

Among jazzmen, as in much of sports and other homosocial environments, sex and women are favored topics of conversation. Male musicians have bonded through their common lifestyle, which involves late hours, travel, and, sometimes, sense of isolation as a result of jazz's lack of widespread popularity. Living in close quarters on the road and interacting intimately in their music, male jazz musicians have tended to reject overt alternative sexualities.[44] On the road I have observed frequent competition among some musicians to score the largest number of female sexual conquests. Conscious of women's gaze, male musicians may intentionally play more lyrically or soulfully, which generally is considered to appeal to women.[45] At the same time, jazzmen risk losing the respect of their fellow band members if they appear to be catering to the women in the audience—

"posin' for the bitches" in Miles Davis's parlance.[46] Despite the competitive masculinism among band members, performance requires cooperative interaction. Some jazzmen see the presence of women in the band (especially women considered attractive) as a potential disruption of the delicate equilibrium of competition and cooperation. Moreover, as long as female instrumentalists in jazz are uncommon, women on the bandstand may draw the audience's attention away from the male members of the band, provoking a jealous reaction. Mayhew suggests that "maybe bandleaders . . . want the attention, or they want the attention to be strictly on the music." Mayhew also mentions a "sexual dynamic" that can intrude on the performance: "If I hang out with a bunch of guys, you know, it can't just be about the music."[47] Jensen, on other hand, seems to thrive on the sexual energy in the band:

> I had musicians in the band and in the audience give me feedback like, 'It's very sexy.' Not sexy in a dirty way, but sexy in a way that it makes sense because there's this energy going on. I think one of the things I've found over the years is that I love men. I flirt with men. I love the energy that I get from them. I've always played mostly with men, except for the DIVA experience, and some all-women things which were usually not that satisfying in comparison.[48]

As these two examples illustrate, the range of women's attitudes toward performing with men should not be underestimated. Flirtatious versus "strictly professional" relationships notwithstanding, integration of women into the homosocial fraternity of jazz, as in other professions, requires a sensitivity among jazzmen that may run counter to masculinist hypersexual tendencies and picaresque traditions. This situation is complicated further by the personal and musically intimate interaction that characterizes jazz performance.

EPILOGUE: PROGRESS OR "ALWAYS EMERGENT"?

In excavating the forgotten or invisible histories of female jazz musicians, Sherrie Tucker exposes a persistent view of women in jazz as "always emergent," or, in her clever phrase, a "perpetual phenomena phenomenon." Because of the lower visibility of women musicians after the peak of all-girl bands during World War II, she writes, it was "possible for women's bands such as Sisters in Jazz and Maiden Voyage to seem like heralds of a brand new phenomenon when they appeared in the 1970s."[49] Criticizing the "common inclusion narrative" that women in jazz "have been vocalists, sometimes pianists, but are only beginning to emerge as horn players, saxophonists, bassists, and drummers," Tucker characterizes this "always emergent" narrative as "a handy disposable container for jazz women."[50]

Contemporary emergence narratives typically credit changes in American society and jazz education for what is widely viewed as increased participation of women in jazz. For example, in her book *Madame Jazz,* Leslie Gourse maintains that "the women's movement has, in general, changed the status and prospects for women in every part of the music world since the 1970s."[51] While acknowledging their many frustrations, she observes that, through this new "psychological orientation" in combination with "musical education," women "began to play more frequently in jazz clubs and concert halls" (9). "By the early 1990s," her narrative continues, "an even more numerous group was coming along, trying its luck in New York," and the West Coast was experiencing "a similar emergence of women" (15). Another important component of emergence narratives is the "critical mass" theory—that women are only beginning to reach levels of participation that will produce a significant number of able practitioners. While the veteran pianist Joanne Brackeen has "marveled at the number of emergent women instrumentalists" currently on the scene, Gourse reports that "only a decade earlier she [Brackeen] had not been very impressed with the relatively few women players."[52] Wynton Marsalis, explaining the absence of women in the Lincoln Center Jazz Orchestra, states, "The more women we have playing jazz, the higher the level of playing gets, the more they audition, and the more women are going to be all over. It will be just like classical music."[53]

Even taking into account Tucker's warning, many things do seem different about the present "emergence" of women in jazz. The women interviewed for this study believe that progress, while agonizingly slow, is tangible. Typical of many, Weisz historicizes her optimism: "More men have been musicians than women in the jazz field. It's a newer thing, that musicians are commonly now women, but it's not like it hasn't existed." With jazz education penetrating elementary schools and Title IX changing attitudes and helping to eliminate barriers, growing numbers of women begin their participation in jazz at a young age when prejudices are less firmly established.[54] In many of the most elite conservatory or college jazz programs women's numbers remain relatively low (especially outside of piano, composition, and voice), but women's participation has become vital at many other schools. In my own experience teaching at two universities, female players, particularly on brass and reed instruments, have formed an integral part of the program. Many young male players not only have become comfortable performing next to women but also have come to expect it as a normal occurrence. Although she worries about the persistence of "a glass ceiling" that still prevents women from entering the highest echelons of jazz, Daly notes that "there's a new generation coming up and they're much more mixed and much more accepting." Perhaps some of these new attitudes can be seen in the experience of Lauren Sevian, a young saxophonist. Since she began playing professionally in New York in 1999, she has felt a great deal of support from the male musicians she has performed and toured with, not only in the Mingus Big Band but in the Artie Shaw and Benny Goodman Tribute Orchestras and other groups as well.

Like other New York City musicians, women are caught up in the demands of carving out a livelihood, which means cultivating a wide array of skills. Weisz notes, "Any musician today cannot think of one thing as being their bread and butter, they have to be freelance players. So all of us do the club date stuff, some of us do Broadway, some of us have our own groups, some of us are involved in the Latin field, classical stuff. Everybody has to be pretty diverse in order to survive." Weisz worries about dwindling opportunities in jazz for both men and women. An economic downturn in 2000 further shrank the amount of work available in the music industry outside jazz.

Despite these obstacles, since leaving Diva in 1998 Daly has discovered "the excitement of really embarking on [her] own." In 2000 she performed in the Mary Lou Williams Women in Jazz Festival with her quartet.[55] The next year she was guest soloist with the Billy Taylor Trio at the Kennedy Center. After releasing her third CD, *Heaven Help Us All* (on her own label, Daly Bread Records), she embarked on a lengthy national tour with Kirpal Gordon, a writer and poet (or "word flinger" in Daly's parlance). She believes that artists must create their own opportunities: "I think anybody who wants to make a living as a player not only needs to use their creativity to learn about the music but has to create opportunities to play. By taking these chances and going out as a leader like this I think I'm going to be more successful than I was in New York."

Creating opportunities requires new skills. "I'm learning a lot of new hats to wear," Daly says. "Tryin' to book a band, be on the road. Now I know even more the trials and tribulations of being a leader."[56] In retrospect, her experience with Diva not only improved her musicianship but also helped her to develop "road chops": "I can appreciate that experience more. I will be forever grateful to Stanley and Sherrie for having that band and doing what they're doing. They are pulling rabbits out of hats. Keeping a big band up and running in this time."

As women join men on the bandstand, some musicians hope that more women will also turn out to hear them. Steve Slagle, lamenting the absence of women musicians in major jazz groups, points out, "Look at the audiences—like so much of the jazz world, the audience is predominantly male." An article that appeared in *Down Beat* in 1941 dismissed women as potential audience members, claiming that it was futile to "try to teach women to like jazz" because "they never will."[57] Such patronizing attitudes have left lasting damage. A 1992 study funded by the NEA found that of Americans who rated jazz their favorite music, two-thirds were male. In classical music and other arts, women's participation rates are significantly higher than men's.[58] For jazz to be successfully recognized as "high culture," worthy of public and private subsidy, women must have a larger role. Will a growing number of male musicians see increased participation of women as not only fair but also in their self-interest? For sexual integration of jazz to be achieved, a critical mass of *male* musicians is also required who believe, with Slagle, that women's participation is "the number one issue as jazz enters the new millennium."

Chapter 11

Blood on the Fields

Wynton Marsalis and the Transformation of the Lincoln Center Jazz Orchestra

Since Martin Williams's call to arms for the repertory movement in 1970, many repertory orchestras have come and gone: the New York Jazz Repertory Company, the National Jazz Ensemble, and the American Jazz Orchestra. Wynton Marsalis and Jazz at Lincoln Center set even loftier goals than establishing a standing orchestra—itself no easy task. Marsalis and company launched a crusade to canonize the great literature of jazz, aiming to bring "real" jazz to millions of new listeners while steering people away from commercially hyped pretenders and corrupted or deluded heretics. Their list of accomplishments is nothing short of spectacular. They have raised tens of millions of dollars, hired dozens of full-time staff, and opened the first concert hall designed specifically for jazz. Hundreds of classic arrangements (in the beginning, primarily Ellington) have been transcribed, and a massive outreach program distributes a few of them annually, free of charge, to high schools around the country. The orchestra's season grew to more than a hundred dates in cities all over the world. The Marsalis name has become virtually synonymous with jazz, as broadcasters and journalists mediate his articulate statements and impeccably tailored image around the world. He has become the Leonard Bernstein of jazz, leading young people's concerts, lecturing on music appreciation.

To become this great and powerful institution, Jazz at Lincoln Center needed more than "strategic planning"; it required a clear philosophical direction and a moral imperative. Jazz at Lincoln Center and Marsalis's discourse have borrowed liberally from the writing and ideas of Albert Murray, novelist, raconteur, observer of American culture, confidant of jazz luminaries, and eminent African American man of letters. His thought, passed directly to Marsalis and filtered through his protégé, Stanley Crouch, has permeated every aspect of Jazz at Lincoln Center: programming, repertoire, personnel, compositional technique, performance practice, education, and style.

The central historical figure in their project is Duke Ellington. To Murray, he is an archetypal hero for his mastery of "elegance in the face of adversity." Ellington's artful resilience, rooted in African American culture, in particular the blues aesthetic, is emblematic of our national character. Though distinctively American, like any profound art Ellington's music has significance for all humanity.[1] Just as the LCJO has made Ellington's music a primary focus, Marsalis has modeled his own compositional style and performance practices on the Ellington orchestra.

Like Theodore Thomas, founder of the Chicago Symphony, Marsalis has embarked on a mission to "make good music popular" and to present "the great works of the great composers greatly performed."[2] Such a crusade would seem to require that the leader hire the best and most experienced musicians available, and, at its inception, Jazz at Lincoln Center engaged some of the most highly regarded names in jazz, including musicians whose pedigrees could be traced directly back to the maestro himself, Ellington. But Marsalis eventually chose a radically different course. Starting in 1993, with a crude attempt to fire everyone over thirty, and culminating in early 1994, when rehearsals began for his three-hour, Pulitzer Prize–winning jazz oratorio, *Blood on the Fields (BOTF),* Marsalis dismantled this all-star band. To the dismay of many established players in New York, Marsalis hired players from outside New York, many of them young and inexperienced.

Interviews with members of the band, arrangers, and other Jazz at Lincoln Center staff, as well as the copious printed words of Marsalis himself and musical examples culled from his massive score for *BOTF,* provide the basis for my examination of Marsalis's controversial transformation of the LCJO from what the *London Times* called the "most elite jazz institution in the world" into what seemed to many contemporary observers a "training band."[3] After laying out the salient issues—including Marsalis's attempts to police the boundaries of jazz and perceptions of him within the jazz community—I explore Murray's theories on jazz and blues as "aesthetic statements." Marsalis, under the tutelage of Murray and Crouch, has tried to make Jazz at Lincoln Center an embodiment of Murray's understandings of jazz and American culture. A central section of this chapter turns to *Blood on the Fields* to examine more closely the influence of both Ellington and Murray on Marsalis's music. The composition and rehearsing of this ambitious work (his first for big band and for which he also created a libretto and assembled a cast of singers) represents an important milestone in the trumpeter's development as a leader and musical thinker and coincided with his transformation of the LCJO. In the conclusion I look at the congruencies between his musical style and his discursive riffs and ideological vamps.

DEFINING JAZZ

Gary Tomlinson has described "canon-building" in jazz as "a strategy for exclusion . . . to define what is and isn't jazz" and specifically faults writings on jazz that "seek its 'essence' primarily or exclusively in its musical features." Such formalist definitions usually begin by assuming that some constant, immutable qualities can be distilled from the works of the ablest practitioners. Tomlinson criticizes the "internalist ideology" inherent to this approach that distances the music from "the complex and largely extramusical negotiations that made it and that sustain it."[4] Krin Gabbard, continuing this line of thought, favors a definition that takes into account shifting tastes, diverse populations, mediated images, and changing historical perspectives. From his point of view (sure to upset many fans and musicians), anything that was ever called jazz may be considered jazz, such as the music of Paul Whiteman ("the king of jazz") and even that of Kay Kyser or Kenny G.[5]

On the face of it, Marsalis would appear to belong to the "formalist" camp. In his words, "To understand the meaning of an art form, you have to find out what the greatest artists have in common."[6] Moreover, he insists that music that has strayed from these essential traits is no longer jazz. Despite the tendency of scholars to see the "formalist" and "sociohistorical" mind-sets as diametrically opposed, closer scrutiny reveals many similarities. Sociocultural backgrounds, views of history, and ideologies determine which "musical features" and "greatest artists" are deemed essential (as well as motivate the search for the "purely musical" or the relevant "extramusical" contexts). Formalist points of view, in jazz as in classical music, though they may be part of a "triumph of an art discourse for the music,"[7] are explicitly bound up with concepts of history and social context.

The discursive formations underpinning the rise of Jazz at Lincoln Center mirror those surrounding American symphony orchestras one hundred years earlier. Theodore Thomas and the other fathers of American orchestras, according to Levine, "owed a great deal to John Sullivan Dwight, the Boston critic, journalist, and editor who had mounted an enduring struggle for such an institution for decades." The purpose of such orchestras, wrote Dwight, was not mere "rendition" but "to keep the standard master works from falling into disregard, to make Bach and Handel, Haydn and Mozart and Beethoven, Schubert, Mendelssohn, and Schumann, and others worthy of such high companionship, continually felt as living presences and blessed influences among us."[8] Similarly, the stated goal of Marsalis and Jazz at Lincoln Center, contrary to the belief of many musicians, has never been to mindlessly ape the original recordings of masters such as Ellington and Basie but to capture their spirit and "keep them alive."[9] The adulatory, almost religious tone of Dwight's language evokes another critic and journalist, Stanley Crouch, who praises Ellington in words like "the peerless giant."[10]

Marsalis states unequivocally, "Ellington codified the music. He put it down, like Bach did for European music. All the characteristics that we've gone through are in Ellington."[11] As early as 1983 Marsalis affirmed in a *Down Beat* blindfold test that "everybody should get down on their knees and thank Duke Ellington."[12] Clearly, the orchestra developers, canon builders, and tastemakers of this, or any age, need their gods and an almost religious zeal.

Essential to Ellington's genius, Crouch writes, was his understanding of "what made [jazz] so different from all other music. It was his grasp of the essences of the idiom that allowed him to maintain superb aesthetic focus throughout his life, no matter how much he developed as a musician and developed the very art itself."[13] Jazz at Lincoln Center attempts to emulate this "aesthetic focus" by emphasizing the "essences of the idiom." David Berger, Crouch's fellow artistic consultant, former LCJO conductor, Ellington scholar, and informal arranging teacher of Marsalis, lists four essential characteristics of jazz: swing, blues feeling, improvisation, and groove. To him, there is nothing ambiguous about "swing." Eighth notes should be played with triplet subdivision. Music in which the eighth notes are equal is "too intellectual" (he gives the example of the Norwegian saxophonist Jan Garbarek). To be "jazz," music must also retain some connection to the blues, if not in form, at least in terms of inflection, timbre, and effect. Berger further explains that jazz always contains improvisation, even in works without soloing, if only in the rhythm section. "Groove" differs from swing and is, according to Marsalis, "the successful coordination of differing parts—like a clock."[14] To these four essences, a fifth is occasionally added. The "Spanish tinge," originally proposed by Jelly Roll Morton ("jazz's first intellectual," as Marsalis refers to him), may be present in the guise of certain rhythms (such as the habanera), thus allowing some jazz-influenced Latin music to be considered jazz. In his paean to the life of the touring jazz musician, *Sweet Swing Blues on the Road* (1994), Marsalis (more than once) offers the following definition, which parsed closely reveals the four essences: "Jazz is musical interplay on blues-based melodies, harmonies, rhythms and textures in the motion of an improvised groove. . . . In jazz it is always necessary to be able to swing consistently and at different tempos."[15] Such clear-cut notions leave little room for musicians to explore modes of playing that do not include every one of these traits. This rigid definition excludes hyphenated or "impure" musical styles such as jazz-rock ("doesn't swing"), Third Stream and classical-influenced jazz ("abandons blues feeling"), much avant-garde ("no groove"), and jazz-flavored music that is entirely composed ("no improvisation"). As Marsalis puts it, "Musical terms are very precise; these terms have histories to them."[16]

Marsalis believes that jazz has suffered under the weight of "misconceptions." Most of the blame can be laid at the feet of the masters who abandoned the true path and the generation that came of age in the 1970s. Asked by an interviewer for *Down Beat* what "moved the music along" during that decade, Marsalis answered unequivocally: "Nothing. Not one thing." What led it "astray" were the twin heresies of fusion and the avant-garde. "Everybody was trying to be pop stars . . . [or play] music that sounds like European music people were writing in the '30s."[17] He deflects charges of purism back toward his accusers: "'Jazz purist' is a term created to preserve the integrity of the corrupted. The purist is scorned as closed-minded and regressive, so that those who lack artistic integrity can get rich and feel persecuted at the same time." Yet, with his spectacular success, can he include himself when he claims "purists have no money, no power, no avenues to disseminate their views, yet they are constantly attacked by those that do"?[18]

In the 1990s, because of this outspokenness, his high visibility as "official" spokesman for jazz, and Jazz at Lincoln Center's gargantuan success at raising money, Marsalis became a lightning rod for jazz's discontents. His self-assuredness rankles many musicians accustomed to looser attitudes; jazz musicians, though opinionated, can be famously tolerant (as long as you play what you hear, man!). "If he simply said he didn't like our music or that it was 'bad jazz,' that would be one thing," complains one trumpeter who performs and records often in more "commercial" jazz forms. "But to totally dismiss it is arrogant. Who is he to say what is or isn't jazz." This musician, fairly representative of many professional jazz musicians in their thirties and forties, admires Marsalis's trumpet playing but sees him as out of touch with the realities faced by musicians who struggle daily to eke out a living. This player views his own forays into funk-jazz and popular Latin styles not as betrayal of his jazz roots but rather as an affirmation of his professional status. He speaks with obvious pride about his command of his instrument and ability to "get it right the first time" and suspects that not many of the LCJO musicians could perform equally well under such pressures: "It's nice for them that they have removed themselves from the 'marketplace' and that they can rehearse endlessly, but most of us don't have that luxury. I'm happy for them, but they shouldn't put down what we do."

What Marsalis and Jazz at Lincoln Center have done, however, is not so much remove jazz from the marketplace as create a new marketplace. They have had to *sell,* to many corporate and private sponsors of the arts, a vision of jazz as a "distinctly American tradition," worthy of support equal to that lavished on classical music. Marsalis is willing to capitalize on its sophisticated image. Jazz is not dying, he concludes, because if it were "musicians—and advertisers—around the world would not profile on the sophistication implied in its name."[19]

Though he is committed to raising the respect and support for jazz to the level found in the classical field, Marsalis has not tried to make jazz *sound* more like classical music. While they recognize the important influence of classical music in the development of jazz (e.g., the French opera in New Orleans), in terms of swing, blues feeling, and other "essential" jazz qualities, Wynton Marsalis and Jazz at Lincoln Center have resisted classicization. As I explore in some detail in the analysis of *Blood on the Fields*, Marsalis ostentatiously has cultivated African American and jazz performance practices. Key elements of the LCJO style are the Ellington aesthetic of an individualized ensemble blend; train sounds, "talking," and other instrumental onomatopoeia; and assorted inflections such as wails, rasps, growls, bends, and glissandos.

Marsalis's music did not always exhibit these traits. Critics commenting on his playing in the early 1980s often heard a resemblance to Miles Davis's work with his "second classic quintet" (with Wayne Shorter, Herbie Hancock, Ron Carter, and Tony Williams) during the mid-1960s.[20] The quintet records prominently featured Shorter's compositions, with their often difficult and convoluted harmonies. During this period, Davis's free and highly chromatic approach merely hinted at the chord changes and occasionally seemed to abandon formal structure entirely. By the late 1980s many listeners noticed a change in Marsalis's style: he was trying to capture the harmonies, tone colors, and special effects (mute work, growls, etc.) of Ellington in his compositions and more of the swing and inflection of Armstrong in his playing. His greatest discovery was the blues, which he realized was the core essence of jazz, proudly proclaimed on *The Majesty of the Blues*, a 1989 CD with his septet.

Although many musicians still express their fondness for his earlier phase of playing (with Art Blakey and the Messengers in 1980–81 and with his own groups in the early 1980s), Marsalis came to view it as superficial. Speaking of this period, he said, "At that point, I wasn't knowing anything." In a July 1984 cover story in *Down Beat*, Marsalis confessed, "I'm embarrassed to admit it, but when I joined Art Blakey's band, I hadn't even listened to Art Blakey's records."[21] For Marsalis, a crucial turning point in his career was meeting Stanley Crouch: "[Crouch was] one of the first people who made me understand the value of the historical perspective in jazz music and the fact that there's a philosophy that goes behind any type of aesthetic achievement."[22] In 1982 Crouch introduced Marsalis to Murray. The young trumpeter began to make frequent pilgrimages to Murray's Harlem apartment. Already a virtuosic trumpeter, Marsalis began to change his playing as he absorbed Ellington, Armstrong, and the "great masters." Perhaps even more significantly, he acquired a philosophy that became the bedrock for his future career and, eventually, Jazz at Lincoln Center.

As a student of Murray and Crouch, as well as of Berger and others, Marsalis proved to be an extremely quick study. In its relatively short history (1989–), change has come rapidly to Jazz at Lincoln Center, sometimes leaving other jazz musicians, academics, and critics behind. Apparently the public tends to be less critical; concerts sell out, tours expand, contributors open their pocketbooks. To better understand Marsalis's transformation from trumpet prodigy to orchestral composer, big band leader, fund-raiser, media spokesman, and educator, let us briefly examine the ideas of the man who has most profoundly influenced him.

ALBERT MURRAY

Albert Murray is the intellectual father of the Lincoln Center project to codify the jazz canon and secure its transmission to future generations. His philosophy is attractive, not least for its emphasis on native cultural forms over more "elitist," European-derived forms of artistic expression. He envisions a distinctly *American* approach to the understanding of arts in which the *"devices of stylization . . . are as vernacular as the idiomatic particulars of the subject itself."* He sees American artists, not just musicians, as, instead of simply "working folk and pop materials into established or classic European forms," "extending, elaborating, and refining (which is to say ragging, jazzing, and riffing and even jamming) the idiomatic into fine art." It is through such "skillful playfulness so characteristic of the blues idiom . . . that the raw material of everyday experience is processed into aesthetic statement."[23] "Skillful playfulness" does not occur in a vacuum but always as part of a larger "discussion." In jazz this dynamic is exemplified best in the music of Ellington, where "the inspiration, no less than the discipline that came from working alongside Ellington the performing composer, conditioned his side men to use their solo space to make meaningful statements as if in the context of a discussion rather than as simply a chance to display their extraordinary technical virtuosity" (111–12). This "individual freedom within group responsibility" is homologous with the American political system: "the orchestration of a veritable jam session of dissonant colonial voices into a constitutional democracy. *E pluribus unum,* human nature permitting" (113). "Discussion" occurs not only "in the moment" with fellow performers but as part of an ongoing dialogue with the past: "All any real orchestra does is keep something alive. Your creativity comes out of the dialogue with the tradition. . . . If you're looking just for innovation, you're flirting with hysteria."[24]

The "raw materials of everyday life" used by artists differ along regional and ethnic lines. But if "the condition of man is always a matter of the specific texture of existence in a given place, time and circumstance," these "regional particulars" have "universal implications": "Beneath the idiomatic surface of your old down-home stomping ground, with all of the ever-so-evocative local color you work so hard to get just right, is the common ground of mankind in general."[25]

While African Americans have faced far more than their share of struggle, adversity is a blessing in disguise, a "challenge to one's creativity." No one should wallow in the "pathology of blackness," as Murray accuses social scientists of doing.[26] The ability to make the best out of a bad situation or "address adversity with elegance" is a heroic stance. He sees "the eternal necessity to struggle not only as the natural condition of mankind but also as a form of antagonistic cooperation without which there is no achievement and fulfillment, no heroic action, no romance." African American experience, then, rather than being of interest only to other black Americans, holds the promise of fulfilling the heroic image for all Americans. African American struggles are an "emblem" of heroism par excellence "for a pioneer people who require resilience as a prime trait."[27]

To Murray, the blues is the quintessential heroic statement: "I don't know of a more valid, reliable, comprehensive, or sophisticated frame of reference for defining and recounting heroic action than is provided by the blues idiom, which I submit enables the narrator to deal with tragedy, comedy, melodrama, and farce simultaneously." Not only is the blues capable of such rich expression or storytelling, but it is also well suited for the juxtaposition of contrasting narrative and musical ideas. The "fully orchestrated blues statement" is "a highly pragmatic and indeed a fundamental device for confrontation, improvisation, and existential affirmation."[28] In the following passage, which I quote in full for its vivid imagery, Murray portrays the big band as the ultimate expression of "the fully orchestrated blues statement."

> Even as the lyrics wail and quaver a tale of woe, the music may indicate the negative mood suggested by the dreadful, or in any case regrettable, details, but even so there will also be tantalizing sensuality in the woodwinds, mockery and insouciance among the trumpets, bawdiness from the trombones, a totally captivating, even if sometimes somewhat ambivalent elegance in the ensembles, plus a beat that is likely to be as affirmative as the ongoing human pulse itself.[29]

Improvisation is central to the storytelling that is at the heart of the blues. Adapting an idea from Kenneth Burke, Murray sees the blues as "fundamental living equipment," a "strategy for acknowledging the fact that life is a lowdown dirty shame and for *improvising* or riffing on the exigencies of the predicament."[30]

Skill in such improvisational storytelling is acquired through direct contact with masters. Murray evokes imagery of the "second line," spectators irresistibly drawn to join with New Orleans street processions, as a metaphor for "a deliberate choice of mentors, role models, functionals and hence *true* fathers." According to Murray, "the second line is an idiomatic reference to an apprenticeship to any given master."[31] Murray himself has carried forward the ideas of Ralph Ellison (Ellison, two years his senior, was a classmate at Tuskeegee Institute during the mid-1930s) and, in turn, has influenced many younger writers and musicians.

In a telling comment, Murray succinctly offers what could be considered the agenda for Jazz at Lincoln Center: "Underneath all of it is that we don't want Americans ever to forget how to swing. We don't ever want them to stop being resilient. We don't ever want them to stop improvising. At the same time, having the precision not to violate the beat."[32] In this single statement Murray vividly reiterates the four essential ingredients in the recipe for jazz. Resilience, as we have seen, is practically a synonym for the blues ("equipment for living"). Jazz must swing; it must contain improvisation; and all the players must contribute to and not violate the groove. The only ingredient missing is Morton's "Spanish tinge" (a seasoning that the recipe apparently makes optional).

Albert Murray's ideas have saturated the music and policies of Jazz at Lincoln Center and continually resurface in its discourse.

"CARRYING THE BEAT": THE LINCOLN CENTER JAZZ ORCHESTRA

The centerpiece of Jazz at Lincoln Center was to be an orchestra devoted to performing the works of "the great jazz artists," Duke Ellington in particular. Because of Marsalis's inexperience with big bands, someone with expertise was needed to lead the band. Crouch recommended David Berger, who had been involved in the repertory movement since 1974.[33] Marsalis and Alina Bloomgarden, founder of Jazz at Lincoln Center, asked Berger whom he wanted to have in the band. Berger recalls, "I started to name some people, and they said, 'No man, you don't understand, you can get *anybody* in the world.' " Berger, trying to think of the biggest names he could, suggested Joe Henderson, Herbie Hancock, Clark Terry, Jimmy Hamilton, Milt Hinton, and others. Although a few, such as Hancock, would turn out to be unavailable, to Berger's amazement most of musicians he suggested were hired. With occasional changes in personnel, Berger conducted this stellar band on tours, television appearances, and a CD's worth of Ellington's music (*Portraits by Ellington,* recorded in 1991).

Bill Easley, who played tenor and clarinet with both Ellington (filling the chair vacated by Jimmy Hamilton) and the Lincoln Center orchestra, remembers fondly:

> That band that they had, with some of those older guys, when Norris [Tierney] and certain people were in the band, that band was the closest to Ellington as any other band ever was. In terms of the spirit and the feel. And I played in all the bands, and I played practically every repertory band there is. When they play things on the radio, they still play some things from that band.

Abruptly, on 31 May 1993,[34] Rob Gibson, who had been hired to manage Jazz at Lincoln Center in 1991, sent a letter to all of the older musicians in the band informing them of a decision to make "across the board changes in the orchestra personnel by hiring an entire band of guys under the age of 30":

> I hope you'll understand that the decision to not utilize your great talents this summer has nothing to do with artistic ability or any personal issues—this is

> simply an attempt on our part to try and get some of the younger musicians to learn more about this music and begin to play it with more authority. Obviously we had that authority with you, and that's why this [decision] has been a tough one.[35]

The ill-conceived letter created a whirlwind of problems for Lincoln Center. The press began contacting Gibson, Marsalis, band members, and other Jazz at Lincoln Center personnel. When it became clear that this maneuver could be considered age discrimination, several band members hired attorneys. Bill Easley recalls, "Everybody had their own way of dealing with it, but I knew that it was also a legal issue." An article that appeared in the *Village Voice,* "Jazz War: A Tale of Age, Rage and Hash Brownies," chronicled the turmoil and even a bizarre alleged attempt during a party to get hostile critics stoned without their knowledge.

With the bad publicity and threatened by lawsuits, Gibson was forced almost immediately to retract the letter. Though his lawyer had suggested Easley could make "a lot of money," the saxophonist dropped his lawsuit after everybody was hired back. He explains, "I figured had I done it, I could have destroyed, pretty much put a big wrench in the whole program. But that wasn't my intention." Some of the older musicians had come to depend on the orchestra for much of their income. But, as Easley notes, even after he was rehired, he knew the victory was temporary: "I knew my days were limited. I'm sure that there was a little fear of me, because I was the one who had really shaken things up. They couldn't necessarily get rid of me right away." Nevertheless, over time the policy was implemented anyway, and all of the older personnel (with the exception of the baritone saxophonist Joe Temperley) gradually were replaced with younger players, mostly members of Marsalis's septet and inexperienced musicians encountered at clinics and festivals. Many came from the South, in particular New Orleans, Marsalis's hometown. "We had a really good band," says Berger, who opposed this personnel change and was dismissed in January 1994 just before a major tour. "He [Marsalis] gradually dismantled it."

As discussed in chapter 3, the earlier version of the LCJO, with its more experienced musicians, had "defeated" the Carnegie Hall Jazz Band in a "Battle Royale" in 1993 but with the new personnel had failed to repeat its victory when the two bands met again just a year later. In the New York jazz community, where this transformation was greeted with little enthusiasm, many theories circulated to explain it. The musicians' union believed Jazz at Lincoln Center merely wanted musicians willing to work for less money. Others maintained that Marsalis, in order to operate dictatorially, needed younger, more pliable musicians. Some theories are more easily dismissed, such as the idea that Marsalis did not want players who might upstage him: he has featured numerous accomplished trumpeters, from Jon Faddis to Ryan Kisor.

Marsalis formed many of his attitudes about leadership early in his career. Although he gained valuable experience as a player and writer during his stint with Art Blakey, he was troubled by Blakey's lax control. According to former bandmates, Marsalis frequently nagged them about their dressing habits and even once challenged Blakey on his heroin habit. Apparently, what bothered him the most was not the leader's drug use but its effect on the music.[36] When he formed his own group in 1982 he sought not only to enforce high musical standards but also to improve the image of jazz. If the musicians respected the music enough to present it in a dignified manner, then the audiences would follow suit.

Being a successful leader required a subtle form of deception. As he described it to a *Down Beat* interviewer, "What you do is hire the cats who can play well enough to tell *you* what to do." But he also realized the importance of not letting the sidemen know how dependent he was on their contribution: "You have to make it seem like you're telling them. It's psychological. You have to be in charge of it, but you don't want to be in charge of it." Both Marsalis and his brother Branford, who worked in his band at the time, disparaged all-star bands because "a band has to have great followers." All-star bands have too many chiefs and "no Indians."[37]

While the media has focused on controversy surrounding the racial and gender makeup of the LCJO,[38] in the New York jazz community musicians seemed more concerned with issues of professionalism. As holders of one of the most prestigious and best-paying gigs in jazz, members of the orchestra found themselves in coveted positions. More than a few New York musicians resented the passing over of older players who had paid extensive dues in favor of youthful novices. Echoing a familiar refrain, Jon Faddis complained that, with a few exceptions, a single member of his band had more experience than all of the LCJO combined.[39] In 1997 Bill Kirchner described "Lincoln Center [as] basically a college-level band leavened with a few seasoned players like [Joe] Temperley and Ted Nash, and Ryan Kisor."

At the heart of Marsalis's decision was the desire to resurrect the apprenticeship system that had served jazz well for most of its history. As a primarily oral/aural cultural form, the transmission of jazz skills traditionally retained important similarities to African practice.[40] In *Stomping the Blues* Murray writes, "To the Africans from whom the dance beat disposition of U.S. Negroes is derived, rhythm was far more a matter of discipline than direct expression of personal feelings. African drummers had to serve a long period of rigidly supervised apprenticeship before being entrusted with such an awesome responsibility as carrying the beat!" To Murray, blues feeling and swing, though vital emblems of African American identity, are learned and are not part of a "racial essence." In Marsalis's words, "Swinging the blues is about culture, not race."[41]

Learning from recordings, books, or school programs is no substitute for a steady gig and direct relationship with a living master. As part of Jazz at Lincoln Center's annual Essentially Ellington competition, after Ellington transcriptions have been distributed, mentors are sent to high schools all over the United States to work with the most promising bands. The winning groups are brought to Lincoln Center for more coaching and several concerts. The recently established jazz program at Juilliard builds on this program by offering students an opportunity to study with Jazz at Lincoln Center musicians.

Although obviously pleased with the expanding number of jazz programs, Marsalis and his colleagues find much to critique in jazz education. Berger voices a frequently heard opinion in the jazz community that "the way we have it now, institutionalized school jazz doesn't work. It turns out players that are at best mediocre." He asks, "How many great players have come through the school system?" Berger believes that the essential characteristics of jazz are being neglected by established jazz programs: "Chord scales are taught and things like that, but rhythm is not addressed, the idea of swing, blues, those areas are not addressed at all." Marsalis, in Berger's view, is "trying to create *jazz* players. . . . Give them opportunities to play and play the same material every day, write material for them and develop a *band*." One standard that Marsalis sees schools regularly failing to meet is the teaching of the Ellingtonian aesthetic of ensemble blend. Instead of enforcing a "kind of clinical sterility" that stifles individuality, Marsalis believes that teachers should "make the students realize that you don't have to sacrifice that ensemble expression because you play with individual expression. That's the thing that's so great about Basie's band or Duke's band: they'd play these tricky passages and it would be precise, but you could still hear the individuals playing it."[42]

With the change of personnel in the LCJO, Marsalis began putting his personal stamp on the orchestra's sound. Berger explains, "He'd rather have young cats that don't have a style so they can develop one. If he thinks you're rushing, he wants to be able to say you're rushing and you'll do what he says and not question it." When I subbed in the sax section of the orchestra, I once saw Marsalis borrow lead trumpeter Roger Ingrams's horn to demonstrate exactly how he wanted a phrase inflected. Would Marsalis have been comfortable asking an experienced player many years his senior to hand over his instrument? The current lead trumpeter, Seneca Black, looked so young (he was just nineteen when he joined in 1997) that the band nicknamed him "90210" after a handsome Beverly Hills high school character in the television series of that name. "Kids step right into this gig," says Berger. "Seneca is a perfect example—lots of raw ability, chops like Jon Faddis. Does he know how to play jazz? No. But where [else] is he gonna work and get the experience."

For the young trombonist Wayne Goodman, who started out as a copyist for the band, the experience of working on *Blood* has become a hazy memory, caught up in the emotions of his first major gig, working with Marsalis, and playing such difficult music. "It was such a whirlwind thing for me. We were working nine hours a day. The most difficult thing that I remember was just reading this new kind of music, because I had never played anything like that before," states Goodman. "He writes what he hears, and he hears very complicated stuff. Very fast runs, . . . it's stuff that he would play on the trumpet, and he just scores it out for the band." Instead of complaining, as seasoned professionals might, Marsalis's young charges forged ahead.

Perhaps even more important than their openness to new ideas was the attitude that younger musicians brought to the orchestra. Marsalis expects players to share his commitment to perfection, his workaholic approach. A Jazz at Lincoln Center administrator confirms that Marsalis seeks to avoid that "union-symphonic musician attitude." Goodman explains, "He doesn't want if it's a ten o'clock rehearsal that people are in their chairs at five to ten and then at one o'clock, they're packing up their horns. That's the way the Philharmonic is; he doesn't want that." Marsalis hates what might be termed a time card mentality, preferring the enthusiasm of youngsters. Gourse reports that Marsalis once confided to Faddis that he "liked their vibe [because] they were eager to play."[43] The LCJO rehearses painstakingly and often. Marsalis constantly attempts, in Goodman's words, to "squeeze one more drop of juice out the orange." Still, his obsessive pursuit of perfection is not intended to stifle spontaneity. Marsalis, according to Goodman, "always talks about how we have to interact and not just stand up there and play. What Wynton is trying to get across to the band is that we're *always* gonna be listening. . . . You get on the bandstand and it's a very sensitive thing—you hear everything that's happening and you're reacting to it."

By the time of the *Blood on the Fields* premier on the first two days of April 1994, Marsalis had assembled a wholly dedicated band of players in their twenties or early thirties who were similar in age and attitude to those in his small groups (and actually included all the members of his septet). The unorthodox performance practices required an orchestra committed to working long hours and open to experimentation.[44] Although he stated that he intended to bring the experienced veterans back for future performances of Ellington's music, most of the new personnel remained with the band.[45]

During this period, the Lincoln Center Jazz Orchestra grew apart from New York City's established networks of musicians. Like Sue Mingus, Wynton Marsalis carved out his own jazz world where none existed. The musicians assembled for *Blood on the Fields,* with a few new additions, evolved into Marsalis's permanent band. In the process Marsalis brought a generation of musicians closer to the music of Ellington and through his "extension, elaboration and refinement" of that tradition in his own music, attempted to put Murray's theories and ideas into practice.

BLOOD ON THE FIELDS

Marsalis has been immersed in Ellington's music since the inception of the *Classical Jazz* series at Lincoln Center in 1988. During much of this time, he benefited from his close association with David Berger. As a leading transcriber and reassembler of Ellington scores, Berger was well qualified to impart elements of the composer's style, such as voicings, orchestrations, and other techniques. The two frequently spoke by telephone and went over scores together. While acknowledging the strong influence of Crouch and Murray and of his own coaching, Berger is quick to make certain that all the credit for the actual composing goes to Marsalis:[46] "You've got to do it, you can't just talk about it. Albert's a teacher, but Wynton is the guy who sits and writes."

Marsalis, perhaps more than any other major figure in jazz, has consciously created music that attempts to embody moral, philosophical, and ideological concepts. In *Blood on the Fields* one finds the influence of both Ellington and Murray. My analysis below compares Marsalis's work to Ellington's opus dealing with similar subject matter, *Black, Brown and Beige,* and relates *BOTF* to Murray's concept of the heroic in American culture, as expressed in his lectures *The Hero and the Blues.*

The Ellington Precedent

Blood on the Fields, Marsalis's first work for big band, was not an arrangement or even a modest original composition but a monumental three-hour oratorio on slavery in the United States. Not surprisingly, Marsalis chose to model his project on a work of Ellington. Besides the maestro's obvious musical influence, the oratorio's narrative closely follows Ellington's original conception for his most famous extended work, *Black, Brown and Beige: A Tone Parallel to the History of the Negro in America.*[47]

While the scope of Ellington's work was appropriately epic—from slavery through emancipation up to the present[48]—his original conception was even more sweeping; he had planned to begin with two movements titled *Africa* and *Slaveship.* In a twenty-nine-page sketch for *BB&B,* Ellington related the story of an African named Boola, beginning with his abduction in Africa and continuing with the horror of the middle passage, where, in "the adjoining cabin a woman is screaming—a symphony of torture." Ultimately, Ellington dropped his plans for these first two movements. John Edward Hasse suggests that the composer's decision "was due to a lack of time, or perhaps . . . his innate patriotism and a desire, especially during wartime, to emphasize positive aspects of American pluralism."[49] Another plausible explanation is that the pain and suffering were simply too great to lend themselves to a musical stage production (just as few composers have attempted to depict the Holocaust in music). Accepting such a work would have been even more difficult for Ellington's audiences and producers than his anti–Jim Crow musical, *Jump for Joy,* which ran for only eleven weeks in Los Angeles during 1941.

Black, Brown and Beige premiered at Carnegie Hall in 1943 to mixed reviews. John Hammond condemned the forty-four-minute work as "pretentious" and questioned the appropriateness of expanding jazz pieces beyond the usual three- or four-minute length. A reviewer for the *New York Times* wrote that though *BB&B* "had many exciting passages, . . . it was in the shorter works like 'Rockin' in Rhythm' and the familiar 'Mood Indigo' that the leader seemed most completely himself."[50] The opening performances of *BOTF,* roughly fifty years later, were greeted more warmly. The *New York Times* critic Jon Pareles, while subtly criticizing the oratorio's three-hour duration, praised it for its "adroit balance" of "fancy gambits with the vernacular of blues and ballads." In 1997 the combined blitz of a twenty-four-city tour, the announcement of the Pulitzer, and the release of a three-CD set (though it had been recorded in 1995) generated a wave of publicity. While the reaction of much of the jazz press was lukewarm and audience fatigue was evident, mainstream critics responded with enthusiasm. A reviewer for *USA Today* proclaimed simply, "*Blood* is magnificent."[51] As the clearest indicator of changed attitudes and of the acceptance of jazz as "serious" music during the intervening years, Marsalis's Pulitzer was the first ever awarded to a jazz musicians (1997)—an honor that was denied Ellington in 1965 when the Pulitzer board voted to reject the recommendation of its music jury. In retrospect, Ellington's reply ("Fate doesn't want me to be famous too young") seems all the more ironic.[52]

Ellington used the term *tone parallel* for his programmatic works or tone poems. His forty-four-minute work, though based on the general historical narrative outlined in his sketch, does not present an explicit plot as does Marsalis's work. As an oratorio, or unstaged vocal drama, rather than a strictly instrumental piece, *Blood on the Fields* allows Marsalis to develop characters. He constructs a narrative in which displaced Africans come to terms with the conditions of bondage through achieving "soul," which Crouch (echoing Murray) defines in the concert's program notes as the "willingness to address adversity with elegance."[53]

Rather than structure his music in three large movements, as did Ellington in *BB&B,* Marsalis constructed a work of twenty-one "sections" separated at about midpoint by an intermission. The suite format, also favored by Ellington in his later extended works,[54] allows short sections, typically connected by some overriding idea or narrative, to be developed independently. This architecture lends itself readily to the repeating chorus structures integral to most jazz. Marsalis has made the historical span narrower than Ellington's by concentrating on the antebellum period rather than the "progress of the race" over two centuries, but he begins with the traumatic event that

Ellington decided to avoid: the middle passage. After an invocation to the "Indians" in section I, the opening scene of the oratorio takes place on a slave ship. Here, in Marsalis's words, "we meet two Africans, Jesse and Leona, who until being forced into relatively equal positions due to their tragic circumstances, occupied very different stations in life—he a prince, she a commoner."[55] "Move Over" (section II) refers to the middle passage and the need for the disparate African tribes summoned in section I to create social solidarity. As in the Ellington sketch, we hear a woman's cries as Leona (Cassandra Wilson), despite the overcrowded conditions, calls out for a comforting touch:

> Pain and evil all around me, O –
> Over, move, move closer over
> Touch me closer

Marsalis evokes the feeling of a floating ship with a swaying 6/4 meter and chromatic runs up and down, some of which have been foreshadowed in the opening section. In section III, "You Don't Hear No Drums," he conveys the nightmare of the mass of sick and dying humanity crammed in a dark, putrid hold through weird sounds collectively improvised by various members of the band and Jesse's (Miles Griffith) increasingly bitter, angry voice. Indicating the impossibility of facing such a situation, Jesse disconnects from the experience. After telling Leona ("Low born woman") several times "I think you better ride this wave on out," he sings (with a little help from the band members singing along), "I've got to get out, got to be way far away, free." He can only escape from the "reeking, foul stench" by "flying high" or by soaring away in his imagination, and the tune breaks into a piano solo in a fast 4/4 swing on a fourteen-bar minor blues. These two sections establish the essential drama of the oratorio—"woman" as a force of social solidarity and "man" as seeker of freedom. Despite their different backgrounds, Leona and Jesse must forge strong bonds in order to face their new life of pain and hardship. In this drama blues and jazz become the expressive equivalents of both impulses—the collective and the individual—and jazz improvisation is closely identified with masculinist individuality.

The fourth movement, divided into two subsections—"The Market Place" and "Soul for Sale"—and the fifth movement—"Plantation Coffle March"—depict facets of the slave trade. In "Soul for Sale" the singer Jon Hendricks portrays a white slave buyer bidding on "a buck whose skin shines" and "brown concubines." His vocal on this medium-tempo swinging tune reveals hardly a trace of condescension or parody of whites. The pleasant, almost jovial feel, with its descending half-time bass line in D minor (somewhat reminiscent of tunes such as "Fever" or "Hit the Road Jack"), belies the disturbing subject matter. Marsalis's tunefulness and ability to write within the conventions of an AABA song format (with a nine-bar A section, however) are very much in evidence. The coffle march of the fifth movement (which, by being in a slow 3/4, feels all the more ponderous) features vocals from both Jesse and Leona. Jesse's continued defiance and first escape attempt are rewarded with a gunshot wound.

With the sixth movement Marsalis reaches the point where Ellington ultimately decided to begin his musical narrative in *BB&B*. "The first thing the Black man did in America was WORK, and there the work song was born[,] . . . a song of burden," Ellington wrote in his sketches.[56] The first movement of *BB&B*, "Black," begins appropriately with a work song. Unlike Ellington's more melodious piece, Marsalis's work song combines eight or nine simple interlocking rhythmic patterns (see Example 46). Both evoke the rhythms of labor with a booming drum hit on beat one. In Marsalis's work song, perhaps signifying their union in coordinated labor, Jesse and Leona sing their first duet. The seventh movement reprises Leona's "I think I hear a drum" and Jesse's "got to be way far away, free" themes, this time in the context of day-to-day imaginings of a people held in bondage.

Marsalis's eighth movement again parallels Ellington's work by turning to the slaves' embrace of Christianity. In the second section of "Black," Ellington's well-known ballad "Come Sunday" (later recorded in 1958 with Mahalia Jackson), Boola finds a Bible and teaches himself to read. For a scene described in the program notes as "'Church Window' mood—the Negroes looked in from outside," Ellington wrote, "Come Sunday, while all the Whites had gone into the church, the slaves congregated under a tree . . . Good souls praying and singing faithfully without a word of bitterness or revenge—'I forgive my past suffering, just let my people go.'" Like Ellington, Marsalis contrasts African American and white religious experiences. Marsalis begins with a slow march in the style of "an old town band" (the out-of-tune notes suggesting white ignorance or ineptitude?). Leona's song of forgiveness, "Oh, We Have a Friend in Jesus," rings hollow. The second part of the eighth movement, "God Don't Like Ugly," with the subheading, "They, however, interpret the word of God differently," ends with Leona singing the words "And the last shall be first," making clear that blacks and whites found different passages of Scripture worth emphasizing.[57]

Covering the period from the Revolutionary War to World War I, *BB&B* celebrates "the contribution made by the Negro to this country in blood." Here Ellington's obvious emphasis on the "Negro heroes" of past wars was motivated in part by wartime patriotism.[58] In *BOTF* Marsalis transfers the blood imagery from the battlefield to the cotton field. Instead of honoring military heroes, Marsalis recognizes African Americans' contributions to feeding, clothing, and building America. Black subjugation and forced labor, "blood on the fields," were fundamental in the economic, cultural, and spiritual development of the United States. In Crouch's words, "The 'peculiar institution' raised high the central issue facing civilization under capitalism, which is bringing together morality and the profit motive."[59]

Ellington's 1943 concert at Carnegie Hall, which premiered *BB&B*, opened with the "Star Spangled Banner." The program notes proclaimed, "Even though the Negro is 'Black, Brown and Beige' he is also 'Red, White and Blue'—asserting the same loyalty that characterized him in the days when he fought for those who enslaved him."[60] *Blood on the Fields* also displays the "red, white and blue" imagery. The CD cover pictures an American flag lightly streaked with bloodstains. In the title piece, "Work Song (Blood on the Fields)," Leona sings:

Blood on the fields
King cotton grow
Brown soil yields
White up above
Red down below

Marsalis explains: "The colors in the piece are the social breakdown of America in the nineteenth century—white above, brown soil, and red down below."[61] Instead of shades of black and brown (*BB&B*), Marsalis transposes the national colors to red, white, and brown. His imagery of cotton fertilized with the blood of African slaves evokes the encounter of Native American, European, and African races in the Americas.

Ellington's first movement, "Black," ends with a section called "Light." This section expresses "the desire for freedom [that] motivated their songs [and] inspired their heroes—real and legendary."[62] In *BOTF* Marsalis expresses this yearning through Jesse's repeated attempts to flee from slavery. The first half of the oratorio closes with Jesse seeking wisdom from the elder Juba. Through him, Jesse learns that he must shed his arrogance and depend more on his brother and sister slaves. Juba outlines three tasks for Jesse: he must love the land, learn to sing with soul, and find a name for his new identity (Negro? Afro-American? black?). In the second half Jesse painfully learns how to survive in this hostile new world and in the process fulfills Murray's vision of American heroism.

The Hero Discovers the Blues

As both musical form and style, the blues were down-home threads that Ellington always wore with ease—comfortable yet sophisticated, never shabby or undignified. A great many of his more than fifteen hundred compositions were out-and-out variants on the twelve-bar blues. Murray believes the blues imbue all Ellington's work: "What an Ellington arrangement or composition represents is . . . the extension, elaboration, and refinement of the basic twelve-bar (and less frequently the eight-, four-, and sixteen-bar) blues idiom statement."[63] Like some mythical hero, a "secular god" in the American pantheon, Ellington confronted the atrocities of racism by "tak[ing] them for granted much the same as the fairy tale princes and dukes of derring-do" faced adversity. Such obstacles were more a test of character, a "dragon to be slayed" on the way to greatness.[64]

Marsalis's 1989 CD, *The Majesty of the Blues,* announced a new era in his music. In the liner notes he described his musical epiphany:

> From my studies I have found out something different from what I thought when I was growing up. In the ignorance of overrefinement, we thought that the blues was the simplest form to play. We didn't even think you had to play blues. We only recognized things like "Giant Steps" because it had a lot of chord changes on it. The only difficulty we recognized was harmonic. But that's a fallacy because you find out through study that blues is the single element that connects the greatest jazz musicians. Why is that? Because blues has the emotional, harmonic, and technical depth to inform whatever you do in this music.[65]

Marsalis's change from his "postbop, Miles Davis" style to the blues-inflected, traditional New Orleans, pan-stylistic jazz of recent years found its first expression on this CD.

In the second half of *BOTF,* Jesse also discovers the blues in spite of himself. Though he still yearns for freedom, for his previous position in life, and perhaps for the cultural purity he had known in Africa, ultimately he must accept his new situation. The blues, as an African *American* form of expression, is his salvation. The second part opens with Jesse on the run again, ignoring Juba's advice. The chorus intones, "Jesse don't care about no Indians, no land, no soul, no singing, and no Leona. It was time for him to go ahead and run." Marsalis conveys his flight musically through Griffith's rapid scat singing interspersed with some scurrying figures in the saxophones. Halfway through this piece, Leona takes over the vocal. Wishing more for his return than his freedom, she sings, "Hope they bring him back to me." Jesse continues his flight by improvising a few more scatted lines. At the end of the piece, the horns begin to improvise wildly over a vamp that gradually builds intensity. Here collective improvisation, used programmatically as in the Mingus band, suggests the frantic chase of the slave hunt. A second part of this movement, labeled Xa, expresses Leona's regret and guilt over wishing for his capture once he is brought back. This episode again portrays woman as a domesticating force inhibiting male freedom and creativity.

Jesse's punishment in section XI, "Forty Lashes," evokes Coltrane's bitter protest against racist oppression, "Alabama." Like Coltrane, Marsalis has composed a meterless "chant" in minor over octave tremolos in the left hand of the piano and pedals in the bass. Marsalis alternates sporadic solos from Anderson on alto and Goines on E♭ clarinet with drum solos by Herlin Riley. Again aiming for programmatic effect, the score directs Riley to make the "'beating' progressively longer and more intense" with each successive solo.

Suggesting that blues were born of such suffering (earlier appearances of blues in sections III and VI were linked to the agony of the middle passage and hard labor on the plantation), the band breaks into a swinging blues. As he drops a semitone to the key of C♯ minor, Marsalis maintains this contrasting 12/8 swing feel for fourteen measures before descending once again into musical chaos. He instructs his players with a single word, *pandemonium,* to create strange sounds on their instruments. At the end two bass clarinets play a bluesy vamp over the band's foot stomping and clapping.

After his capture and punishment, Jesse is a changed man. In section XII he sings, "Oh, what a fool I've been. [I'm] not no prince, just a man, just a lonely man." On his two final words, "No more!" as if to signify this change, the music moves from C minor to C major. The second part of section XII, "Back to Basics," taken at a medium swing or "bounce" tempo, expresses Jesse's transformation instrumentally. Nearly all of the ensemble parts in this eleven-and-a-half-minute piece are in unison. Various members make animal sounds, and at one point Marsalis instructs the trumpets to sound like an elephant, a chicken, and a rooster and to "stutter." Brass players rapidly switch between straight, harmon, and plunger mutes and effect moaning, laughing, and crying sounds. The writing here especially shows Ellington's influence in the plunger effects, the prominence of the reeds in the "mix," and the extended unison line (reminiscent of "Schwiphti" in Ellington's *Suite Thursday*). Even the one concerted ensemble passage, a long string of chromatically descending thirteenth chords from G to B♭, sounds very Ellingtonian (e.g., "Concerto for Cootie").

Marsalis expresses Jesse's changing social relationships through orchestration. On trumpet, Marsalis, playing the role of Jesse, engages in a dialogue with the rest of the ensemble, their solidarity suggested by their playing in unison. Then, in the first extended solo section, he "converses" with each member of the group by trading fours with them. On the repeat of this solo section, Ron Westray and Wycliffe Gordon hold their own unique style of musical conversation on trombone, trading growling, mocking, four-bar insults. A forty-measure interlude featuring laughing and taunting horns, more unison, and more Marsalis leads into another solo section. Now all four saxophones alternate fours for one chorus, followed by another chorus of trades with Marcus Printup and Russell Gunn on trumpet. In these segments Marsalis seems to have self-consciously employed Murray's aesthetic of "discussion" to create "a veritable jam session of dissonant colonial voices." The piece goes out with a long vamp featuring all the horns on a unison line in

EXAMPLE 45. *Blood on the Fields,* Section XV, blues riff (Wynton Marsalis).

A minor and the "laughing" trumpet of Marsalis. In section XIII Jesse finally surrenders to Leona's love and discovers soul. Leona sings of their unity, "when our hearts are swaying at one tempo that is soul." Within this communal groove, Jesse echoes that "soul is the giving without want." The piece develops into a D major blues as Jesse and Leona sing a scat duet and ends as they trade a few short phrases back and forth in B major.

Juba returns in section XIV to continue riffing on the theme of solidarity and brotherhood:

> Look and see
> to learn and be
> one part of we
> and not just ye
> if you'd be free.

Marsalis changes the feel drastically with this up-tempo swinging tune. He deploys the horns sparingly, only in the first four bars and in a shout chorus. After a couple of extended scat solos, Juba (Jon Hendricks) returns on the bridge singing "don't fall in love with the weight of your pain," a line that expresses a point of view congruent with Murray's lessons on the "fakelore of black pathology."[66] As Jesse learns to face trials and tribulations with courage, he begins to search for small pleasures in his life of bondage. In a short subsection of XIV titled "The Sun Is Gonna Shine," Jesse scats a joyous melody and solo over an AABA structure that once again displays Marsalis's penchant for avoiding "four square forms."[67] The A sections are nine bars, and the bridge is eleven bars—a five-bar and a six-bar phrase.

Section XV is a slow blues in D major preceded by a short rubato section (Example 45). Leona sings, and the pianist Eric Reed ad libs on a down-home boogie pattern that evokes southern rural plantation or Delta blues.

Although the next section is not a blues (it is in fact based on the tune in section XIV), its subheading reads, "Jesse has learned to play the blues." A middle section is open for solos, and we hear from five of the horn players.

TABLE 4 Blues in *Blood on the Fields*

	Section Title	*Key & Form*	*Soloist(s)*	*Instrument*
III	"You Don't Hear No Drums"	E♭ minor; 12 bar	Marsalis	trumpet
III	"You Don't Hear No Drums"	G minor; 14 bar	Reed	piano
IV	"Work Song"	E♭ major; 8 bar	Ensemble	winds
XI	"Forty Lashes"	C♯ minor; 12 bar	Reed	piano
XIII	"I Hold Out My Hand"	D major; 11 bar	Jesse, Leona	voices
XV	"Will the Sun Come Out?"	D major; 12 bar	Leona, Reed	voice, piano
XVIII	"Calling the Indians Out"	C major; 12 bar	Ward	violin

A lead clarinet and plunger wah-wah's in the trombones once more remind the listener of Ellington.

The next section (XVIII), "Calling the Indians Out," sounds very different from *BOTF*'s opening section of the same title. Marsalis introduces a violinist, Michael Ward, who plays a melody freely over rich harmonies in the rhythm section. The piece then breaks into some fast, romping fiddling in two, before finally launching into yet another blues. The introduction of this new instrument late in the work is reminiscent of the way Ellington sometimes brought in Ray Nance on violin.[68] Ward improvises numerous choruses on a C blues that retains some of its "foot-stomping" quality by remaining in two.

This final blues of *BOTF* demonstrates that Jesse has indeed learned the blues. Perhaps the fiddle is meant to imply that the blues has become an integral part of the American musical landscape, an "emblem for a pioneer people who require resilience as a prime trait." Table 4 shows the blues currents that run through the entire work. Significantly, almost all appearances of the blues up through Jesse's beating in section XI are in minor. After his awakening all three instances of blues are in major.

In section XIX, "Follow the Drinking Gourd," Marsalis reinforces the connection between musical improvisation and freedom through Griffith's scat singing. Jesse escapes once more, this time with Leona. Marsalis repeats the same device he used earlier: collective improvisation to suggest the frenzy of the hot pursuit. Again the escape fails, but as the next to last section, "Freedom Is in the Trying," reminds us, "even for the righteous, success is never certain."

The last vocal number in *BOTF*, section XX, like the end of the first half, features Juba. The entire ensemble joins in on the refrain, "Oh Lord Juba!"

As the group sings his praises, Juba clearly represents the survival of traditions that extend all the way back to Africa—respect for griots and their wisdom and the relevance of such knowledge for survival in a hostile land.

Throughout *Blood on the Fields,* Marsalis draws on material from his native city, New Orleans. The presence of elder New Orleans musicians on the suite "The New Orleans Function" on *The Majesty of the Blues* (1989) announced his rediscovery of his roots. On this recording he tried to depict the experience of "growing up in New Orleans, that kind of fraternity, of humor, of style, food, dances, parades, churches, ribbing, family, sports, girls—all of it." Reflecting on his recent "enlightenment," he added, "I can do this better right now because I think I'm at a place where I really understand what jazz is."[69]

The oratorio's opening section, "Calling the Indians Out," refers to the social clubs and mutual-aid societies in the black neighborhoods of New Orleans, the Mardi Gras Indians. These rival groups or "gangs," whose members dress in elaborate Indian costumes, historically resisted the city's prevailing order. By invoking these tribes as a metaphor for African ethnic groups, Marsalis makes a connection between cultural practices in the black diaspora and the mother continent. Much later, in "Chant to Call the Indians Out" (section XVIII), Marsalis, perhaps as a way of indicating Jesse's rediscovery and reinterpretation of his African roots, again relies on the Indian imagery. Jesse sings to a beat, labeled as African in the composer's score: "Oh! Who wants to help their brother dance this dance." By this time he has shed (or had beaten out of him) much of his aristocratic demeanor and has begun to identify with the other slaves. Marsalis draws more overtly on New Orleans material for the "second line," or street processional groove, underlying the elder Juba's songs—the last section before the intermission ("Juba and a O'Brown Squaw") and the penultimate section of the work ("Freedom Is in the Trying"). These marching beats, along with "Dixieland" polyphony and other New Orleans practices, crop up throughout *BOTF.* While alluding to his apprenticeship to Murray and other elders, Marsalis follows Murray's edict on crafting local experiences into universal aesthetic statements.

Some aspects of *Blood on the Fields* evolved during the extensive rehearsals. Berger recalls that little of the singing and clapping by the ensemble had been planned. As the band often rehearsed without the singers, Marsalis sang the vocalists' parts. When some band members joined in, Marsalis, according to Berger, decided to incorporate their singing into the performance. For example, the entire ensemble sings the refrain "I think you better ride this wave on out" (in section III, "You Don't Hear No Drums"). In Berger's view, singing by band members, which has been "out of the jazz experience for a long time," resonates with earlier eras, especially the 1930s, when it was fairly common. "Imagine how difficult it would be," he says, "to get players today to do that. They're all too uptight to do simple things like this. It's very sophisticated and 'country' at the same time."

Even more difficult were the dramatic effects that Marsalis rehearsed to perfection. Goodman recalls that he often wanted the band to "sound like different things—like having it sound like *people* crying, or having the whole band sound like a banjo. He would tell us what he was hearing." The musical dialogue, or "discussions," required "talking" effects from the instruments, similar to Bubber Miley's, Joe Nanton's, and Cootie Williams's in the the Ellington orchestra. Goodman says, "He likes a very vocal quality, he's always saying 'more vocal quality in the sound.' He wants it to sound like human voices instead of just like different groups of instruments." Everyone needed to be aware of the story line and of his specific role. "He wanted it to be expressed that way, not just, 'OK now you're gonna play a *solo.*' " Goodman likens the process to a director working with actors.[70]

Jesse's painful adjustment and eventual triumph of the spirit is the raw material of legend, the heroism celebrated by Murray in *The Hero and the Blues* (1973). Jesse is the archetypal hero "whose playful creativity is his stock in trade, and also the salvation of his people."[71] Though he may not have decided what to call himself, Jesse is transformed from African to African American. In the process he learns the "playful creativity" of song and dance provide the tools for survival.

BOTF is also a very personal story. Marsalis's discovery of jazz traditions and past heroes such as Armstrong and Ellington reshaped his music. Marsalis *is* the African prince, who, in spite of "royal birth" into a musical family, must learn the blues in order to achieve mastery. Similarly, the elder Juba represents Marsalis's gurus, Albert Murray and Stanley Crouch. Juba, with his clowning and tomfoolery, suggests the struggle that Marsalis initially had appreciating the roles of early black entertainers he found "tommish."[72] Marsalis connects his awakening to a new respect for his elders: "I was always around older people, my great-uncle and great-aunt. They were just soulful. I didn't realize that until I left home and got around other people. . . . So with Mr. Murray, it was a natural progression. I've been to his house hundreds of times. Now I take my kids up to see him. It's like we're family."[73] Marsalis has cast himself perfectly for his multiple roles in *Blood on the Fields.* As trumpeter, composer-bandleader, and young artist, he plays the heroes Armstrong and Ellington as well as Jesse, the proud African prince.

JAZZ AND IDEOLOGY

The jazz produced at Lincoln Center is drenched in its makers' understandings of history, perspectives on American culture, and ambitions for the future. Unlike some jazz musicians, especially those of the 1960s and 1970s, who challenged existing power relations, sometimes venting frustration and rage in the process, Marsalis works within the existing political order. Instead of seeking radical change, Jazz at Lincoln Center wishes to assume its rightful place among other elite cultural institutions. While Marsalis may be "rejecting the aesthetic boundary between jazz and classical music,"[74] he maintains a vigorous antiassimilationist stance musically by accentuating the "essential" characteristics that distinguish jazz from classical music. A related project is rebuilding support and participation within the black community.

In a convenient reversal, unlike the founding fathers of American symphony orchestras, Marsalis emphasizes the "Americanness" of his art form and its adoption by *Europeans*. Although Murray cautiously explains that his ideas should not "be confused with nationalism[,] . . . for it has nothing to do with the flag-waving, chauvinism, and Fourth of July jingoism," Jazz at Lincoln Center has not hesitated to appeal to patriotic instincts in its fundraising and its efforts to expand the audience of jazz. For Marsalis and Jazz at Lincoln Center, jazz is unmistakably American, not only because it relies on, in Murray's words, "indigenous raw material," but also because it is homologous to the American sociopolitical system. Marsalis describes the connection: "In democracy as in jazz, you have freedom with restraint. It's not absolute freedom, it's freedom within a structure. . . . Played properly, jazz shows you how the individual can negotiate the greatest amount of personal freedom and put it humbly at the service of a group conception."[75] Political and social structure is equated with musical structure: chord changes and groove. The operative words are *played properly*. This statement, clearly meant to disparage "free jazz" and its lack of structure, illustrates how, with characteristic circularity, ideology both expresses and enforces stylistic constraint.

Jazz was born out of the tension between the promise of freedom and the reality of its denial. After the abolition of slavery, says Marsalis, "these people, these Americans, these niggers willed an art into existence to objectify the most precious aspirations of democratic thought, and to validate those same conceptions so compromised in their daily lives as to seem absurd."[76] Structurally, *Blood on the Fields* equates improvisational freedom with human freedom. "As the piece progresses, as the characters become freer," Marsalis notes, "there is more room for people to play. In the beginning it is all written out."[77] Improvisation always takes place over a framework of chord changes, except for a few instances where soloists are instructed to play freely. In these cases it is usually meant to suggest depravity or horror—as in section II on the slave ship, when Marsalis calls for the "sparse wild sounds" from the first tenor.

Marsalis expresses "individuality at the service of group conception" compositionally in his ensemble textures. Two particularly striking examples in *BOTF* are the "hockets" in sections III and VI. In "Work Song (Blood on the Fields)," almost all the instruments are given distinct pitches, rhythms, and timbres (Example 46). The orchestration calls for two bass clarinets in the

EXAMPLE 46. *Blood on the Fields,* Section VI, "Work Song (Blood on the Fields)" (Wynton Marsalis).

saxophone section and for two different kinds of mutes in the brass in addition to special effects such as vibrato and "wahs." In this highly individuated orchestration, each instrument can be heard separately, but collectively they sound like one continuous vamp. The musically coordinated labor represents the uniting of individuals in a common groove (recall Marsalis's definition of groove: "the successful coordination of differing parts—like a clock").

"Freedom within a structure" leaves plenty of room for competition. Competitive improvisation occurs throughout *BOTF* as illustrated in the "fours" traded in "Back to Basics." As one Jazz at Lincoln Center administrator notes,

"Wynton likes to fire up the competition between members of the band." In Marsalis's philosophy, competitive individualism, a basic tenet of capitalism and the American socioeconomic structure, remains an essential impulse in jazz, contributing much of its musical vitality.

Blood on the Fields teaches that the righteous do not necessarily succeed, that blind resistance in the face of overwhelming odds is foolhardy. The clever hero learns to outwit his "massa" by keeping "his head in the east but his mind in the west."[78] Successful change comes from working within tradition. When an interviewer asked him who most embodies his mentors' concept of the heroic, Marsalis named Harriet Tubman because "she never got caught." "I think Robeson and DuBois got tired," he adds. Marsalis seems to be referring to their turn toward communism. Little in the Murray-Crouch-Marsalis philosophy challenges prevailing capitalist "free market" discourse. Apparently because of her ability to stay within the system, Harriet Tubman didn't get tired. Marsalis also explains John Coltrane's rejection of mainstream jazz in his later music in similar terms. "Cats get tired," he says, ". . . . constantly trying to come up with something new. . . . The tradition of the new is suicidal."[79] He recognizes, however, that his predecessors lived in different times; even some of the greatest heroes could not face the unceasing struggle and pain. Rather than work within traditional musical or social structure, they advocated radical change.

In winter 1998 Marsalis appeared at a press conference with Mayor Rudolph Giuliani to announce plans for a new concert hall for Jazz at Lincoln Center to be built at the site of the old Coliseum on Columbus Circle. In reflecting on his achievements, Marsalis stated that he had been "motivated by a desire to help jazz musicians like his father, who had so much to give and found so little acceptance."[80] "They are old oak tree[s] of men," he writes in a chapter of *Sweet Swing Blues* dedicated to Stanley Crouch, "strong, proud, with far reaching roots deeply imbedded, sucking nourishment from the original stream, their branches stretching out boldly against the sky to proclaim the majesty of the blues."[81]

Overlooking the fact that it comes from a man who fired all his musicians over the age of thirty, the effusive prose serves to place Marsalis at the heart of a patrilineage that he sees as extending back to the almost mythical New Orleans trumpeter, Buddy Bolden.[82] In establishing the jazz canon, he seeks to erase "the supposed generation gaps that have bedeviled jazz since musicians began to emerge who were able to play with authority in only one style." A familiar refrain, echoed throughout the fall 1999 tour, was "All Jazz Is Modern." Having absorbed the sounds of Armstrong and New Orleans tradition in his playing and adapted the style of Ellington in his composing, Marsalis is laying the groundwork for what may become the jazz musician of the twenty-first century, conversant in all styles from the turn of the century to the 1960s (except, in his case, free jazz and fusion).

Marsalis has spoken eloquently and profusely on a wide range of subjects. In almost the same breath, his speech traverses lofty ideals and rustic metaphors ("Knocks in the head, feet in the butt can beget recognition," section XII, *BOTF*). Like Murray and Crouch, he enjoys mythological allusion, but he still appreciates tough talk and folksy slang. *Sweet Swing Blues on the Road* contains profuse references to Hannibal, Gabriel, David and Goliath, and Ethiope ("who they called Aesop"). He also speaks with obvious admiration of Crouch's willingness to "hang his foot into somebody's ass if provoked" and of a former bassist's carrying of a firearm.[83] When she first heard him speak, Candace Stanley, Marsalis's former mate and the mother of two of his children, expected that someone who played classical music and dressed conservatively would "talk like white people." Instead, to her pleasant surprise, she found, "Wow, he talks like a brother." In his book Marsalis blends romantic words ("sweetness, tenderness and lovingness") with not-so-subtle sexual allusion ("in-out-in-out"). He can rail against a "society in which from the time you are twelve, everything is telling you fuck fuck fuck fuck fuck fuck and get as much pussy as you can"[84] and still enjoy his own reputation for sexual conquest (a chapter in his book, "Sweet Release," offers photographic documentation). Like Jesse, the hero of *Blood on the Fields,* Marsalis has resisted the domesticating influence of women, seeking refuge "in a world defined by the creativity of men."[85] He speaks of his respect for women's rights, but his musical sphere, like most of jazz, continues to be nearly all-male. He nurtures young jazz musicians in his orchestra but refuses to hire women until they reach a "higher . . . level of playing."[86] His language constantly refers to jazz*men* and draws on imagery of warriors and battle as his traveling fraternity of musicians appear in arenas throughout the world.

It is tempting to dwell on his obvious contradictions and inconsistencies.[87] A few obvious examples are his tight control over his band members while celebrating their "individuality," his firing of the veteran players despite his "new found respect" for the elders of jazz, his strident policing of the boundaries of jazz while professing to move jazz forward, his apparent desire to keep his touring orchestra all-male despite an upswing of participation of women in jazz generally, his cocksure explication of jazz history (as in the recent Ken Burns film, *Jazz*) without recognizing other points of view, and his emphasis on the Americanness of the idiom at the expense of its international currency.

What is perhaps more revealing is the extent to which the ideology and rhetorical strategies of Jazz at Lincoln Center have contributed to its remarkable success. Clifford Geertz has described the process by which "ideologies render otherwise incomprehensible situations meaningful" and "make it possible to act purposefully within them." Ideology is expressed in symbolic language involving a "subtle interplay" of "referential connections," which "concepts like 'distortion,' 'selectivity,' and 'oversimplification' are simply incompetent to formulate."[88] Scholars may have an obligation to point out distortions and inconsistencies, but to assess the literal truth of ideological statements is to miss the point. The richer in symbolism the language, regardless of internal contradictions, the more effective it is in rallying the troops.

While reaffirming the masculinist individualism of jazz, Marsalis and Crouch have attempted to rearticulate the meaning of jazz away from the subcultural status it increasingly acquired from the bebop era forward. Their complex rhetorical strategies invoke sociomusical homologies that resonate with the dominant discourse of our society—the ideal of American meritocracy. Figures of speech, repetitive phrases, and allusions to Murray and mythology are consciously employed much the same as riffs and vamps in his musical discourse. The language weds opposites in the same way Murray sees the blues juxtaposing the contradictions embedded in American culture. As Marsalis writes in *Sweet Swing Blues on the Road,* "The blues has psychological complexity. . . . You put something beautiful right on top of something ugly. Take something from the whorehouse and put it right next to something from the church. . . . [T]he blues reconciles opposites" (17–18). He describes jazz musicians, paraphrasing Murray, as "grown men engaged in child's play."[89] Like his speech, his performance styles and those of his players range from refined to "gutbucket," often in the same tune.

Marsalis is very conscious not only of history but also of his place *in* it. His language reveals an acute awareness of his trajectory through a unique time in jazz and American cultural history. He views jazz in transition, in a phase where it is struggling to shed itself of "misconceptions."[90] In this sense he could easily be seen as a fin-de-siècle figure, simultaneously looking backward and forward. He is attempting to anthologize and codify the achievements of the first hundred years of jazz. At the same time, his work anticipates a new era in which jazz, especially through extended works like *Blood on the Fields,* takes advantage of the opportunities of the concert hall setting while accentuating and perhaps even fetishizing those characteristics that make it distinctive. His short book *Sweet Swing* contains dozens of references to "this part of the 20th century" (20), "modern life late in the 20th" (160), and the "end of the 20th century" (87, 90). These phrases are often coupled with terms that seem borrowed from the discourse of neoconservatism, such as "social decay" (152, 160, 165), culture "wars" (145, 161), and decline of values ("the fake air of informality put on to cloak a lack of grace and style"). The emphasis on jazz as an *American* art form has made it particularly relevant to the culture wars fought in the last decades of the twentieth century. Marsalis relishes the role of cultural crusader. Alluding to his mentor, Marsalis explains that "as Mr. Murray says, culture is life style, and wars are fought over what style of life a society will lead" (145).

Rather than become identified with any partisan cause, however, in order to remain successful as a fund-raiser Marsalis must remain aloof from politics. He directs much of his cultural criticism at the black community.[91] Here the decline of social values has led to a lack of respect for elders, especially neglected jazz heroes. He decries the situation in which these "seasoned warriors walk unrecognized and disrespected through any and every Afro-American neighborhood" (160).

Marsalis believes, following Murray's mantra, that he is pushing to "extend, elaborate and refine" jazz traditions. His ideology does not confine; it inspires. Most artists seem to work best when, unencumbered by doubts or second-guessing, they can create with the confidence that comes from total conviction. While celebrating their "individuality" and "personal freedom within group responsibility," Marsalis enforces an intense work ethic, constantly trying "to squeeze one more drop out of the orange." Over time, Marsalis's approach yielded results. Despite their initial misgivings, even some of the most diehard critics admitted that by 1999 the LCJO had found a distinctive voice. Some paid it the highest compliment: it played like a *band!*

By transforming the most prominent cultural symbol of jazz into a young, mostly black orchestra, Marsalis aims to not only teach a new generation of musicians to "carry the beat" but also change audiences' perception of jazz. As Berger says Marsalis explained to him as he was being fired, "There's nothing unusual about old guys playing jazz, but a young band playing this music with authority, that's news!"

Outro

Following a suitelike structure common to many extended jazz works, the chapters of this book have journeyed through a series of jazz scenes chosen as much for their contrast as for their representativeness. My work has depended on the contributions of many different people. Like a good jazz arrangement, this narrative has tried to preserve the musicians' distinctive voices, drawing much of its power from their knowledge and brilliance.

The big band, as any jazz musician in New York knows, far from representing nostalgia or sterility, offers composers, arrangers, leaders, and players a chance to participate in forms of individual and large-scale collective expression unlike anything else in the jazz experience. While it has served as vital social and musical nexuses for many jazz musicians, to outsiders this activity has remained hidden in plain sight.

Contributing to the marginalization of orchestral jazz has been the tendency of jazz writers and scholars to prioritize characteristics, such as improvisation and swing, that clearly differentiate jazz from classical music. From the earliest years of jazz, emphasis on its "otherness" has extolled the oral mode over written texts, the "freedom" of small group over the "regimentation" of the large group, the spontaneity of improvisation over the fixedness of the composition. Rather than see stark choices between these oppositions, jazz composers found fertile terrain in which to create music in which their voices and the voices of their musicians are heard in conversation. While skillfully exploiting the collaborative aspects of jazz composition, jazz composers positioned themselves within existing Western standards of musical ownership. Composers such as Mingus and Ellington freely adopted the image, procedures, and roles of the Western composer, at times engaging in playful competition with their classical counterparts by highlighting what they saw as jazz musicians' superior technical and creative prowess. In contemporary orchestral jazz, this conversation continues among composers and players, musicians and their audiences, and jazz and other idioms.

Despite the best intentions of most musicians, much of the musical dialogue occurs within worlds separated by race and gender. The breadth and depth of jazz scenes in New York enable musicians to circulate in social networks where they find common ground with other musicians. As they perform together, their similar training and experience tends to reinforce their sense of distinctiveness from other groups. Homophily, the tendency of likes to attract, seems an especially powerful force in big bands because of the emphasis on differing styles of blending and standards of ensemble cohesion. While we have heard many musicians voice their desires for freer movement between scenes, to some extent their relative isolation feeds this rich stylistic variegation. Their different musical styles and practices cross-fertilize and influence each other, but their very separateness helps to incubate further stylistic innovation and differentiation.

One of the main criticisms leveled at big bands has been that they betray ideals of individualism in jazz and in African American culture. Rather than attempt to understand the wide range of creative solutions to the problem of balancing individual and collective expression in large jazz ensembles, listeners, critics, and historians, like many of the musicians, seem confined by their own socialization in specific blending styles. Ideology plays an important role, with rhetoric linking styles of group interaction to social ideals, celebrating the ensemble that promotes the greatest individual freedom, the ensemble that protects individual liberty within "group responsibility" (with or without references to American democracy), or the ensemble that glorifies individual achievement supported by a highly cohesive group. In these diverse patterns of musical interaction, do the musicians model utopian social structures, in Christopher Small's words, "the world as it ought to be," or enact the class interests and social relationships of their respective subgroups?[1] By staying within the relatively prescribed orbits of their respective jazz worlds, many musicians seem to confirm the interdeterminacy of social and musical structure. But what do we make of the small but growing number of jazz musicians who take pleasure in the full range of sociomusical interactions big bands can offer, from tightly coordinated ensembles such as the Vanguard or Maria Schneider orchestras to looser, sometimes anarchic ensembles such as the Mingus or Andrew Hill orchestras? Are they less confined by ideology or less committed to social ideals? Contemporary ethnomusicological models emphasize music's "formative role in the construction, negotiation, and transformation of sociocultural identities."[2] Perhaps, while taking a more playful approach to musical identity through their involvement in different musical worlds, these musicians affirm values of social mobility and pluralism.

While I have emphasized individual agency and the *performative* aspects of musical identity, to the musicians involved, artistic choices are rarely described as free or conscious and are experienced as rising ineluctably from personal dispositions and experience. We do well to remember Thad Jones's advice to John Mosca, "I want you to play it the way *you* would play it," or Mingus's constant prodding of his musicians, "Play yourself." Their counsel suggests that, rather than look externally to styles, traditions, and pedagogy, jazz musicians consider introspection and expression of *pre*formed internal subjectivities the ultimate goal in their *per*formance of musical identity. "Every tub sits on its own bottom."

In response to a dehumanizing culture that constructed African Americans as a homogeneous, undifferentiated mass, jazz musicians asserted identities based on individual autonomy and self-reliance. Within the mostly male space of jazz, as men defined themselves in relation to each other and to their audiences, this individual expression involved the exploration of masculine roles. For black men, jazz offered opportunities to compose and improvise new riffs over stereotypical images imposed from above. For white men, jazz was also liberating, opening up possible explorations of masculinity inflected by the perceived or imagined differences of race and class. Throughout the history of jazz women have faced discrimination and expectations as to the form and extent of their participation. The formation of all-women bands opened a space for women to define themselves not only in relation to men but also in relation to other each other. While these bands seem at times to reproduce the competitive, hypermasculinist relations of more patriarchal jazz worlds (i.e., Buddy Rich), we also have seen their role in nurturing solidarity and mutual support among female jazz musicians. Ultimately, jazz's emphasis on individual autonomy and cooperation has attracted musicians of diverse backgrounds all over the globe.

While in their relationships with leaders, composers, and each other musicians open up spaces to assert individual identities, we should harbor no illusions regarding music's ability to reinforce dominant constructions of race, gender, and other categories. Persistence of images that "blacks don't read well," that white groups play in a more polished ensemble style, that black groups swing harder indicate the degree to which race is still perceived in musical performance. As an example of gender politics, women are seen as just beginning to emerge as jazz musicians even after many decades of participation. Some musicians battle the most pernicious stereotypes. Eddie Allen's formation of a black rehearsal band and Diva's credo ("This is how girls play") are two examples that come immediately to mind. Other musicians play on perceived differences. Maria Schneider has "explored her feminine side" in her music, and the soft pastels and floral imagery of her album covers and her musical statements have constructed her image in traditional feminine terms. In the blues inflections, growls, and programmatic effects of his music, Wynton Marsalis fetishizes racial specificity even as he promotes jazz's universalism and timeless appeal in his rhetoric.

The work of the best jazz composers retains much of the polyvocal and collaborative qualities of Afro-modernist art: Jim McNeely's highly developed concerto that nevertheless gives the soloist complete freedom; Maria Schneider's counting on the improviser "to carry the piece to another place"; Andrew Hill's noncommittal conducting style balanced with his performers' obsessive need to find out what he wants; William Parker's broadening of the concept of free jazz to include "inside" playing and efforts to communicate this to his musicians; Carla Bley's rejection of all things maternal but dependence on her partners and soloists. By participating in the performance of their works, these jazz musicians often spontaneously recompose their works by remaining open to the "happy accident" or by responding to unforeseen circumstances. This openness is especially characteristic of more "experimental" or avant-garde big bands.

In their contributions to the production of orchestral jazz, to varying extents arrangers, leaders, and improvisers are all part of the compositional process of "putting together." As leaders, Jon Faddis's and Dean Pratt's lack of timidity in tweaking compositions runs counter to Western tendencies to treat musical scripts as inviolable. Sue Mingus negotiates public and private spheres in her re-creation of the Mingus ethos. The VJO stresses freedom while insisting that the highly demanding music is their leader. In arranging, Ron Horton's reticence to alter Andrew Hill's material led him to work more closely with the composer. Meanwhile, in the Carnegie Hall Jazz Band, arrangers virtually "recomposed" some of the most esteemed classics of the jazz canon. Latin jazz arrangers signify on standard melodies and harmonies of jazz by rearranging them to fit the rhythmic matrices of clave. Contributions of soloists vary from band to band. In the VJO, improvisers' extended solos give relief from the complex patterns of leading and following in the ensemble work. In contrast, Schneider's and Marsalis's more programmatic compositions tend to shape improvisers' contributions to fit within the overall compositional narrative. Carla Bley relies on a small group of regular soloists for much of her music's identity.

This study raises several important issues that have broad implications for jazz education. With the rise of the repertory movement, a growing number of jazz musicians are able to improvise in a range of historical styles. Is it realistic, or even desirable, to expect musicians also to master the wide variety of performance practices required by radically different standards of ensemble cohesion? Does this versatility come at the expense of innovation or of finding one's own voice? Not surprisingly, my research (and my experience directing and performing in ensembles) suggests that musicians trained and experienced in more cohesive blending practices adapt more easily to freer styles than vice versa. (After all, participants in freer styles are, by definition, supposedly more receptive to different approaches.) If this observation is true, then perhaps jazz education's emphasis on "mainstream" ensemble styles is not misplaced. At the same time, repertoire involving freer collective expression should not be excluded; aspiring musicians must learn that individuated styles of ensemble playing don't need "fixing." One of the most common criticisms of jazz education is that it produces "generic" musicians. As we have seen, an important criterion for becoming a *band* is development of a signature repertoire and performance style. This customization usually is arrived at through active collaboration of composers, arrangers, bandleaders, and performers. Formal jazz composition and arranging classes typically discourage such interaction. Students work in isolation and bring in their charts for a quick and perfunctory reading by the student ensemble. Instead, jazz students could frequently attend rehearsals, compose and arrange with their student peers in mind, revise and adapt their works, receive feedback from performers—in sum, develop a more dialogic relationship with their musicians. While being able to churn out quickly a generic arrangement on demand may be an important skill for students to develop for careers in the commercial music industry, more important to the vitality of the jazz idiom is that composers and performers learn from each other, much as they have throughout the history of jazz.

Rather than seek "tonal resolution" as in classical sonata form, this coda, or "outro" in jazz arrangers' parlance, ends on an altered dominant seventh chord. While this book's scope is limited to large ensembles within a relatively narrow time frame, it examines a wider range of styles and social groups than attempted by many studies in jazz. Inevitably, a study that aspires to the comprehensiveness sought in the preceding pages raises as many questions as it answers. A basic premise of this book is that masculine identity formation has been central to the process of individuation so highly valued in jazz, particularly by African Americans. How is recontextualization of jazz through institutionalization changing this process? How will women's greater presence alter this fundamentally masculinist orientation? Will women continue to be seen in some quarters as disrupting or restricting male individuality, as implied in Jesse and Leona's relationship in *Blood on the Fields?* Is the intimate interaction typical of jazz performance threatened by more open exploration of alternative sexualities? Much of the evidence gathered in this book suggests that jazz musicians are more open to exploration of gender and sexual identity than is commonly believed.

Although big bands are unlikely ever to come back in the sense of regaining mass popularity, perhaps greater recognition of the widespread involvement of jazz musicians in big bands can eventually lead to more general support of big band jazz as a vital and ongoing part of the jazz scene. Europe, with its long traditions of support for composers and orchestras, has encouraged production of orchestral jazz through "radio orchestras" and generous subsidies. Does billing jazz as "America's music" threaten to keep jazz musicians in the United States parochial at a time when some of the most interesting jazz is emerging from Europe and other countries? Do jazz musicians from other countries feel less constrained by tradition than Americans? Does the success of Jazz at Lincoln Center portend a jazz that, along with its governmental and corporate support, reinforces the existing social order? Or will a more Mingusian point of view prevail, one that challenges people's assumptions, that is politically provocative, that brings together people of widely varying backgrounds?

Some big bands in New York have benefited from the rising status of composers such as Ellington and Mingus, but the success of a few prominent big bands (e.g., the Lincoln Center Jazz Orchestra and the Mingus Big Band) leaves unanswered questions as to whether other jazz orchestras will find enough public and private support, or good-paying gigs, to maintain steady employment, and, if they do, what will they perform? Compared to the classical symphonic canon, the existing repertoire for big bands seems rather meager—hardly sufficient to sustain the repertory movement indefinitely. For orchestral jazz to remain vital, production of new works as well as rearrangements of classic scores must continue. The 1990s may prove to be watershed years in jazz for the groundswell of interest in composition and big bands. The involvement of so many musicians—more than eighty-five big bands in New York alone, most playing original music—suggests that a foundation for the creation of substantial new orchestral jazz repertoire already exists.

APPENDIX

Some New York City Big Bands Active in 1997–1998

(not including many dance bands)

Toshiko Akiyoshi
Bob Alexander
Grisha Alexiev
Lew Anderson All-American Big Band
Wayne Andre
Ron Aprea
BMI New York Jazz Orchestra
Nancie Banks
Count Basie
David Berger
Sam Burtis
Jaki Byard Apollo Stompers
Carnegie Hall Jazz Band
Chuck Clark Little Big Band
Tony Corbiscello (NJ)
Paquito D'Rivera, UN Orchestra
DMP Big Band
James L. Dean (NJ)
Diva
Duke Ellington Famous Orchestra
Gil Evans Orchestra (Miles Evans)
Andy Farber
John Fedchock New York Big Band
Fitzko/Kinslow
Frank Foster Loud Minority
Satoko Fujii
George Gee
Dave Glenn Little Big Band
Dizzy Gillespie All-Star Big Band
Larry Gillespie
Lionel Hampton
Roy Hargrove
Jimmy Heath
Peter Herborn
Woody Herman
Jeff Holmes
Mike Holober Gotham Jazz Orchestra
Richie Iacona Bad Little Big Band
Illinois Jacquet
Neil Kirkwood
Guillermo Klein Big Van
Oliver Lake
Nick Levinovsky
Lincoln Center Jazz Orchestra
Jason Lindner
Manhattan Symphony Jazz Orchestra (Dennis Mackrel)
John Mastroianni (CT)
Kit McClure
Mike Migliore
Mingus Big Band
Bob Mintzer
Bill Mobley/ Frank Griffith
Mosaic Orchestra
Diane Moser's Jazz Composers Orchestra (NJ)
New England Jazz Ensemble (CT)
Next Legacy
NewYorkestra

Chico O'Farrill Afro-Cuban Jazz Orchestra
Tim Ouimette
Ed Palermo
William Parker's Little Huey Creative Music Orchestra
Charli Persip and Supersound
Pratt Brothers
Tito Puente
Sam Rivers
Joe Roccisano
Stan Rubin
Ray Santos
Loren Schoenberg
Maria Schneider
Don Sebesky
Joey Sellers Aggregation
Peter Silver
Magali Souriau
Spirit of Life
Alex Stewart
Tom Talbert
McCoy Tyner
Bobby Watson Tailor-Made Big Band
Bill Warfield
Scott Whitfield
Howard Williams
Gary Wofsey
Phil Woods
Vanguard Jazz Orchestra
Roland Vazquez

NOTES

PREFACE

1. John Birks "Dizzy" Gillespie, with Al Fraser, *To Be or Not to Bop: Memoirs* (1979), 134. Ralph Ellison, *Shadow and Act* ([1964] 1995), 206–7.

INTRO

1. These dates, commonly given for the swing era, coincide with Benny Goodman's appearance at the Palomar Ballroom (August 1935) and the breakup of seven prominent bands in just a few weeks beginning in December 1946.
2. While acknowledging the coarseness of these categories, for lack of better terms, *mainstream* will refer to bebop and closely related styles generally characterized by cyclical harmonic structures, steady pulse, and improvisation more or less *inside* these frameworks; *avant-garde* denotes movement *outside* these frameworks. Both of these terms have less than static histories. Interestingly, "mainstream" as first used by Stanley Dance in the mid-1950s referred to styles of players from swing bands such as Basie's, Goodman's, and Ellington's. As bebop became the lingua franca of jazz, it gradually became considered mainstream. *Avant-garde* designates a very broad range of musical practices. David G. Such points out that "the labels are as inventive and divergent as the music itself" and provides examples of the many names given to this music: "free jazz," "the new wave," "black classical music," "post-bop," and "out jazz" (*Avant-Garde Jazz Musicians: Performing "Out There"* [1993], 17). More recently, the idiom-neutral terms *creative music* and *cutting edge* have come into vogue.
3. All this activity did not pass completely unnoticed in the jazz press. By the late 1990s big bands in New York had become so widespread that articles in the *New York Times,* a "Special Big Band Issue" of *Down Beat,* and feature articles in *Jazz Times* asked the age-old question, are the big bands coming back? See Dave Helland, "Repertory Big Bands: Jazz's Future-Past," *Down Beat* 64.1 (January 1997): 34–37; John McDonough "Doin' 'Em Proud: How the Mingus and Basie Big

Bands Thrive on More than Just Nostalgia," *Down Beat* 64.1 (January 1997): 16–21; Bob Blumenthal, "The Future for Big Bands: Bleak or Bright?" *Jazz Times* 28.7 (September 1998): 28–31, 35, 50; and Ben Ratliff, "The Peal of Horns Aplenty from a Big Band Cornucopia," *New York Times*, 16 January 1998, E1, 34.

4. Ben Ratliff, "The Solo Retreats from the Spotlight in Jazz," *New York Times*, 28 May 2000, II:23.
5. Francis Davis, *Outcats: Jazz Composers, Instrumentalists, and Singers* (1990), 210.
6. Interview. As indicated in "A Note on Sources" at the beginning of this book, quotations from individuals I interviewed appear without formal citation.
7. In 1997, in a step seen as largely symbolic, New York's Local 802 moved its jazz contract negotiators into its classical department.
8. See Bruno Nettl, "Orchestras," in *The Western Impact on World Music* (1985), 57–61, for a discussion of the significance of large ensembles. As discussed in chapter 3, from the 1960s well into the 1990s, hoping to capitalize on the economic benefits and revitalize decaying urban centers, smaller cities and communities established arts organizations and built performance venues at an accelerating pace.
9. David W. Stowe, in *Swing Changes: Big-Band Jazz in New Deal America* (1994), quotes these figures, which he acknowledges are "imprecise" and "varying by source" (107, 112–13). See his chapter "The Incorporation of Swing" (94–140) for further discussion of swing industry economics.
10. George T. Simon, *The Big Bands* ([1967] 1981); Albert J. McCarthy, *Big Band Jazz* (1974).

In *Early Jazz* (1968) Gunther Schuller traces the development of jazz composition and arranging techniques from Ferdinand "Jelly Roll" Morton ("the first great composer") through Don Redman ("the first great arranger") and early Ellington. Schuller's *Swing Era* (1989) continues this project until 1945 and the emergence of bebop. This 919-page volume covers a vast amount of material, including a "fairly comprehensive study" of "white swing bands," which Schuller believed most jazz histories had ignored (*Swing Era*, ix). Also beginning in New Orleans with Jelly Roll Morton's Red Hot Peppers, which he considers stylistically close to big bands, Joachim Berendt (*The Jazz Book* [1975]) offers a concise history of big bands through the 1970s. Useful information and overviews can be gleaned from the booklets accompanying the three Smithsonian collections of big band jazz (Gunther Schuller and Martin Williams, *Big Band Jazz: From the Beginnings to the Fifties* [1983]; Mark Tucker, *Swing That Music: The Big Bands, the Soloists, and the Singers, 1929–1956* [(1987) 1993]; and Bill Kirchner, *Big Band Renaissance: The Evolution of the Jazz Orchestra: The 1940s and Beyond* [1995]). *Lost Chords: White Musicians and Their Contribution to Jazz, 1915–1945* (1999), by Richard Sudhalter, discusses white big bands in detail. John Storm Roberts relates the history of Latin bands in *The Latin Tinge: The Impact of Latin American Music on the United States* (1985). Several recent books offer fresh perspectives on big band music of the swing era. Lewis A. Erenberg in *Swingin' the Dream: Big Band Jazz and the Rebirth of American Culture* (1998) and David Stowe in *Swing Changes* see swing music as reflecting the political ethos of New Deal America—"a new optimism about democratic culture, an appreciation of ethnic and racial pluralism, and a delight in the utopian promise of urban life" (Erenberg, *Swingin' the Dream,* xvi). Sherrie Tucker's *Swing Shift: "All-Girl" Bands of the 1940s* (2000) challenges "dominant swing discourse" by relating the "forgotten history" of all-women bands such as the International Sweethearts of Rhythm. Tucker shows how members of the "all-girl" bands, far from regarding themselves as temporary substitutes for men during the war years, struggled to be respected musicians.

11. Winthrop Sargeant, *Jazz: Hot and Hybrid* (1938), 200–201. See also Rudi Blesh, *Shining Trumpets: A History of Jazz* (1946).
12. Barry Ulanov, "It's Not the Book, It's the Attitude," *Metronome,* March 1942, 11.
13. Harry Henderson and Sam Shaw, "And Now We Go Bebop!" *Colliers,* 20 March 1948; reprinted in *Jazz: A Century of Change* (1997), ed. Lewis Porter, 174.
14. Bernard Gendron discusses the similar discursive formations, binary oppositions such as "art—commerce," "authenticity—artificiality," "jazz—swing," and "black—white," that were used, with minor modifications, by both factions in "Moldy Figs and Modernists: Jazz at War (1942–1946)," in *Jazz among the Discourses* (1995), ed. Krin Gabbard, 31–56.
15. Barry Ulanov, "Moldy Figs vs. Moderns," *Metronome,* November 1947, 15, 23. The battles were broadcast from WOR Mutual Studios, New York City, on Saturday, 13 September 1947; and Saturday, 20 September 1947. The rest of the "moldy figs" were Edmond Hall, Jimmy Archey, Ralph Sutton, Danny Barker, and Pops Foster; the other "moderns" were John LaPorta, Billy Bauer, Ray Brown, and Max Roach.
16. Gendron, "Moldy Figs," 33.
17. Scott DeVeaux, "The Emergence of the Jazz Concert, 1935–1945," *American Music* 7.1 (1989): 6–29, 11.
18. Ross Russell, "Bebop," in *The Art of Jazz: Essays on the Nature and Development of Jazz* (1959), ed. Martin Williams, 202.
19. Ibid., 201, 196.
20. Hsio Wen Shih, "The Spread of Jazz and the Big Bands," in *Jazz: New Perspectives on the History of Jazz by Twelve of the World's Foremost Jazz Critics and Scholars* (1959), ed. Nat Hentoff and Albert J. McCarthy, 187.
21. LeRoi Jones (Amiri Baraka), *Blues People* (1963), 184.
22. Jones, ". . . Enter the Middle Class," in *Blues People,* 122–41. "Swing demonstrates . . . that the only assimilation that society provided [the Negro] was toward the disappearance of the most important things the black man possessed, without even the political and economic reimbursement afforded the white American" (186).
23. Ben Sidran, *Black Talk* (1971), 8.
24. Jones, *Blues People,* 183; Sidran, *Black Talk,* 93; Russell, "Bebop," 210.
25. To Gendron's binary oppositions mentioned above, we might add oral–literate, spontaneous–controlled, individualistic–conformist, listening–dancing, communal–corporate, and combo–big band.
26. Scott DeVeaux, "Constructing the Jazz Tradition: Jazz Historiography," *Black American Literature Forum* 25 (1991): 544. Williams's selection of a number by the Gene Krupa Orchestra for the *Smithsonian Collection of Classic Jazz* seems based mostly on its featuring of the trumpeter Roy Eldridge.
27. Gunther Schuller, "Arrangement," in *The New Grove Dictionary of Jazz,* 2d ed., ed.

Barry Kernfeld ([1988] 2002), 1:79–80; Scott DeVeaux, *The Birth of Bebop: A Social and Musical History* (1997), 2.

28. Bruno Nettl, *Heartland Excursions: Ethnomusicological Reflections of Schools of Music* (1995), 93, 107; see also David Ake, *Jazz Cultures* (2002), 113–14.
29. Gary Kennedy, "Jazz Education," in *The New Grove Dictionary of Jazz,* 2:398. Mike Vax, "Report to the American Federation of Jazz: The State of Jazz Education in the United States in 1998," www.mikevax.com/afjs.html, accessed May 2001.
30. Barry Kernfeld, "Festivals," in *The New Grove Dictionary of Jazz,* 1:753.
31. Kirchner, *Big Band Renaissance.*
32. Paul F. Berliner, *Thinking in Jazz: The Infinite Art of Improvisation* (1994), 808.
33. Wynton Marsalis in Dick Russell, *Black Genius* (1998), 67; see also Ellison, *Shadow and Act,* 234; and Albert Murray, *The Blue Devils of Nada: A Contemporary American Approach to Aesthetic Statement* (1996), 111–13.
34. Ingrid Monson, *Saying Something: Jazz Improvisation and Interaction* (1996), 66–67. The situation is further complicated when the researcher expands the field of inquiry to include the widest range of jazz styles. Berliner, Monson, and, more recently, Travis A. Jackson ("Jazz Performance as Ritual: The Blues Aesthetic and the African Diaspora," in *The African Diaspora* [2003], ed. Ingrid Monson, 23–82), have concentrated primarily on "mainstream" jazz.
35. Ellington recorded a tune named "Every Tub" in London on 13 July 1933, but the tune was released under the title "Hyde Park." During his legendary Decca sessions (1937–39), Count Basie recorded "Every Tub," a tune based on " 'Rhythm' Changes" featuring Lester Young. Zora Neale Hurston used the expression in *Dust Tracks on a Road* ([1942] 1984), 324–25.
36. For discussions of individuality in African American music, see Samuel Floyd Jr., *The Power of Black Music* (1995), 6; Lawrence Levine, *Black Culture and Black Consciousness: Afro-American Folk Thought from Slavery to Freedom* (1977); Jones, *Blues People;* Murray, *Blue Devils;* Jackson, "Jazz Performance as Ritual." In *Every Tub Must Sit on Its Own Bottom: The Philosophy and Politics of Zora Neale Hurston* (1995), 93–115, Deborah G. Plant traces the tradition of African American individualism to the black folk preacher.
37. In Mark Tucker, *The Duke Ellington Reader* (1993), 135.
38. In his ambitious Cantometrics project, *Folk Song Style and Culture* (1968), Alan Lomax attempted both to analyze the vocal characteristics of most of humankind according to "individualized" and "integrated" styles and to correlate these data with cultural traits such as degree of social stratification and cohesiveness. The obvious problem with this approach is that by treating cultures monolithically, interesting variations will be averaged out and disappear. If big band jazz were analyzed in this manner, the wide range of blending styles would likewise vanish. If, however, each musical scene is examined individually, certain characteristic styles of instrumental blend emerge.

    Discussion of blending styles figures prominently in Anthony Seeger's *Why Suyá Sing: A Musical Anthropology of an Amazonian People* (1987). *Ngere,* unison songs in which men and/or women try to blend their voices, are contrasted with *akia,* distinct, individual songs in which, when sung together, men attempt to remain recognizably different so that each singer can be distinguished by their female audiences. In developing the theory of "participatory discrepancies,"

Charles Keil, J. A. Prögler, and others have concentrated mostly on microlevel rhythmic factors to explain how performance practices contribute to "groove." See Charles Keil, "The Theory of Participatory Discrepancies: A Progress Report," *Ethnomusicology* 39.1 (1995): 1–19; J. A. Prögler, "Searching for Swing: Participatory Discrepancies in the Jazz Rhythm Section," *Ethnomusicology* 39.1 (1995): 21–54. This book concentrates on pitch, timbre, and textures—areas that Keil didn't have "much to say yet about" ("Participatory Discrepancies," 7).

39. It also must be noted that historically black and white players in the United States received different training and used different equipment, such as mouthpieces, and, for economic reasons, blacks sometimes played inferior-quality instruments.

40. In addition to Jones, *Blues People;* Sidran, *Black Talk;* and Keil, "Participatory Discrepancies," see John Shepherd, *Music as Social Text* (1991); Olly Wilson, "The Heterogeneous Sound Ideal in African-American Music," in *New Perspectives on Music: Essays in Honor of Eileen Southern* (1992), ed. Josephine Wright, 327–38; and Ingrid Monson, "Riffs, Repetition, and Theories of Globalization," *Ethnomusicology* 43.1 (1999): 31–65.

41. Ronald Radano and Philip V. Bohlman, *Music and the Racial Imagination* (2000), 37. See also Georgina Born and David Hesmondhalgh, introduction to *Western Music and Its Others: Difference, Representation, and Appropriation in Music,* ed. Georgina Born and David Hesmondhalgh (2000), 1–58; and Richard Middleton, "Musical Belongings: Western Music and Its Low-Other," in *Western Music and Its Others,* 59–85.

42. William Russell, in *Jazz Music,* October 1943. Quoted by Charles Edward Smith in "New Orleans and Traditions in Jazz," in *Jazz,* 29. Parts of this quote also appear in Jones, *Blues People,* 145. In the Dixieland revival much of Bunk Johnson's appeal to traditionalists was his "authenticity," which, while encouraging Johnson to pursue stylistic devices associated with difference, also accentuated their perception in the racial imaginary. Questions about Johnson's birthdate led to disputes over his claims to have actually been a member of Bolden's band.

43. Sidran, *Black Talk,* 74.

44. A few of many possible examples are the late saxophonist Jim Pepper's jazz on American Indian themes, Asian American saxophonist Fred Ho's use of Chinese instruments, Vijay Iyer's drawing from South Asian traditions, and clarinetist Ivo Papasov's odd-metered Bulgarian jazz.

45. Suzanne G. Cusick, "Feminist Theory, Music Theory, and the Mind/Body Problem," in *Music/Ideology: Resisting the Aesthetic* (1998), ed. Adam Krims, 43. In her article "On Musical Performances of Gender and Sex," in *Audible Traces: Gender, Identity, and Music* (1999), ed. Elaine Barkin and Lydia Hamessley, while looking for traces of the seventeenth-century composer Francesca Caccini's gendered identity and body in her music, Cusick explores the vocal qualities of the Indigo Girls and Pearl Jam. She writes, "The intelligibility of [musicians'] gender performances depends on the audiences' experience of the 'background' of cultural norms" ("On Musical Performances," 38). Citing Butler, Cusick also notes that the "field of possible individual performances is extremely broad" (38). Judith P. Butler, *Gender Trouble: Feminism and the Subversion of Identity* (1990), 17. For a few examples of feminist work in classical music, see Jane Bowers and Judith Tick,

eds., *Women Making Music: The Western Art Tradition, 1150–1950* (1986); Susan C. Cook and Judy S. Tsou, eds., *Cecelia Reclaimed Feminist Perspectives on Gender and Music* (1994); and Susan McClary, *Feminine Endings: Music, Gender, and Sexuality* (1991).

46. Examples of recent work discussing gender in jazz are Sherrie Tucker, "Big Ears: Listening for Gender in Jazz Studies," *Current Musicology* 71–73 (Spring 2001–Spring 2002): 375–408; Krin Gabbard, *Jammin' at the Margins: Jazz and the American Cinema* (1996); Hazel Carby, "Playin' the Changes," in her book *Race Men* (1998), 159–61; and Nichole T. Rustin, "Mingus Fingers: Charles Mingus, Black Masculinity, and Postwar Jazz Culture" (Ph.D. diss., 1999).
47. Lucy Green, *Music, Gender, Education* (1997), 138.
48. See, e.g., Carby, *Race Men;* and Monique Guillory, "Black Bodies Swingin': Race, Gender, and Jazz," in *Soul: Black Power, Politics, and Pleasure* (1998), ed. Monique Guillory and Richard C. Green, 191–215. Tucker characterizes this "men and masculinity school of gender analysis" as "Miles Davis Studies" (Tucker, "Big Ears," 389).
49. Green, *Music, Gender, Education,* 108.
50. Hardin Armstrong, Williams, and Akiyoshi all played piano as well, an instrument that was often considered feminine, as evidenced in Jelly Roll Morton's worries that, as a pianist, people might consider him a sissy.
51. Numerous instances of direct involvement of classical composers with groups of performers can be cited, such as Bach at Cöthen, Haydn at Esterházy, and Boulez at the Institut de Recherche et Coordination Acoustique/Musique (IRCAM). The difference in jazz, however, is the degree and frequency of collaborative relationships.
52. Jim McNeely, "Current Directions in Composing for the Jazz Orchestra," handout (1998).
53. Classical composers, of course, also have written for specific soloists. Collaboration between composers and performers, however, diminished as the composer gained more authority and control in the nineteenth century. Depending on the leader, orchestral jazz can also be produced with minimal collaboration. Still, even though jazz seems to be becoming more like classical music in certain aspects (discussed further throughout this book), it is difficult to imagine a "jazz" that does not have improvisation and in which direct collaboration never occurs.
54. The NEA study found "age a significant factor affecting affiliation among jazz musicians. . . . The homophily of older musicans is greater, so older musicians exclude younger ones to a rather substantial greater degree, whereas younger musicians are more inclusive of older musicians." The networks of older musicians are also larger, "reflect[ing] their greater professional experience and recognition" (Joan Jeffri, *Changing the Beat: A Study of the Worklife of Jazz Musicians* [2002], 3:56–57).
55. My term *jazz scenes* is indebted to Howard S. Becker's influential book, *Art Worlds* (1982). Becker analyzes the social and cooperative basis of art production. He defines an "art world" as "all the people whose activities are necessary to the production of the characteristic works" (34). In this book, the word "scene," much as it is commonly used by musicians, refers to the different, often fractious social networks involved in jazz rather than the "jazz community" as a whole. Indeed, be-

cause of these tensions, some jazz musicians object to the word *community* in reference to the jazz universe. In many ways each scene is a "world" unto itself, with its own venues, record labels, practitioners, promoters, and critical advocates. Although Becker takes "art world" as his "basic unit of analysis," he concedes that both the " 'artness' and the 'worldness' are problematic," and he acknowledges that works "may be produced in a variety of cooperating networks and under a variety of definitions. Some networks are large [and] complicated" while "in the limiting case, the world consists only of the person making the work" (36–37). Rather than a rigid concept, his use of the term seems flexible and adaptable to a variety of circumstances. For valuable discussion of a similar theoretical construct that includes the consumers as well as the producers, see Mark Slobin's analysis of musical subcultures in *Subcultural Sounds: Micromusics of the West* (1993).

56. Jeffri, *Changing the Beat,* 3:52, 54–56.

57. For their survey of jazz musicians in New Orleans, San Francisco, and New York, *Changing the Beat,* a team of researchers led by Joan Jeffri conducted two surveys, one based on a random sample of members of the American Federation of Musicians (AFM) and another based on respondent-driven sampling (RDS) procedures that have been used to study "hidden populations." An initially selected group of jazz musicians referred other musicians, who in turn gave others, "until statistically sound sample sizes" were produced. One advantage of the RDS method is that it also allowed researchers to study patterns of affiliation among jazz musicians (Jeffri, *Changing the Beat,* 1:6; see also Douglas D. Heckathorn and Joan Jeffri, "Finding the Beat: Using Respondent-Driven Sampling to Study Jazz Musicians," *Poetics* 28.4 [2001]: 307–29). The seemingly large population of jazz musicians may be due, in part, to the fairly broad standard used. Jazz musicians were defined as anyone who "answered yes to the question, 'Do you ever play or sing jazz music?' " (Jeffri, *Changing the Beat,* 1:6).

    The survey is not without problematic areas. For example, the researchers claim that piano and voice are the most popular primary "instruments" in New York. Saxophonists were offered the choices "alto saxophone," "baritone saxophone," or simply "saxophone" (what happened to "tenor" and "soprano" saxophones?). If all three saxophone categories are combined, saxophone actually becomes far and away the most popular instrument in New York (20.1%) and also tops the list in New Orleans (15.4%) and San Francisco (16.7%) (cf. Jeffri, *Changing the Beat,* 3:42–43). Stylistic categories, as always, present thorny issues. Did musicians consistently equate "traditional" with early jazz or Dixieland styles, or could they have meant "mainstream" as opposed to avant-garde? Musicians could choose the rubric "cool jazz," despite the fact that I have never heard a musician say he or she plays "cool" jazz (cf. Jeffri, *Changing the Beat,* 3:59). Would "cool jazz" refer to the style of jazz that emerged in the 1950s in the aftermath of bop or to contemporary styles of jazz/rock fusion that have co-opted the term?

58. For a discussion of the "downtown" and "uptown" classical music scenes, see Samuel Gilmore, "Schools of Activity and Innovation," *Sociological Quarterly* 29.2 (1988): 203–19.

59. See Andre Craddock-Willis, "Jazz People: Wynton Marsalis vs. James Lincoln Collier," *Transition* 65 (1995): 140–76, for the transcription of a particularly acrimonious debate that occurred at Lincoln Center on 7 August 1994.

60. Pierre Bourdieu has studied the production and reception of art in the context of the larger social order. His concept of field is useful for understanding the relationships of jazz scenes not only to each other but also from the perspectives of critics, academics, record companies, and others. Each field valorizes characteristic forms of capital. In the jazz field the primary form of capital is knowledge (or in Bourdieu's terms, "cultural capital") and, secondarily, prestige (or "symbolic capital"). In the critical field, as economic capital rises, symbolic capital falls; in other words, "musicians sell out." See Pierre Bourdieu, *Outline of a Theory of Practice* ([1972] 1977) and *The Logic of Practice* ([1980] 1990).
61. Bruno Nettl, "Thoughts on Improvisation: A Comparative Approach," *Musical Quarterly* 60.1 (1974): 1–19.
62. Stephen Blum, "Recognizing Improvisation," in *In the Course of Performance: Studies in the World of Musical Improvisation,* ed. Bruno Nettl with Melinda Russell (1998), 27.
63. Nettl, "Thoughts on Improvisation."
64. The U.S. Copyright Act of 1976 extended copyright protection to sound recordings fixed and published on or after 15 February 1972. Holders of the recording copyright, most frequently the record company, not the musicians, may license parts of the recording (including improvisations) for sampling and other uses but do not enjoy the rights to publication, mechanical royalties, and other more expansive privileges retained by owners of the copyright on the "composition."
65. On parody in postmodern expression, see Fredric Jameson, *Postmodernism; Or, The Cultural Logic of Late Capitalism* (1995), 16–21. On "signifyin(g)" see Henry Louis Gates Jr., *The Signifying Monkey: A Theory of Afro-American Literary Criticism* (1988). For an example applying this theory to jazz analysis, see Robert Walser, " 'Out of Notes': Signification, Interpretation, and the Problem of Miles Davis," *Musical Quarterly* 77.2 (1993): 343–65; reprinted in Gabbard, ed., *Jazz among the Discourses,* 165–88.
66. The markings on Ellington's scores and parts housed at the Smithsonian reveal only a fraction of the countless details that evolved during constant performances of his orchestra.
67. James Lincoln Collier, *Duke Ellington* (1987), 303–4.
68. Paul Gilroy, *The Black Atlantic: Modernity and Double Consciousness* (1993), 36. Instead of focusing on national black cultures, Gilroy argues for a more inclusive heuristic unit (the "black Atlantic"), on the basis of shared oppression, common goals, and hybrid cultures (double consciousness) rather than an immutable "African essence."
69. In a cogent analysis, drawing on the work of W. E. B. DuBois, Houston Baker Jr., and others, Richard Middleton compares the compositional approaches of Mozart, Gershwin, Ellington, and Ibrahim. Middleton, "Musical Belongings," 59–85. For his discussion of "double consciousness" related to Ellington, see p. 71.
70. Musicians also categorize bands according to stylistic criteria, i.e., "swing," "Latin," "avant-garde," etc.; or makeup of personnel, "black," "white," "all-girl" or "all-woman," "old-timer" or "Geritol" bands.
71. In his anthology of modern big band jazz, *Big Band Renaissance,* Kirchner has organized the recordings according to a similar plan. Our typologies differ, how-

ever, in several respects. First, I am only peripherally concerned with road bands, although the few that remain draw much of their membership from New York. Their decreasing number has made them even less of a force in contemporary big band music (of the sixteen bands included by Kirchner, only three, the Basie and Ferguson bands and the U.S. Air Force Airmen of Note, still tour with any regularity). Second, for similar reasons, discussed below, studio bands have become less relevant to the big band scene. Kirchner's category of avant-garde bands is based on stylistic rather than functional criteria. Since they seldom gather except for some kind of regular or impending gig, avant-garde bands are treated here as working bands.

72. In 1997 the Doris Duke Charitable Foundation awarded a $2 million grant to Jazz at Lincoln Center to "help preserve the music of Duke Ellington."

CHAPTER 1. NEW YORK CITY BIG BAND SCENES

1. The following account is based loosely on an evening tour by the ethnomusicologist Stephen Blum and the author.
2. In 2001 the name was officially changed to Boys and Girls Harbor.
3. Until the April 1997 contract, in which minimums were cut substantially, the number of players required in the larger ballrooms of New York hotels ranged from sixteen in the Marriott Marquis Broadway Ballroom to twelve in the Waldorf Astoria Grand Ballroom.
4. See Jack Bower's long-running column "Big Band Report" at www.allaboutjazz.com for reviews of big bands, especially from outside New York.
5. In the trumpeter Rex Stewart's version of this often-repeated story, Goldkette "fixed the fight" by keeping Henderson's band off the stand (Stewart, *Boy Meets Horn* [1991], 113).
6. Samuel B. Charters and Leonard Kunstadt, *Jazz: A History of the New York Scene* (1962), 159–64; Sudhalter, *Lost Chords,* 212–14. William Howland Kenny, *Chicago Jazz: A Cultural History, 1904–1930* (1993), 148–61.
7. Linda Dahl, *Stormy Weather: The Music and Lives of a Century of Jazz Women* (1984).
8. Tucker, *Swing Shift,* 195–224. In the 1970s the so-called second wave of all-female big bands emerged mostly outside of New York. At the University of North Texas (then North Texas State), Yes M.A.A.M (Musicians Ain't Always Men) was formed as an alternative to the official (and all- or mostly male) lab bands for which the school is renowned. In 1976 the trumpeter-flugelhornist Clark Terry put together an all-women big band for the Wichita Jazz Festival. Terry recruited women from the many campuses he visited as a clinician and guest soloist (pers. com., 7 February 1999). One of the first bands to achieve recognition was Maiden Voyage, which began in 1979 as a rehearsal band for female musicians in the Los Angeles area and went on to appear on the *Tonight Show,* in various clubs, and at jazz festivals including a special tribute to the Sweethearts of Rhythm at the Women's Jazz Festival in 1980. See James A. Liska, "Maiden Voyage," *Down Beat* 48.11 (November 1981): 53–54.
9. Most commercial "rhumbas" were actually not authentic Cuban *rumbas* (without the *h*) but *sones.*
10. Roberts, *Latin Tinge,* 76–126.

11. Count Basie and Albert Murray, *Good Morning Blues: The Autobiography of Count Basie* (1985), 178–206, 217–19.
12. Kirchner, *Big Band Renaissance,* 7.
13. Sonny Rollins, *Brass and Trio* (Metro Jazz 1002, Verve MV-8430, 1958); John Coltrane, *Africa/Brass* (Impulse IMPD 2–168, 1961); Thelonious Monk, *The Thelonious Monk Orchestra at Town Hall* (Riverside RLP12–300, 1959).
14. Other less commonly used brass instruments are flugelhorns, tubas, and French horns.
15. Jazz musicians refer to a passage that features a section of the band playing a melodic line in block harmony as a "soli." In this context the term *soli* is singular; hence the apparent redundancy of the plural. Solis are typically in the style of an improvised solo and are made up mostly of eighth note or smaller note values. They can be quite challenging to play, especially the inner voices. Famous examples are Ellington's "Cottontail" (1940), possibly the first extended sax soli and based on a solo line by Ben Webster (according to David Berger), Thad Jones's "Three and One" (1966), and Sammy Nestico's "Basie—Straight Ahead" (1969). In the 1970s, in several recordings that epitomize this sound, the group Supersax played arrangements of Charlie Parker solos in four-part block harmony with the lead doubled at the octave in the baritone sax. Slide Hampton's arrangement of "Shiny Stockings" on the Carnegie Hall Jazz Band's recent recording (1996) carries this procedure to a new extreme by featuring in succession lengthy sax, trombone, and trumpet solis.
16. In Bret Primack, booklet accompanying *The Complete Roulette Recordings of the Maynard Ferguson Orchestra* (1994), 2.
17. Ibid., 3.
18. Bob Belden, liner notes to *Treasure Island* (Sunnyside SCC 1041D, 1990).
19. William Parker, liner notes to *Mayor of Punkville* (AUMO 15/16, 2000).
20. In Raymond Horricks, *Gil Evans* (1984), 21.
21. Maria Schneider, "Interview with Maria Schneider," in *Evanesence: Complete Scores,* ed. Fred Sturm (1998), vi–xii.
22. In an appearance at Birdland on 27 April 1999 Sue Mingus made these remarks to the audience when she took the microphone to apologize for a new piece that "didn't work." Sy Johnson had just directed the orchestra in a lengthy and difficult orchestration of an improvised piano solo by Mingus called "Myself When I Am Real."
23. As the use of this metaphor illustrates, associations of gender with certain musical qualities—masculine/dynamic : feminine/lyrical—seem never to be far from the surface. Issues of gender representations in jazz are explored in chapter 10.
24. Lewis Porter and Michael Ullman, *Jazz: From Its Origins to the Present* (1997), 410.
25. Charles Mingus, "What Is a Jazz Composer?" Liner notes to *Let My Children Hear Music* (Columbia KC3 1039, 1971). Reprinted in *Charles Mingus: More Than a Fake Book,* ed. Sue Mingus (1991), 155–57.
26. Dean Pratt, liner notes to *Groovy Encounters* (Amosaya AM-2532-CD, 1997).
27. Simon, *Big Bands,* 17.

CHAPTER 2. BEHIND THE SCENES

1. D'Rivera's words appear in the liner notes to a CD he recorded in Germany, *Paquito D'Rivera & The WDR Band: Big Band Time* (Timba Records 59773-2, 2002). In my interview with him he in effect quoted himself.
2. Gary Giddins, "Joe Lovano (The Long Apprenticeship)," *Visions of Jazz: The First Century* (1998), 613.
3. See, e.g., Robin Pogrebin, "Battling the Chaos in Schools' Arts Classes," *New York Times,* 5 June 2003, B1, 6.
4. On Long Island, a Jazz and Commercial Music Program begun in 1972 by the privately owned Five Towns College attempted to follow the Berklee model, without nearly the success. Another more highly regarded program began in 1977 just outside New York City at William Paterson University in New Jersey. Although other schools offered jazz ensembles and courses as part of their curriculum, MSM was the first New York City jazz program to achieve widespread notoriety.
5. In the course of performing in and researching New York big bands, I have occasionally heard players criticize alumni of this school for their lack of large ensemble experience. In about 2000 the New School instituted a Latin big band under the direction of Bobby Sanabria.
6. As of 2006, from 9:00 A.M. to 5:00 P.M. the hourly rate was $10. After 5:00 P.M. the rate increases to $20 per hour, still substantially lower than most other comparable facilities. In Los Angeles, according to the Local 802 union official in charge of booking 802's facility, *all* the musicians using the space must be members. Joey Sellers says this provision is not always enforced. At Local 802 only the leader must be a member. If the Los Angeles rule were in force in New York, a large number of bands would be excluded.
7. Jeffri, *Changing the Beat,* 1:16. This projection is based on a sample of 592 Local 802 members.
8. An estimated 43.6 percent of all New York jazz musicians earn the majority of their incomes outside of performance (teaching, as well as music and non-music-related occupations) (Jeffri, *Changing the Beat,* 3:13).
9. In 1998 two hours cost $40, and three hours, $50. As of 2006 these rates had risen by $5.
10. In November 2002, after this was written, Nancie Banks was found dead in her apartment. The precise date of her death is not known.
11. The third set was eliminated sometime after the Vanguard's original owner, Max Gordon, died in 1989. Gordon would fall asleep in the back room, but his wife Lorraine, who now manages the club, prefers to go home earlier.
12. Up until the 1980s the money frequently went to big bands for summer park dates in local communities. Some bands, such as that led by the late trumpeter Sonny Land, performed as many as twenty dates each season. In recent years, in an attempt to widen the appeal of these concerts and reduce expenses, communities have hired smaller, more versatile units (i.e., those adept at rock)—such as club date bands. Communities have also balked at the union's requirement that the musicians be paid even if the performance is rained out.
13. Richard Primus, quoted in "Where Race Matters," by Jodi Wilgoren (*New York Times,* 4A, p. 20, 13 April 2003), talks about his class, Introduction to Constitu-

tional Law: "Critical mass means enough minorities so that they are not pigeonholed as racial spokesmen and are allowed to illustrate that black and Hispanic and Asian students have a range of experiences and views, just like white students. . . . In an environment where you have one person, every time he talks they'll think, 'Yes, it's him, he's black and he's talking,' said Professor Primus. 'If you have seven or eight, that starts to go away.' "

14. Since 2000 the Mingus Big Band occasionally has included a woman on its regular weekly gig or on short tours.
15. Lawrence Levine (*Highbrow/Lowbrow: The Emergence of Cultural Hierarchy in America* [1988]) documented the bifurcation of American culture into class-related high and low forms of entertainment in emulation of European standards of sacralized art.

CHAPTER 3. THE RISE OF REPERTORY ORCHESTRAS

1. Martin Williams, "What to Do about Jazz in Our August Cultural Centers," *New York Times,* 25 January 1970, II34.
2. *Living jazz museum* was a term often used in the 1970s and 1980s to describe the repertory movement. Bill Kirchner has criticized some of the more obsessive practices of the repertory movement as "musical necrophilia."
3. See DeVeaux, "Emergence of the Jazz Concert." Paul Whiteman's *Experiment in Modern Music* that included the premier of *Rhapsody in Blue* in New York's Aeolian Hall 1924, part of his project to "make a lady out of jazz," was more of an effort to *transform* jazz than simply *transplant* it. Still, as the similarity of their titles suggests *(Rhapsody in Blue* and *Symphony in Black),* Ellington was influenced by Whiteman and Gershwin's work. See also Mark Tucker, "The Genesis of *Black, Brown and Beige,*" *Black Music Research Journal* 13.2 (1993): 67–86; and Middleton, "Musical Belongings."
4. Jones, *Blues People.*
5. Max Roach, "What Jazz Means to Me," *Black Scholar* 3 (Summer 1972): 4.
6. In a famous incident Mingus had his band "trade fours" (alternate four-measure passages) with a noisy audience.
7. See "Musicians Disrupt TV Show," *Down Beat* 37.19 (1 October 1970): 11; and "Jazz and the Peoples Movement," *Down Beat* 37.22 (12 November 1970): 11.
8. John S. Wilson, "The Great Jazz Dream—Can It Come True?" *New York Times,* 18 November 1973, 19, 33; and "If the Symphonies Can Do It, So Can Jazz," *New York Times,* 20 January 1974, 15, 18.
9. Les Ledbetter, "The Pop Life: All-Star Jazz Group Set for First Concert, "*New York Times,* 18 January 1974, 24.
10. Under the rent remission system the Carnegie Hall Corporation paid rent to the city of New York and received half of it back as long as it spent the money on new programming projects.
11. John S. Wilson, "Jazz Company's 2d Season to Be Test," *New York Times,* 5 November 1974, 29.
12. Performances included the Grand Parade du Jazz in Nice in 1975 and 1976, a three-part Ellington concert series at the 1976 Newport New York Jazz Festival, the 1978 re-creation of W. C. Handy's 1928 Carnegie Hall concert in New York

and at the Kennedy Center, Washington, D.C., and a European tour in 1980. The band included Jim Maxwell, Joe Newman, Ernie Royal, Pee Wee Erwin, and Sudhalter (trumpets); Britt Woodman, Eddie Bert and Mike Zwerin (trombones); Norris Turney, Bob Wilber, Budd Johnson, Eddie Barefield, and Cecil Payne (reeds); Dick Hyman (piano); Bucky Pizzarelli (guitar); George Duvivier (bass); and Bobby Rosengarden (drums).

13. Mike Zwerin, *Close Enough for Jazz* (1983), 175–76.
14. Wilson, "Great Jazz Dream."
15. *The National Jazz Ensemble 1975–1976* (Chiaroscuro CR(D) 140/151).
16. Quoted in Wilson, "Great Jazz Dream," 19.
17. John S. Wilson, "Jazz Goes to the New School," *New York Times,* 18 February 1977, 67.
18. Gary Giddins, *Rhythm-a-ning: Jazz Tradition and Innovation in the 80's* (1985), 281.
19. Quoted in Dave Helland, "Repertory Big Bands: Jazz's Future-Past," *Down Beat* 64.1 (January 1997): 34.
20. In John Edward Hasse, *Beyond Category: The Life and Genius of Duke Ellington* ([1993] 1995), 392.
21. Giddins, *Rhythm-a-ning,* 277.
22. Ibid., "Afterword: An Orchestra Is Born," 279–86. Note that this chapter was added to the 1986 edition and is not found in the 1985 edition.
23. Giddins, *Rhythm-a-ning,* 281.
24. Davis, *Outcats,* 210; original emphasis.
25. Peter Watrous, "When a Repertorial Show Stays True to the Repertory," *New York Times,* 11 October 1994, C16.
26. LCJO press release n.d. [? June 1988].
27. Jon Pareles, "Lincoln Center Adding Jazz to Its Repertory," *New York Times,* 10 January 1991, A1, C2.
28. LCJO Stagebill, September 1998, 20.
29. Richard Harrington, "The Canon Wars Come to Jazz," *Washington Post,* 20 February 1994, G1.
30. "Jazz Debate at Lincoln Center," *Sonneck Society Bulletin* 21.1 (Spring 1995): 11.
31. Lara Pellegrinelli, "Dig Boy Dig," *Village Voice,* 14 November 2000, 65–67.
32. Ibid., 65.
33. Harrington, "Canon Wars," G1.
34. George Wein, liner notes to *The Carnegie Hall Jazz Band* (Blue Note CDP 724383672820, 1996).
35. Gary Marmorstein, "Shoulders Broad Enough for the Band to Lean On," *New York Times,* 17 October 1993, H34.
36. Peter Watrous, "Making the Repertory of the Hallowed Past into Something New," *New York Times,* 23 October 1993, 11.
37. Peter Watrous, "Choral Effects Enhance Quiet Bernstein Pleasures," *New York Times,* 15 November 1997, B11.
38. A majority of CHJB members also played in the Thad Jones/Mel Lewis or Vanguard orchestra, and nearly everyone served time in Lionel Hampton's band.
39. Peter Watrous, "Ellington Revered and Revised," *New York Times* 25 January 1999, E7.

40. Some of my account is based on an interview with Gino Francesconi, Carnegie Hall Archivist and Museum Director, on 6 May 2003.
41. Peter Watrous, "Another War of the Titans, Fought Now with Trumpets," *New York Times,* 30 June 1994, C13.
42. Peter Watrous, "The Battle of the Bands, Part Two," *New York Times,* 3 July 1995, 15.
43. Charles J. Gans, "Carnegie Hall Jazz Band Bids 'Goodbye,' " Associated Press Newswires, 22 June 2002.
44. Ted Panken, "Lights out for Carnegie Hall Jazz Band," *Down Beat* 69.5 (May 2002): 18.
45. Ibid.
46. Jon Faddis, "In My Own Words: The Legacy of the Carnegie Hall Jazz Band," *Down Beat* 69.6 (June 2002): 14–15.
47. Stanley Crouch, "The Problem with Jazz Criticism," *Newsweek,* Web Exclusive, 5 June 2003, www.msnbc.com/news/922745.asp.
48. Peter Watrous's words mentioned above condemning a CHJB concert featuring Dave Grusin, "Choral Effects Enhance Quiet Bernstein Pleasures."
49. Although he goes a bit far in lumping together "Jesse Helms, Ayatollah Khomeinei, Ronald Reagan, Pat Robertson, and Wynton Marsalis," Gary Carner noted the link between the rise of "post-1970s conservatism" and the success of their calls for "traditional values." Introduction to a special edition on jazz of the *Black American Literature Forum* 25.3 (Fall 1991): 441.
50. Philip H. Ennis, *The Seventh Stream: The Emergence of Rocknroll in American Popular Music* (1992), 345.
51. Albert McCarthy, "The Jazz Scene," *Jazz Monthly,* no. 186 (August 1970): 3.
52. Kevin F. McCarthy et al., *The Performing Arts in a New Era* (2001), xviii–xxii.
53. Rep. Howard W. Smith of Virginia, a leading opponent of arts funding, quoted in Kevin V. Mulcahy and C. Richard Swaim, *Public Policy and the Arts,* 148–49.
54. Alice Goldfarb Marquis, *Art Lessons: Learning from the Rise and Fall of Public Arts Funding* (1995), 93.
55. Gerald D. Yoshitomi, "Cultural Democracy" in *Public Money and the Muse,* ed. Stephen Benedict (1991), 202.
56. Paul J. DiMaggio, "Decentralization of Arts Funding from the Federal Government to the States," in Benedict, ed., *Public Money and the Muse,* 230.
57. Marquis, *Art Lessons,* 122.
58. Quoted in Peter Watrous, "To Clint, with Love, from Jazz," *New York Times,* 17 October 1996, 15, 20.
59. McCarthy et. al., *Performing Arts in a New Era,* 85–88.
60. Bruce Weber, "Arts: A Shifting American Landscape. In the Heartland. A Cornucopia of Culture," *New York Times,* 6 December 1998, AR44.
61. Teri Agins, "Brooks Brothers Wines, Dines Potential New Customers," *Wall Street Journal,* 9 July 2001, B4.
62. Weber, "Arts: A Shifting American Landscape."
63. Source: NEA statements: 1995 "Music," 85–89; 1996 "Music Awards," 87; 1996 "Grants to Individuals," 111.
64. McCarthy et.al., *Performing Arts in a New Era,* 88.
65. Robin Pogrebin, "ChevronTexaco to Stop Sponsoring Met's Broadcasts," *New York Times,* 21 May 2003, B1, 8.

66. http://jazzatlincolncenter.com/jalc/facility/archrend.html. Accessed April 2003.
67. www.birdlives.com/. Accessed July 1998.
68. McCarthy et.al., *Performing Arts in a New Era,* 45, 109.
69. Ibid., 109.
70. Ibid., *New Era,* xxv.
71. www.lilawallace.org/. Accessed April 2003.
72. http://fdncenter.org/grantmaker/dorisduke/arts.html#jazz. Accessed April 2003.
73. www.chamber-music.org/programs/newworks.html. Accessed April 2003.
74. Stephen Kinzer, "As Funds Disappear, So Do Orchestras," *New York Times,* 14 May 2003, B1, 9.
75. Ibid. Kinzer quotes various individuals involved in orchestra management and direction.

CHAPTER 4. ON THE INSIDE

1. Throughout this chapter "Vanguard band" and "VJO" will occasionally refer to the Thad Jones/Mel Lewis Orchestra, Mel Lewis Orchestra, and Vanguard Jazz Orchestra collectively. The context should make clear whether they are used in this cumulative sense or not.
2. *The Fabulous Thad Jones* (1954, Debut 12) and *The Magnificent Thad Jones* (1956–57, Blue Note 1527, 1546). Some of these recordings have been rereleased on *The Complete Blue Note/UA/Roulette Recordings of Thad Jones* (Mosaic MD-172, 1997).
3. Mingus, quoted in Brian Priestley, *Mingus: A Critical Biography* (1982), 57. The Bartók quote is taken from "Of Thad and Mel," in Gary Giddins's *Faces in the Crowd: Players and Writers* (1992), 143.
4. For a brief discussion of the music played by Boyd Raeburn and his orchestra, see Kirchner, *Big Band Renaissance,* 12–13.
5. Barry Kernfeld, "Mel Lewis," in *The New Grove Dictionary of Jazz,* 2:586.
6. Barry Kernfeld, "Thad Jones," in *The New Grove Dictionary of Jazz,* 2:438. Kirchner, booklet accompanying *Complete Solid State Recordings of the Thad Jones/Mel Lewis Orchestra,* 2.
7. John S. Wilson, "2 New Big Bands Here Appeal to More than Old Memories," *New York Times,* 12 February 1966, 17.
8. Jerry Dodgion insists that the TJ/ML band was never a rehearsal band: "They started the band to have a full-time band. They did not want a rehearsal band. And they only rehearsed three times for Christ's sake. . . . They didn't just want Monday night. They hated that. Thad and Mel were really offended by it. They thought it was really a derogatory term."
9. A cooperatively run orchestra is not new in jazz. In 1929 the members of the Casa Loma Orchestra dismissed their frontman and reorganized as a cooperative orchestra with one of their saxophonists, Glen Gray, as president and the rest of the band as board of directors and stockholders (Schuller, *Swing Era,* 633).
10. In March 2005, after this chapter was written, many New York jazz musicians were shocked by the news that three trumpeters, with collectively seventy-seven years of experience playing in the band, had been abruptly fired. Lead trumpeter Earl

Gardner, along with second and third trumpeters Joe Mosello and Glenn Drewes, received almost simultaneously via Federal Express a terse form letter on Saturday morning, 19 March, stating: "After a meeting of our Board of Directors on March 17, 2005, we are terminating your relationship as musicians with Sixteen As One Music, Inc. / Vanguard Jazz Orchestra effective immediately. We regret this action is necessary." This change reflects the board of directors' desire to cut back on the frequency of subbing and enforce a renewed commitment to the band. As a result performance traditions developed over many years have been lost, but the potential remains for the new trumpet section to develop a distinctive style of its own.

11. Thad Jones interview quoted extensively in Giddins, "Of Thad and Mel," 141–50.
12. Rayburn Wright, *Inside the Score* (1982), 182.
13. Jazz musicians typically spell harmonies quite loosely. In sharped-ninth chords the altered ninth is most often spelled as a minor third (as in this example with a c-natural instead of b-sharp). This spelling better indicates its actual function: the superimposing of a minor third over a major third. The simultaneous use of major and minor thirds, in some contexts, seems related to the idea of the "blue" third. Moreover, the "sharped ninth" rarely resolves upward—as the terminology would imply—instead resolving downward, through the flatted-ninth, to the fifth of the tonic (i.e., D: c–b♭–a)
14. In jazz harmony C/A^7 means a C major triad combined with an A dominant seventh chord.
15. In the early 1980s two members of the Mel Lewis Orchestra were fired reportedly for complaining, "This shit doesn't swing. Let's play some real jazz."
16. For an in-depth study of the arranging of Jones, Brookmeyer, and others, see Wright's classic work *Inside the Score.* Also valuable is Fred Sturm's study of arranging techniques through comparing several versions of the same tunes ("King Porter Stomp," "The Chant of the Weed," "All of Me," and "Take the 'A' Train") in *Changes over Time: The Evolution of Jazz Arranging* (1995).
17. Rereleased on the compilation *Swing, Swing, Swing: Cavalcade of Vitaphone Shorts, Vol.* 2 (MGM/UA VHS M204696).
18. Louis Armstrong and, more recently, Freddie Hubbard are two examples of trumpet players who suffered apparently irreparable damage to their chops.
19. Gabbard, *Jammin' at the Margins,* 143. See pp. 71–72 and 138–59 for his discussion of "how the trumpet functions to establish the virility of those who play it." His argument "that the instrument is not just a phallic symbol, but that it effectively functions as the phallus . . . , the grand signifier of power and masculinity that all men seek but can never really possess," may contain more than a grain of truth but risks resulting in a one-sided and stereotypical view of trumpeters. Mark Tucker, in response to Gabbard, suggests that, other than certain obvious sonic qualities such as its penetrating sound, there is no reason the trumpet should be considered any more "phallic" than other jazz horns ("Musicology and the New Jazz Studies," *Journal of the American Musicological Society* 51.1 [1998]: 137–38). Gender representation in jazz is discussed more fully in chapter 10.
20. James Harvey relates a story that may sound familiar to many trombonists. When he bought a plunger at a hardware store in Oakland, CA, he removed the handle

and placed it on the checkout counter saying, "I don't use this." As he popped the rubber plunger into his knapsack, the clerk "looked at him with revulsion."

21. Leon Petruzzi, "Lead Trumpet Performance in the Thad Jones/Mel Lewis Jazz Orchestra: An Analysis of Style and Performance Practices" (Ph.D. diss., 1993), 180–82. To hear some of the contrast Snooky Young was capable of producing, Petruzzi suggests listening to the contrast in Young's sounds between Letters B and C in "Don't Git Sassy."
22. Players often invoke these terms to distinguish players who play more diatonically within each chord change (or "inside") from those who constantly use notes "outside" the regular chord changes (often through chord substitution).
23. Primack, booklet accompanying *Complete Roulette Recordings of the Maynard Ferguson Orchestra,* 2. Sebesky played trombone for the Ferguson and Kenton bands in the late 1950s before giving up the instrument to devote himself entirely to writing. See chapter 1, "Size and Instrumentation," for Sebesky's comparison of his experiences arranging for the Ferguson band, which had only two trombones, and the Kenton band, which had five.
24. Kirchner, liner notes to *The Complete Solid State Recordings of the TJ/ML Orchestra,* 8. The composer, Thad's brother, pianist Hank Jones, copyrighted the tune as simply "That's Freedom."
25. John Mosca, "Reflection," *Vanguard Jazz Orchestra [Newsletter],* 1998, 1.
26. During the swing era, sections of the band stood up when they were featured. Modern big bands frequently abandoned this practice, as players seemed to think such concessions to showmanship were corny. Saxophonists, in particular, may find it harder to read because of their distance from the music, but the gains in sound projection may justify standing.
27. See Basie and Murray, *Good Morning Blues,* for further discussion of the competition between tenor players Lester Young and Hershel Evans (171, 194–96).
28. Perry thinks the last arrangement featuring a tenor battle that the band performed was Frank Foster's chart on "Giant Steps": "When I first joined the band [in 1977] they were still playing that."
29. Maria Schneider's band also follows this configuration: the darker-toned Perry and the brighter one (Rick Margitza) sit in the same respective positions.
30. In his sketch scores Ellington devoted an entire staff to Carney out of the four staves he typically used (the other three were allotted one each to the brass, the other reeds, and the rhythm section).
31. Although Gerry Mulligan, a few years his senior, was better known and won more polls, among many musicians Adams was considered a more exciting and resourceful soloist.
32. The bandleader, clinician, and saxophonist Bob Mintzer extols the virtues of rehearsing the rhythm section apart when learning new charts. Mintzer discussed this during a rehearsal and concert with the Nite Life big band on Long Island, ca. 1993.
33. For further discussion of subdivision in jazz and popular music, see my article " 'Funky Drummer': James Brown, New Orleans, and the Rhythmic Transformation of American Popular Music," *Popular Music* 19.3 (2000): 293–318.
34. A few examples of small-group playing from Lewis's later discography are *Mel Lewis and Friends* (1976, A&M Horizon 716), *The Lost Art* (1989, Music Masters

6022–2), and, as a sideman with Joe Lovano, *Tones, Shapes, Colors* (1985, Soul Note 121–2).

35. For further details of Lewis's views on equipment and technique, see the entire interview reprinted from the February 1985 *Modern Drummer* in Rick Mattingly, *The Drummer's Time: Conversations with the Great Drummers of Jazz* (1998), 38–45. The quote appears on p. 40.
36. The drummer Kenny Clarke related how he discovered how to break up time with loud accents by "dropping bombs" (which became a marker of the bebop style) during his time in the Edgar Hayes band during 1937–38. Ira Gitler, *Swing to Bop: An Oral History of the Transition in Jazz in the 1940s* (1985), 54–56.
37. This technique bears Green's name not because he originated the style but because he became its most renowned practitioner. The playing of chords on every beat by banjo as well as guitar players is heard on many early jazz recordings. Green's name became synonymous with this technique not only because he was so good at it but also because it was practically all he did. An often-related story illustrates this. Basie would announce that the next tune would feature "our guitarist, Freddie Green." Throughout the entire tune Green would do his usual quarter-note chording. At the end of the tune on the break before the final chord, however, *he* would play Basie's signature three-chord ending instead of Basie.
38. Andy Farber, who frequently includes guitar in his ensembles, has written arrangements for Jazz at Lincoln Center, Anne Hampton Callaway, Frankie Lane, and many others.
39. LaLama made this point during an arranging class at Manhattan School of Music in fall 1989.
40. Hanna's first long-term job was with the TJ/ML Orchestra. According to Mark Tucker, "Hanna served an important apprenticeship there, finding ways to accommodate a fully formed solo style to the challenges of fellow Michiganer Thad Jones's tricky charts." For a discussion of Hanna's career and his tenure with the TJ/ML Orchestra, see Mark Tucker, "Seven Steps to Piano Heaven: The Artistry of Sir Roland Hanna," *ISAM Newsletter* (Fall 2000); reprinted in *Behind the Beat: Jazz Criticism by Mark Tucker,* ed. Ray Allen and Jeff Taylor (2003), 46–48.
41. Norman David, *Jazz Arranging* (1998), 157–8.
42. Reviewers often use military or mechanistic analogies when writing about precise ensemble playing. For example, in 1997 a writer in the *New York Times* called the band one of the most . . . *highly drilled* big bands in the country [my emphasis]." These words imply a kind of regimentation that seems not in the spirit of the VJO (Ben Ratliff, "Not Grandpa's Big Band Records," *New York Times,* 23 December 1997, E5).

CHAPTER 5. MAKING IT WORK

1. Although arrangers were seldom put on salary, and thus could hardly be considered "staff" (except during the height of the swing era), leaders often referred to them in this manner.
2. In Denmark Jones formed his own big band, the Thad Jones Eclipse, from 1979 to 1980, and briefly returned to the United States to lead the Count Basie Or-

chestra (after its leader died in 1984) until February 1986. In August of that year Jones also passed away.

3. Jones also left his wife behind and began a new family with his European girlfriend.
4. The tenor saxophonist Billy Mitchell told me a similar story about Basie, who apparently also took away solos as a form of "punishment." Once on a gig in Mitchell's hometown, Basie didn't let him take a single solo. Mitchell was especially incensed because, as he recalls, it was also his birthday and all "his people were there" (pers. com., ca 1993).
5. John Mosca was kind enough to loan me videotape of two television performances: one from Stockholm in 1969 and another from Munich in 1976.
6. Stanley Crouch, "1000 Nights at the Village Vanguard," *Village Voice* 31 (4 March 1986): 79.
7. Giddins, *Faces in the Crowd,* 149.
8. *VJO Newsletter* 1.1 (1998): 4.
9. Crouch, "1000 Nights," 79.
10. Although it sounds easy to perform, the piece is extremely difficult for young musicians to perform without rushing (speeding up the tempo), as many school band directors have discovered.
11. Dean Pratt, liner notes to *Groovy Encounters* (Amosaya Music AM2532-CD 1997), 5, 8.
12. Watrous, "Ellington Revered and Revised."
13. The performance would have benefited from a few more rehearsals—the entire work was put together in just two lengthy practice sessions (one of which I attended at Carroll's studios).
14. Watrous, "Ellington Revered and Revised."
15. Charles Ives, *Memos* (1972), 71.

CHAPTER 6. NEW DIRECTIONS IN JAZZ COMPOSITION

1. The relationship of jazz to popular music also figures prominently in this equation. In early jazz, when the influence of ragtime and marches was more immediate, more complex structures were the norm. As popular music became more standardized in the form of repeating chorus structures, jazz followed suit.
2. Jackson, "Jazz Performance as Ritual."
3. See, e.g., "Maria Schneider's Orchestral Jazz Adventures," a cover article in *Jazz Times* (September 1998). Of course, recognition does not necessarily bring financial rewards. A recent *New York Times* article begins: "In the last decade, Maria Schneider, who regularly wins prizes for best composer and best big band arranger in jazz, has made three albums on the Enja record label. Each sold about 20,000 copies—very good numbers for jazz. She didn't make a dime off any of them" (Fred Kaplan, "D.I.Y. Meets N.R.L. [No Record Label]," *New York Times,* 4 July 2004, II23).
4. "Dance You Monster to My Soft Song" and "Wyrgly" appear on *Evanescence* (Enja ENJ 8048 2, 1994). "Bombshelter Beast" is on *Coming About* (Enja ENJ-9069–2, 1996).
5. Schneider, liner notes to *Evanescence.*

6. Schneider, *Evanescence: Complete Scores,* ed. Fred Sturm (1998), xii.
7. Ibid., x.
8. This section is notated as eighteen measures of actual double-time for the saxophones, trumpets, and second trombone and as nine measures of double-time *feel* for the rhythm section and third and fourth trombones.
9. Schneider, *Complete Scores,* x.
10. Ibid.
11. McClary, *Feminine Endings,* 15–16, 64.
12. Marcia J. Citron, "Feminist Approaches to Musicology," in Cook and Tsou, eds., *Cecelia Reclaimed,* 21–22.
13. I presented much of this analysis to a special session of the Society for Music Theory (SMT) in Columbus, Ohio, on 1 November 2002, titled "Women in Jazz: Voices and Roles," in which Maria Schneider was the respondent. Although the composer should never be considered the "ultimate" authority in such matters, Schneider stated, "The boogie part is *definitely* masculine."
14. McClary, *Feminine Endings,* 160.
15. Schneider, *Complete Scores,* vii.
16. Schneider's comments were made during a special session of the SMT, 1 November 2002.
17. J. Bradford Robinson and Barry Kernfeld, "Carla Bley," in *The New Grove Dictionary of Jazz,* 1:239.
18. Several of Ellington's concertos could be considered Concerti Grossi (e.g., "Battle of Swing" and "Launching Pad") because they feature a group of soloists in opposition to the orchestra. Bley's "On the Stage in Cages" fails to meet this criterion because, although a group of soloists is featured individually, they never perform autonomously orchestrated passages, i.e., as a group within a group.
19. André Hodeir, "A Masterpiece: *Concerto for Cootie,*" in Tucker, ed., *Duke Ellington Reader,* 278.
20. In a similar vein Gunther Schuller found that "organic unity" in Ellington's longer works was only achieved when improvisation was "virtually suppressed." Schuller, *Swing Era,* 150.
21. Robert Walser, editor's notes to "Sonny Rollins and the Challenge of Thematic Improvisation" by Gunther Schuller, in *Keeping Time: Readings in Jazz History,* ed. Robert Walser (1999), 213. See also Lawrence Gushee, "Musicology Rhymes with Ideology," *Arts in Society* 7.2 (Summer1970): 230–36; and Robert Walser, "Deep Jazz: Notes on Interiority, Race, and Criticism," in *Inventing the Psychological: Toward a Cultural History of Emotional Life in America,* ed. Joel Pfister and Nancy Schnog (1997), 271–96.
22. Jim McNeely, "Current Directions."
23. Ibid.
24. Jim McNeely, liner notes to *Lickety Split* (New World Records 80534-2, 1997), 4.
25. See Peter van der Merwe, *Origins of the Popular Style: The Antecedents of Twentieth-Century Popular Music* (1989), 120–25, 177–83. Van der Merwe also describes these kinds of figures as "pendular thirds" (131–32).
26. McNeely, liner notes to *Lickety Split,* 9.
27. McNeely's work also shares with Milhaud's the chromaticism between the fourth degree and minor third, transposition of this idea to the fifth where it becomes

alteration of the seventh, bitonal use of triads, and other characteristics. A central focus of both pieces also involves developing the themes in fugal polyphony.

28. McNeely later mentioned to me that when, because of melodic or voice leading considerations, he chose a chord tone from the triad for the bass note, he added the second in order to keep the weight of the voicings consistent.
29. In conversation several band members have suggested playfully that the title "Sticks" is actually an abbreviation of "Ed Sticks It In."
30. In June 2006 McNeely informed me that the band had stopped performing the piece.
31. Gunther Schuller's first article on jazz, "The Future of Form in Jazz," published in 1957 for the *Saturday Review of Literature,* traced this trend to Ellington and "Reminiscing in Tempo" (1935), where it provoked many of the same charges of "not jazz" in the late 1950s as it sometimes did at the end of the twentieth century (reprinted in *Musings: The Musical Worlds of Gunther Schuller* [1986], 19).
32. McNeely, "Current Directions."
33. Schneider, *Complete Scores,* xii.
34. Green, *Music, Education, Gender,* 108.

CHAPTER 7. ON THE EDGE

1. In November 2004 the band left this downtown club and began a Tuesday residency at a Midtown location, the Iridium at 1650 Broadway (Fifty-first Street).
2. Susan Graham Mingus, *Tonight at Noon: A Love Story* (2002), 266.
3. Joseph Hooper, "Mingus Lives! New Adventures In Big-Band Chaos Theory," *New York Observer,* 26 January 1998. In another example, in a review of the Mingus Big Band, Hentoff writes, "[I]t was if the larger-than-life, volcanic Charles Mingus was there—shouting at his musicians to keep stretching themselves and never fake true improvisation" ("Mingus Lives," *Wall Street Journal,* 18 April 1997, A16). Perhaps the ultimate fetishization occurs with Mingus's bass. Treating it as a sacred object, on special occasions Sue has his famous lion's head bass brought to gigs and recording sessions for the band's bassist to play.
4. According to Nat Hentoff, Mingus often shared with him "his dream of having a big band regularly rehearsing and playing his works" ("Mingus Lives"). For an in-depth view of Mingus's life and his compositions and recorded output, see Brian Priestley's excellent book, *Mingus: A Critical Biography.* Mingus himself offers a rich account of his life in *Beneath the Underdog* (1991), though, as his longtime drummer and companion Dannie Richmond points out, it often seems as much fantasy as fact (in Priestley, *Critical Biography,* xi). *L'Amérique de Mingus: Musique et politique: Les "Fables of Faubus" de Charles Mingus* (1991), by Didier Levallet and Denis-Constant Martin, discusses Mingus's music, personality, and politics in the context of the civil rights movement and social order of the 1950s and 1960s. *Charles Mingus: Sein Leben, seine Musik, seine Schallplatten* (1984), by Horst Weber and Gerd Filtgen, contains a brief biography, testimonials from his colleagues, and a short annotated discography. Gene Santoro provides another account of the bassist's life with some new anecdotes in *Myself When I Am Real: The Life and Music of Charles Mingus* (2000) and Sue Mingus offers an intimate view of their sometimes turbulent relationship in *Tonight at Noon.* A short closing

chapter in *Tonight at Noon* describes some of Sue Mingus's experiences leading Mingus ensembles after her husband's death.

5. Rustin, "Mingus Fingers." See also Kevin McNeily, "Charles Mingus Splits, or, All the Things You Could Be by Now if Sigmund Freud's Wife Was Your Mother," *Canadian Review of American Studies* 278.2 (1997): 45–70.
6. Susan Mingus, *Tonight at Noon*, 265–66.
7. As Rustin aptly points out, "middle-class respectability" was all the more difficult for Mingus to achieve through his domestic partnerships because of the prejudice faced by interracial couples (216–19). See chapter 4, "*Pithecanthropus Erectus:* Debut Records, Domesticating Jazz, and Working Women," in "Mingus Fingers" (183–243). In a section titled "Women's Role," Valerie Wilmer discusses various roles women have played in jazz musicians' careers including, in some detail, Shirley Brown's vital role in providing artistic and emotional support to her husband, the bassist Ray Brown (*As Serious as Your Life: The Story of the New Jazz* [1977 (1980), 189–209). See also Patricia Sunderland, "Cultural Meanings and Identity: Women of the African-American Art World of Jazz" (Ph.D. diss., 1992).
8. He had originally considered the title *Memoirs of a Half-Schitt-Colored Nigger* for his autobiography. Because of his mixed background (his paternal grandmother was Swedish and his maternal grandmother was of Chinese descent), he sometimes referred to himself as a "mongrel" and "outcast" (Susan Mingus, *Tonight at Noon*, 38).
9. The connection between prostitution and the commercial pressures of the music industry are made throughout the text. Nowhere is this clearer than when Fats Navarro suggests black jazz musicians have only two options, "Play for money or be a pimp." Mingus responds, "I tried being a pimp, Fats. I didn't like it." Navarro: "Then you gonna play for money." See " 'Passions of a Man': The Poetics and Politics of Charles Mingus," in Eric Porter, *What Is This Thing Called Jazz? African American Musicians as Artists, Critics, and Activists* (2002), 101–48, for further discussion of the sexual politics in *Beneath the Underdog*. See also Rustin and McNeily.
10. See, e.g., his inability to follow through in "turning out" Pam (*Underdog*, 212–17).
11. In Priestley, *Critical Biography*, 95.
12. In their banter during "Fables of Faubus," Mingus and Dannie Richmond, his longtime drummer and confidant, ridicule Arkansas Governor Orval Faubus (who attempted to block desegregation in Little Rock High School in 1957).
13. During this period of "semiretirement" Mingus was heavily medicated much of the time (see "Put Me in That Dungeon," in Priestley, *Critical Biography*, 172–93).
14. "Open Letter from Sue Mingus," www.mingusmingusmingus.com. Accessed March 2000.
15. Best Big Band Awards in this single year were received from the *Jazz Times* Readers Poll, the *Down Beat* Critics Poll and Readers Poll, and the New York Jazz Critics Circle.
16. Sharon Lerner, "New York Woman: The Big Band Plays On (The Widow of Charles Mingus Jazzes up the Club Scene)," *New York Post*, 15 July 1997.
17. Susan Mingus, *Tonight at Noon*, 258, 260.
18. In Lerner, "New York Woman."
19. In January 1978 Mingus entered the studio with a big band that included Randy

and Michael Brecker, Steve Gadd, George Coleman, Slide Hampton, and many other well-known players. These recordings were released on *Something Like a Bird* (Atlantic SD 8805) and *Three Worlds of Drums* (Atlantic F 50571).

20. "Baby Take a Chance with Me" and "This Subdues My Passion" were transcribed for a Mingus tribute at Lincoln Center.
21. Schuller and Homzy edited and reconstructed *Epitaph,* a huge eighteen-movement work that Mingus had worked on for many years and attempted to record in a concert at Town Hall in 1962 (which can be heard on Blue Note CDP 7243 8 28353 2 5). Their version was performed in 1989 at Lincoln Center. Schuller later adapted two pieces from *Epitaph* for the Mingus Big Band, "Started Melody" and "Please Don't Come Back From the Moon," both of which can found on *Gunslinging Birds.*
22. Charles Mingus, liner notes to *Mingus Ah Um* (Columbia CK 40648, [1959] 1998).
23. Jazz musicians often refer to unnotated arrangements as "head charts."
24. Charles Mingus, liner notes to *Mingus Dynasty* (Columbia CK 65513, [1959] 1999), 9.
25. Ibid., 10.
26. John Berry, *The Jazz Ensemble Director's Handbook* (1990), 21.
27. In addition to the three-way split of his personality in *Underdog,* the title suggests Mingus's triracial heritage—African American, white, and Chinese.
28. Ingrid Monson discusses another riff-based tune recorded by Basie, "Sent for You Yesterday" ("Riffs, Repetition, and Theories of Globalization").
29. Mingus describes an encounter with twenty prostitutes in a Mexican brothel (*Underdog,* 174–79).
30. Mingus, *Let My Children.*
31. In *Underdog* Mingus describes playing cello in a youth orchestra. Believing he could not read music, the white conductor kicked him out when he played the correct original version of a Beethoven symphony instead of the simplified version the others were playing (31–32).
32. In Sue Mingus, liner notes to *Live in Time* (Dreyfus Jazz FDM 36583–2, 1996).
33. Interview with Herb Nolan in *Down Beat,* 25 January 1975, quoted in Priestley, *Critical Biography,* 219.
34. www.dreyfusrecords.com/discs_ns.php?a=18. Accessed June 2003.

CHAPTER 8. "IN THE CRACK" TO "TOTALLY OUTSIDE"

1. John Litweiler, *The Freedom Principle: Jazz after 1958* (1984), 13. Litweiler outlines some of these developments in his first chapter, "Steps in a Search for Freedom." Eric Porter distinguishes between "universalist" and "black nationalist" orientations. Noting that the "rejection of the restrictive elements of jazz (particularly the escape from European harmonic conventions) could easily be read as a rejection of the limitations imposed on black people by white society," the views expressed by prominent musicians such as Coltrane, Dolphy, and Coleman "presented a challenge to those who wished to limit the meaning and function of [avant-garde] music to an African American context" (*What Is This Thing Called Jazz?* 197).

2. LeRoi Jones [Amiri Baraka], *Black Music,* "The Changing Same (R&B and New Black Music)" (1967), 207.
3. Wilmer, *As Serious as Your Life,* 14.
4. Sun Ra quoted in Wilmer, *As Serious as Your Life,* 87–88.
5. John Szwed, *Space Is the Place: The Lives and Times of Sun Ra* (1997), 113, 97.
6. Porter discusses the "Black Arts imperative," which linked avant-garde music and black nationalism, with a particular focus on the Collective Black Artists in New York in his chapter, "Practicing 'Creative Music': The Black Arts Imperative in the Jazz Community" (*What Is This Thing Called Jazz?* 191–239).
7. George E. Lewis, "Improvised Music after 1950: Afrological and Eurological Perspectives" (1996), 91–122.
8. Szwed, *Space Is the Place,* 120.
9. Liner notes to *Inspiration,* by Sam Rivers's Rivbea All-Star Orchestra (BMG France 74321–64717–2, 1999), 2.
10. Ibid., 7.
11. Szwed, *Space Is the Place,* 119.
12. Ibid., 115.
13. Ibid., 124.
14. Ibid., 115.
15. Ibid., 124.
16. Ibid., 116.
17. Ed Hazel and Barry Kernfeld, "Andrew Hill," in *The New Grove Dictionary of Jazz,* 2:238.
18. Nat Hentoff, liner notes to *Point of Departure* (Blue Note BLP 4167, 1964).
19. Ibid.
20. Gary Kennedy, "William Parker," in *The New Grove Dictionary of Jazz,* 3:237–38.
21. William Parker, liner notes to *Sunrise in the Tone World,* 1997.
22. The New School concert was held on 18 May 2000.
23. See my review of Lewis Porter, *John Coltrane: His Life and Music,* in *Annual Review of Jazz Studies* (2000–2001): 237–52, in which I discuss the utility of analyzing Coltrane's "atonal" playing in terms of set theory.
24. In the classical or "Eurological" universe, since the 1950s Earle Brown also experimented with "hand gestures and an elegant way of sculpting sound on the spur of the moment into tactile forms." Kyle Gann characterizes such practices and his dependency "on intelligent performer interpretation" as "not a surprising fact" given Brown's background as a jazz trumpeter (Kyle Gann, *American Music in the Twentieth Century* [1997], 145–48).
25. John Murphy, "The African Big Band Aesthetic of Sam Rivers," Paper read at the 2002 Annual Meeting of the Society for Ethnomusicology, Estes Park, CO. Original emphasis.
26. Liner notes to *Inspiration,* 6.
27. Murphy, "African Big Band Aesthetic."
28. www.velocity.net/~bb10k/PARKER.disc.html. Accessed June 2004.
29. At his seventy-fifth birthday celebration at Sweet Basil on 25–27 September 1998, Sam Rivers fielded an all-star big band that featured solos by nearly every member on every tune.

CHAPTER 9. JAZZ AND CLAVE

1. Christopher Washburne, "Latin Jazz: The Other Jazz," *Current Musicology* 71–73 (2001–2): 409–26.
2. Jeffri, *Changing the Beat,* 3:136.
3. Wilson A. Valentín Escobar analyzes the rise of Latin jazz in the Nuyorican and Latino communities in New York during the 1960s and 1970s in "Freedomland at the New Rican Village: Latin Jazz and the Making of a Latino Avant-Garde Arts Scene in New York City" (Ph.D. diss., 2004). For discussion of the role of Latin popular music in the formation of Latino identity, see Roberta Singer, " 'My Music Is Who I Am and What I Do': Latin Popular Music and Identity in New York City" (Ph.D. diss., 1982); Peter Manuel, "Puerto Rican Music and Cultural Identity: Creative Appropriation of Cuban Sources from Danza to Salsa," *Ethnomusicology* 38.2 (1994): 249–80; Ruth Glasser, *My Music Is My Flag: Puerto Rican Musicians and Their New York Communities, 1917–1940* (1995); Juan Flores, *From Bomba to Hip Hop: Puerto Rican Culture and Latino Identity* (2000); Lise Waxer, *Situating Salsa: Global Markets and Local Meaning in Latin Popular Music* (2002); Marisol Berríos-Miranda, "Is Salsa a Musical Genre," in *Situating Salsa,* ed. Lise Waxer (2002), 23–50; and Wilson A. Valentín Escobar, "El Hombre que Respira Debajo del Agua: Trans-*Boricua* Memories, Identities, and Nationalisms Performed through the Death of Héctor Lavoe," in Waxer, ed., *Situating Salsa,* 161–86.
4. Washburne, "Latin Jazz," 420.
5. Leonardo Acosta discusses the cross-fertilization of jazz and blues with Cuban music from both the Cuban and the U.S. perspective. One of the earliest Cuban musicians thought to play jazz was one Pedro Stacholy who had spent time in New York and founded a band in Cuba in 1914. See *Cubana Be Cubana Bop: One Hundred Years of Jazz in Cuba* (2003), 16–17, 27.
6. Acosta, *Cubana Be,* 58.
7. Stan Kenton, one of the most visible exponents of "Afro-Cuban" jazz, commissioned numerous arrangements from Pete Rugulo and, eventually, O'Farrill. Although the Kenton legacy has suffered in scholarly and critical discourse, his orchestra exerted a tremendous influence on Cuban jazz and is still held in high regard by many Cuban musicians.
8. Roberts, *Latin Tinge,* 102.
9. In Roberts, *Latin Tinge,* 101.
10. Socarrás was probably the first important flute soloist to play on jazz recordings ("Have You Ever Felt That Way" by Clarence Williams in 1928).
11. Mireya Navarro, "A Master of Latin Jazz Is Rediscovered at 79; after Lean Decades, Chico O'Farrill Revels in His Late-Blooming Fame," *New York Times* 30 December 2000, B1.
12. Acosta, *Cubana Be,* 140.
13. Some writers have given the location of the school as Florida (Cristóbal Díaz Ayala, "Chico O'Farrill," in *The New Grove Dictionary of Jazz,* 3:185). Arturo insists that his father went to Riverside Military Academy in Gainesville, GA.
14. This pc set [0347] is listed by Allen Forte in *The Structure of Atonal Music* (1973), as set 4–17 (179). Forte gives two examples: Ives, *Unanswered Question* (10), and

Stravinsky, *Le Roi des etoiles* (115). Stefan Kostka in *Materials and Techniques of Twentieth-Century Music* (1990) describes it as a triad with "split third" (55) and offers as a musical example, Debussy: *Preludes, Book II* (1913), "La Puerta del Vino" mm. 9–15, where it comes equipped with a "blue" minor seventh (56).

15. Navarro, "A Master of Latin Jazz Is Rediscovered," B1.
16. The quote is taken from Ray Santos's promotional literature. Charlie Parker's first recordings with Machito were on 20 December 1948 ("No Noise Pt. 1," No Noise Pt. 2," and "Mongo Mangüé").
17. Glasser, *My Music Is My Flag,* 113.
18. Ibid., 84–85.
19. www.jazzconclave.com/i-room/santos.htm. Accessed April 2004.
20. Glasser, *My Music Is My Flag,* 58.
21. "Bernie's Tune," written by Washington, DC, pianist Bernie Miller, was popular among jazz musicians in the 1950s. Gerry Mulligan recorded the most famous version with Chet Baker in his pianoless quartet in 1952.
22. See Peter Manuel, "The Anticipated Bass in Cuban Popular Music," *Latin American Music Review* 6.2 (1985): 249–61; and Rebecca Mauleón, *Salsa Guidebook for Piano and Ensemble* (1993), for transcriptions and analysis of basic patterns played by the rhythm section in *son,* mambo, and salsa.
23. See Flores, *From Bomba to Hip Hop,* 81.
24. As further confirmation of the centrality of music to Latino identity and nationalism, heated controversy has swirled around the relative importance of Puerto Rican elements in salsa. See Manuel, "Puerto Rican Music and Cultural Identity"; and Berríos-Miranda, "Is Salsa a Musical Genre?"
25. Navarro, "A Master of Latin Jazz Is Rediscovered," B1.
26. Ibid.
27. Ibid.
28. Richard Jenkins, *Pierre Bourdieu* (1992), 75–76. See Pierre Bourdieu, *The Logic of Practice,* trans. R. Nice ([1980] 1990), 161.
29. This hierarchy reproduces the distinctive patterns of nationalism in the Americas described by Benendict Anderson (*Imagined Communities: Reflections on the Origin and Spread of Nationalism* [1983]). Administration of the colonies could only be entrusted to emissaries sent directly from Spain. Anderson discusses a hypothetical child born in the Americas one week after his father's migration from Spain: "[T]he accident of birth in the Americas consigned him to subordination—even though in terms of language, religion, ancestry, or manners, he was largely indistinguishable from the Spain-born Spaniard. There was nothing to be done about it: he was *irremediably* a creole. . . . [H]idden inside the irrationality was this logic: born in the Americas, he could not be a true Spaniard; *ergo* born in Spain, the *penninsular* could not be a true American" (59). This logic was reinforced by Vico, Herder, Rousseau, and other Enlightenment writers who argued for the importance of climate and environmental factors over heredity in the formation of national character.
30. A play on the term *chitlin' circuit* that refers to poor black audiences (mostly in the South), *cuchifrito circuit* is often used by musicians to refer to venues that cater to Puerto Ricans. Cuchifrito, a small deep-fried cube of pork, is an important characteristic national dish of Puerto Rico. Such common pairings of food and

music confirm the close connection between cooking and music making, between ethnic dishes and musical identity.

31. See Glasser, *My Music Is My Flag,* for discussion of the effect of U.S. colonialism on Puerto Rican musical traditions.
32. Valentín Escobar, "Freedomland at the New Rican Village."
33. Flores, *From Bomba to Hip Hop,* 144. 2000 U.S. Census data found at http://web.gc.cuny.edu/lastudies/Latinodatabases.htm.
34. For further discussion of this topic, see Flores, *From Bomba to Hip Hop,* 178–79.
35. See Gillespie with Fraser, *To Be or Not to Bop,* 320–22; and Katherine Dunham, *Les danses d'Haïti* (1950). Monson has discussed African American jazz musicians' indirect connections to Africa through the Caribbean in terms of a triangulating dynamic (introduction, *The African Diaspora* [2000], 1–19).
36. Eduardo Sánchez de Fuentes, *La música aborigen en América* (1938).
37. A few examples of white reaction to jazz have been reprinted in Robert Walser's *Keeping Time.* See, e.g., "The Location of 'Jass' " (7–8), "Does Jazz Put the Sin in Syncopation" (32–36), and "The Jazz Problem" (41–54). As several other articles in this volume reveal, if it was not being co-opted or scorned, jazz was celebrated as "African" music.
38. In his seminal work, *Music in Cuba* ([1946] 2001), Alejo Carpentier wrote: "attempts to create a work of national expression always return, sooner or later, to Afro-Cuban and mestizo genres or rhythms" (267). See Victoria Eli Rodríguez, "Cuban Music and Ethnicity: Historical Considerations," in *Music and Black Ethnicity: The Caribbean and South America,* ed. Gerard Béhague (1994, 91–108). In "Representations of Afrocuban Expressive Culture in the Writings of Fernando Ortiz," *Latin American Music Review* 15.1 (1994): 32–54, Robin Moore, while noting Ortiz's prejudices and ambivalence toward many "primitive" Afro-Cuban cultural forms, particularly in his earliest writings, nonetheless concludes that Ortiz and the Grupo Minoristas "recognize[d] the value of depicting the nation as ethnically and culturally mixed in their struggle to create artistic forms acceptable to all Cubans" (48). Although they may have "failed to receive widespread support, . . . [their] primary achievement . . . was to articulate themselves to the vanguard of Cuban academics who began to reformulate tentative conceptions of Hispanic culture and identity so as to accommodate aspects of Afrocuban culture as well" (47). Moore explores these issues in greater detail in *Nationalizing Blackness: Afrocubanismo and Artistic Revolution in Havana, 1920–1940* (1997).
39. During the 1930s and 1940s, throughout much of the French- and Spanish-speaking Caribbean, the *negritud* movement promoted African cultural heritage as emblematic of Caribbean identity.
40. Antonio Benítez-Rojo, *The Repeating Island: The Caribbean and the Postmodern Perspective* (1996), 51–55, 68–69. For a more expansive view of this rich creole culture, see Antonio García de León Griego, *El mar de los deseos: El Caribe hispano musical. Historia y contrapunto* (2002).
41. Acosta, *Cubana Be,* 30.
42. Many theories have been put forward to explain the greater retention of African cultural forms in Latin America than in the United States. Tannenbaum credited differences in the Anglo and Iberian managing of slavery and intervention by the Catholic church, which encouraged, among other things, manumission and co-

optation rather than eradication of African religious practices (*Slave and Citizen* [1946]). Fearing that Tannenbaum had grossly underestimated the cruelty of Latin slave systems, subsequent views have emphasized the high concentration of homogeneous African ethnic groups in large sugar plantations and the later banning of the slave trade and emancipation in Cuba and the rest of Latin America. Importation of slaves to the United States was forbidden in 1807 (although trade continued clandestinely) before the huge buildup of the Cuban sugar industry in the nineteenth century brought a massive influx of African slaves. By the twentieth century, when almost no former slaves in the United States could claim African birth, many Cubans had direct memories of Africa. See Marvin Harris, *Patterns of Race in the Americas* (1964); George Eaton Simpson, *Black Religions in the New World* (1978); and H. Hoetink, " 'Race' and Color in the Caribbean," in *Caribbean Contours,* ed. Sidney Mintz and Sally Price (1985), 55–84.

43. The efforts of Bobby Sanabria, percussionist, educator, and scholar, have been primarily connected with educational institutions such as the Manhattan School of Music and the New School.
44. Von Kleist was a student in the Jazz Diploma program at Juilliard next door.

CHAPTER 10. GOING FOR IT

1. Jeffri, *Changing the Beat,* 1:7.
2. Ibid., 3:56.
3. By the time of a follow-up interview in September 2004, Weisz stated that she had not played with McClure "for a long time."
4. Two recent books feature extensive interviews with women musicians. See Leslie Gourse, *Madame Jazz: Contemporary Women Instrumentalists* (1995); and Wayne Enstice and Janis Stockhouse, *Jazzwomen: Conversations with Twenty-one Musicians* (2004).
5. 1998: www.jazzcorner.com/diva.html. Accessed June 1998.
6. Liner notes to *Something's Coming,* Diva (No Man's Band) (Perfect Sound PSCD1216, 1995).
7. Lee Kavanaugh, "Diva: Girls Playing in the Boys' Club," *Windplayer* 54.14 (1996): 20.
8. Interview with Virginia Mayhew (1 August 2000), in Enstice and Stockhouse, *Jazzwomen,* 220–21.
9. The title is a takeoff on the classic Woody Herman arrangement, "Four Brothers," by Jimmy Giuffre.
10. Kavanaugh, "Diva," 15, 17.
11. In Kavanaugh, "Diva," 19.
12. Quoted in Mike Hennessey, "The Kit McClure Big Band (Fighting Sexism, Playing Jazz)," *Jazz Now* 7.6 (1997): 13.
13. Hennessey, "Kit McClure," 13.
14. Interview with Ingrid Jensen (8 September 1999), in Enstice and Stockhouse, *Jazzwomen,* 152.
15. Carol Neuls-Bates, "Women's Orchestras in the United States, 1925–45," in *Women Making Music,* ed. Jane Bowers and Judith Tick (1986), 349. See also Green, *Music, Gender, Education,* 69, 71–72.
16. A survey in the early 1970s by *Music Journal* found only 38 out of 527 musicians

(7 percent) in five of the country's leading orchestras were women, and most of them were in the string section. (Data quoted in Malcolm E. Bessom, ed., "You Won't Have Lady Musicians to Kick Around Much Longer," *Music Educators Journal* 62.7 [1972]: I). In September 2004 I conducted an informal survey of the same orchestras and found 160 women members out of a total of 528.5, or 30 percent. Interestingly, the New York Philharmonic had a substantially higher percentage (40%) than the others. In the five orchestras strings still comprise the vast majority of women members (81%). (Besides the New York Philharmonic, the other four orchestras were Philadelphia, Chicago, Boston, and Cleveland.)

17. Sherrie Tucker stresses the displacement of women after the war years. But, like the female musicians Tucker describes in detail, male musicians also struggled to find "ways to incorporate music into their lives" (Tucker, *Swing Shift,* 330). Because they had comprised the majority of big band musicians before the contraction, most of the musicians who lost their gigs were white men. Of course, they enjoyed certain advantages in finding employment alternatives outside of music that were not available to women and African American men.
18. Judith Tick, "Passed Away Is the Little Piano Girl," in Bowers and Tick, eds., *Women Making Music,* 327. Green notes that while female singers are in tune with their bodies, for female instrumentalists "the instrument which she wields or controls interrupts the centrality of the appearance of her in-tuneness with her body" (*Music, Gender, Education,* 53).
19. "Why Women Musicians Are Inferior," *Down Beat* 5.2 (February 1938): 4; reprinted in Walser, ed., *Keeping Time,* 112. Walser's chapter, "Jazz and Gender during the War Years," usefully brings together several articles on women and jazz published in *Down Beat* in the years 1938–41.
20. Judith K. Delzell and David A. Leppla, "Gender Association of Musical Instruments and Preferences of Fourth-Grade Students for Selected Instruments," *Journal of Research in Music Education* 40.2 (Summer 1992): 100–101. Harold F. Abeles and Susan Yank Porter, "The Sex-Stereotyping of Musical Instruments," *Journal of Research in Music Education* 26.2 (Summer 1978): 65–75.
21. Malcolm E. Bessom, ed., "Eliminating Sex Discrimination from School Music Programs," *Music Educators Journal* 62.7 (March 1976): 75. See also Delzell and Leppla, "Gender Association of Musical Instruments," 95.
22. Green, *Music, Gender, Education,* 109.
23. In Dahl, *Stormy Weather,* 55. This quotation should not be taken to indicate a complete absence of improvisation. Tucker notes that the African American all-girl bands "tended to emphasize improvisation more than white bands." In the white bands often "there were two or three good improvisers, who were featured" (Tucker, *Swing Shift,* 52–53).
24. Ted Toll, "The Gal Yippers Have No Place in Our Jazz Bands," *Down Beat* 6.11 (15 October 1939): 16; reprinted in Walser, ed., *Keeping Time,* 115.
25. In Kavanaugh, "Diva," 17–18.
26. Green, *Music, Gender, Education,* 220–21.
27. In conversation female musicians often remind me of the lack of female musicians in many big bands. See also Lara Pellegrinelli's critique of the Lincoln Center Jazz Orchestra hiring policies, "Dig Boy Dig."
28. In Kavanaugh, "Diva," 18.

29. Judith Tick, drawing mostly from music criticism, discusses "masculine" and "feminine" traits in classical music at the turn of the century (see especially her chart " 'Femininity' and 'Masculinity' in Music c. 1900," in "Piano Girl," 337).
30. For more discussion of "tensions" and "emancipated dissonances" in jazz, see Steve Larson, "Schenkerian Analysis of Modern Jazz: Questions about Method," *Music Theory Spectrum* 20.2 (1998): 209–41, esp. 217–18. See also Stephen Strunk, "Harmony," in *The New Grove Dictionary of Jazz,* 2:160–61. In classical music French Impressionist styles were sometimes disparaged as unmasculine partly for their departure from functional harmony.
31. David Ake, "Re-Masculating Jazz: Ornette Coleman, 'Lonely Woman,' and the New York Jazz Scene in the Late 1950s," *American Music* 16.1 (Spring 1998): 34, 36. As discussed in earlier chapters, playing outside the changes, or "free," most frequently has been associated with political liberation movements. Free jazz seems to have been analyzed for gender performance even less than mainstream jazz.
32. This statement glosses Charles Mingus's statements discussed in chapter 7.
33. Tucker, "Big Ears," 387, 394, 380. See also Herman Gray, "Black Masculinity and Visual Culture," *Callaloo* 18.2 (1995): 401–5; and Ingrid Monson, "The Problem with White Hipness: Race, Gender, and Cultural Conception in Jazz Historical Discourse," *Journal of the American Musicological Society* 48.3 (1995): 396–422.
34. Guillory, "Black Bodies Swingin'," 193, 192.
35. I have expanded Rustin's point here about Mingus's subjectivities to include black jazz musicians more generally. Rustin, "Mingus Fingers," 29.
36. Gray, "Black Masculinity," 401. This passage has been quoted widely. See, for example, Rustin, "Mingus Fingers," 101–2; and Tucker, "Big Ears," 390–91.
37. Gabbard has made the point that "Part of what has made jazz so intriguing is the number of alternatives it has offered to conventional notions of masculinity and male sexuality" (*Jammin' at the Margins,* 7).
38. Alan Lomax and Ferdinand "Jelly Roll" Morton, *Mister Jelly Roll: The Fortunes of Jelly Roll Morton, New Orleans Creole and "Inventor of Jazz"* ([1949] 1993), 77, 81.
39. Tucker points to a 1956 *Down Beat* article in which Horace Silver describes cool jazz as "faggot-type jazz . . . with no guts." Silver suggests a list of jazz masters (all black) whom musicians should listen to. In "Big Ears," 404n.
40. Ron Wellburn *[sic],* "The Black Aesthetic Imperative," in *The Black Aesthetic,* ed. Gayle Addison (1971), 136–37. Welburn's quote illustrates the instability of certain musical codes of "whiteness" or "blackness" and how they also could be reversed. Ironically, Lester Young frequently acknowledged his debt to white C-melody saxophonist Frankie Trumbauer. Trumbauer's influence seems most evident (but not exclusively) in Young's tone. In Young's hands, a white-influenced sound—blues and rhythmically reinflected—could be rearticulated as "black." Young's sound and style then spawned a whole generation of imitators, white and black. Discussion of "white" and "black" sounds should in no way be taken as expressing inherent "racial essence." That white players are as capable of learning "black" styles as black players are of learning "white" ones has been proven in many blindfold tests in which the listener has mistaken the player's race. Incidentally, John Gennari interviewed Welburn in 1997. Apparently the

views in *Black Aesthetic* were very much influenced by the political climate of the 1960s and 1970s. Reportedly, he is "no longer satisfied by 'the old nationalistic arguments about jazz and race' " (see John Gennari, *Blowin' Hot and Cool: Jazz and Its Critics* [2006], chap. 6).

41. In Enstice and Stockhouse, *Jazzwomen,* 224, 157, 158.
42. Interview with Terri Lyne Carrington (29 July 1997), in Enstice and Stockhouse, *Jazzwomen,* 61.
43. For discussion of some of the difficulties faced by an African American woman entering the jazz universe, see Porter's chapter on Abbey Lincoln's decision to become a "serious" jazz singer, in *What Is This Thing Called Jazz?* 149–90.
44. Hazel Carby discusses the music and memoirs of Miles Davis in the context of the work of gay writer, Samuel R. Delany. In a striking juxtaposition, given the strong heteromasculinist currents in jazz, Carby moves from Delany's graphic description of a gay orgy to a performance of the Miles Davis Quintet. Carby suggests that intimate musical interaction among male musicians may produce a compensatory hyperheterosexuality or homophobia. Carby, *Race Men,* 159–61.
45. For example, working in a funk band, I heard horn players deride each other for playing "pussy licks"—musical ideas thought to appeal to women in the audience. One-up-manship banter of this sort—"busting chops"—is, of course, common in groups of males.
46. Rustin discusses Charles Mingus's concern with the female gaze ("Mingus Fingers," 24, 104–5).
47. In Enstice and Stockhouse, *Jazzwomen,* 221.
48. Ibid., 158.
49. Tucker, *Swing Shift,* 330.
50. Tucker, "Big Ears," 385.
51. Gourse, *Madame Jazz,* 7.
52. Ibid., 22.
53. In Pellegrinelli, "Dig Boy Dig," 65. In her "emergence narrative" regarding the classical field, McClary sees "the political climate of the 1980s [as] more hospitable to participation and experimentation by women artists than any previous moment in music history. For the first time there exists something like a critical mass of women composers and musicians." McClary writes that scholarly and critical work have "cleared a space where women feel freer to choose to write music that foregrounds their sexual identities without falling prey to essentialist traps" (*Feminine Endings,* 32–33).
54. For example, Abeles and Porter found that "sex-stereotyping behavior in musical instrument preference is not very strong in young children (kindergarten) but is more pronounced in children beyond grade 3" ("Sex-Stereotyping," 72).
55. Daly's trio comprises Dave Hofstra, Eli Yamen, and Peter Grant.
56. As part of her tour, Daly is filming a documentary on local jazz musicians, who, though so important to the development and history of the music, have been largely unrecognized in favor of nationally and internationally recognized figures. She explains, "Part of the idea of this trip is that I bought a video camera, and I'm looking to document some of the elder statesmen and women of the music. Some of what I would call the hidden treasures of the jazz world. 'Cause

every time I go on the road somewhere I meet these amazing people. And I feel like nobody knows who they are, but they tell all these interesting stories."

57. Marvin Freedman, "Here's the Lowdown on Two Kinds of Women," *Down Beat* (1 February 1941): 9; reprinted in Walser, ed., *Keeping Time,* 120.
58. Scott DeVeaux, "Jazz in America: Who's Listening?" *Research Division Report #31* (1995); reprinted in Walser, ed., *Keeping Time,* 391–92.

CHAPTER 11. *BLOOD ON THE FIELDS*

1. Eric Porter shows how "Marsalis, like the generations before him, has plotted jazz along the axes of African American cultural achievement, American exceptionalism, and universal expression" (*What Is This Thing Called Jazz?* 288). See Murray, *Blue Devils,* esp. 11–12, for statements regarding African American and American particularism and universalist art.
2. In Levine, *Highbrow/Lowbrow,* 118–19.
3. The *London Times* quote appears in numerous Jazz at Lincoln Center brochures and promotional materials.
4. Gary Tomlinson, "Cultural Dialogics and Jazz: A White Historian Signifies," *Black Music Research Journal* 11 (1991): 247–48.
5. See Gabbard's "Policing the Boundaries," in *Jammin' at the Margins,* 19–33; and "The Jazz Canon and Its Consequences," in *Jazz among the Discourses,* 14–18. See also Tomlinson "Cultural Dialogics," 245–49. Lewis Porter devotes a chapter of his book *Jazz: A Century of Change* (1997) to discussing various definitions of jazz offered by Jelly Roll Morton, Harvey Pekar, Mark Gridley, and others ("Definitions," 13–38). He distinguishes between "strict definitions" and a "family resemblances approach" in which (invoking Wittgenstein) "the use of the word [is] its meaning" (29). Gabbard traces the etymology of the word *jazz* in his article for *The New Grove Dictionary of Jazz,* 2d ed. (2002), 2:389–93.
6. In Stanley Crouch, liner notes to *The Majesty of the Blues* by Wynton Marsalis (Columbia CK 45091, 1989), 6.
7. Gabbard, "Policing," 23.
8. In Levine, *Highbrow/Lowbrow,* 121.
9. "I'm realizing," said Marsalis in 1989, "that a musician should not ape or imitate these styles." On his own interest in composition, he added, "The direction I am going in now allows me to address more of the fundamentals of the music and to dig deeper into my own experiences" (quoted in Crouch, *Majesty,* 5).
10. Crouch praised Ellington effusively in a twenty-minute sermon titled "Premature Autopsies" that he wrote for Marsalis's 1989 CD, *The Majesty of the Blues.* The sermon, accompanied by a musical background, was delivered by the Reverend Jeremiah White Jr., imported from Chicago just for the date.
11. In Russell, *Black Genius,* 62.
12. In Fred Bouchard, "Wynton Marsalis Blindfold Test," *Down Beat* 50.12 (December 1983): 53.
13. Liner notes to *Levee Low Moan* by Wynton Marsalis (Columbia CK 47975, 1992), 1.
14. Wynton Marsalis (and Frank Stewart), *Sweet Swing Blues on the Road* (1994), 149.
15. Marsalis, *Sweet Swing,* 129, 141, 148–49.

16. In Howard Mandel, "The Wynton Marsalis Interview," *Down Beat* 51.7 (July 1984): 64.
17. Ibid., 18.
18. Marsalis, *Sweet Swing,* 147–48.
19. Marsalis and his staff are well aware that the sophisticated image of jazz makes it attractive to advertisers of luxury products (Marsalis, *Sweet Swing,* 141) and have wooed sponsorships from makers of designer perfumes to suits.
20. Davis's so-called first classic quintet (1955–57) included John Coltrane, Red Garland, Paul Chambers, and Philly Joe Jones.
21. In Leslie Gourse, *Wynton Marsalis: Skain's Domain: A Biography* (1999), 107; and in Mandel, "Interview," 17.
22. In Gourse, *Wynton Marsalis,* 108.
23. Murray, *Blue Devils,* 93, 107; original emphasis.
24. In Russell, *Black Genius,* 61.
25. Murray, *Blue Devils,* 11–12.
26. Porter discusses "pathology of blackness" and notions of a supposed "black matriarchy" in Daniel Patrick Moynihan's *The Negro Family: A Case for National Action,* issued by the U.S. Department of Labor's Office of Policy Planning and Research in 1965 (Porter, *What Is This Thing?* 183). Porter also discusses "cultural Moynihanism" in the context of conservative social policies of the 1980s and 1990s and the "resonance" of Marsalis's "aesthetic vision" (316–19).
27. Murray, *Blue Devils,* 43, 53. Here Murray is making reference to a phrase from Constance Rourke's *American Humor: A Study of the National Character* (1931).
28. Murray, *Blue Devils,* 4, 5.
29. Ibid., 5.
30. Ibid., 2, 4; emphasis added. Murray's words are reminiscent of Bourdieu's discussion of improvisation in a social context: "the 'art' of the *necessary improvisation* which defines excellence" (Bourdieu, *Outline of a Theory of Practice,* 8).
31. Murray, *Blue Devils,* 104–5.
32. In Russell, *Black Genius,* 61.
33. Berger's association with Chuck Israels and the National Jazz Ensemble is described in detail in chapter 3.
34. Gourse incorrectly gives the year as 1992 (Gourse, *Wynton Marsalis,* 234).
35. In Richard B. Woodward, "Jazz War: A Tale of Age, Rage and Hash Brownies," *Village Voice,* 9 August 1994, 27–34.
36. Gourse, *Wynton Marsalis,* 69–82.
37. In James A. Liska, "Interview: Wynton and Branford Marsalis: A Common Understanding," *Down Beat* 49.12 (December 1982): 15.
38. Pellegrinelli, "Dig Boy Dig," Many other examples could be cited. A few: Peter Applebome, "A Jazz Success Story with a Tinge of the Blues (at Lincoln Center, Defining the Canon Draws Fire)," *New York Times,* 22 September 1998, E1, 10; Craddock-Willis, "Jazz People"; Harrington, "The Canon Wars Come to Jazz."
39. Pers. com., 18 March 2000. A former member of the Lincoln Center Afro-Latin Jazz Orchestra made a nearly identical complaint (see chap. 9).
40. Many writers have contrasted the tradition of oral transmission in jazz with the

written means of preservation in Western art music (e.g., Berliner, *Thinking in Jazz,* 774). Some have made a connection to African practices (e.g., Alfred Wilmot Fraser, "Jazzology: A Study of the Tradition in Which Jazz Musicians Learn to Improvise" [Ph.D. diss., 1983]).

41. Albert Murray, *Stomping the Blues* (1976), 106; Marsalis, *Sweet Swing,* 142.
42. In Willard Jenkins, "School's In: Wynton Marsalis on What's Right and What's Wrong with Jazz Education," *Jazz Times 1998–1999 Jazz Education Guide,* 20.
43. Gourse, *Wynton Marsalis,* 181.
44. Even the sole remaining veteran in the current band, the baritone saxophonist Joe Temperley (b. 1929), was not used in the performance of *Blood.* Temperley, one of the few baritone saxophonists who has mastered the sound of Ellington's baritonist, Harry Carney, returned to the band after these performances. Because Marsalis wanted slap-tonguing and other unconventional effects on baritone and bass clarinet on *Blood,* he turned to James Carter.
45. Gourse, *Wynton Marsalis,* 236. Gourse seems to miss the point when she says, "Exactly who the personnel would have been in the temporary orchestra was never stated " (236). There was no *temporary* orchestra; the idea of hiring a different band just to play Ornette Coleman's music was probably a smoke screen intended to obfuscate Marsalis's real agenda—the establishment of a younger orchestra. Gourse does nothing to challenge what seems like a bit of disingenuousness on Marsalis's part. The older players maintain (and nothing in the letter corroborates Marsalis's version) that there was never any indication they would be brought back.
46. In the period following the premier of *Blood,* New York was rife with rumors of outside involvement in the composing of the oratorio. Some suggested that much of the composing, arranging, and orchestration was actually done by people other than Marsalis. Although Berger, Joe Muccioli of King Brand, and others certainly participated in "processing" Marsalis's scores and sketches (correcting obvious mistakes, fixing orchestrations, etc., the full extent of which may never be known), such roles are not unusual in the collaborative communities that produce orchestral jazz and other arts. Both Berger and Muccioli are adamant that Marsalis did the actual composing.
47. Other large-scale works by Ellington that treat slavery within a historical narrative are *Symphony in Black* (1934), *A Drum Is a Woman* (1956), and *My People* (1963).
48. Mark Tucker traces this type of historical narrative to nineteenth-century minstrel shows, particularly those staged by post–Civil War black companies. These scenarios were continued in Broadway shows and musical reviews such as Lew Leslie's *Blackbirds.* Ellington may have also been influenced by pageants celebrating black history such as *The Star of Ethiopia* that appeared in Washington, DC, in 1915. Black composers such as James P. Johnson *(Yamekraw)* and William Grant Still *(Afro-American Symphony)* produced extended works on similar themes, which may have served as models for Ellington ("The Genesis of *Black, Brown and Beige*").
49. Hasse, *Beyond Category,* 261.
50. John Hammond, "Is the Duke Deserting Jazz?" *Jazz* 1.8 (May 1943); reprinted in

Mark Tucker, ed., *The Duke Ellington Reader* (1993), 171–73. "Duke Ellington at Carnegie Hall," *New York Times,* 24 January 1943, 45. For other responses to *BB&B,* including Leonard Feather's heated rebuttal of Hammond, see Tucker, ed., *Ellington Reader,* 153–204. See also Hasse, *Beyond Category,* 261–65; and Schuller, *Swing Era,* 75–76, 83, 90–93.

51. Jon Pareles, "Wynton Marsalis Takes a Long Look at Slavery," *New York Times,* 4 April 1994, C13, 14; Steve Jones, "Ambitious 'Blood' Is Magnificent," *USA Today,* 17 June 1997, 6D. Most jazz critics found something to praise in the epic oratorio; see, e.g., Larry Birnbaum, "Blood on the Fields," *Down Beat* 64.9 (September 1997): 45; and Francis Davis, "Marsalis: Blood on the Fields," *Stereo Review* 62.10 (October 1997): 103–4. For two more critical reviews, see Gary Giddens, "Classic Ambition," *Village Voice,* 1 July 1997, 80; and Roberta Penn, " 'Blood' Overlong, Lyrically Anemic," *Seattle Post-Intelligencer,* 10 July 1997, C4.

52. In 1999, the centennial year of his birth, a Pulitzer was bestowed posthumously on Ellington.

53. Stanley Crouch, liner notes to *Blood on the Fields* by Wynton Marsalis (adapted from original program notes for concerts on 1 and 2 April 1994) (Columbia CXK 57694, 1997), 8.

54. Besides *BOTF,* Marsalis has used this structure in *Jazz: 6 1/2 Syncopated Movements* (recorded in 1993), *Jump Start—The Mastery of Melancholy* (recorded in 1995), *Big Train* (recorded in 1999), and others. Ellington composed numerous suites. A few examples are *Liberian Suite* (1947), *Such Sweet Thunder* (1957), *The Queen's Suite* (1959), *Suite Thursday* (1960), *The Far East Suite* (1966), and *The Uwis Suite* (1972).

55. In Crouch, liner notes to *Blood on the Fields,* 8.

56. In Hasse, *Beyond Category,* 261.

57. In distinguishing between antebellum and post–Civil War attitudes toward salvation among African Americans, Lawrence Levine made the same observation a cornerstone of his study *Black Culture and Black Consciousness.*

58. Just two years earlier his dreams of taking on the road a more socially critical work, *Jump for Joy,* had quickly evaporated.

59. Crouch, liner notes to *Blood,* 7–8.

60. In Tucker, *Reader,* 162.

61. In Russell, *Black Genius,* 65.

62. Ellington in Hasse, *Beyond Category,* 262.

63. Murray, *Blue Devils,* 80.

64. Murray, *Blue Devils,* 80, 87. The "dragon," a favorite trope of Murray's that has been picked up by Crouch and Marsalis, is a metaphor for racism and probably is meant to suggest the "Grand Dragon" of Ku Klux Klan infamy.

65. In Crouch, liner notes to *Majesty,* 6.

66. Murray, *Blue Devils,* 43.

67. Gunther Schuller would probably approve of this facet of Marsalis's composing. In a discussion of Ellington's *Reminiscing in Tempo* (1935), he describes thirty-two- or twelve-bar jazz forms as imposed by "the limitations of mass public taste." Instead of seeing their usefulness to jazz musicians, particularly for improvisation, he derisively equates "8-bar phrases" with "pop-tune mentality." Because of its

breaking free of these "pre-set molds," *Reminiscing* represented "gigantic forward strides . . . not only in jazz but in the history of black music in America" (*Swing Era,* 75). Murray, on the other hand, rather than see these moves as attempts to "break free" of these structures, prefers to see Ellington's "extension, elaboration, and refinement of the traditional twelve-bar blues chorus and standard thirty-two bar pop song form" as resulting in "a steady flow of incomparable twentieth-century American music" (*Blue Devils,* 93).

68. Nance, whose multifaceted talents (on trumpet and violin and in dance) earned him the name "Floorshow," is featured on violin in the last movement of Ellington's *Suite Thursday.* He also performed several numbers on this instrument in the 1943 concert at Carnegie Hall that premiered *BB&B.*
69. In Crouch, liner notes to *Majesty,* 5.
70. The difficulty of the music also required lengthy rehearsals with the singers. Partially to solve this problem, Marsalis doubled many of the vocal parts with a wind instrument, a procedure common in opera perhaps but unusual in jazz. For more comments from the musicians on rehearsals and on the 1997 tour, see Zan Stewart, "Blood Brothers," *Down Beat* 64.5 (May 1997): 26–28.
71. Murray, *Blue Devils,* 16.
72. In the liner notes to *The Majesty of the Blues,* Marsalis, speaking of his decision to use some older musicians from his hometown on the recording, states: "In my early years I thought that New Orleans music was just about some Uncle Tomming. I was around it all the time, but I wasn't involved on the level I now know I should have been" (in Crouch, liner notes to *Majesty,* 7).
73. In Russell, *Black Genius,* 67.
74. Porter, *What Is This Thing Called Jazz?* 321.
75. In Russell, *Black Genius,* 67.
76. Marsalis, *Sweet Swing,* 156.
77. In Gourse, *Wynton Marsalis,* 263.
78. *BOTF,* section XX, "Freedom Is in the Trying."
79. In Russell, *Black Genius,* 63, 66.
80. In Gourse, *Wynton Marsalis,* 268.
81. Marsalis, *Sweet Swing,* 150.
82. No recordings of Bolden (1877–1931) are known to exist. Contemporaries noted the bluesy quality of his playing and his powerful sound.
83. Marsalis, *Sweet Swing,* 116, 27.
84. Gourse, *Wynton Marsalis,* 115, 252.
85. Carby's quote refers to Miles Davis (*Race Men,* 138).
86. In Pellegrinelli, "Dig Boy Dig," 65.
87. Porter also makes numerous references to contradictions between Marsalis's discourse and goals, noting that "this vision remains consistent, in some ways, with the ideological projects it seeks to refute" (*What Is This Thing Called Jazz?* 316, 319, 320, 326, 327, 328, 334).
88. Clifford Geertz, *The Interpretation of Cultures* (1973), 213, 220.
89. See Murray, *Blue Devils,* 13. Marsalis, *Sweet Swing,* 41, 50, 59.
90. Marsalis, *Sweet Swing,* 141–42.
91. See Marsalis, *Sweet Swing,* 136–37, for an "imaginary" dialogue with a resident of "the street."

OUTRO

1. Christopher Small, "Responses," *Ethnomusicology* 39.1 (Spring 1995): 91.
2. Born and Hesmondhalgh, *Western Music and Its Others,* 31. For discussion of how theories of homology tend toward reductionism in emphasizing one or the other, or the "circularity" of these "structural resonances," see also Richard Middleton, *Studying Popular Music* (1990), 9–10, 159–66.

SOURCES

INTERVIEWS

Allen, Eddie (trumpet, leader, composer-arranger). 28 May 2003.
Ballou, Dave (trumpeter). 10 August 1998.
Banks, Nancie (singer, leader, composer). 25 August 1998.
Batiuchok, Margaret (president, New York Swing Dance Society). 21 March 2003.
Berger, David (leader, composer-arranger, conductor, educator). 25, 29 July 1998.
Bley, Carla (pianist, composer, leader). 29 June 2004.
Brandford, Jay (saxophone). 24 May 2003.
Burtis, Sam (trombonist, composer-arranger). 24 July 1998.
Daly, Claire (saxophonist). 30 August 1998, 17 September 2004.
Davies, Rick (trombone, composer). 10 February 2004.
Dodgion, Jerry (saxophonist, composer). 23 January 1999.
Drewes, Glenn (trumpeter). 1 February 1999.
D'Rivera, Paquito (saxophonist, clarinetist, composer, leader). 25 April 2003.
Easley, Bill (saxophonist, clarinetist). 26 May 2003.
Eidem, Bruce (trombonist). October 2002.
Farber, Andy (saxophonist, leader, composer). Numerous conversations, 1998–99.
Fitzko, Steve (trumpeter, bandleader). 28 July 1998.
Frahm, Joel (saxophonist). 26 September 1998.
Francesconi, Gino (archivist and museum director, Carnegie Hall). 6 May 2003.
Goodman, Wayne (trombonist). 10 August 1999.
Grillo, Bob (guitarist). 9 February 1999.
Harvey, James (trombonist, pianist, drummer, composer, leader). October 2002.
Horton, Ron (trumpeter, composer-arranger). 6 May 2004.
Israels, Chuck (bassist, bandleader, composer). 1 April 2003.
Jazz at Lincoln Center administrator. 8 September 1998.
Johnson, Richard (saxophonist). 28 July 1998.
Keller, Bob (saxophonist). 17 August 1998, 27 May 2003.

Kenyon, Steve (saxophonist, composer). 24 July 1998.
Kirchner, Bill (saxophonist, composer-arranger, leader, educator). 25, 29 July 1998.
Labor organizer, Local 802 American Federation of Musicians. 7 October 1998.
Labor organizer, Local 802 American Federation of Musicians. 9 October 1998.
Lake, Oliver (saxophonist, composer, performance artist). 14 March 2002.
Lovano, Joe (saxophonist). 29 March 2003.
Madison, Jimmy (drummer, leader). 11 March 2003.
Middleton, Rob (saxophonist, leader, composer). 25 August 1998.
Millikan, Bob (trumpeter). 3 March 2003.
Mosca, John (trombonist, leader). 1 March 1999.
Moser, Diane (pianist, leader, composer). 2 September 1998.
Mossman, Michael (trumpeter, composer-arranger, educator). 15 June 1999.
Muccioli, Joe (conductor, copyist, composer-arranger). Numerous conversations, 1999–2005.
Oatts, Dick (saxophonist). 4 February 1999.
O'Farrill Jr., Arturo (pianist, leader, composer). 17 March 2003.
Palermo, Ed (saxophonist, guitarist, leader, composer-arranger). 29 July 1998.
Parker, William (bassist, leader, composer). 24 April 2003.
Perry, Rich (saxophonist). 7 October 2004.
Persip, Charli (drummer, leader). 25 August 1998.
Pratt, Dean (trumpeter, leader, copyright administrator). 26 August 1998.
Press, Red (woodwind doubler, Broadway contractor). 27 May 2003.
Public question and answer session with members of the Mingus Big Band: Clark Gayton (trombone), Earl McIntyre (bass trombone), Alex Norris (trumpet), Boris Kozlov (bass), David Kikoski (piano). 25 October 2000.
Rieckenberg, Dave (saxophonist). 10 August 1998.
Riley, John (drummer). 18 March 2003.
Rosengard, Dan (pianist). 31 July 1998.
Roullier, Ron (pianist, leader, composer). 29 July 1998.
Russell, Benny (saxophonist, leader, composer, educator). 2 September 1998.
Santos, Ray (saxophonist, composer-arranger, leader). 10 February 2004.
Schoenberg, Loren (saxophonist, leader, educator). 25 August 1998.
Sellers, Joey (trombonist, leader, composer). Numerous conversations, 1998–99.
Sevian, Lauren (saxophonist). 29 September 2004.
Silvester, Jorge (saxophonist, leader, composer). 25 August 1998.
Slagle, Steve (saxophonist, composer-arranger). 10 August 1999, November 2004.
Slaughter, Harriet (Human Resources, League of American Theaters and Producers). 28 May 2003.
Stubblefield, John (saxophonist). 25 October 2000.
Terry, Clark (trumpeter, leader, composer). 7 February 1999.
Vega, Ray (trumpeter, composer, educator). 12 February 2004.
Warfield, Bill (trumpeter, leader, composer-arranger, educator). Numerous conversations, 1998–99.
Wein, George (impresario). 25 March 2003.
Weisz, Deborah (trombonist). 4 May 1999, 17 September 2004.

WORKS CITED

Abeles, Harold F., and Susan Yank Porter. "The Sex-Stereotyping of Musical Instruments." *Journal of Research in Music Education* 26.2 (Summer 1978): 65–75.

Acosta, Leonardo. *Cubana Be Cubana Bop: One Hundred Years of Jazz in Cuba.* Washington, DC: Smithsonian Books, 2003.

Agins, Teri. "Brooks Brothers Wines, Dines Potential New Customers." *Wall Street Journal,* 9 July 2001, B4.

Ake, David. "Re-Masculating Jazz: Ornette Coleman, 'Lonely Woman,' and the New York Jazz Scene in the Late 1950s." *American Music* 16.1 (Spring 1998): 25–44.

———. *Jazz Cultures.* Berkeley: University of California Press, 2002.

Anderson, Benedict. *Imagined Communities: Reflections on the Origin and Spread of Nationalism.* New York: Verso, 1983.

Applebome, Peter. "A Jazz Success Story with a Tinge of the Blues (At Lincoln Center, Defining the Canon Draws Fire)." *New York Times,* 22 September 1998, E1, 10.

Basie, Count, and Albert Murray. *Good Morning Blues: The Autobiography of Count Basie.* New York: Donald I. Fine, 1985.

Becker, Howard S. *Art Worlds.* Berkeley: University of California Press, 1982.

Benítez-Rojo, Antonio. *The Repeating Island: The Caribbean and the Postmodern Perspective.* 2d ed. Durham: Duke University Press, 1996.

Berendt, Joachim. *The Jazz Book.* New York: Lawrence Hill & Co., 1975.

Berliner, Paul F. *Thinking in Jazz: The Infinite Art of Improvisation.* Chicago: University of Chicago Press, 1994.

Berríos-Miranda, Marisol. "Is Salsa a Musical Genre?" In *Situating Salsa,* edited by Lise Waxer, 23–50. New York: Routledge, 2002.

Berry, John. *The Jazz Ensemble Director's Handbook.* Milwaukee, WI: Jenson Publications, 1990.

Bessom, Malcolm E., ed. "You Won't Have Lady Musicians to Kick Around Much Longer." *Music Educators Journal* 59.1 (September 1972): I.

———, ed. "Eliminating Sex Discrimination from School Music Programs." *Music Educators Journal* 62.7 (March 1976): 75.

Birnbaum, Larry. "Wynton Marsalis & the Lincoln Center Jazz Orchestra: *Blood on the Fields.*" *Down Beat* 64.9 (September 1997): 45.

Blesh, Rudi. *Shining Trumpets: A History of Jazz.* New York: Knopf, 1946.

Blum, Stephen. "Recognizing Improvisation." In *In the Course of Performance: Studies in the World of Musical Improvisation,* edited by Bruno Nettl with Melinda Russell, 27–45. Chicago: University of Chicago Press, 1998.

Blumenthal, Bob. "The Future for Big Bands: Bleak or Bright?" *Jazz Times* 28.7 (September 1998): 28–31, 35, 50.

Born, Georgina, and David Hesmondhalgh. Introduction to *Western Music and Its Others: Difference, Representation, and Appropriation in Music,* 1–58. Berkeley: University of California Press, 2000.

Bouchard, Fred. "Wynton Marsalis Blindfold Test." *Down Beat* 50.12 (December 1983): 53.

Bourdieu, Pierre. *Outline of a Theory of Practice.* Translated by R. Nice. Cambridge: Cambridge University Press, [1972] 1977.

———. *The Logic of Practice.* Translated by R. Nice. Stanford, CA: Stanford University Press, [1980] 1990.

Bowers, Jane, and Judith Tick, eds. *Women Making Music: The Western Art Tradition, 1150–1950.* Urbana and Chicago: University of Illinois Press, 1986.

Butler, Judith P. *Gender Trouble: Feminism and the Subversion of Identity.* New York: Routledge, 1990.

Carby, Hazel. *Race Men.* Cambridge, MA: Harvard University Press, 1998.

Carner, Gary. Introduction to "Literature of Jazz Issue." *Black American Literature Forum* 25.3 (Fall 1991): 441–48.

Carpentier, Alejo. *Music in Cuba.* Translated by Alan West-Durán. Minneapolis: University of Minnesota Press, [1946] 2001.

Charters, Samuel B., and Leonard Kunstadt. *Jazz: A History of the New York Scene.* New York: Da Capo Press, 1962.

Citron, Marcia J. "Feminist Approaches to Musicology." In *Cecelia Reclaimed Feminist Perspectives on Gender and Music,* edited by Susan C. Cook and Judy S. Tsou, 15–34. Urbana: University of Illinois Press, 1994.

Collier, James Lincoln. *Duke Ellington.* New York: Oxford University Press, 1987.

Cook, Susan C., and Judy S. Tsou, eds. *Cecelia Reclaimed: Feminist Perspectives on Gender and Music.* Urbana and Chicago: University of Illinois Press, 1994.

Craddock-Willis, Andre. "Jazz People: Wynton Marsalis vs. James Lincoln Collier." *Transition* 65 (1995): 140–78.

Crouch, Stanley. "1000 Nights at the Village Vanguard." *Village Voice* 31 (4 March 1986): 79.

———. Liner notes to *The Majesty of the Blues* by Wynton Marsalis. Columbia CK 45091, 1989.

_____. Liner notes to *Blood on the Fields* by Wynton Marsalis (adapted from original program notes for concerts on 1 and 2 April 1994). Columbia CXK 57694, 1997.

———. "The Problem with Jazz Criticism." *Newsweek,* Web Exclusive, 5 June 2003. www.msnbc.com/news/922745.asp.

Cusick, Suzanne G. "Feminist Theory, Music Theory, and the Mind/Body Problem." In *Music/Ideology: Resisting the Aesthetic,* edited by Adam Krims, 37–55. Amsterdam: G+B Arts International, 1998.

———. "On Musical Performances of Gender and Sex." In *Audible Traces: Gender, Identity, and Music,* edited by Elaine Barkin and Lydia Hamessley, 25–48. Zurich: Carciofoli Verlagshaus, 1999.

Dahl, Linda. *Stormy Weather: The Music and Lives of a Century of Jazz Women.* New York: Limelight Editions, 1984.

David, Norman. *Jazz Arranging.* New York: Ardsley House, 1998.

Davis, Francis. *Outcats: Jazz Composers, Instrumentalists, and Singers.* New York: Oxford University Press, 1990.

———. "Wynton Marsalis & and Lincoln Center Jazz Orchestra: *Blood on the Fields.*" *Stereo Review* 62.10 (October 1997): 103–4.

Delzell, Judith K., and David A. Leppla. "Gender Association of Musical Instruments and Preferences of Fourth-Grade Students for Selected Instruments." *Journal of Research in Music Education* 40.2 (Summer 1992): 93–103.

DeVeaux, Scott. "The Emergence of the Jazz Concert, 1935–45."*American Music* 7.1 (1989): 6–29.

———. "Constructing the Jazz Tradition: Jazz Historiography." *Black American Literature Forum* 25 (1991): 525–60.

———. "Jazz in America: Who's Listening?" *Research Division Report #31* (National Endowment for the Arts, 1995). Reprinted in *Keeping Time: Readings in Jazz History,* edited by Robert Walser, 389–95. New York: Oxford University Press, 1999.

———. *The Birth of Bebop: A Social and Musical History.* Berkeley: University of California Press, 1997.

Díaz Ayala, Cristóbal. "Chico O'Farrill." In the *New Grove Dictionary of Jazz,* 2d ed., vol. 3, edited by Barry Kernfeld, 185. London: Macmillan, 2002.

DiMaggio, Paul J. "Decentralization of Arts Funding from the Federal Government to the States." In *Public Money and the Muse,* edited by Stephen Benedict, 216–52. New York: Norton, 1991.

Dunham, Katherine. *Les danses d'Haïti.* Paris: Fasquelle, 1950.

Ellison, Ralph. *Shadow and Act.* New York: Vintage International, [1964] 1995.

Ennis, Philip H. *The Seventh Stream: The Emergence of Rocknroll in American Popular Music.* Hanover, NH: University Press of New England, 1992.

Enstice, Wayne, and Janis Stockhouse. *Jazzwomen: Conversations with Twenty-one Musicians.* Bloomington: Indiana University Press, 2004.

Erenberg, Lewis A. *Swingin' the Dream: Big Band Jazz and the Rebirth of American Culture.* Chicago: University of Chicago Press, 1998.

Faddis, Jon. "In My Own Words: The Legacy of the Carnegie Hall Jazz Band." *Down Beat* 69.6 (June 2002): 14–15.

Flores, Juan. *From Bomba to Hip Hop: Puerto Rican Culture and Latino Identity.* New York: Columbia University Press, 2000.

Floyd, Samuel, Jr. *The Power of Black Music.* New York: Oxford University Press, 1995.

Forte, Allen. *The Structure of Atonal Music.* New Haven: Yale University Press, 1973.

Fraser, Alfred Wilmot. "Jazzology: A Study of the Tradition in Which Jazz Musicians Learn to Improvise." Ph.D. diss., University of Pennsylvania, 1983.

Freedman, Marvin. "Here's the Lowdown on Two Kinds of Women." *Down Beat* 8.3 (1 February 1941): 9. Reprinted in *Keeping Time: Readings in Jazz History,* edited by Robert Walser, 120. New York: Oxford University Press, 1999.

Gabbard, Krin, ed. *Jazz among the Discourses.* Chicago: University of Chicago Press, 1995.

———. *Jammin' at the Margins: Jazz and the American Cinema.* Chicago: University of Chicago Press, 1996.

———. " 'Jazz': Etymology." In the *New Grove Dictionary of Jazz,* 2d ed., vol. 2, edited by Barry Kernfeld, 389–93. London: Macmillan, 2002.

Gann, Kyle. *American Music in the Twentieth Century.* New York: Schirmer Books, 1997.

Gans, Charles J. "Carnegie Hall Jazz Band Bids 'Goodbye.' " Associated Press Newswires, 22 June 2002.

García de León Griego, Antonio. *El mar de los deseos: El Caribe hispano musical. Historia y contrapunto.* México and Bueno Aires: Siglo XXI Editores, 2002.

Gates, Henry Louis, Jr. *The Signifying Monkey: A Theory of Afro-American Literary Criticism.* New York: Oxford University Press, 1988.

Geertz, Clifford. *The Interpretation of Cultures.* New York: Basic Books, 1973.

Gendron, Bernard. "Moldy Figs and Modernists: Jazz at War (1942–1946)." In *Jazz among the Discourses,* edited by Krin Gabbard, 31–56. Durham: Duke University Press, 1995.

Gennari, John. *Blowin' Hot and Cool: Jazz and Its Critics.* Chicago: University of Chicago Press, 2006.

Giddins, Gary. *Rhythm-a-ning: Jazz Tradition and Innovation in the 80's.* New York: Oxford University Press, 1985.

———. *Faces in the Crowd: Players and Writers.* New York: Oxford University Press, 1992.

———. "Classic Ambition." *Village Voice,* 1 July 1997, 80.

———. *Visions of Jazz: The First Century.* New York: Oxford University Press, 1998.

Gillespie, John Birks "Dizzy," with Al Fraser. *To Be or Not to Bop: Memoirs.* Garden City, NY: Doubleday, 1979.

Gilmore, Samuel. "Schools of Activity and Innovation." *Sociological Quarterly* 29.2 (1988): 203–19.

Gilroy, Paul. *The Black Atlantic: Modernity and Double Consciousness.* Cambridge, MA: Harvard University Press, 1993.

Gitler, Ira. *Swing to Bop: An Oral History of the Transition in Jazz in the 1940s,* New York: Oxford University Press, 1985.

Glasser, Ruth. *My Music Is My Flag: Puerto Rican Musicians and Their New York Communities, 1917–1940.* Berkeley: University of California Press, 1995.

Gourse, Leslie. *Madame Jazz: Contemporary Women Instrumentalists.* New York: Oxford University Press, 1995.

———. *Wynton Marsalis: Skain's Domain: A Biography.* New York: Schirmer Books, 1999.

Gray, Herman. "Black Masculinity and Visual Culture." *Callaloo* 18.2 (1995): 401–5.

Green, Lucy. *Music, Gender, Education.* Cambridge: Cambridge University Press, 1997.

Guillory, Monique. "Black Bodies Swingin': Race, Gender, and Jazz." In *Soul: Black Power, Politics, and Pleasure,* edited by Monique Guillory and Richard C. Green, 191–215. New York: New York University Press, 1998.

Gushee, Lawrence. "Musicology Rhymes with Ideology." [Review of *Early Jazz,* by Gunther Schuller.] *Arts in Society* 7.2 (Summer 1970): 230–36.

Harrington, Richard. "The Canon Wars Come to Jazz." *Washington Post,* 20 February 1994, G1.

Harris, Marvin. *Patterns of Race in the Americas.* New York: Walker, 1964.

Hasse, John Edward. *Beyond Category: The Life and Genius of Duke Ellington.* New York: Da Capo Press, [1993] 1995.

Hazel, Ed, and Barry Kernfeld. "Andrew Hill." In the *New Grove Dictionary of Jazz,* 2d ed., vol. 2, edited by Barry Kernfeld, 238. London: Macmillan, 2002.

Heckathorn, Douglas D., and Joan Jeffri. "Finding the Beat: Using Respondent-Driven Sampling to Study Jazz Musicians." *Poetics* 28.4 (2001): 307–29.

Helland, Dave. "Repertory Big Bands: Jazz's Future-Past." *Down Beat* 64.1 (January 1997): 34.

Henderson, Harry, and Sam Shaw. "And Now We Go Bebop!" *Colliers,* 20 March 1948. Reprinted in *Jazz: A Century of Change,* edited by Lewis Porter, 174. New York: Schirmer Books, 1997.

Hennessey, Mike. "The Kit McClure Big Band (Fighting Sexism, Playing Jazz)." *Jazz Now* 7.6 (October 1997): 13, 22.

Hentoff, Nat. "Mingus Lives." *Wall Street Journal,* 18 April 1997, A16.

Hodeir, André. "A Masterpiece: *Concerto for Cootie.*" In *The Duke Ellington Reader,* edited by Mark Tucker, 276–88. New York: Oxford University Press, [1954] 1993.

Hoetink, H. " 'Race' and Color in the Caribbean." In *Caribbean Contours,* edited by Sidney Mintz and Sally Price, 55–84. Baltimore: Johns Hopkins University Press, 1985.

Hooper, Joseph. "Mingus Lives! New Adventures In Big-Band Chaos Theory." *New York Observer,* 26 January 1998.

Horricks, Raymond. *Gil Evans.* New York: Hippocrene Books, 1984.

Hurston, Zora Neale. *Dust Tracks On a Road.* Urbana: University of Illinois Press, [1942] 1984.

Ives, Charles. *Memos.* New York: Norton, 1972.

Jackson, Travis A. "Jazz Performance as Ritual: The Blues Aesthetic and the African Diaspora." In *The African Diaspora,* edited by Ingrid Monson, 23–82. New York: Routledge, 2003.

Jameson, Fredric. *Postmodernism. Or, the Cultural Logic of Late Capitalism.* Durham: Duke University Press, 1995.

"Jazz and the Peoples Movement." *Down Beat* 37.22 (12 November 1970): 11.

"Jazz Debate at Lincoln Center." *Sonneck Society Bulletin* 21.1 (Spring 1995): 10–11.

Jeffri, Joan. *Changing the Beat: A Study of the Worklife of Jazz Musicians.* 3 vols. NEA Research Division Report #43, 2003.

Jenkins, Richard. *Pierre Bourdieu.* New York: Routledge, 1992.

Jenkins, Willard. "School's In: Wynton Marsalis on What's Right and What's Wrong with Jazz Education." *Jazz Times 1998–1999 Jazz Education Guide,* 18–26.

Jones, LeRoi (Amiri Baraka). *Blues People.* New York: Morrow Quill Paperbacks, 1963.

———. *Black Music.* New York: William Morrow, 1967.

Kaplan, Fred. "D.I.Y. Meets N.R.L. (No Record Label)." *New York Times,* 4 July 2004, II 23.

Kavanaugh, Lee. "Diva: Girls Playing in the Boys' Club." *Windplayer* 54.14 (1996): 14–23.

Keil, Charles. "The Theory of Participatory Discrepancies: A Progress Report." *Ethnomusicology* 39.1 (1995): 1–19.

Kennedy, Gary "Jazz Education." In *New Grove Dictionary of Jazz,* 2d ed., vol. 2, edited by Barry Kernfeld, 396–98. London: Macmillan, 2002.

———. "William Parker." In *New Grove Dictionary of Jazz,* 2d ed., vol. 3, edited by Barry Kernfeld, 237–38. London: Macmillan, 2002.

Kenny, William Howland. *Chicago Jazz: A Cultural History, 1904–1930.* New York: Oxford University Press, 1993.

Kernfeld, Barry. "Mel Lewis." In *New Grove Dictionary of Jazz,* 2d ed., vol. 2, edited by Barry Kernfeld, 586. London: Macmillan, 2002.

———. "Thad Jones." In *New Grove Dictionary of Jazz,* 2d ed., vol. 2, edited by Barry Kernfeld, 438. London: Macmillan, 2002.

———. "Festivals." In *New Grove Dictionary of Jazz,* 2d ed., vol. 1, edited by Barry Kernfeld, 753. London: Macmillan, 2002.

Kinzer, Stephen. "As Funds Disappear, So Do Orchestras." *New York Times,* 14 May 2003, B1, 9.

Kirchner, Bill. Booklet accompanying *The Complete Solid State Recordings of the Thad Jones/Mel Lewis Orchestra.* Mosaic MD5-151, 1994.

———. *Big Band Renaissance: The Evolution of the Jazz Orchestra: The 1940s and Beyond.* Washington, DC: Smithsonian Institution Press, 1995.

Kostka, Stefan. *Materials and Techniques of Twentieth-Century Music.* Englewood Cliffs, NJ: Prentice Hall, 1990.

Larson, Steve. "Schenkerian Analysis of Modern Jazz: Questions about Method." *Music Theory Spectrum* 20.2 (1998): 209–41.

Ledbetter, Les. "The Pop Life: All-Star Jazz Group Set for First Concert." *New York Times,* 18 January 1974, 24.

Lees, Gene. *Leader of the Band: The Life of Woody Herman.* New York: Oxford University Press, 1995.

Lerner, Sharon. "New York Woman: The Big Band Plays On (The Widow of Charles Mingus Jazzes up the Club Scene)." *New York Post,* 15 July 1997.

Levallet, Didier, and Denis-Constant Martin. *L'Amérique de Mingus. Musique et politique: Les "Fables of Faubus" de Charles Mingus.* Paris: P.O.L., 1991.

Levine, Lawrence. *Black Culture and Black Consciousness: Afro-American Folk Thought from Slavery to Freedom.* New York: Oxford University Press, 1977.

———. *Highbrow/Lowbrow: The Emergence of Cultural Hierarchy in America.* Cambridge, MA: Harvard University Press, 1988.

Lewis, George E. "Improvised Music after 1950: Afrological and Eurological Perspectives." *Black Music Research Journal* 16.1 (1996): 91–122.

Liska, James A. "Maiden Voyage." *Down Beat* 48.11 (November 1981): 53–54.

———. "Interview: Wynton and Branford Marsalis: A Common Understanding." *Down Beat* 49.12 (December 1982): 14–16, 64.

Litweiler, John. *The Freedom Principle: Jazz after 1958.* New York: William Morrow, 1984.

Lomax, Alan. *Folk Song Style and Culture.* Washington, DC: American Association for the Advancement of Science, 1968.

Lomax, Alan, and Ferdinand "Jelly Roll" Morton. *Mister Jelly Roll: The Fortunes of Jelly Roll Morton, New Orleans Creole and "Inventor of Jazz."* New York: Pantheon Books, [1949] 1993.

Lopes, Paul. *The Rise of a Jazz Art World.* Cambridge: Cambridge University Press, 2002.

Mandel, Howard. "The Wynton Marsalis Interview." *Down Beat* 51.7 (July 1984): 16–19, 67.

Manuel, Peter. "The Anticipated Bass in Cuban Popular Music." *Latin American Music Review* 6.2 (1985): 249–61.

———. "Puerto Rican Music and Cultural Identity: Creative Appropriation of Cuban Sources from Danza to Salsa." *Ethnomusicology* 38.2 (1994): 249–80.

Marmorstein, Gary. "Shoulders Broad Enough for the Band to Lean On." *New York Times,* 17 October 1993, H34.

Marquis, Alice Goldfarb. *Art Lessons: Learning from the Rise and Fall of Public Arts Funding.* New York: Basic Books, 1995.

Marsalis, Wynton (and Frank Stewart). *Sweet Swing Blues on the Road.* New York: Thunder's Mouth Press, 1994.

Mattingly, Rick. *The Drummer's Time: Conversations with the Great Drummers of Jazz.* Cedar Grove, NJ: Modern Drummer Publications, 1998.

Mauleón, Rebecca. *Salsa Guidebook for Piano and Ensemble.* Petaluma, CA: Sher Music, 1993.

McCarthy, Albert J. "The Jazz Scene." *Jazz Monthly,* August 1970, 3.

———. *Big Band Jazz.* New York: G. P. Putnam Sons, 1974.

McCarthy, Kevin F., et al. *The Performing Arts in a New Era.* Santa Monica, CA: RAND, 2001.
McClary, Susan. *Feminine Endings: Music, Gender, and Sexuality.* Minneapolis: University of Minnesota Press, 1991.
McDonough, John. "Doin' 'Em Proud: How the Mingus and Basie Big Bands Thrive on More than Just Nostalgia." *Down Beat* 64.1 (January 1997): 16–21.
McNeely, Jim. "Current Directions in Composing for the Jazz Orchestra." Handout for lecture given at the IAJE 25th Annual Conference, 9 January 1998, New York City.
McNeily, Kevin. "Charles Mingus Splits, or, All the Things You Could Be by Now if Sigmund Freud's Wife Was Your Mother." *Canadian Review of American Studies* 278.2 (1997): 45–70.
Middleton, Richard. *Studying Popular Music.* Philadelphia: Open University Press, 1990.
———. "Musical Belongings: Western Music and Its Low-Other." In *Western Music and Its Others: Difference, Representation, and Appropriation in Music,* edited by Georgina Born and David Hesmondhalgh, 59–85. Berkeley: University of California Press, 2000.
Mingus, Charles. "What Is a Jazz Composer?" Liner notes to *Let My Children Hear Music.* Columbia KC3 1039, 1971. Reprinted in *Charles Mingus: More Than a Fake Book,* edited by Sue Mingus, 155–57. Milwaukee, WI: Hal Leonard, 1991.
———. *Beneath the Underdog.* New York: Random House, 1991.
Mingus, Susan Graham, ed., with Andrew Homzy. *Charles Mingus: More than a Fake Book.* Milwaukee, WI: Hal Leonard, 1991.
———. *Tonight at Noon: A Love Story.* New York: Pantheon, 2002.
Moore, Robin. "Representations of Afrocuban Expressive Culture in the Writings of Fernando Ortiz." *Latin American Music Review* 15.1 (1994): 32–54.
———. *Nationalizing Blackness: Afrocubanismo and Artistic Revolution in Havana, 1920–1940.* Pittsburgh: University of Pittsburgh Press, 1997.
Monson, Ingrid. "The Problem with White Hipness: Race, Gender, and Cultural Conception in Jazz Historical Discourse." *Journal of the American Musicological Society* 48.3 (1995): 396–422.
———. *Saying Something: Jazz Improvisation and Interaction.* Chicago: University of Chicago Press, 1996.
———. "Riffs, Repetition, and Theories of Globalization." *Ethnomusicology* 43.1 (1999): 31–65.
———. Introduction to *The African Diaspora: A Musical Perspective,* 1–19. New York: Garland, 2000.
Mosca, John. "Reflection." *Vanguard Jazz Orchestra [Newsletter],* 1998.
Mulcahy, Kevin V., and C. Richard Swaim, eds. *Public Policy and the Arts.* Boulder. CO: Westview Press, 1982.
Murphy, John. "The African Big Band Aesthetic of Sam Rivers." Paper read at the 2002 Annual Meeting of the Society for Ethnomusicology, Estes Park, CO.
Murray, Albert. *Stomping the Blues.* New York: Da Capo Press, 1976.
———. *The Blue Devils of Nada: A Contemporary American Approach to Aesthetic Statement.* New York: Pantheon Books, 1996.
"Musicians Disrupt TV Show." *Down Beat* 37.19 (1 October 1970): 11.
Navarro, Mireya. "A Master of Latin Jazz Is Rediscovered at 79; after Lean Decades,

Chico O'Farrill Revels in His Late-Blooming Fame." *New York Times,* 30 December 2000, B1.

Nettl, Bruno. "Thoughts on Improvisation: A Comparative Approach." *Musical Quarterly* 60.1 (1974): 1–19.

———. "Orchestras." In *The Western Impact on World Music,* 57–61. New York: Schirmer Books, 1985.

———. *Heartland Excursions: Ethnomusicological Reflections on Schools of Music.* Urbana: University of Illinois Press, 1995.

Neuls-Bates, Carol. "Women's Orchestras in the United States, 1925–45." In *Women Making Music,* edited by Jane Bowers and Judith Tick, 349–69. Urbana: University of Illinois Press, 1986.

Panken, Ted. "Lights Out for Carnegie Hall Jazz Band." *Down Beat* 69.5 (May 2002): 18.

Pareles, Jon. "Lincoln Center Adding Jazz to Its Repertory." *New York Times,* 10 January 1991, A1, C2.

Pellegrinelli, Lara. "Dig Boy Dig." *Village Voice,* 14 November 2000, 65–67.

Petruzzi, Leon. "Lead Trumpet Performance in the Thad Jones/Mel Lewis Jazz Orchestra: An Analysis of Style and Performance Practices." Ph.D. diss, New York University, 1993.

Plant, Deborah G. *Every Tub Must Sit on Its Own Bottom: The Philosophy and Politics of Zora Neale Hurston.* Urbana: University of Illinois Press, 1995.

Pogrebin, Robin. "ChevronTexaco to Stop Sponsoring Met's Broadcasts." *New York Times,* 21 May 2003, B1, 8.

———. "Battling the Chaos in Schools' Arts Classes." *New York Times,* 5 June 2003, B1, 6.

Porter, Eric. *What Is This Thing Called Jazz? African American Musicians as Artists, Critics, and Activists.* Berkeley: University of California Press, 2002.

Porter, Lewis. *Jazz: A Century of Change.* New York: Schirmer Books, 1997.

Porter, Lewis, and Michael Ullman. *Jazz: From Its Origins to the Present.* Englewood Cliffs, NJ: Prentice Hall, 1993.

Priestley, Brian. *Mingus: A Critical Biography.* New York: Da Capo Press, 1982.

Primack, Bret. Booklet accompanying *The Complete Roulette Recordings of the Maynard Ferguson Orchestra.* Stamford, CT: Mosaic Records, 1994.

Prögler, J. A. "Searching for Swing: Participatory Discrepancies in the Jazz Rhythm Section." *Ethnomusicology* 39.1 (1995): 21–54.

Radano, Ronald, and Philip V. Bohlman. *Music and the Racial Imagination.* Chicago: University of Chicago Press, 2000.

Ratliff, Ben. "Not Grandpa's Big Band Records." *New York Times,* 23 December 1997, E5.

———. "The Peal of Horns Aplenty from a Big Band Cornucopia." *New York Times,* 16 January 1998, E1, 34.

———. "The Solo Retreats from the Spotlight in Jazz." *New York Times,* 28 May 2000, II23.

Roach, Max. "What 'Jazz' Means to Me." *Black Scholar* 3 (Summer 1972): 2–6.

Roberts, John Storm. *The Latin Tinge: The Impact of Latin American Music on the United States.* Tivoli, NY: Original Music, 1985.

Robinson, J. Bradford, and Barry Kernfeld. "Carla Bley." In *New Grove Dictionary of Jazz,* 2d ed., vol. 1, edited by Barry Kernfeld, 239. London: Macmillan, 2002.

Rodríguez, Victoria Eli. "Cuban Music and Ethnicity: Historical Considerations." In *Music and Black Ethnicity: The Caribbean and South America,* edited by Gerard Béhague, 91–108. Boulder, CO: Lynne Rienner, 1994.

Rourke, Constance. *American Humor: A Study of the National Character.* New York: Harcourt, Brace and Company, 1931.

Russell, Dick. *Black Genius.* New York: Carroll & Graf, 1998.

Russell, Ross. "Bebop." In *The Art of Jazz: Essays on the Nature and Development of Jazz,* edited by Martin Williams, 187–214. New York: Oxford University Press, 1959.

Rustin, Nichole T. "Mingus Fingers: Charles Mingus, Black Masculinity, and Postwar Jazz Culture." Ph.D. diss., New York University, 1999.

Sánchez de Fuentes, Eduardo. *La música aborigen en América.* Havana: Molina, 1938.

Santoro, Gene. *Myself When I Am Real: The Life and Music of Charles Mingus.* New York: Oxford University Press, 2000.

Sargeant, Winthrop. *Jazz: Hot and Hybrid.* New York: Arrow, 1938.

Schneider, Maria. *Evanescence: Complete Scores.* Edited by Fred Sturm. n.p.: Universal Edition, 1998.

Schuller, Gunther. *Early Jazz.* New York: Oxford University Press, 1968.

———. "The Future of Form in Jazz." In *Musings: The Musical Worlds of Gunther Schuller,* 18–25. New York: Oxford University Press, 1986.

———. *The Swing Era.* New York: Oxford University Press, 1989.

———. "Arrangement." In *The New Grove Dictionary of Jazz,* 2d ed., vol. 1, edited by Barry Kernfeld, 75–81. London: Macmillan, [1988] 2002.

Schuller, Gunther, and Martin Williams. *Big Band Jazz: From the Beginnings to the Fifties.* Washington, DC: Smithsonian Institution Press, 1983.

Seeger, Anthony. *Why Suyá Sing: A Musical Anthropology of an Amazonian People.* Cambridge: Cambridge University Press, 1987.

Shepherd, John. *Music as Social Text.* Cambridge: Polity Press, 1991.

Shih, Hsio Wen. "The Spread of Jazz and the Big Bands." In *Jazz: New Perspectives on the History of Jazz by Twelve of the World's Foremost Jazz Critics and Scholars,* edited by Nat Hentoff and Albert J. McCarthy, 171–87. New York: Da Capo Press, 1959.

Sidran, Ben. *Black Talk.* New York: Da Capo Press, 1971.

Simon, George T. *The Big Bands.* New York: Macmillan, [1967] 1981.

Simpson, George Eaton. *Black Religions in the New World.* New York: Columbia University Press, 1978.

Singer, Roberta. " 'My Music Is Who I Am and What I Do': Latin Popular Music and Identity in New York City." Ph.D. diss., Indiana University, 1982.

Slobin, Mark. *Subcultural Sounds: Micromusics of the West.* Hanover, NH: University Press of New England, 1993.

Small, Christopher. "Responses." *Ethnomusicology* 39.1 (Spring 1995): 91.

Smith, Charles Edward. "New Orleans and Traditions in Jazz." In *Jazz: New Perspectives on the History of Jazz by Twelve of the World's Foremost Jazz Critics and Scholars,* edited by Nat Hentoff and Albert J. McCarthy, 21–41. New York: Da Capo Press, 1959.

Stewart, Alexander. " 'Funky Drummer': James Brown, New Orleans, and the Rhythmic Transformation of American Popular Music." *Popular Music* 19.3 (2000): 293–318.

———. Review of Lewis Porter, *John Coltrane: His Life and Music. Annual Review of Jazz Studies* 11 (2000–2001): 237–52.

Stewart, Rex. *Boy Meets Horn.* Ann Arbor: University of Michigan Press, 1991.

Stewart, Zan. "Blood Brothers." *Down Beat* 64.5 (May 1997): 26–28.

Stowe, David W. *Swing Changes: Big-Band Jazz in New Deal America.* Cambridge, MA: Harvard University Press, 1994.

Strunk, Stephen. "Harmony." In *The New Grove Dictionary of Jazz,* 2d ed., vol. 2, edited by Barry Kernfeld, 160–61. London: Macmillan, 2002.

Sturm, Fred. *Changes over Time: The Evolution of Jazz Arranging.* Rottenburg, Germany: Advance Music, 1995.

Such, David G. *Avant-Garde Jazz Musicians: Performing "Out There."* Iowa City: University of Iowa Press, 1993.

Sudhalter, Richard. *Lost Chords: White Musicians and Their Contribution to Jazz, 1915–1945.* New York: Oxford University Press, 1999.

Sunderland, Patricia. "Cultural Meanings and Identity: Women of the African-American Art World of Jazz." Ph.D. diss., University of Vermont, 1992.

Szwed, John. *Space Is the Place: The Lives and Times of Sun Ra.* New York: Pantheon Books, 1997.

Tannnenbaum, Frank. *Slave and Citizen.* Boston: Beacon Press, 1946.

Tick, Judith. "Passed Away Is the Little Piano Girl." In *Women Making Music: The Western Art Tradition, 1150–1950,* edited by Jane Bowers and Judith Tick, 325–48. Urbana: University of Illinois Press, 1986.

Toll, Ted. "The Gal Yippers Have No Place in Our Jazz Bands." *Down Beat* 6.11 (15 October 1939): 16. Reprinted in *Keeping Time: Readings in Jazz History,* edited by Robert Walser, 115. New York: Oxford University Press, 1999.

Tomlinson, Gary. "Cultural Dialogics and Jazz: A White Historian Signifies." *Black Music Research Journal* 11 (1991): 229–64.

Tucker, Mark. *Swing That Music: The Big Bands, the Soloists, and the Singers, 1929–1956.* Washington, DC: Smithsonian Institution Press, [1987] 1993.

———. *The Duke Ellington Reader.* New York: Oxford University Press, 1993.

———. "The Genesis of *Black, Brown and Beige.*" *Black Music Research Journal* 13.2 (1993): 67–86.

———. "Musicology and the New Jazz Studies." *Journal of the American Musicological Society* 51.1 (1998): 131–48.

———. "Seven Steps to Piano Heaven: The Artistry of Sir Roland Hanna" *ISAM Newsletter,* Fall 2000. Reprinted in *Behind the Beat: Jazz Criticism by Mark Tucker,* edited by Ray Allen and Jeff Taylor, 46–48. Brooklyn, NY: Institute for Studies in American Music, Brooklyn College, CUNY, 2003.

Tucker, Sherrie. *Swing Shift.* Durham: Duke University Press, 2000.

———. "Big Ears: Listening for Gender in Jazz Studies." *Current Musicology* 71–73 (Spring 2001–Spring 2002): 375–408.

Ulanov, Barry. "It's Not the Book, It's the Attitude." *Metronome,* March 1942, 11.

———. "Moldy Figs vs. Moderns." *Metronome,* November 1947, 15, 23.

Valentín Escobar, Wilson A. "El Hombre que Respira Debajo del Agua: Trans-*Boricua* Memories, Identities, and Nationalisms Performed through the Death of Héctor Lavoe." In *Situating Salsa,* edited by Lise Waxer, 161–86. New York: Routledge, 2002.

———. "Freedomland at the New Rican Village: Latin Jazz and the Making of a Latino Avant-Garde Arts Scene in New York City." Ph.D. diss., University of Michigan, 2004.

van der Merwe, Peter. *Origins of the Popular Style: The Antecedents of Twentieth-Century Popular Music.* New York: Oxford University Press, 1989.

Vax, Mike. "Report to the American Federation of Jazz: The State of Jazz Education in the United States in 1998." www.mikevax.com/afjs.html, 2001.

VJO Newsletter 1.1 (1998).

Walser, Robert. " 'Out of Notes': Signification, Interpretation, and the Problem of Miles Davis." *Musical Quarterly* 77.2 (1993): 343–65. Reprinted in *Jazz among the Discourses,* edited by Krin Gabbard, 165–88. Durham: Duke University Press, 1995.

———. "Deep Jazz: Notes on Interiority, Race, and Criticism." In *Inventing the Psychological: Toward a Cultural History of Emotional Life in America,* edited by Joel Pfister and Nancy Schnog, 271–96. New Haven: Yale University Press, 1997.

———, ed. *Keeping Time: Readings in Jazz History.* New York: Oxford University Press, 1999.

Washburne, Christopher. "Latin Jazz: The Other Jazz." *Current Musicology* 71–73 (2001–2): 409–26.

Watrous, Peter. "Making the Repertory of the Hallowed Past into Something New." *New York Times,* 23 October 1993, 11.

———. "Another War of the Titans, Fought Now with Trumpets." *New York Times,* 30 June 1994, C13.

———. "When a Repertorial Show Stays True to the Repertory." *New York Times,* 11 October 1994, C16.

———. "The Battle of the Bands, Part Two." *New York Times,* 3 July 1995, 15.

———. "To Clint, with Love, from Jazz." *New York Times,* 17 October 1996, 15, 20.

———. "Choral Effects Enhance Quiet Bernstein Pleasures." *New York Times,* 15 November 1997, B11.

———. "Ellington Revered and Revised." *New York Times* 25 January 1999, E7.

Waxer, Lise. *Situating Salsa: Global Markets and Local Meaning in Latin Popular Music.* New York: Routledge, 2002.

Weber, Bruce. "Arts: A Shifting American Landscape. In the Heartland. A Cornucopia of Culture." *New York Times,* 6 December 1998, AR1, 44.

Weber, Horst, and Gerd Filtgen. *Charles Mingus: Sein Leben, seine Musik, seine Schallplatten.* Gauting-Buchendorf: Oreos, 1984.

Wellburn *[sic],* Ron. "The Black Aesthetic Imperative." In *The Black Aesthetic,* edited by Gayle Addison, 132–49. Garden City, NY: Doubleday, 1971.

"Why Women Musicians Are Inferior." *Down Beat* 5.2 (February 1938): 4. Reprinted in *Keeping Time: Readings in Jazz History,* edited by Robert Walser, 112. New York: Oxford University Press, 1999.

Wilgoren, Jodi. "Where Race Matters." *New York Times,* 13 April 2003, 4A20.

Williams, Martin, ed. *The Art of Jazz: Essays on the Nature and Development of Jazz.* New York: Oxford University Press, 1959.

———. "What to Do about Jazz in Our August Cultural Centers." *New York Times,* 25 January 1970, II34.

Wilmer, Valerie. *As Serious as Your Life: The Story of the New Jazz.* Westport, CT: Lawrence Hill, [1977] 1980.

Wilson, John S. "2 New Big Bands Here Appeal to More than Old Memories." *New York Times,* 12 February 1966, 17.

———. "The Great Jazz Dream—Can It Come True?" *New York Times,* 18 November 1973, 19, 33.
———. "If the Symphonies Can Do It, So Can Jazz." *New York Times,* 20 January 1974, 15, 18.
———. "Jazz Company's 2d Season to Be Test." *New York Times,* 5 November 1974, 29.
———. "Jazz Goes to the New School." *New York Times,* 18 February 1977, 67.
Wilson, Olly. "The Heterogeneous Sound Ideal in African-American Music." In *New Perspectives on Music: Essays in Honor of Eileen Southern,* edited by Josephine Wright, 327–38. Warren, MI: Harmonie Park Press, 1992.
Woodward, Richard B. "Jazz War: A Tale of Age, Rage and Hash Brownies." *Village Voice,* 9 August 1994, 27–34.
Wright, Rayburn. *Inside the Score.* Delevan, NY: Kendor Music, 1982.
Yoshitomi, Gerald D. "Cultural Democracy." In *Public Money and the Muse,* edited by Stephen Benedict, 195–215. New York: Norton, 1991.
Zwerin, Mike. *Close Enough for Jazz.* London: Quartet Books, 1983.

SELECTED DISCOGRAPHY OF CONTEMPORARY NEW YORK CITY BIG BAND MUSIC, 1990–2005

Not intended to be exhaustive, this discography emphasizes New York City composers or bands as well as original arrangements. Dates are years of release.

Afro-Latin Jazz Orchestra, Jazz at Lincoln Center's (with Arturo O'Farrill). 2005. *Una Noche Inolvidable.* Palmetto 2111.

Akiyoshi, Toshiko. 2003. *Hiroshima: Rising from the Abyss.* True Life Jazz 10008.

Anderson, Lew. 1992. *Fired Up.* Sovereign Records CDSOV 504.

———. 1998. *Live at the Blazer!* Sovereign Records CDSOV 506.

Banks, Nancie. 1992. *Waves of Peace.* Consolidated Artists Productions CAP 902.

———. 1994. *Bert's Blues.* Consolidated Artists Productions CAP 904.

———. 1999. *Ear Candy.* GFI Records

———. 2001. *Out of It.* GFI Records.

Basie, Count, Orchestra (under the direction of Grover Mitchell). 1996. *Count Basie Orchestra with the New York Voices.* MCGJ 1002.

———. 1998. *Count Plays Duke.* Mama Foundation MMF 1024.

———. 1999. *Swing Shift.* Mama Foundation MMF 1027.

Bauzá, Mario, and His Afro-Cuban Jazz Orchestra. 1992. *Tanga Suite.* Messidor 15819.

———. 1993. *My Time Is Now.* Messidor 15824.

———. 1994. *944 Columbus.* Messidor 15828.

Belden, Bob. 1990. *Treasure Island.* Sunnyside SSC 1041D.

———. 1998. *La Cigale: Live in Paris.* Sunnyside 1079.

Berger, David (and the Sultans of Swing). 1999. *The Harlem Nutcracker.* Such Sweet Thunder SST 1001.

———. 2000. *Doin' the Do!* Such Sweet Thunder SST 1002.

———. 2004. *Marlowe.* Such Sweet Thunder SST 1003.

Bley, Carla. 1991. *The (Very) Big Carla Bley Band.* ECM Records/WATT23.

———. 1993. *Big Band Theory.* ECM Records/WATT25.

———. 1996. *Goes to Church.* ECM Records/WATT27.

———. 2003. *Looking for America.* ECM Records/WATT31.

Boras, Tom. 1995. *Three Houses.* MMC Recordings 2011.
Brown, Anita. 2003. *27 East.* Lasheda Records.
Byard, Jaki (and the Apollo Stompers). 1991. *Phantasies II.* Soul Note 121175.
Carnegie Hall Jazz Band. 1996. *The Carnegie Hall Jazz Band.* Blue Note CDP 7243 8 36728 2 0.
Diva (No Man's Band). 1995. *Something's Coming.* Perfect Sound PSCD1216.
———. 1999. *I Believe in You.* Arbors Records. ARCD-19231.
D'Rivera, Paquito. 1996. *Portraits of Cuba.* Chesky Records 145.
———. 1999. *Tropicana Nights.* Chesky Records 186.
——— (and the United Nations Orchestra). 1994. *A Night in Englewood.* Messidor CD 15829–2.
——— (and the United Nations Orchestra). 1997. *Live at the Manchester Craftsman's Guild.* MCGJ 1003.
——— (with the WDR Big Band, Bill Dobbins, arranger). 2003. *Big Band Time.* Universal Music Latino 360 599.
Fedchock, John. 1995. *John Fedchock New York Big Band.* Reservoir RSR CD 138.
———. 1997. *On the Edge.* Reservoir RSR CD153.
———. 2002. *No Nonsense.* Reservoir RSR CD170.
Fugii, Satoko. 1998. *South Wind.* Leo Lab Records LIBRA 215–104.
———. 2000. *Double Take.* ewcd-0019/0020 2CD (includes one disc of her Orchestra East recorded in Japan and one disc of her Orchestra West recorded in New York).
———. 2000. *Jo.* ZZ 7608.
———. 2003. *The Future of the Past.* Enja Records ENJ-9457 2.
———. 2005. Blueprint. MTCJ-3016.
Gillespie, Dizzy (the Alumni All-Star Big Band, directed by Jon Faddis). 2002. *Things to Come.* Telarc MCGJ1009
Gillespie, Larry. 1998. *Contour.* Blue Lion Music CDB0535690012.
Henderson, Joe. 1996. *Joe Henderson Big Band.* Verve 314 533 451–2.
Herborn, Peter. 1999. *Large One.* Jazzline Records 1154–2.
———. 2002. *Large Two.* Jazzline Records 1162–2.
Hill, Andrew. 2002. *A Beautiful Day.* Palmetto Records PM 2085.
Holland, Dave. 2002. *What Goes Around.* ECM 1777.
———. 2005. *Overtime.* Sunnyside 3028.
Hollenbeck, John, Large Ensemble. 2004. *A Blessing.* OmniTone 15209.
Holober, Mike, and the Gotham Jazz Orchestra. 2004. *Thought Trains.* Sons of Sound SSPCD030.
Klein, Guillermo, & Big Van. 1997. *El Minotauro.* Candid CCD79706.
Levinovsky, Nick. 1997. *Listen Up.* NLO 97.
——— (with Kathy Jenkins). 2003. *Swing Madness.* NLO 2003.
Lewis, Mel. 1990. *To You: A Tribute to Mel Lewis.* Music Masters 5054–2C.
Liebman, Dave. 2003. *Beyond the Line.* OmniTone 12204.
Lindner, Jason. 2000. *Premonition.* Concord SCD-9026–2.
Longo, Mike, and the New York State of the Art Jazz Ensemble. 2004. *Oasis.* CAP 982.
Marsalis, Wynton, and the Lincoln Center Jazz Orchestra. 1997. *Blood on the Fields.* Columbia CXK 57694.
———. 1999. *Big Train.* Columbia/Sony Classical CK69860.
———. 2005. *A Love Supreme.* Palmetto PM 2106.

———. 2005. *Don't Be Afraid: The Music of Charles Mingus.* Palmetto PM 2114.
Mingus Big Band. 1993. *Mingus Big Band 93 (Nostalgia in Times Square).* Dreyfus Jazz FDM 36559–2.
———. 1995. *Gunslinging Birds.* Dreyfus Jazz FDM 36575–2.
———. 1996. *Live in Time.* Dreyfus Jazz FDM 36583–2.
———. 1997. *¡Que Viva Mingus!* Dreyfus Jazz FDM36593–2.
———. 1999. *Blues and Politics.* Dreyfus Jazz FDM36603–2.
———. 2001. *The Essential Mingus Big Band.* Dreyfus Jazz FDM 36628–2.
——— (Big Band and Orchestra). 2002. *Tonight at Noon: Three or Four Shades of Love.* Dreyfus Jazz FDM 36633–2.
——— (Big Band, Orchestra, and Dynasty). 2005. *I Am Three.* Sunnyside 3029.
Mintzer, Bob. 1991. *Art of the Big Band.* DMP 479.
———. 1993. *Departure.* DMP 493.
———. 1994. *Only in New York.* DMP 501.
———. 1995. *The First Decade.* DMP 510.
———. 1996. *Big Band Trane.* DMP 515.
———. 1998. *Latin from Manhattan.* DMP 523.
———. 2000. *Homage to Count Basie.* DMP 529.
———. 2003. *Gently.* DMP 534.
———. 2004. *Live at MCG with Special Guest Kurt Elling.* MCG Records 1016.
Mobley, Bill. 1998. *Live at Smalls, Vol. 1.* Space Time BG 9805.
———. 1998. *Live at Smalls, Vol. 2.* Space Time BG 9809.
——— (and Space Time Big Band). 2001. *New Light.* Space Time Records BG2117.
Morgan, Gary, and PanAmericana. 2003. *Live at Birdland.* Cap Records CAPR 976.
Mosaic Orchestra. 2001. *The Journey.* The Orchard 751.
Moser, Diane (Diane Moser's Composers Big Band). 1999. *LIVE! At Tierney's Tavern.* New Arts NA-001.
Murray, David. 1991. *David Murray Big Band. Conducted by Lawrence "Butch" Morris.* Columbia DIW CK48964.
——— (Latin Big Band). 2003. *Now Is Another Time.* Justin Time JUST 161–2.
NewYorkestra Big Band. 2003. *Urban Soundscape.* Seabreeze SEAB 2134.
O'Farrill, Chico (The Chico O'Farrill Afro-Cuban Jazz Big Band). 1995. *Pure Emotion.* Milestone MCD-9239–2.
———. 1999. *Heart of a Legend.* Milestone MCD-9299–2.
———. 2000. *Carambola.* Milestone MCD-9308–2.
Palermo, Ed. 1997. *The Ed Palermo Big Band Plays the Music of Frank Zappa.* Astor Place TCD 4005.
Parker, William, and the Little Huey Creative Music Orchestra. 1997. *Sunrise in the Tone World.* AUM 002/3.
———. 2000. *Mayor of Punkville.* AUM 015/16.
———. 2002. *Raincoat in the River.* Eremite MTE 036.
———. 2002. *Spontaneous.* Splasc(h) Records CDH 855.2.
Persip, Charli. 1994. *Original Superband.* Natasha Imports NI-4028.
Pierson, Tom. 1996. *Planet of Tears.* Auteur Records.
———. 2003. *The Hidden Goddess.* Auteur Records.
Pratt Brothers Big Band. 1997. *Groovy Encounters.* Amosaya AM-2532-CD.
Rivers, Sam. 1999. *Culmination.* RCA Victor 74321–68311–2.

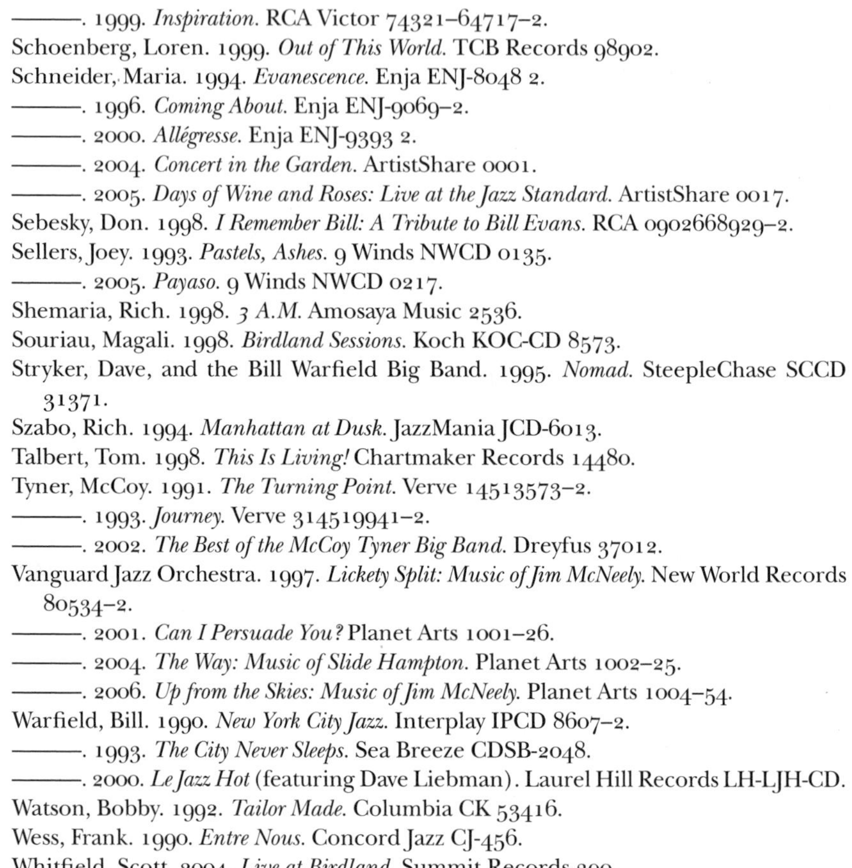

———. 1999. *Inspiration.* RCA Victor 74321–64717–2.
Schoenberg, Loren. 1999. *Out of This World.* TCB Records 98902.
Schneider, Maria. 1994. *Evanescence.* Enja ENJ-8048 2.
———. 1996. *Coming About.* Enja ENJ-9069–2.
———. 2000. *Allégresse.* Enja ENJ-9393 2.
———. 2004. *Concert in the Garden.* ArtistShare 0001.
———. 2005. *Days of Wine and Roses: Live at the Jazz Standard.* ArtistShare 0017.
Sebesky, Don. 1998. *I Remember Bill: A Tribute to Bill Evans.* RCA 0902668929–2.
Sellers, Joey. 1993. *Pastels, Ashes.* 9 Winds NWCD 0135.
———. 2005. *Payaso.* 9 Winds NWCD 0217.
Shemaria, Rich. 1998. *3 A.M.* Amosaya Music 2536.
Souriau, Magali. 1998. *Birdland Sessions.* Koch KOC-CD 8573.
Stryker, Dave, and the Bill Warfield Big Band. 1995. *Nomad.* SteepleChase SCCD 31371.
Szabo, Rich. 1994. *Manhattan at Dusk.* JazzMania JCD-6013.
Talbert, Tom. 1998. *This Is Living!* Chartmaker Records 14480.
Tyner, McCoy. 1991. *The Turning Point.* Verve 14513573–2.
———. 1993. *Journey.* Verve 314519941–2.
———. 2002. *The Best of the McCoy Tyner Big Band.* Dreyfus 37012.
Vanguard Jazz Orchestra. 1997. *Lickety Split: Music of Jim McNeely.* New World Records 80534–2.
———. 2001. *Can I Persuade You?* Planet Arts 1001–26.
———. 2004. *The Way: Music of Slide Hampton.* Planet Arts 1002–25.
———. 2006. *Up from the Skies: Music of Jim McNeely.* Planet Arts 1004–54.
Warfield, Bill. 1990. *New York City Jazz.* Interplay IPCD 8607–2.
———. 1993. *The City Never Sleeps.* Sea Breeze CDSB-2048.
———. 2000. *Le Jazz Hot* (featuring Dave Liebman). Laurel Hill Records LH-LJH-CD.
Watson, Bobby. 1992. *Tailor Made.* Columbia CK 53416.
Wess, Frank. 1990. *Entre Nous.* Concord Jazz CJ-456.
Whitfield, Scott. 2004. *Live at Birdland.* Summit Records 390.

CREDITS

Afro-Cuban Jazz Suite composed and arranged by Chico O'Farrill. Copyright 1950 Chico O'Farrill. Taken from a score graciously provided by Lupe O'Farrill.

"A-That's Freedom" arranged by That Jones. Copyright 1965. Renewal Copyright: D'Accord Music c/o Publishers' Licensing Corporation, P.O. Box 5807, Englewood, NJ 07631. Transcribed by the author from Thad Jones/Mel Lewis Orchestra, *Live at the Village Vanguard,* Solid State 18016.

"Azulito" composed and arranged by Ray Santos. Copyright 1962 Nena Music. Taken from a score graciously provided Ray Santos.

Blood on the Fields composed and arranged by Wynton Marsalis. Copyright 1997 Wynton Marsalis. Taken from an unpublished score.

"Diane" composed by Charles Mingus. Copyright 1975 Jazz Workshop, Inc. Taken from *Charles Mingus: More than a Fake Book,* edited by Susan Graham Mingus with Andrew Homzy, 22. Milwaukee, WI: Hal Leonard, 1991.

"Ecclusiastics" composed by Charles Mingus. Copyright 1975 Jazz Workshop, Inc. Transcribed by the author from *Mingus Big Band 93,* Dreyfus FDM 36559–2.

"E's Flat Ah's Flat Too" composed by Charles Mingus. Copyright 1979 Jazz Workshop, Inc. Adapted from *Charles Mingus: More than a Fake Book,* edited by Susan Graham Mingus with Andrew Homzy, 34–36. Milwaukee, WI: Hal Leonard, 1991.

"Jump Monk" composed by Charles Mingus. Copyright 1979 Jazz Workshop, Inc. Adapted from *Charles Mingus: More than a Fake Book,* edited by Susan Graham Mingus with Andrew Homzy, 66–67. Milwaukee, WI: Hal Leonard, 1991.

"The Man Who Never Sleeps" composed by Charles Mingus. Copyright 1975 Jazz Workshop, Inc. Taken from *Charles Mingus: More than a Fake Book,* edited by Susan Graham Mingus with Andrew Homzy, 63. Milwaukee, WI: Hal Leonard, 1991.

"Number 29" composed by Charles Mingus. Copyright 1973 Jazz Workshop, Inc. Transcribed by the author from *Live in Time,* Dreyfus FDM 36583–2.

"On the Stage in Cages" composed and arranged by Carla Bley. Copyright 1993 Alrac Music (BMI). Taken from a score graciously provided by Carla Bley.

"Second Race" composed and arranged by Thad Jones. Copyright 1965, 1980 D'Accord Music c/o Publishers' Licensing Corporation, P.O. Box 5807, Englewood, NJ 07631. Taken from a score published by Kendor.

"Sticks" composed and arranged by Jim McNeely. Copyright 1995 Wu Wei Music (BMI). Taken from a score graciously provided by Jim McNeely.

"Sunny Ray" composed and arranged by Ray Santos. Copyright 1958 Nena Music. Taken from a score graciously provided Ray Santos.

"Tijuana Gift Shop" composed by Charles Mingus. Copyright 1952 Jazz Workshop, Inc. From a score graciously provided by Michael Mossman.

"Wyrgly" composed and arranged by Maria Schneider. Copyright 1989 Maria Schneider Music, MSF Music (ASCAP). Taken from Maria Schneider, *Evanescence: Complete Scores.* Edited by Fred Sturm. n.p.: Universal Edition, 1998.

INDEX

Text: 10/12 Baskerville
Display: Baskerville
Compositor: Binghamton Valley Composition, LLC
Printer and binder: Maple-Vail Manufacturing Group